AMERICAN NEGRO
SLAVE REVOLTS

AMERICAN NEGRO SLAVE REVOLTS

HERBERT APTHEKER

Generously Donated to

The Frederick Douglass Institute

By Professor Jesse Moore

Fall 2000

INTERNATIONAL PUBLISHERS

New York

TO FAY

AUTHOR'S PREFACE TO THE 1963 EDITION

THE volume now before the reader was first published, in February 1943, by the Columbia University Press as No. 501 in the *Studies in History, Economics and Public Law*, edited by the Faculty of Political Science of that University. A second printing was issued the next year, and a third in 1945, but the volume has been out of print now for several years. Naturally, it is very gratifying to the author that a publisher feels the continuing demand for this work merits its re-publication, just twenty years after it first saw the light of day.

This edition appears, too, in the Centennial Year of the issuance of the Final Emancipation Proclamation by Abraham Lincoln. But as these words are written, the news from the nation in general, the South in particular and Mississippi most particularly, indicates that both the enslavement and the struggle against it—which this book describes—are by no means simply "past history."

The galleys of the original edition of this book were examined by the author while he was in the United States Army, and under field conditions which were not conducive to careful proof-reading. I have noted a number of typographical errors in a separate *Errata*.

Generally speaking, this book has weathered some heavy attacks launched by individuals to whom white supremacy and the magnolia-moonlight-molasses mythology that adorns it were sacred. Still, neither this nor the notoriously radical political sympathies of its author have succeeded in consigning the work to damnation—that is, to oblivion. Probably the dominant view in academic circles is that expressed by Professor Carlton C. Qualey, writing on "Newer Interpretations of American History to 1860."* Noting that the "seemingly adequate" work of the late Ulrich Bonnell Phillips was being

---

* In, R. E. Thursfield, ed., *The Study and Teaching of American History* (17th Yearbook, National Council for the Social Studies, 1946), p. 116.

re-examined, Professor Qualey wrote that the present book was part of this re-examination and that while it "is marked by reforming zeal," still it "succeeds in proving that the contentedness of the Negro slave as suggested by southern writers has no considerable basis in fact, and that the prevailing sentiment of the Negro was a melancholy longing for freedom, marked by frequent rebellions. . . ."

Again, Professor Kenneth M. Stampp, of the University of California (Berkeley), writing on "The Historian and Southern Negro Slavery," in *The American Historical Review* (April, 1952, p. 617), notes: "There were individual acts of violence against masters and overseers, and cases of conspiracy and rebellion. If the significance of these cases has been overstated by Herbert Aptheker, it has been understated by many of his predecessors." Happily, in his own book, published in 1956 (*The Peculiar Institution: Slavery in the Ante-Bellum South*, Knopf, N. Y.), Professor Stampp certainly does not align himself with those guilty of "under-statement."

The present writer is proud that Negro scholars have greeted this work with enthusiasm; two who so reacted were his revered mentors—I mean, the late Dr. Carter G. Woodson, and Dr. W. E. B. Du Bois. Professor John Hope Franklin, now Chairman of the History Department in Brooklyn College, in his *From Slavery to Freedom: A History of American Negroes* (N. Y., 1947, Knopf, p. 603), finds that this book is "the best account of resistance to slavery."

In addition to the works mentioned above, it may be useful to note those books and articles that have been published since 1943 which deal particularly with the response of the American Negro to his enslavement:

ADDINGTON, W. G., "Slave Insurrections in Texas," *The Journal of Negro History*, October, 1950, XXXV, pp. 408–434.

APTHEKER, H., "Notes on Slave Conspiracies in Confederate Mississippi," *The Journal of Negro History*, January, 1944, XXIX, pp. 75–79.

APTHEKER, H., *To Be Free: Studies in American Negro History* (N. Y., 1948, International Publishers).

CLARKE, T. W., "Negro Plot, 1741," *New York History*, April, 1944.

EVERETT, D. E., "Free Persons of Color in New Orleans, 1803–1815," *The Journal of Negro History*, October, 1953, XXXVII, pp. 377–402.

FRANKLIN, J. H., *The Militant South* (Cambridge, 1956, Harvard Univ. Press).

HOFSTADTER, R., "U. B. Phillips and the Plantation Legend," *The Journal of Negro History*, April, 1944, XXIX, pp. 109–124.

LOFTON, JOHN M., "Vesey's Call to Arms," *The Journal of Negro History*, October, 1948, XXXIII, pp. 395–417.

LOFTON, J. M., "Negro Insurrectionist," *The Antioch Review*, Summer, 1958.

McKIBBEN, D. B., "Negro Slave Insurrections in Mississippi," *The Journal of Negro History*, January, 1949, XXXIV, pp. 73–90.

MILES, E. A., "The Mississippi Slave Insurrection Scare of 1835," *The Journal of Negro History*, January, 1957, XLII, pp. 48–60.

REDDING, J. SAUNDERS, *They Came In Chains* (Phila., 1950, Lippincott), especially chapter 5.

RUSSELL, M. J., "American Slave Discontent in Records of the High Courts," *The Journal of Negro History*, October, 1946, XXXI, pp. 411–434.

TOWNER, L. W., " 'A Fondness for Freedom': Servant Protest in Puritan Society," *William and Mary Quarterly*, April, 1962, XIX, pp. 201–219.

So much by way of a new preface to a work chronicling the aspirations and actions of Negro slaves seeking freedom, formally heralded by the President in his New Year's Day Proclamation in 1863, ratified by the Government of the United States with the adoption of the Thirteenth Amendment to the Constitution in December 1865, and still being passionately sought in its fullness ten decades later.

HERBERT APTHEKER

January, 1963

ERRATA

Page 57, line 19, read "last" for "least."

Page 85, note 18, line 3, read "Caroline" for "Carolina."

Page 121, note 25, line 2, read "Brodnax" for "Brodaax."

Page 127, note 43, line 3, read "Caroline" for "Carolina."

Page 134, note 63, line 3, read "Frederic" for "Frederick."

Page 228, note 69, line 2, read "this is in the" for "this is the."

Page 241, line 8, read "1805" for "1804."

Page 271, line 24, read "Charleston" for "Charles."

Page 274, note 28, line 2, read "War" for "Was."

Page 294, note 4, line 2, read "104" for "1044."

Page 318, line 2, read "Witcher" for "Witches."

Page 319, line 6, read "our" for "out."

Page 334, note 33, line 1, read "Northrup" for "Northup."

ACKNOWLEDGMENT

I HAVE received assistance from many people in the preparation of this work. Professors Allan Nevins, Frank Tannenbaum, William L. Westerman, Harry J. Carman, Joseph Dorfman and Louis M. Hacker, all of Columbia University, have corrected errors and offered valuable suggestions. Professor Melville J. Herskovits of Northwestern University, Professor Clement Eaton of Lafayette College, and Dr. Harvey Wish of De Pauw University have also been generous in encouraging and aiding me. The staffs of several libraries, as the New York Public Library, the Brooklyn Public Library, the Boston Public Library, the Congressional Library, the libraries of Columbia University and the University of North Carolina, of the Historical Societies of Maryland and Virginia, the State Library and Archives of Virginia, the State Library and Archives of North Carolina, and the State Library and Memorial Building of South Carolina, were uniformly helpful and considerate.

The work was done under the supervision of Professor John A. Krout of Columbia University. Without his advice and criticism the monograph, had it ever been published, would certainly have contained many more errors and failings than it now does. Those errors and failings that may yet remain are, however, of my own making, and responsibility for them and for all opinions and ideas expressed herein is mine alone.

CONTENTS

CHAPTER I

INTRODUCTION

IN preparing, several years ago, a detailed study [1] of the slave rebellion of 1831 in Virginia under the leadership of Nat Turner, the present writer came to the conclusion that this event was not an isolated, unique phenomenon, but the culmination of a series of slave conspiracies and revolts which had occurred in the immediate past. These antecedents had largely gone unreported and, apparently, uninvestigated, the result naturally being a poor focussing of the Turner Rebellion, and an incomplete understanding of the events and trends which that outbreak evoked or accelerated.

It seemed probable, furthermore, that a similar situation might exist in respect of the other outstanding insurrections and plots, such as those of Cato in 1739, Gabriel in 1800, and Vesey in 1822; that other unknown or practically unknown major outbreaks might have taken place and that an intensive study of the entire subject might uncover hitherto neglected aspects of the life of the Negro people, and the role of the institution of slavery in the history of the United States.

There has been, and there still is a notable lack of agreement, both in contemporary and secondary accounts, concerning the details of the subject and its relative importance. Many commentators declare that they observe a considerable degree of contentedness and docility among the Negro slaves (not a few ascribing the latter characteristic to alleged inherent " racial " qualities), while some, especially contemporaries, assert that they see a notable absence of both. A few examples may be offered.

1 " Nat Turner's Revolt," unpublished master's thesis, 1937, Columbia University.

Some regional historians,[2] while implying that discontent and disaffection may have been common elsewhere, affirm that in the locality of their particular interest these conditions were rare or non-existent. Others, dealing with a brief period of time, declare [3] that signs of unrest are lacking therein, but they often admit that this may not be true for other eras.

Many eminent historians, discussing more general subjects, have assumed a similar position on this particular question, a few expressing very strong opinions. Thus John Fiske thought [4] that the rarity of manifestations of slave unrest was " one of the remarkable facts in American history." James Schouler, reaching a similar conclusion, based it upon " the innate patience, docility, and child-like simplicity of the negro " who, he felt, was " an imitator and non-moralist ", learning " deceit and libertinism with facility," being " easily intimidated, incapable of deep plots "; in short Negroes were " a black servile race, sensuous, stupied, brutish, obedient to the whip, children in imagination . . .".[5]

2 Caleb P. Patterson, *The Negro in Tennessee, 1790-1865,* p. 49; Ivan E. McDougle, *Slavery in Kentucky, 1792-1865,* p. 43; Harrison A. Trexler, *Slavery in Missouri, 1804-1865,* p. 72; J. M. Batten, " Governor John Floyd " in *John P. Branch Historical Papers of Randolph-Macon College,* 1913, IV, p. 39.

3 James Parton, *Life of Andrew Jackson,* II, p. 397; John S. Bassett, *Slavery in the State of North Carolina,* p. 94; W. E. B. DuBois, *The Suppression of the African Slave Trade,* p. 6; Benjamin Brawley, *A Social History of the American Negro,* p. 17; James T. Adams, *Provincial Society, 1690-1763,* p. 103; Asa H. Gordon, " The struggle of the slave for freedom," in *The Journal of Negro History,* XIII, p. 35; Luther P. Jackson, " Religious instruction of Negroes, 1830-1860, with special reference to South Carolina," in *ibid.,* XV, p. 112; Walter H. Mazyck, *George Washington and the Negro,* p. 42.

4 *Old Virginia and Her Neighbors,* II, p. 196.

5 James Schouler, *History of the United States of America under the Constitution,* II, pp. 264-267. See also, A. M. Simons, *Social Forces in American History,* p. 274; Claude H. VanTyne, *The War of Independence,* p. 203; Maury Maverick, *A Maverick American,* p. 315; James G. Randall, *The Civil War and Reconstruction,* p. 53; John D. Hicks, *The Federal Union,* p. 496; H. J. Eckenrode, " Negroes in Richmond in 1864," *The Virginia Magazine of History and Biography,* 1938, XLVI, p. 194.

Not a few specialists in the field of American slavery have published similar sentiments. One, who has referred to a few of the uprisings, decided [6] that the fact of their revelation was of greater importance than their existence, and concluded that there was not discontent, but rather "a fine devotion on the part of the majority of the slaves." Another, the late Ulrich B. Phillips, who is generally considered the outstanding authority on the institution of American Negro slavery, expressed it as his opinion that "slave revolts and plots very seldom occurred in the United States." This conclusion coincided with, indeed, was necessary for the maintenance of, Professor Phillips' racialistic notions that led him to describe the Negro as suffering from "inherited ineptitude", and as being stupid, negligent, docile, inconstant, dilatory and "by racial quality submissive." [7]

By no means all commentators, however, have accepted this viewpoint. Several first-hand observers of the slaves were struck by their restlessness, discontent, and rebelliousness. Thus, for example, the preamble to a Virginia law of 1669, which made the killing of slaves by owner or overseer as a result of "correction" a non-criminal act, declared that this measure was needed because "the only law in force for the punishment of refractory servants resisting their master, mistris or overseer [lengthening the term of servitude] cannot be inflicted upon negroes, nor the obstinacy of many of them by other than violent meanes supprest." [8] The same idea was implicit in some of the earliest protests of certain Quakers against slavery. Both the famous Germantown Protest of 1688 and the argument pre-

6 Francis P. Gaines, *The Southern Plantation*, p. 225.

7 The cited phrases and words are from *The Course of the South to Secession*, p. 101; *American Negro Slavery*, pp. 341-42; *A History of Transportation in the Eastern Cotton Belt*, p. 25; *Life and Labor in the Old South*, p. 196; "The economic cost of slaveholding in the cotton belt," in *Political Science Quarterly*, 1905, XX, p. 270. For Phillips' background see Wood Gray's paper on him in William T. Hutchinson, ed., *The Marcus W. Jernegan Essays in American Historiography*, pp. 355 ff.

8 William W. Hening, ed., *The Statutes at Large being a collection of the laws of Virginia*, II, p. 270.

sented to the Concord, Pennsylvania Monthly Meeting ten years later by Robert Pyle made a point of the belligerent spirit of the Negroes as an argument against slavery since it proved the suffering of the victims and necessitated armed might for purposes of suppression.[9]

Governor Drysdale in his message to the General Assembly of Virginia in 1723 (immediately following the crushing of a slave conspiracy) urged the enactment of further precautionary measures with the remark: [10] " I am persuaded you are too well acquainted with the Cruel dispositions of these Creatures, when they have it in their power to destroy or distress, to let Slipp this faire opportunity of making more proper Laws against them." A leading inhabitant of the same Colony, Colonel William Byrd, in a letter to Lord Egmont dated July 12, 1736, appealed for an end to the slave trade on the grounds of the acute danger arising from the increasing number of slaves for, he said,[11] " Numbers make them insolent, and then foul Means must do what fair will not ... But these base Tempers require to be rid with a tort Rein, or they will be apt to throw their Rider."

The Negro leaders, Absalom Jones and Richard Allen, in a pamphlet published in 1794, also referred [12] to " the dreadful insurrections that have been made when opportunity offered" and felt these were sufficient " to convince a reasonable man that great uneasiness and not contentment is the inhabitant of their

9 See the present writer's " The Quakers and Negro Slavery " in *The Journal of Negro History*, XXV, pp. 336-38.

10 *The Virginia Historical Register and Literary Notebook,* 1851, IV, p. 63.

11 *The American Historical Review,* 1895, L, p. 89; quoted by Edward Channing, *A History of the United States,* II, p. 377. See also Alexander Hewatt, *An Historical Account of the Rise and Progress of the Colonies of South Carolina and Georgia,* II, p. 97; and Verner W. Crane, " Benjamin Franklin on slavery and American liberties," in *Pennsylvania Magazine of History and Biography,* LXII, p. 8.

12 Absalom Jones and Richard Allen, *A Narrative of the Proceeding of the Black People during the Awful Calamity in Philadelphia in the Year 1793,* p. 24; quoted in Charles H. Wesley, *Richard Allen,* p. 108.

breasts." Occasionally white Southerners, even in the nineteenth century, but prior to the flowering of the Abolitionist movement, published similar sentiments. Thus Hugh M'Call, one of the earliest historians of Georgia, remarked [13] that " the Negroes could not be supposed to be content in slavery, [and] would grasp with avidity at the most desperate attempts which promised freedom." Again, a South Carolina publicist, writing just after the Vesey conspiracy, while maintaining that the slaves were well off, nevertheless admitted: [14] " We regard our negroes as the *'Jacobins'* of the country, against whom we should always be upon our guard, and who, although we fear no permanent affects from any insurrectionary movements on their part, should be watched with an eye of steady and unremitting observation."

Among anti-slavery leaders there were some who were aware of part of the rebellious record of the slaves, although even in this group there were others who believed that docility was characteristic. Of the former may be mentioned Joshua Coffin,[15] Horace Greeley,[16] and John Brown,[17] while among the latter

---

13 *The History of Savannah*, I, p. 125, quoted, not quite correctly, by Ruth Scarborough, *The Opposition to Slavery in Georgia prior to 1860*, p. 190.

14 [E. C. Holland] *A Refutation of the Calumnies circulated against the Southern & Western States respecting the Institution and Existence of Slavery among Them...*, p. 61; see also Gov. Gibbes' message to the South Carolina Assembly in 1711, in *ibid.*, p. 28; and Anonymous, *Letter to a Member of the General Assembly of Virginia, on the Subject of the late Conspiracy of the Slaves*, p. 6; C. W. Janson, *The Stranger in America...*, p. 361; Helen T. Catterall, ed., *Judicial Cases concerning American Slavery and the Negro*, III, p. 568.

15 Joshua Coffin, a Massachusetts Quaker Abolitionist and the historian of Newburyport, was the author of the first extended study of American slave revolts. This appeared as Appendix A to Amos A. Phelps' *Lectures on Slavery and its Remedy*, and was reprinted in New York in 1860 as *An Account of Some of the Principal Slave Insurrections*.

16 See editorial in N. Y. *Weekly Tribune*, Sept. 16, 1854. It is typical of the lack of accuracy with which the subject has been handled that this dates the Vesey plot as 1820 and the Turner revolt as 1832.

17 Oswald G. Villard, *John Brown*, p. 362.

were Richard Hildreth[18] and, for a time, Thomas Wentworth Higginson.[19]

Although American historians have generally tended to minimize or deny the discontent among the Negro slaves of the United States, it is nevertheless true that from time to time recognition of its existence has appeared. Certain Negro scholars,[20] for example, have demonstrated an awareness of the phenomenon, and a few white investigators [21] of the question have also denied that meekness or docility was characteristic of the slaves. Within very recent years there has been a notable increase in the number adopting this viewpoint.[22]

Yet there is no thorough, documented study of many phases of the problem, and until this is undertaken one who is anxious

18 R. Hildreth, *Despotism in America*, pp. 69, 164. It is worth noting that the one passing reference to an actual slave revolt that Hildreth makes in his massive historical work is (by inference, not by name) to Gabriel's conspiracy in Virginia, and this is misdated—an unusual mistake for that meticulous worker. *The History of the United States of America*, V, p. 341.

19 On November 30, 1858, Thomas W. Higginson wrote to Lysander Spooner, "The great obstacle to anti-slavery action has always been the apparent feebleness & timidity of the slaves themselves." Lysander Spooner Papers, Boston Public Library. Later, however, Higginson wrote articles on slave revolts for the *Atlantic Monthly* expressing a different opinion.

20 John W. Cromwell, *The Negro in American History*, pp. 12-17; Carter G. Woodson, *The Negro in Our History*, pp. 78-79, 90-93, 177-85, and reviews by Dr. Woodson of a book by U. B. Phillips in *The Mississippi Valley Historical Review* (1919), pp. 480-82, and of a book by W. B. Hesseltine, in *The Journal of Negro History* (1937), XXII, p. 243.

21 H. Catterall, ed., *op. cit.*, I, p. 54 n., Frederic Bancroft, *Slave-Trading in the Old South*, pp. 17, 277, 283-84.

22 Examples are: Robert Minor, "The black ten millions," in *The Liberator*, VII, pp. 7-9; Hollie E. Carter, "Negro insurrections in American history," unpublished master's thesis, 1936, Howard University; Harvey Wish, "American slave insurrections before 1861," in *The Journal of Negro History* (1937) XXII, pp. 299-320; Joseph C. Carroll, *Slave Insurrections in the United States, 1800-1865*; C. L. James, *A History of Negro Revolt* (*Fact*, London, Sept., 1938); letter by Melville J. Herskovits in *The South Atlantic Quarterly* (1940), XXXIX, pp. 350-51; Louis M. Hacker, *The Triumph of American Capitalism*, pp. 295-96; Henrietta Buckmaster, *Let My People Go, passim*.

to know the facts concerning the institution of slavery in American life is very largely groping in the dark. The present work represents an attempt to meet this need.[23]

23 In the words of L. D. Reddick: " Since the work of Mrs. Catterall, there are but two important aspects of the field unexplored. First, there is need for a thorough study of the attempts to break the system by the slaves through suicide, flight, individual resistance and group insurrection. Secondly, there is not yet a picture of the institution as seen through eyes of the bondsman himself." "A new interpretation for Negro history," in *The Journal of Negro History* (1937), XXII, p. 20.

CHAPTER II

THE FEAR OF REBELLION

WHILE there is a difference of opinion as to the prevalence of discontent amongst the slaves, one finds very nearly unanimous [1] agreement concerning the widespread fear of servile rebellion. This is true not merely among those historians who show some awareness of mass unrest, but even among the larger number who either ignore or positively deny widespread plots and revolts.

Thus, references to this fear, not infrequently joined with an expression of wonder at its presence, are to be found in works [2] dealing with the institution of slavery in Massachusetts, New York, Tennessee, Virginia, North Carolina, South Carolina, Georgia, Louisiana, and Texas. The same is true of more extended studies by such scholars [3] as James Schouler, Herbert L. Osgood, William E. Dodd, Carl R. Fish, Emory Q. Hawk,

1 Occasional exceptions occur, as Joseph Cobb, *Mississippi Scenes*, pp. 160-61; Joseph H. Ingraham, *The Southwest by a Yankee*, II, pp. 260-262.

2 George H. Moore, *Notes on the History of Slavery in Massachusetts*, pp. 69, 129; Edwin V. Morgan, *Slavery in New York*, p. 12; James C. Ballagh, *History of Slavery in Virginia*, pp. 74-75; John S. Bassett, *Slavery and Servitude in the Colony of North Carolina*, pp. 60-61; J. S. Bassett, *Slavery in the State of North Carolina*, p. 94; Rooser H. Taylor, " Slaveholding in North Carolina: an economic view," in *James Sprunt Historical Publications*, 1926, XVIII, p. 27; H. M. Henry, *The Police Control of the Slave in South Carolina*, p. 148; U. B. Phillips, *Georgia and State Rights*, pp. 153, 186; Arthur P. Whitaker, *The Mississippi Question, 1795-1803*, pp. 41-42; Harold Schoen, " The free Negro in the Republic of Texas," in *Southwestern Historical Quarterly*, 1937, XLI, p. 101.

3 James Schouler, *History of the United States*, II, pp. 64, 66, 262; Herbert L. Osgood, *The American Colonies in the Eighteenth Century*, IV, pp. 83, 85, 99; William E. Dodd, " The emergence of the first social order in the United States," in *The American Historical Review*, 1935, XL, p. 230; Carl R. Fish, *The American Civil War an interpretation* (edited by W. E. Smith), pp. 44-45; Emory Q. Hawk, *Economic History of the South*, p. 86; Ulrich B. Phillips, " Racial problems, adjustments and disturbance," in *The South in the Building of the Nation*, IV, p. 236.

and Ulrich B. Phillips. Very recently Clement Eaton devoted [4] several pages to a discussion of this phenomenon. Of course, the discovery of a plot or the suppression of a rebellion, if publicized, invariably evoked fear—indeed, terror—but these manifestations will be noted as they occurred. There is also evidence that this fear existed quite independent of any connection with an actual outbreak.

Military activity frequently provoked expressions of alarm concerning the Negroes. Thus one of the prime concerns of the officials of Virginia in 1673 during the war with the Dutch was the possible development of disaffection among the indentured servants and the slaves.[5] Difficulties with Indians, particularly of the Yamasee tribe, aroused fears among South Carolinians as to the behavior of their slaves at various intervals during the first third of the eighteenth century. This reached panic proportions, particularly in Granville County, when it was discovered that fugitive Negro slaves were actively aiding the Yamasee and Lower Creek Indians in border forays during 1727 and 1728.[6]

During the French and Indian War pronounced worry concerning the Negroes was evident in Maryland, Virginia and South Carolina. James Glen, governor of the last of these colonies, in a message to the legislature on January 27, 1756, acknowledged the existence of these fears, and made use of it in a letter to the London Board of Trade on April 14, 1756 protesting against the contemplated landing within South Carolina of about nine hundred Acadians.[7]

Alarm appears to have been even more acute in Virginia, the locale of much of the fighting especially during the early and, for the British, the disastrous years of the struggle. In

4 Clement Eaton, *Freedom of Thought in the Old South*, Chapter IV.

5 Philip A. Bruce, *Institutional History of Virginia in the Seventeenth Century*, II, pp. 199-200.

6 Verner W. Crane, *The Southern Frontier, 1670-1732*, pp. 184, 247.

7 Ruth A. Hudnut and Hayes Baker-Crothers, "Acadian transients in South Carolina," *American Historical Review*, 1938, XLIII, pp. 500-503.

the summer of 1755 Colonel Charles Carter had informed
Lieutenant-Governor Robert Dinwiddie of setbacks inflicted
by the French and their allies, and also, of stirrings on the part
of the slaves. Dinwiddie replied, July 18, 1755, that he felt the
news of the French successes had been exaggerated, but he went
on: [8]

The Villany of the Negroes on any Emergency of Gov't is w't
I always fear'd. I greatly approve of Y'r send'g the Sheriffs with
proper Strength to take up those y't appear'd in a Body at Y'r
Son's House, and if found guilty of the Expressions mention'd I
expect You will send for a Com'o to try them, and an Example of
one or two at first may prevent those Creatures enter'g into Com-
binat's and wicked Designs ag'st the Subjects . . . In the mean
Time You (must) act consist't with Y'r good Sense in keeping
Patrollers out for the Peace of Y'r Co'ty. I shall order an Adver-
tisem't in the Papers as You Desire, but with't Y't I think the
Sheriffs sh'd seize all Hourses used by Negroes in the Night Time.

Five days later Dinwiddie informed the Earl of Halifax
that he found it necessary to [9] " leave a proper number of soldiers in each county to protect it from the combinations of the
negro slaves, who have been very audacious on the defeat on
the Ohio. These poor creatures imagine the French will give
them their freedom." The next year this same official wrote [10]
at least two letters to his superiors in England containing refer-
ernces to similar fears and mentioning the fact that the presence
of over 120,000 Negroes in a total population of some 295,000

8 R. A. Brock, ed., *The Official Records of Robert Dinwiddie*, II, pp. 102-
103. For evidence that the same events provoked concern in Maryland, see
the letter from Gov. Horatio Sharpe to Lord Calvert, July 15, 1755 in
W. H. Browne, ed., *Archives of Maryland*, VI, p. 251; and the minutes
of the Maryland Council, dated August 15, 1755, in *ibid.*, XXXI, p. 72.

9 John C. Fitzpatrick, ed., *The Writings of George Washington*, I, p. 151 n.

10 *Ibid.*, I, p. 336 n.; Brock, *op. cit.*, II, p. 474; see also Louis K. Koontz,
The Virginia Frontier, 1754-1765, p. 45 n.; Walter H. Mazyck, *George Washington and the Negro*, p. 24; Charles H. Ambler, *George Washington and
the West*, p. 112; Hayes Baker-Crothers, *Virginia and the French & Indian
War*, p. 82.

made it unwise to order the militia " to any great Distance from the pres't settlem'ts."

The next period of major military activity, that of the Revolutionary War, also produced expressions of alarm concerning the slave. John Adams recorded in his diary for November 24, 1775, the visit of two Southern delegates to the Continental Congress, Archibald Bulloch and John Houston, and noted [11] that these men felt grave concern over the possibility that a British army might wage a war in the South under an antislavery banner, which, they said, would lead to twenty thousand slaves flocking to it in a few weeks. These men remarked that, " The Negroes have a wonderful art of communicating intelligence among themselves; it will run several hundreds of miles in a week or a fortnight."

There are recurrent instances of this type of fear during the Revolution. Major-General Charles Lee, for example, wrote five letters during the month of April, 1776, while at Williamsburg, Virginia, stressing the importance of maintaining a firm control over the slaves.[12] The last letter in this series, dated April 16, and addressed to Robert Morris, mentioned the possibility of a servile revolt and urged Morris to have three or four regiments from the middle colonies ready for reinforcing the southern front in case it should materialize. When, during the summer, Lee moved his headquarters to Charlestown, South Carolina, he was visited, at his request, by citizens from Georgia. These people brought him information about the extreme weakness of their region, the ravages of the British Navy, the use of Florida by Indians as their base for marauding at-

11 Charles F. Adams, ed., *The Works of John Adams*, II, p. 428. Fears of Negro uprising were experienced in Framingham, Massachusetts in 1775.— Temple, *History of Framingham*, p. 275; Lorenzo J. Greene, *The Negro in Colonial New England, 1620-1776* (Columbia University Press, 1942), p. 198.

12 " The Charles Lee Papers," *Collections of the New York Historical Society*, I, pp. 369, 372, 379, 410, 424-25. Lee during April and May received letters from subordinates telling of unrest and flight among the slaves, *ibid.*, I, pp. 390, 462.

tacks, and the wholesale flight of the slaves.[13] "Add to these considerations the vast Numbers of Negroes we have, perhaps of themselves Sufficient to subdue us—in Point of Numbers the Blacks exceed the Whites; and the ready channel of Supply and secure retreat which St. Augustine affords render them much to be dreaded."

A letter written July 31, 1776, by Henry Wynkoop, a resident of Bucks County, Pennsylvania, to the local Committee of Safety requested [14] the dispatching of ammunition in order to quiet " the people in my Neighborhood [who] have been somewhat alarmed with fears about Negroes & disaffected people injuring their families when they are in the Service."

Conditions in South Carolina are illuminated by the report of the Congressional Committee on the circumstances in the Southern States submitted [15] on March 29, 1779. The Committee reported that according to information furnished it by South Carolina's delegates, and by Mr. Huger, who had been sent north by that State's Governor in order to present up-to-the-minute data, South Carolina could not effectively employ its militia against the British. This was so because much of that force was needed as a home guard to prevent rebellion and flight amongst the slaves. It was this report that led the Congress to suggest the freeing and arming of three thousand South Carolina slaves and their use against the English. This was spurned by the state authorities and led the Council to recommend South Carolina's withdrawal from the conflict, a suggestion which was not followed because of General Moultrie's refusal to surrender.

Another bit of evidence, this time involving Virginia, ap-

13 *Ibid.*, II, pp. 114-115, Charles Lee to John Hancock, July 2, 1776. According to the figures given by Evarts B. Greene and V. D. Harrington in *American Population before the Census of 1790*, p. 182, there were about 17,000 whites and 15,000 Negroes in Georgia in 1774.

14 Samuel Hazard, ed., *Pennsylvania Archives*, First Series, IV, p. 792. See also *ibid.*, second series, edited by William H. Egle, XV, p. 368.

15 W. C. Ford, ed., *Journals of the Continental Congress*, XIII, p. 385; W. H. Mazyck, *op. cit.*, pp. 720-76; see also Charles Elliot, *Sinfulness of American Slavery*, II, p. 153.

peared in a letter by a Colonel Wooding dated Halifax County, July 21, 1781. The writer lamented a lack of military equipment, and remarked [16] that some good guns were owned by several of the inhabitants, " but the owners I am told secrete them and Say they will do it for their own Defence against insurrections of Slaves or Tories—Reasons that seem to carry weight (with me at least) . . .".

Very much the same situation prevailed during the years of the War of 1812. Just before the outbreak of hostilities, in December, 1811, a Virginia slaveholder and Congressman, John Randolph, " dwelt on the danger arising from the black population." [17] " He said he would touch this subject as tenderly as possible ; it was with reluctance that he touched it at all . . . While talking of taking Canada, some of us are shuddering for our safety at home. I speak from facts when I say, that the night bell never tolls for fire in Richmond, that the mother does not hug the infant more closely to her bosom. I have been a witness of some of the alarms in the capital of Virginia."

A letter written by a resident of Charleston, South Carolina, in the summer of 1812, makes reference to the fears in these words, [18] " Consider, I beseech you, that the coast of S. Carolina and Georgia is principally inhabited by a black population, which it is not to be denied, the whites are not able to controul . . . A regiment of militia has been sent us from the interior for our protection, but they have mutinied . . . tho' the mutiny is arrested for the moment, the spirit of it is by no means quelled."

During the first year of the conflict with England, slaveholders in Georgia were distraught because of events centering in East Florida. From that Spanish possession Indians and fugitive slaves carried on a guerrilla warfare against Georgia's

16 Samuel McRae, ed., *Calendar of Virginia State Papers*, II, p. 233. Later volumes edited by William Palmer. Hereafter cited as *C.V.S.P.*

17 H. A. Garland, *The Life of John Randolph of Roanoke*, I, pp. 293-95. Randolph was in Richmond during the great Gabriel conspiracy of 1800. See William C. Bruce, *John Randolph*, II, pp. 250-51.

18 New-York *Evening Post*, August 4, 1812.

inhabitants. Moreover, American-born residents of East Florida, supported by United States soldiers and gunboats, attempted, unsuccessfully, to overthrow the Spanish rulers. The
forces mustered by the Spaniards to resist this attack included
Negro soldiers, and this caused alarm among neighboring slaveholders.[19]

In far-off Mississippi Territory, news of the outbreak of war
also accentuated the ever-present dread of slave rebellion. Governor David Holmes in a letter dated Town of Washington,
July 22, 1812, appealed [20] to Brigadier-General James Wilkinson for a considerable quantity of muskets, rifles, powder, and
lead. One factor behind this request was the possibility that the
attitude of the Choctaw Indians would change from friendship
to hostility, but of greater importance were the slaves. Of these,
said the Governor

I entertain much stronger apprehensions. Scarcely a day passes
without my receiving some information relative to the designs of
these people to insurrect.[21] It is true that no clear or positive evidence of their intentions has been communicated; but certain facts,
and expressions of their views have justly excited considerable
alarm amongst the citizens. For my own part I am impressed with
the belief that real danger exists, and that it is my duty to lose
no time in procuring arms for the defence of the Country . . . If
you should not deem it correct to comply wholly with my request,
I hope you will do so in part; for I assure you, Sir, it is my firm
belief that the safety of the citizens here may depend upon my procuring a sufficient number of arms to enable them to defend themselves against the dangers apprehended.

When, several weeks later, the Territory was called upon to
dispatch a portion of its militia outside its borders, Governor

19 Julius W. Pratt, *Expansionists of 1812*, pp. 192-95, 207-212; T. F. Davis,
"United States troops in Spanish East Florida, 1812-1813," in *The Florida
Historical Society Quarterly* (1930-31), IX, pp. 3-12, 96-109, 133-55, 259-78.

20 Clarence E. Carter, ed., *The Territorial Papers of the United States*,
VI, p. 299.

21 For one such piece of information see, *post*, p. 253.

Holmes again wrote [22] to General Wilkinson and stressed the same problem:

Remonstrances and petitions have been presented to me stating the danger to be apprehended from the Negroes & Indians, should the Militia be marched out of the Territory. To these representations I have given no answer. But I am of opinion that if you can dispense with the service of the Cavalry, and furnish us with two hundred Muskets for the use of the Militia that will remain at home, it would make the country secure against any probable difficulties, and quiet the fears of many good citizens. The Detachment now encamped near the Cantonment of Washington consists of one fourth of the physical force of the Counties comprising the Mississippi district. Nearly one half of the entire population are Slaves and the frontier Counties are thinly inhabited. These considerations, I am confident, will have with you their just weight. In Slave Countries the Danger of insurrection always exists, and the Inhabitants should be prepared to meet the event.

John Randolph testified in the summer of 1813 that his forecast of panic made two years before was accurate, since precisely that condition had befallen the people of Virginia upon the Governor's call for militia to meet the British. " The distress and alarm occasioned by this requisition ", he wrote,[23] " do not arise from *fear* of the prowess of the *enemy,* but of the effects of the *climate* and *water* of the low country, especially *at this season,* and the danger from *an internal foe,* augmented by the removal of so large a portion of our force. Of the result you can form no conception."

One year later General Philip Stuart of the Maryland militia wrote to President Madison that many of the inhabitants of his state were in dire distress because of the fighting, and driven to

---

22 Letter dated Washington, October 19, 1812, in *ibid.*, VI, pp. 328-29.

23 John Randolph to Josiah Quincy, Roanoke, July 4, 1813, in Edmund Quincy, *Life of Josiah Quincy of Massachusetts*, p. 333. Three days later Brigadier-General Robert B. Taylor wrote the Governor of Virginia of acute fears of Negro revolt in Nansemond County—*C.V.S.P.*, X, p. 241.

distraction by fears as to what the slaves might do. He noted that, as a special precaution,[24]

The negroes are ordered, at night, to retire to the heights lest the Enemy from his facility of movement, should capture them. Here, projects may be engendered at which humanity shudders . . . if no aid is afforded us, I shall be compelled to disband my militia, to the end that by removing their families and remaining property into the interior of the Country, they may have something from that general ruin that threatens them, and also that the Enemy may not be strengthened by a species of force, by us the most to be dreaded of any within his means.

Many citizens of Caroline County, Virginia, protested [25] on August 3, 1814, against the Governor's call upon their militia for extra-county duty, " on account of apprehension of negro insurrection." At about the same time the Governor of Louisiana, Edward Tiffin, received a letter from a resident of New Feliciana commenting [26] upon the dangerous state of affairs, what with the militia in a poor condition, many citizens disloyal, and the slaves exceedingly dangerous. " Many of the People declare they will not serve a tour of duty, and leave their Family's to be plundered and butchered by the Negro's &c."

A letter from the prominent Virginian, Walter Jones, to James Monroe, the Secretary of State, dated December 20, 1814, commented [27] upon the flight of hundreds of slaves, the

24 Letter dated July 29, 1814 in Papers of James Madison, Library of Congress.

25 C.V.S.P., X, p. 367, also p. 388.

26 John Smith to Edward Tiffin, August 28, 1814, in Papers of James Monroe, Library of Congress. It may be noted that these conditions were cited by Congressman William O. Butler of Kentucky, who served at the Battle of New Orleans, in justifying Andrew Jackson's declaration of martial law preceding that struggle, and in arguing for the refunding of the fine to which the General had been subjected for that action—The Congressional Globe, 1843, 27 Cong., 3rd Sess., XII, 118-19.

27 James Monroe Papers, Library of Congress. A South Carolinian who strongly favored the war took the trouble to deny the vital importance of the slaves' presence as an argument against its prosecution—Benjamin Elliott, A Sketch of the Means and Benefits of prosecuting this War against Britain, p. 19.

poor behavior of the militia and their inadequate supplies. He declared that the last two factors " render our general welfare as ludicrous, as severe disaster can be made " and added:

The disaffection of the blacks is daily gaining extent & boldness which may produce effects, at the approaching festival of Xmas, that may bring to men minds, the Sicilian vespers of times past. The same heedless Imbecility that destroys our Efforts against the external Enemy, paralyses every thing like vigilance & Police, in respect to the more dangerous internal population, public hope has been highly raised, & much rooted on the aid of the Regiment, under Colo. Hamilton. it would with Certainty restrain the internal Evil. where is he? we hear not a word about him. I beseech you, my dear Sir, to hasten his march.

Evidences of such fears recurred with the outbreak of the " Second American Revolution." James L. Petigru, an outstanding South Carolinian, learned [28] with regret and surprise in January, 1861, that his sister seemed unwilling to return home from the North for " she says she lives in fear of insurrection." The wife of Senator James Chestnut, Jr., of South Carolina, felt the same way, as did the wife of Senator Louis T. Wigfall of Texas. Mrs. Chestnut noted in her diary in March, 1861, that William Henry Trescott, a former United States Assistant Secretary of State, spoke French at the dinner table and explained,[29] " we are using French against Africa. We know the black waiters are all ears now, and we want to keep what we have to say dark. We can't afford to take them into our confidence, you know."

Further evidences of sharp suspicions recur, the most striking coming from Louisiana. There, a lady in mortal terror of Negro uprisings had provided herself with " a hatchet, a tomahawk, and a vial of some kind of spirits " with which she in-

28 Petigru to Mrs. Jane P. North, dated Charleston, January 29, 1861, in James P. Carson, *Life, Letters, and Speeches of James Louis Petrigru the Union Man of South Carolina*, p. 367.

29 Isabella D. Martin and Myrta L. Avary, eds., *A Diary from Dixie*, as written by Mary Boykin Chestnut, pp. 1, 24-25, 33.

tended to blind the dreaded rebels when and if the fatal day arrived.[30]

Two fundamental considerations in the minds of the rulers of the South, territorial annexation and the question of secession, evoked a third, the problem of slave control. Whenever the first two were discussed the third frequently entered the picture, and this fact again shows the constant presence of the fear and its all-pervading quality.

Data demonstrating the relationship of the former, territorial expansion, with fears concerning the slaves' behavior are numerous. Thus, while it is, of course, true that American political and economic interests together with Napoleon's financial distress, and his defeat in St. Domingo, were of basic importance in the acquisition of the Louisiana Territory, it is also a fact that another factor was present. Contemporary material demonstrates that a consideration, so far as the United States was concerned, that appears to have had some importance was the fear that France of the liberty, equality, fraternity slogan might use Louisiana not only to detach western lands from the United States, but also to revolutionize the adjacent slave population.

While the area was still in the weak hands of Spain a newspaper correspondent had written: [31] " If the French once get an establishment upon the Spanish territory, in the vicinity of the southern states, it will behove the planter to look well to his own household. Should the example of St. Domingo be caught ... [there] shall be great tribulation."

The same consideration is stressed [32] in the instructions given

30 Kate M. Rowland and M. L. Croxall, eds., *The Journal of Julia Le Grand, New Orleans, 1862-1863*, p. 58, entry of December 31, 1862. See also, F. B. Simkins and J. W. Patton, *The Women of the Confederacy*, pp. 1-2; F. L. Owsley, " Local defense and the overthrow of the Confederacy," in *Mississippi Valley Historical Review* (1925), XI, pp. 490-91. For rumors of similar situations throughout the South, see, *The Liberator*, May 10, Aug. 16, Dec. 20, 1861; N. Y. *Daily Tribune*, Feb. 1, 20, March 19, May 3, June 8, 1861; Jan. 23, 1862.

31 " Gustavus," in the Hartford *Connecticut Courant*, August 21, 1797.

32 See Arthur B. Darling, *Our Rising Empire, 1763-1803*, p. 423.

September 28, 1801 by James Madison, the Secretary of State, to Robert Livingston, the newly-appointed Minister to France. Above all else, said Secretary Madison, Mr. Livingston was to impress upon the French nation the " momentous concern " of the United States over the reported cession of adjacent lands by Spain to France. And, among other things, Mr. Livingston was " to point to the unrest which would occur among the slaves in the Southern States, for they had been taught to regard the French as patrons of their cause."

Fear became acute when it was definitely known that the area was in France's possession. This is, in part, what Hamilton had in mind when, in 1803, he wrote [33] concerning the transfer of sovereignty, " This event threatens the early dismemberment of a large portion of the country; more immediately the safety of all the Southern States; and remotely, the independence of the whole Union." The same year Senator Wells of Delaware declared: [34]

Let the French be but once settled [in Florida and Louisiana] and they will have the whole of your Southern States at their mercy. Unhappily, there is an inveterate enemy in the very bosom of those States. You might as well attempt to stop the course of the plague, as to arrest the subtle and dangerous spirit they would the moment it suited their interests, let loose among the helots of that country. Then you would have lighted up there a domestic war, which would only be extinguished in the blood of your citizens.

Another aspect of the question that received some attention [35]

[33] The " Pericles " letter, in Henry C. Lodge, ed., *The Works of Alexander Hamilton*, VI, p. 334. For this letter's authenticity see A. P. Whitaker, *The Mississippi Question*, p. 315 n.

[34] In the Senate, February 24, 1803, *Annals of Congress*, XII, 156. Senator Gouverneur Morris of New York said the same thing on this day, *ibid.*, XII, 194. Wells, Hamilton, and Morris were, of course, enemies of the new France, so that a political motive was not lacking in the expression of the above fears.

[35] Such a use of Louisiana is dwelt on in an obscure pamphlet by an anonymous author as early as 1795, *Tyrannical Libertymen. A Discourse upon Negro-Slavery* composed at ——; in Newhampshire, Hanover, 1795; and is mentioned in the wellknown work by the Virginian, St. George Tucker,

was the possibility of using this western territory as a Negro colonization area, especially for the disposal of slaves who had already been shown to be dangerous.[36]

The foreign ownership of Florida had, ever since the early part of the eighteenth century, disturbed slaveholders in Georgia and South Carolina. The fact, moreover, that the Spaniards made a point of aiding fugitive slaves, and often enlisted them as soldiers, was particularly annoying. The same condition and practices continued after the American Revolution and were immediately sources of irritation between the United States and Spain.[37] This continued for several decades, and the necessity of stopping it was one of the causes of an American-inspired revolt in East Florida in 1812 and 1813, which received considerable support from the United States, particularly from Georgia.[38]

The chain of military events that finally culminated in Florida's annexation in 1819 was, to a great extent, created by the desire to wipe out the nests of hostile Indians and runaway slaves who used the swamps of Florida as havens of refuge and as bases from which to launch lightning-like attacks upon plantations across the border. These activities, in turn, increased the restlessness of the slave population.

A Dissertation on Slavery: with a proposal for the gradual abolition of it, in the State of Virginia, first published in Phila., 1796, reprinted, N. Y., 1861. The same thought is in the anonymous pamphlet published in Baltimore, 1801, *A Letter to A Member of the General Assembly of Virginia* ..., pp. 18-19. In 1805 the Virginia legislature asked for the use of Louisiana for this purpose—C. G. Woodson, *The Negro in our History*, p. 282. As an expansionist, however, Thomas Jefferson expressed a preference for Africa— Gilbert Chinard, *Thomas Jefferson*, p. 399. See also Mary S. Locke, *Antislavery in America, 1619-1808*, p. 193.

36 It is to be remembered that the Lewis and Clark expedition ended in 1806, and that for years after this much of the newly acquired territory was unknown and considered a wasteland. The federal policy of settling Indians here indicates this well. See R. S. Cotterill, *The Old South*, pp. 130-133.

37 See John C. Fitzpatrick, *The Diaries of George Washington*, IV, pp. 103, 181-82.

38 *Supra*, p. 24; see also H. Aptheker, "Maroons within the present limits of the United States," in *The Journal of Negro History*, 1939, XXIV, pp. 172-73.

A typical statement of the case, one which preceded American military invasion under Colonel Clinch by but a few days, appeared in the Savannah, Georgia, *Journal* [39] of June 26, 1816. This paper pointed to the existence of a strong and dangerous force of runaway slaves in the Florida fort at Appalachicola Bay recently abandoned by the British officer, Colonel Nicholls, and declared:

It was not to have been expected, that an establishment so pernicious to the Southern States, holding out to a part of their population temptations to insubordination, would have been suffered to exist after the close of the war. In the course of the last winter, several slaves from this neighborhood fled to that fort; others have *lately* gone from Tennessee and the Mississippi Territory. How long shall this evil, requiring immediate remedy be permitted to exist?

The anti-slavery policy of the Mexican Government was a prime cause of dissension between that state and American slaveholders resident in Texas.[40] The Negroes of Texas learned of the Mexican anti-slavery regulations, and grew restless so that their masters had to resort to barbarous methods of pun-

39 Quoted in Richmond *Enquirer*, July 10, 1816. It is to be observed that the British chargé in East Florida, J. P. Morier, had, in a note to his foreign office in January, 1811, suggested that American pretensions to the Floridas might well be hindered by causing outbreaks among the slaves and by importing Negro soldiers from Havana to assist them in their struggle for freedom, J. F. Rippy, *Rivalry of the United States and Great Britain over Latin-America 1808-1830*, p. 37. Professor Isaac J. Cox has remarked, " Confusion and anarchy in the neighboring Spanish province might affect his [the Amercan's] slaves or the near-by Indians. This stuation formed a real reason for action by the American authorities."—*The West Florida Controversy*, p. 666.

40 The Hartford *Connecticut Courant* of November 20, 1826, quoting the Arkansas *Gazette* of October 10, tells of an exodus of slaveholders from Texas into Louisiana and Arkansas due to the anti-slavery attitude of the Mexican nation. See the interesting prophecy in [W. W. Blane] *An Excursion through the United States*, p. 208.

ishment in order to retain them.[41] The desire to hold human property more securely is not to be overlooked in considering causes of the Texas Revolution, or in evaluating the reasons for American interest in the success of that effort and in ultimate annexation.

During the actual fighting between Texas and Mexico fears concerning the slaves were great indeed, and the belief that the Mexicans would stir them to rebellion was widespread. These worries may be found expressed in the writings of such leading insurrectionists as Benjamin R. Milam, Horatio A. Allsbury, Thomas J. Pilgrim, and Henry Austin.[42] Stephen F. Austin himself, in a letter [43] to his sister, Mrs. Mary Austin Holley, dated New Orleans, August 2, 1835, succinctly stated the feelings and fears of the group when he wrote that Texas had to be Americanized and *" Texas must be a slave country. It is no longer a matter of doubt.* The interest of Louisiana requires that it should be, a population of fanatical abolitionists in Texas

41 See the report of Don Manuel Mier y Teran to President Guadalupe Victoria, June 30, 1828 in Alleine Howren, " Causes and origin of the decree of April 6, 1830 " in *The Southwestern Historical Quarterly*, 1913, XVI, pp. 397-98. The State constitution of Coahuila-Texas adopted March, 1827, declared that none thereafter born was to be a slave, and forbade the introduction of more slaves after a six month period. A law of May, 1828 recognized the legality of labor contracts made between employer and worker prior to arrival in Texas. In September, 1829, however, a Mexican decree abolished slavery, but in November this was made inapplicable as concerned Texas— *ibid.*, pp. 387-91.

42 Eugene G. Barker, ed., *The Austin Papers*, Austin, 1926, 3 vols., III, pp. 82-83, 108, 162, 318. See also Abigail Curlee, " The history of a Texas slave plantation," in *The Southwestern Historical Quarterly*, 1922, XXVI, p. 93; Harold Schoen, " The free Negro in the Republic of Texas," *ibid.*, 1937, XL, p. 171. Andrew Jackson favored the annexation of the Texas Republic by the United States, pointing out that, otherwise English influence there would grow, England and Texas might form an alliance, and Great Britain could then, in case of war with the United States, use Texas as an excellent base from which to arouse slave rebellions—Jackson to A. V. Brown, December 12, 1843, in John B. McMaster, *A History of the People of the United States from the Revolution to the Civil War*, VII, pp. 314-15.

43 E. C. Barker, *op. cit.*, III, p. 102.

would have a very pernicious and dangerous influence on the overgrown population of that state." [44]

A similar line of reasoning was used by the American envoys to England, France, and Spain who, meeting in Ostend in 1854, let the world know that in their opinion Cuba " ought " to belong to the United States. An important argument for this, they declared,[45] lay in the possibility that the slaves of the Pearl of the Antilles might emulate their brethren of St. Domingo. Were that prize within the strong hand of the United States she would not permit " the flames to extend to our own neighboring shores, seriously to endanger or actually to consume the fair fabric of our Union."

Fear of the slave population offered still another type of argument for territorial expansion that was occasionally used: namely, the idea that this expansion made possible the diffusion of the Negro inhabitants and thus lessened the possibility of a serious slave rebellion.

The Virginia Congressman, William Branch Giles, for example, made much of this point while arguing in March, 1798, against the prohibition of slavery in the Territory of Mississippi[46] and it cropped up again in the speeches of those favoring

44 Yet observe Professor Barker's own statement, " there is no evidence of purpose on the part of the emigrants, or of the slaveholding leaders in the United States, to wrest Texas from Mexico to enlarge the slave area of the south . . . it does not appear that anxiety concerning the status of slavery played an appreciable part in producing the Texas revolution."—" The influence of slavery in the colonization of Texas," in *The Mississippi Valley Historical Review*, 1924, XI, p. 35. Note Jackson's statement, *supra*, and John C. Calhoun's note of April 27, 1844 to the British Minister defending the treaty of annexation he negotiated with Texas (later rejected by the Senate) because of his country's need of that area " in order to preserve domestic institutions."—Enoch W. Sikes and W. M. Keener, *The Growth of the Nation*, 1837-1860, being volume 13 of *The History of North America*, edited by G. C. Lee, p. 132. See Samuel F. Bemis, *A Diplomatic History of the United States*, pp. 224, 229.

45 Frederic Bancroft, *Life of William H. Seward*, I, p. 472; Bemis, *op. cit.*, p. 321.

46 Dice R. Anderson, *William Branch Giles*, p. 59.

slavery in Illinois,[47] and those urging the annexation of Texas in 1845.[48] It was used, too, by Representative Albert Gallatin Brown of Mississippi, when, in January, 1853, he called [49] for the acquisition of Cuba.

Lieutenant Matthew F. Maury, a leading personality in bringing about the exploring trip of the Americans, Herndon and Gibbons, in the Amazon Valley in the 1850's, which had as an ultimate aim the absorption of that tremendous area by the United States, used the following language to justify this objective:[50]

I cannot be blind to what I see going on here. It is becoming a matter of *faith*—I use a strong word—yes a matter of faith among leading Southern men, that the time is coming, nay that it is rapidly approaching when in order to prevent this war of races and its horrors, they will in self-defense, be compelled to conquer parts of Mexico, and central America, & make slave-territory of that—and that is now free [while, of course, slavery still prevailed in Brazil].

When the rulers of the Old South " calculated the value of the Union," one of their prime considerations was the question of slave control. Some felt that it was not wise to repudiate a constitution which provided for the assistance of the entire nation, if needed, to suppress an insurrection; others, that secession, even if peaceably accomplished, would accentuate the discontent of the Negroes, and if resulting in war, would certainly have that effect and thus weaken the South.

47 N. D. Harris, *The History of Negro Servitude in Illinois*, p. 19.

48 J. B. McMaster, *op. cit.*, VII, p. 401.

49 James B. Ranck, *Albert Gallatin Brown*, p. 130. Brown used the same argument in opposing the reopening of the slave trade in 1859, *ibid.*, p. 173.

50 Maury to Mrs. William M. Blackford, December 24, 1851, in Whitfield J. Bell, Jr., " The relation of Herndon and Gibbon's exploration of the Amazon to North American slavery, 1850-55," in *The Hispanic-American Historical Review*, XIX, p. 500.

James Monroe made this point in a letter to John C. Calhoun at the height of the latter's agitation against a high tariff. The elder statesman wrote: [51]

As to the Union all movements which menace, or even suggest the least danger to it, cannot fail to have an ill effect. None of the States are so deeply interested, according to my best judgment, in its preservation, as the Southern. Rivalry, restraints on intercourse, would immediately ensue, under partial confederacies, or any other arrangements, which could be formed, the pernicious consequences of which may easily be conceived. Hostility and wars would be inevitable whereby our free system of government would be overwhelmed. The Southern States would soon become a scene of the most frightful calamities, because their slaves would be excited to insurrection. It is my candid opinion if there is any portion of the Union which ought to feel peculiar solicitude for its preservation, it is these States.

Several months later Monroe again wrote [52] to Calhoun to reaffirm these sentiments. " They were formed on long reflection, founded in experience and a particular consideration of the state of the Southern country, & especially in the article of slaves, the number of which, in most of them, exceeds that of the white population."

Again, James Madison in a letter to Henry Clay, dated June, 1833, assured [53] the latter that he was right in believing that few Northern people possessed " unconstitutional designs on the subject of the slaves." Madison, moreover, as was his wont, emphasized the economic factors tying the North to the South as a guarantee that the former would not deliberately antagonize the latter to the extent of forcing disunion. " On the other hand," he went on, " what madness in the South, to look for

51 Monroe to Calhoun, August 4, 1828, in S. M. Hamilton, ed., *The Writings of James Monroe*, VII, p. 175. Monroe was governor of Virginia during the very considerable slave unrest of 1800-1802. See also, on this point, Basil Hall, *Travels in North America . . . 1827-1828*, III, pp. 242-52.

52 *Ibid.*, VII, pp. 242-43.

53 Gaillard Hunt, ed., *The Writings of James Madison*, IX, p. 517.

greater safety in disunion. It would be worse than jumping out
of the Frying-pan into the fire: it wd. be jumping into the fire
for fear of the Frying-pan."

During the secession scare of 1850 the same concern was frequently expressed by persons with a political axe to grind. The
best example of this occurs in the speech [54] of Horace Mann
delivered February 15, in his capacity as a Representative from
Massachusetts. Mr. Mann warned that were the line of Mason
and Dixon to be transformed into an international boundary
the problem of fugitive slaves would mount to tremendous proportions so that " slavery would melt away upon your borders
like an iceberg in the tropics." And, he asked, " will separation
bring relief and security?", immediately replying:

No, sir;—it will enhance the danger a myriad fold . . . if agitation
and instigation are evils now, woe to those who would seek to
mitigate or to repress them by the remedies of disunion and civil
war. Let men who live in a powder mill beware how they madden
pyrotechnists . . . civil war between the North and the South, anything that brings the quickening idea of freedom home to the mind
of the slave . . . will unleash the bloodhounds of insurrection. Can
you master armies in secret, and march them in secret, so that
the slave shall not know that they are mustered and marched to
perpetuate his bondage, and to extend the bondage of his race?

An Alabama fire-eater, William J. Alston, replied [55] to this
type of argument by minimizing the dangers flowing from the
slave population, and declaring that in any case the Negroes
were unarmed and unaccustomed to the use of arms, and so
could be suppressed without too much difficulty.

The following decade of crisis brought forth a large crop of
speeches, articles, and pamphlets more or less devoted to a con-

54 Separately printed as *Speech of Horace Mann, of Massachusetts, on the
subject of slavery in the territories, and the consequences of a dissolution of
the Union*, delivered in the House of Representatives, February 15, 1850,
Boston, 1850, pp. 21, 25, 31-32.

55 *Speech of Hon. Wm. J. Alston, of Alabama, in the House of Representatives. April 18, 1850*, n. p., p. 7.

sideration of the effect of secession upon the slaves' behavior. The aged Josiah Quincy aptly remarked [56] that the slaveholders' " studies, thoughts, councels are absorbed and directed to two objects,—how to keep their negroes in subjection; and, as subsidiary to this end, how to keep the control of the Free States. By this control, they present to the fears of their slaves the arm of the Union, ever in readiness to keep them in subjection,[57] and also relieve themselves from the apprehension that that arm might be extended for the relief of their slaves."

The months just preceding the Civil War witnessed particularly full discussions of the pros and cons of secession as a method of securing the ownership of human property. On one side [58] it was held that even peaceful and successful secession, by establishing a hostile border nation and by withdrawing the financial and armed support of the Northern States, would increase the difficulty of slave control; while, if military action followed secession this difficulty would increase a hundred-fold, and might well prove a decisive element in the South's defeat—it thus not only failing to gain independence but also losing slavery.

The other school [59] emphasized the hostility of the North, its agitating, propagandizing citizens, its anti-slavery laws, and

56 Josiah Quincy, *Address Illustrative of the Nature and Power of the Slave States, and the Duties of the Free States*; delivered at the request of the inhabitants of the town of Quincy, Mass., June 5, 1856, p. 26. See also an anonymous pamphlet, *The South: a letter from a friend in the North*, pp. 23, 30.

57 The fact that the States of the Union, as a whole, were pledged to suppress efforts of the slaves to achieve their liberty was a major practical factor behind the cry of the Garrisonians for a dissolution of that Union. See the remarks of the Reverend Samuel J. May at the first anniversary meeting of the American Anti-Slavery Society, held in New York, May, 1834, in *First Annual Report* of that Society, N. Y., 1834, p. 20; Moncure D. Conway, *Testimonies Concerning Slavery*, p. 48, as examples of this. Charles Sumner's attitude early in his career was similar—Laura A. White, " Charles Sumner and the crisis of 1860-61," in Avery Craven, ed., *Essays in honor of William E. Dodd*, p. 147.

58 Emerson D. Fite, *The Presidential Campaign of 1860*, pp. 172-73.

59 Carl Russell Fish, *The American Civil War an interpretation*, edited by William E. Smith, pp. 44-46. Laura A. White has remarked that "Alabama's decision in favor of secession was doubtless greatly influenced by fear of

the unlikelihood that that region *would* aid in suppressing servile insurrections—supposing such assistance to be needed—; and, on the positive side, extolled the alleged power of an homogenous, vast, expanding empire founded upon and pledged to the maintenance of chattel slavery.

The Augusta, Georgia, *Daily Constitutionalist* of November 16, 1860, succcinctly summed up an influential viewpoint in these words: [60]

Some of the Southern States see, in the tremendous popular majorities which have elevated Lincoln to the Presidency, the huge mountainous waves that are beating down on the South with resistless force, and if she supinely waits for the deluge, must engulph the whole social system of the South in the relentless waters of anti-slavery fanaticism. With them the question is, secession from the Union, and a self-defending, homogenous southern Republic, or submission to the Union, and the fate of Jamaica and St. Domingo.

On the other hand the anti-secessionist Raleigh *North Carolina Standard* of February 5, 1861, emphasized the difficulties of slave control in case of Civil War and warned:

The negroes will know, too, that the war is waged on their account. They will become restless and turbulent . . . Strong governments will be established, and will bear heavily on the masses . . . The end will be—Abolition! There are other considerations touching slavery which we shall not refer to here,—every intelligent mind will at once understand us, and will weigh these considerations for itself.

In his last annual message to Congress on December 3, 1860, President James Buchanan declared that the unrest of the slaves and the terror this produced were prime causes of the apparent

Negro insurrection" heightened by the uncovering of plots there in 1860— "The South in the 1850's as seen by British consuls," *The Journal of Southern History*, 1935, I, p. 47.

60 This and the following newspaper quotations are from Dwight L. Dumond, ed., *Southern Editorials on Secession*, pp. 179, 245, 446. See also pp. 143, 273, 285, 325, 432.

collapse of the Union. The efforts of territorial legislatures and of Congress to prevent the expansion of slavery, and of Northern people and their local governments to prevent the enforcement of the fugitive slave act were " evils " which the South might have endured " without danger to the Union (as others have been) in the hope that time and reflection might apply the remedy." But, he went on: [61]

The immediate peril arises not so much from these causes as from the fact that the incessant and violent agitation of the slavery question throughout the North for the last quarter of a century has at length produced its malign influence on the slaves and inspired them with vague notions of freedom. Hence a sense of security no longer exists around the family altar. This feeling of peace at home has given place to apprehension of servile insurrections . . . Should this apprehension of domestic danger, whether real or imaginary, extend or intensify itself until it shall pervade the masses of the Southern people, then disunion will become inevitable.[62]

The foregoing by no means exhausts the evidence establishing the fact that widespread fear of slave rebellion was characteristic of the South. Many miscellaneous events also evoked from time to time expression of this dread.

61 James D. Richardson, ed., *A Compilation of the Messages and Papers of the Presidents*, VII, pp. 3157-58. See Buchanan's letter to William Flinn, dated Wheatland, August 8, 1849, in P. G. Auchampaugh, *James Buchanan and his Cabinet on the Eve of Secession*, p. 17. The New Orleans *Bee*, December 10, 1860, decidedly protested against Buchanan's emphasis upon the danger from the slaves—Dumond, *op. cit.*, p. 315. Two recent writers, of an extremely conservative viewpoint, S. A. Ashe and L. G. Tyler, take a position very similar to that of Buchanan in *Secession, Insurrection of the Negroes, and Northern Incendiarism*, revised and reprinted from *Tyler's Quarterly Historical and Genealogical Magazine* (1935), *passim*. See Arthur C. Cole, *The Irrepressible Conflict*, pp. 77-78.

62 See, in addition, Thomas Williams, *The Negro in American Politics*, pp. 20, 32-33; [John Townsend] *The Doom of Slavery in the Union: its safety out of it, passim.*; speech of Senator Louis T. Wigfall of Texas, Dec. 12, 1860. *Congressional Globe*, 36 Cong., 2nd Sess., 73; *Letter of Hon. Joseph Segar, to a friend in Virginia, in vindication of his course in declining to follow his state into secession*, pp. 24, 55.

Thus, fear of the Negroes formed one of the main justifications used by the Trustees of the Georgia Settlement in first forbidding and then opposing the establishment of slavery therein during the early decades of the eighteenth century.[63]

Again, one of the arguments South Carolinians urged upon English officials in 1769 to support their claim for a more westerly boundary for their province than that provided in the line of 1764, was that this would add many whites to its population and thus reduce the pressing danger flowing from the large slave population.[64] This expansion of territory would, too, bring the Catawba Indians within South Carolina's borders which, it was asserted, would be valuable since they were extremely useful in suppressing slave outbursts and capturing runaways.

The same fear was a prominent factor behind the laws passed by Southern colonies from time to time blocking the slave trade, and their petitions to the King for the same purpose, particularly just prior to the Revolution.[65] It fills, too, the writings aimed at bringing about the outlawry of that nefarious business, as, for example, those penned by the indefatigable and influential Quaker, Anthony Benezet.[66] This was true, although, as Benezet wrote: [67]

I know it is the general opinion, that nothing ought to be published whereby the Negroes may be made acquainted with their own strength & the apprehension of danger the whites are in from them, for this reason in every publication I have made, I have guarded against it, but I am persuaded this fear may be carried too far,

63 A. D. Candler, ed., *Colonial Records of Georgia*, I, p. 50; *Collections of the Georgia Historical Society*, I, pp. 170-71; R. Scarborough. *op. cit.*, pp. 9, 12, 37, 73.

64 Lord Charles G. Montagu to Earl of Hillsborough, Charles Town, April 19, 1769, in Walter Clark, ed., *State Records of North Carolina*, XI, pp. 225-27.

65 W. E. B. DuBois, *The Suppression of the African Slave Trade*, pp. 9-10, 209, 211; James C. Ballagh, *History of Slavery in Virginia*, pp. 11-12.

66 Ant[hony] Benezet, *A Caution to Great Britain*, p. 5; George S. Brookes, *Friend Anthony Benezet*, p. 292.

67 Benezet to Robert Pleasants, Phila., April 8, 1773, in Brookes, *op. cit.*, p. 301.

for it is certainly yet more dangerous to withhold from the generality of people the knowledge of danger they will be in, thro' a continued importation of Negro Slaves.

Much of the same argument was made by George Mason at the Constitutional Convention in a speech of August 22, 1787 denouncing the slave trade,[68] and two years later James Madison cited [69] the weakness and danger arising from a slave population in pressing Congress for the passage of a ten-dollar duty on each slave imported. The same body tabled in 1790 a Quaker anti-slavery memorial; and one of the main points of the opponents of commitment or consideration of the paper was the fear that anything else than outright rejection " would," according to Representative Aedanus Burke of Georgia, " sound an alarm and blow the trumpet of sedition through the Southern States." [70]

American slaveholders trembled for their own security as they followed the tremendous revolutionary activity of the French West Indian slaves in the 1790's.[71] And their always precarious sense of ease was further jeopardized by the appearances and tales of refugees arriving at Charleston, Norfolk, Baltimore, and Richmond.[72]

The analogy was too plain to be missed and led to the expression of sentiments like those contained in a letter by Thomas Jefferson:

68 Helen Hill, *George Mason Constitutionalist*, p. 202. Economic motivation was, of course, not absent in Virginia's opposition to the African slave trade.

69 Richard Hildreth, *The History of the United States*, IV, p. 95.

70 *Ibid.*, IV, p. 179; John Page of Virginia disagreed, p. 181. Statements similar to that by Burke were uttered in 1797 in Congress by John Rutledge, Jr., of South Carolina and Nathaniel Macon of North Carolina, *ibid.*, V, pp. 179-83.

71 Charles H. Ambler, *Thomas Ritchie a study in Virginia politics*, p. 25.

72 Duke de la Rochefoucault Liancourt, *Travels Through the United States*, translated by H. Neuman, I, p. 584; II, p. 17; Isaac Weld, Jr., *Travels Through the States of North America*, I, p. 176; Mary Treudley, " The United States and St. Domingo," *The Journal of Race Development*, VII, pp. 112-114, 124.

I become daily more & more convinced that all the West India Islands will remain in the hands of the people of colour, & a total expulsion of the whites sooner or later will take place. It is high time we should foresee the bloody scenes which our children certainly, and possibly ourselves (south of Potomac), have to wade through, & try to avert them.[73]

There was also persistent concern lest the rebellious slaves of these islands, inspired by a desire to free their brethren to the north, or, as was thought more likely, provoked by the French, might surreptitiously stir up slaves in the United States, or actually invade the mainland for that purpose. An early example of such rumors is a letter from Thomas Jefferson, then Secretary of State, dated Philadelphia, December 23, 1793, to Governor John Drayton of South Carolina: [74]

It is my duty to communicate to you a piece of information, although I cannot say I have confidence in it myself. A French gentleman, one of the refugees from St. Domingo, informs me that two Frenchmen, from St. Domingo also, of the names Castaing and La Chaise, are about setting out from this place for Charleston, with a design to excite an insurrection among the negroes. He says that this is in execution of a general plan, formed by the Brissotine party at Paris, the first branch of which has been carried into execution at St. Domingo. My informant is a person with whom I am well acquainted, of good sense, discretion and truth, and certainly believes this himself. I inquired of him the channel of his information. He told me it was one which had never been found to be mistaken. He explained it to me; but I could by no means consider

73 Jefferson to James Monroe, Philadelphia, July 14, 1793, in Paul L. Ford, ed., *The Writings of Thomas Jefferson*, VI, pp. 349-50. See also his letter to St. George Tucker, dated Monticello, August 28, 1797, *ibid.*, VII, p. 168. The fears of American slaveholders were sharpened, of course, by plots at home, to be detailed later.

74 H. A. Washington, ed., *The Writings of Thomas Jefferson*, IV, pp. 97-98. See also Nathaniel Russell to Ralph Izard, Charleston, June 6, 1794 in U. B. Phillips, " The South Carolina Federalists," *The American Historical Review*, XV, p. 734; and the report of a mass meeting of worried citizens of Savannah, Georgia, in 1795 in the Charleston *City Gazette and Daily Advertiser*, July 9, 1795.

it as a channel meriting reliance; and when I questioned him what could be the impulse of these men, what their authority, what their means of execution, and what they could expect in the result; he answered with conjectures which were far from sufficient to strengthen the fact. However, were anything to happen, I should deem myself inexcusable not to have made the communication. Your judgment will decide whether injury might not be done by making the suggestion public, or whether it ought to have any other effect than excite attention to these persons, should they come into South Carolina. Castaing is described as a small dark mulatto, and La Chaise as a Quateron of a tall fine figure.

The fear that France would use Negro troops from St. Domingo to liberate the slaves in the United States, and in the British West Indies, and then annex the latter, if no more, was an important factor behind American and British diplomacy, particularly in 1799. A belief that a St. Domingo politically independent of France, but economically dependent upon Great Britain and the United States, would be less dangerous to the slave holdings of both was vital in bringing those two nations to the support of Toussaint.[75] In June, 1799 the three Powers signed an agreement giving English and American ships exclusive trading privileges, and requiring Toussaint to see to it that no persons dangerous to the slave regions of the United States or the British Empire left his domain. According to Edward Stevens,[76] the United States consul-general at St. Do-

[75] See correspondence between Rufus King, United States Minister to England and Timothy Pickering, Secretary of State, during 1799, and letter from Lord Grenville to Rufus King in Charles King, ed., *The Life and Correspondence of Rufus King*, II, pp. 499-501, 504-505, 557, III, p. 46; Mary S. Locke, *op. cit.*, p. 196; Arthur B. Darling, *op. cit.*, pp. 355, 362. Note, in addition, the interesting letter from a certain Michael Walton to Thomas Jefferson dated Baltimore, December 14, 1807, in which the writer describes himself as an English-born American citizen. Mr. Walton declares he was in Paris "after the last Peace" (of Amiens ?) and learned of French plans to sever the United States, send Negro troops into Florida, "to keep up a communication with the Negroes of Carolina & Georgia; to strike a formidable blow in those States, whilst Troops marched [into] Kentucky Va from Louisiana." Jefferson Papers, Library of Congress.

[76] "Letters of Toussaint Louverture and of Edward Stevens, 1798-1800," *Documents, American Historical Review*, XVI, pp. 73, 82, 92.

mingo, Toussaint kept his part of the bargain, notwithstanding proddings from France to aid in an attack upon Jamaica and, possibly, the southern portion of the United States.

Serious worry concerning the possible activities of these island rebels, independently or at the behest of France, was expresssed from 1797 to 1800 by outstanding Americans [77] including George Washington, Harrison Gray Otis, Charles C. Pinckney, Albert Gallatin, and Henry Lee. Three others,[78] George Keith Taylor of Virginia, and John Rutledge and Robert Goodloe Harper, both of South Carolina, (and all firm Federalists, which makes their aspersions on the new France subject to a considerable dash of salt) flatly asserted that agents of that government were sowing seeds of revolution among the Negroes.[79]

This concern was a factor in the rearmament program of the federal government from 1797 to 1799,[80] and in the anti-slave

77 Their statements may be found in, respectively, Worthington C. Ford, ed., *The Writings of George Washington*, XIV, p. 34; Hildreth, *op. cit.*, V, p. 72; *Annals of Congress*, January 22, 23, 1799, IX, 2752, 2766-67; January 7, 1800, X, 268, 276-77.

78 Their statements are, respectively, in Henry H. Simms, *Life of John Taylor*, p. 79; *Annals of Congress*, January 3, 1800, X, 242; Elizabeth Donnan, ed., " Papers of James Bayard," in *Annual Report of the American Historical Association*, 1913, II, p. 89. Rutledge's statement may be cited as representative: " There have been emissaries amongst us in the Southern States, they have begun their war upon us ... [the slaves] have been tampered with, and this is going on ... " The alleged implication of two Frenchmen in the Gabriel Plot eight months after these words were uttered was to embarrass the Republicans in the political campaign of 1800.

79 In considering these assertions it is to be borne in mind that professional Jacobin-baiters were legion, and these led credulous souls to search under their beds and behind their cupboards for French revolutionists. See [William Cobbett] *Porcupine's Works*, VIII, pp. 199, 199, 224-25; J. B. McMaster, *op. cit.*, II, p. 441; L. L. Montague, *Haiti and the United States, 1714-1938*, p. 39.

80 Speech of Albert Gallatin, Jan. 7, 1800, *Annals of Congress*, X, 276-77; R. Hildreth, *op. cit.*, V, pp. 212, 223; George Gibbs, *Memoirs of the Administrations of Washington and John Adams*, II, p. 60.

trade laws passed by that government in 1794 and 1800,[81] and by various state governments from 1792 to 1801.[82]

A Southerner, writing [83] in the year 1801, in discussing the "reality" and "magnitude" of the danger from the slaves declared that all were as convinced of both as they were of the existence of a Heaven and Hell—a simile of very great strength at the time it was drawn. It is this quality of the fear that is most impressive—its pervasiveness, deepness—which seemed to add a distinctive element, an electrical current, to the very atmosphere of the slave regions.

Speaking under the stimulus of recently suppressed conspiracies in the south, Governor Winthrop Sargent of the Territory of Mississippi urged [84] the legislature in January, 1801, to enlarge the militia. He warned that each passing day witnessed an addition to the number of slaves and therefore, he went on, "to the number of our most inveterate enemies also." The Governor proceeded to hint that local slaveholders had recently experienced difficulties in controlling their slaves, and concluded that "in a war with any European, or even Indian power, they [the slaves] might be irresistibly stimulated to vengeance."

81 DuBois, *op. cit.*, pp. 73, 84; M. Locke, *op. cit.*, p. 142.

82 As previously stated, trouble with local slaves was also important in causing the enactment of these laws. See W. Kilty, *The Laws of Maryland* (Annapolis, 1800), II, chap. LXVIII; H. Marbury and W. H. Crawford, *Digest of the Laws of Georgia*, p. 440; Brevard, *Public Statute Law of South Carolina*, II, pp. 250, 256-57; Edward Channing, *A History of the United States*, IV, p. 433 n. It was a settled policy in the south during these years to forbid the importation of slaves from South America and the West Indies. There are interesting letters concerning this from Governor Drayton of South Carolina to Chancognie, French commercial agent, Sept. 9, 1802, and to Jefferson, Sept. 12, 1802. "Force of arms" was threatened by Drayton to prevent this trade.—Papers of Thomas Jefferson, Library of Congress.

83 *Letter to a Member of the General Assembly of Virginia, on the Subject of the Late Conspiracy of the Slaves* (Baltimore, 1801), p. 3.

84 Dunbar Rowland, *History of Mississippi*, II, p. 631. For evidence on these unhappy experiences, see D. Rowland, ed., *The Mississippi Territorial Archives, 1798-1803*, I, p. 312.

The next governor of this area, William C. C. Claiborne, was keenly aware of the same dangers in 1802. Because of this he attempted, vainly, to curb the importation of adult male slaves, succeeded in strengthening the militia, and in bringing about the establishment of Fort Dearborn at the town of Washington about six miles east of Natchez.[85]

In 1802 and 1803 an influential Quaker, Zachariah Dicks,[86] thought by his fellow-religionists to possess the gift of prophecy, created among them in Georgia and South Carolina a condition approximating panic by his warning of an impending slave rebellion and a bloody servile war. Scores of Quaker families, obsessed with fear, migrated to the free Northwest.

While traveling through the South in 1805 Jonathan Mason, a former Senator from Massachusetts, sensed the tenseness and wrote,[87] " The citizens live in fear, and [to] avert the evil, to lessen the danger, and to thin their population employs the time and expense of the Government [of Virginia] annually." A resident of Baltimore versed in military science was so impressed in 1807 with the danger that he penned [88] an extremely long letter to the President of the United States giving detailed proposals for protection against slave insurrections, proposals

85 See the letters from Claiborne to James Madison, Secretary of State, and to General James Wilkinson, during January and February, 1802, in Rowland, ed., *op. cit.*, I, pp. 373-79. Indians were also a source of concern. Claiborne was corresponding with Wilkinson about these worries as late as the spring of 1803, see Clarence E. Carter, ed., *op. cit.*, V, p. 217.

86 Louis T. Jones, *The Quakers of Iowa*, p. 36; C. V. Woodward, *Tom Watson*, pp. 8-9.

87 Diary entry dated Richmond, January 13, 1805, in *Proceedings of the Massachusetts Historical Society*, 2nd series, 1885-86, II, p. 19. See also [Ann Alexander], *An Address to the Inhabitants of Charleston, South Carolina*, Phila., 1805, p. 7.

88 Michael Walton to Thomas Jefferson, Baltimore, December 14, 1807 in Jefferson Papers, Library of Congress. The threat of war with Great Britain heightened Mr. Walton's concern. See also the letters from John Page, dated Richmond, July 12, 1807, and Governor James Sullivan of Massachusetts, dated Boston, January 7, 1808 to Jefferson, quoted in Louis M. Sears, *Jefferson and the Embargo*, pp. 56, 58.

arrived at, he said after considerable experience in combating
such uprisings in the West Indies.

The American-inspired revolution of 1810 in Spanish-held
West Florida evoked expressions of fear of the slave population
both there and in the neighboring Mississippi Territory. So
many of the West Florida settlers had left their homes to take
part in the successful storming of the Baton Rouge fort in September, 1810, that their families appealed to the American officer, Colonel Hugh Davis, stationed in nearby Homochitto in
Mississippi, for troops to prevent slave uprisings. Davis relayed
this request to Governor David Holmes on September 25 and
remarked that he feared a " St. Domingo " across the border
unless a display of forces were made.[89] Three days later the
Governor gave the army commander, Colonel Thomas Cushing,
orders to station a company of soldiers at the West Florida
border in order to ensure the good order of the slaves both
north and south of that line.[90]

The question of Missouri's admission into the Union brought
slavery to the fore, led to heated debates in Congress and, as
usual, brought expressions of concern over the Negro population. An example of this is contained in a letter [91] dated February 20, 1820, stating that the passage of the Missouri Compromise would lead to Northern domination and " I have no
doubt, from the language ascribed to Mr. King,[92] would sound

89 Isaac J. Cox, *The West Florida Controversy*, p. 406.

90 Charles E. Carter, ed., *op. cit.*, VI, p. 121; Cox, *op. cit.*, pp. 406-407
points out, however, that the troops were useful, too, in overawing opposition
within West Florida to the revolutionists. In October, 1810, the area was
annexed by the United States.

91 Linn Banks to James Barbour, Richmond, in " Letters to Senator
Barbour," *William and Mary College Quarterly*, 1901, X, p. 21. There is
evidence that these debates did reach the ears of some of the Negroes concerned in the great Vesey plot of 1822, see *post*, p. 81.

92 Reference is here made to the rather mild anti-slavery expressions of
Senator Rufus King of New York in Congress, November, 1819, which may
be found in Charles R. King, ed., *op. cit.*, VI, pp. 690-703. The remarks of
Representative James Tallmadge of New York at the same time were much
stronger—see William Chambers, *American Slavery and Colour*, p. 43.

the tocsin of freedom to every negro of the South, and we may live to see the tragical events of Santo Domingo repeated in our own land."

At the end of 1820 the Charleston *Courier* [93] noted that " Three interesting papers from an unknown writer under the signature of 'A Carolinian,' were laid on the desks of the Members of the State Legislature a few days since," which pointed to the danger of permitting the continued growth of the Negro population and urged the adoption of measures to check this alleged menace to the secure possession of human property.

The depth of this concern is well indicated in a letter written to Thomas Jefferson by an old friend, Thomas Law. Mr. Law remarked [94] that he was greatly unnerved by terrible personal afflictions, including the death of two children. Yet, he went on, he felt that he " could lay down in peace " if he could but see his country actively promote manufacturing, better its transportation facilities, and "A System introduced to check the rapid increase of slaves to the South, who may be aided by Hayti & Cuba to the West [sic] & the motley Crew West of the Sabine ... I have a plan long considered to accomplish the latter important object, but there is too much warmth on this subject for calm discussion."

A prominent South Carolina slaveholder placed considerable stress in 1825 on this danger and, what was unusual, did so in a public address, warning [95] " that the tenure by which we hold our slaves, is daily becoming less secure." A Virginia slaveowner

93 Charleston *Courier*, December 12, 1820. In 1821 a law forbidding manumissions, and containing other restrictive measures was passed.

94 Letter dated March 7, 1823, n. p., in Jefferson Papers, Library of Congress. It is interesting to observe that Mr. Law found it difficult, as early as 1823, to freely discuss the subject of slavery.

95 Whitemarsh B. Seabrook, *A Concise View of the Critical Situation, and Future Prospects of the Slave-holding States, in Relation to their Coloured Population,* read before the Agricultural Society of St. John's Colleton on the 14th of September, 1825, p. 3. This pamphlet will make instructive reading for the many who assert that the defense of slavery originated as a result of the Abolitionist attack of the 1830's.

and politician the next year also publicly and even more strongly admitted [96] the presence of this deep fear. Warning of the possibility of a tremendous Negro uprising, even of a successful one, he went on, " I wish I could maintain, with truth . . . that it was a small danger, but it is a great danger, it is a danger which has increased, is increasing, and *must* be diminished, or it must come to its regular catastrophe."

It is an arresting coincidence—probably based on increasing evidence of slave unrest—that in the months just before the Turner rebellion and its aftermath of turmoil there were several striking prophecies of impending catastrophe. Thus, an English visitor to New Orleans in 1830 remarked [97] that the evils of slavery were " beginning to re-act upon the Christians, who are latterly in a constant state of alarm, which threatens at no far distant period to overwhelm the south with some dreadful calamity."

Again, the Reverend Samuel J. May in July, 1831, warned,[98] " The slaves are men. They have within them that inextinguishable thirst for freedom, which is born in man. They are already writhing in their shackles. They will, one day, throw them off with vindictive violence, if we do not unloose them." Benjamin Lundy, in his Baltimore monthly paper [99] for August, 1831 de-

96 John Randolph in the Senate, objecting to delegates from the United States being sent to a planned Panama conference, March 2, 1826, *Register of Debates*, II, 117. See also Basil Hall, *op. cit.*, III, pp. 229, 242-43. The attempt during these years of Mexico and Colombia, apparently backed by France and England to get rid of Spanish rule and slavery in Cuba and Puerto Rico was a source of worry. See above speech, and Theodore E. Burton, " Henry Clay," in Samuel F. Bemis, ed., *The American Secretaries of State and their Diplomacy*, IV, pp. 134, 143.

97 S. A. Ferrall, *A Ramble of six thousand miles through the United States of America*, p. 196. The distinction here made between Christians and slaves was common and generally accurate four or five generations before, but hardly at this time.

98 *A Discourse on Slavery*, delivered July 3, 1831, p. 16.

99 *The Genius of Universal Emancipation*, 3rd series, II, pp. 54-55. As previously remarked, in this chapter panic or fear coming as a direct result of an uprising will not be considered, so that the abject terror that followed the Turner Rebellion will be discussed later.

clared—before news of Turner's uprising had reached him—
" Vengeance is accumulating in the land of despotism; and it
will assuredly burst forth with tremendous fury, if Justice be
not admitted to a participation in the councils of those in authority."

The great English actress, Frances Anne Kemble, who spent
several months in 1838 and 1839 as the mistress of a large
Georgia slave plantation, wrote [100] while there, " I know that
the southern men are apt to deny that they do live under an
habitual sense of danger, but a slave population, coerced into
obedience, though unarmed and half-fed, *is* a threatening source
of constant insecurity, and every southern *woman* to whom I
have spoken on the subject, has admitted to me that they live
in terror of their slaves."

A New Orleans newspaper felt,[101] in 1841, that " the enmity
between the white and black race is rapidly maturing," noted
recent " repeated attacks of the negro upon the white man in
our city," and wondered " whether they be not the piquet guard
of some stupendous conspiracy among the blacks, to fall upon
us unawares." The paper urged various measures of repression,
as the forbidding of manumission and of religious gatherings,
and concluded, " Let us always be on our guard, and grant no
indulgence to the negro, but keep him strictly and vigorously
within his sphere."

Indication of anxiety comes from Maryland early in 1843 in
that agitation for the outlawing of all secret Negro organizations was considerable, and the Baltimore Grand Jury presented [102] the Negro Masonic lodges as particularly dangerous.
Again, a letter from Clarksville, Georgia, of February 2, 1844
demonstrates the existence of very acute fear.[103] A sentence here

100 F. A. Kemble, *Journal of a Residence on a Georgia Plantation in 1838-
1839*, p. 379. See also Margaret Armstrong, *Fanny Kemble a Passionate
Victorian*, p. 244.

101 New Orleans *Advertiser*, n. d., in *The Liberator*, October 15, 1841.
A slave plot had been crushed in Louisiana in July.

102 Reported in *The Liberator*, March 17, 1843.

103 John W. H. Underwood to Senator Howell Cobb, in U. B. Phillips, ed.,
" The correspondence of Robert Toombs, Alexander H. Stephens, and Howell

indicates an interesting appreciation of the profoundly revolutionary implications of the entire Abolitionist movement in that the writer remarks that " the same torch " which he fears will consume the fabric of the slave South " will also cause the northeastern horizon to coruscate with the flames of northern palaces." Let us, then, he urges, secede now, for:

What will it avail us at the South for the incendiaries to cease their work after our throats are cut and our houses burned? Sir, the negroes in Georgia are already saying to each other that great men are trying to set them free and will succeed, and many other expressions of similar import. And if the agitation of the subject is continued for three months longer we will be compelled to arm our Militia and shoot down our property in the field. If the thing is not already incurable, tell the agitators we had rather fight them than our own negroes, and that we will do it too.

As one might expect the critical decade prior to the Civil War presents much evidence of the presence of this enveloping sense of impending calamity. Emily P. Burke declared [104] that she was a witness of this while in Georgia and remarked that she had " known ladies that would not dare to go to sleep without one or two pistols under their pillows." Frederika Bremer, a famous Scandinavian writer, reported [105] a conversation with a former planter in Louisiana at about the same time, during which the gentleman declared, " People are becoming compelled to more justice and gentleness towards their slaves, for their own safety. I have known times here, when there was not a single planter who had a calm night's rest; they then never lay down to sleep without a brace of loaded pistols at their side." James Stirling, an English traveller, was in New Orleans at such a time, the winter of 1856, and noted,[106] " at this moment the planter lays himself to bed with pistols under his pillow, never knowing

Cobb, *Annual Report of the American Historical Association, 1911*, II, pp. 54-55.

104 E. P. Burke, *Reminiscences of Georgia*, pp. 156-58.

105 F. Bremer, *The Homes of the New World*, II, p. 451.

106 J. Stirling, *Letters from the Slave States*, p. 59.

when the wild whoop of insurrection may awaken him to a bloody fight . . . Is it pleasant to live in such a country? I have slept for nights over the boiler, and can tell you it is very far from pleasant."

Another visitor, Frederick Law Olmsted, during approximately the same time, repeatedly commented [107] upon the pervasiveness of this fear, finding " no part of the South where the slave population is felt to be quite safe from a contagion of insurrectionary excitement." He, too, as Stirling, reported that upon retiring with his roommate in a Louisiana public inn the man carefully loaded his gun, and barricaded the door, with the remark, " You don't know there may be runaways around." The same condition impressed the shrewd Edwin Lawrence Godkin [108] while in the South during 1856 and 1857, to whom an unnamed ex-Governor of Mississippi also hinted at rather restless sleeping. The politician lamented the disproportionate growth of the slave as compared with the free population, and asserted that the difference " was now felt to be so alarmingly great that many people never lay down at night without fears that their throats might be cut in this sleep."

A Missouri newspaper in arguing for the adoption of a policy of emancipation stressed [109] the sense of ever-present danger which was, it maintained, characteristic of the system it wished to see ended. It demanded to know, " Who that watches passing events and indications, is not sensible of the fact that great internal convulsions await the slave States?" And it held it " better to grapple with the danger in time, if danger there be, and avert it, than wait until it becomes formidable. One thing is certain, or history is no guide: that is, that slavery cannot be perpetuated anywhere."

107 F. L. Olmsted, *A Journey in the Back Country, pp.* 30, 474; see also Charles Elliott, *op. cit.,* II, p. 155; William Chambers, *op. cit.,* p. 118.

108 Rollo Ogden, ed., *Life and Letters of Edwin Lawrence Godkin,* I, pp. 149-50; also pp. 136-37. A different attitude is noted on page 143.

109 Editorial in the St. Louis *Democrat,* January 28, 1857; quoted in Hinton R. Helper, *The Impending Crisis of the South,* p. 371. See also, John S. C. Abbott, *South and North*; or *Impressions Received during a Trip to Cuba and the South,* pp. 124, 172, 175-77.

CHAPTER III

THE MACHINERY OF CONTROL

A RULING class, often subjected to periods of panic arising from doubt of its ability to maintain its power, may be expected to develop very complex and thorough systems of control. The American slaveocracy did develop numerous psychological, social, juridical, economic, and militaristic methods of suppression and oppresion.

One of the most basic devices of control was the fostering of a belief in the innate inferiority of the Negro people. Theologians assured all and sundry—including the slaves themselves —that the Negroes were the accursed of God, either the descendants of Cain or else of the "snake" (nachash) who tempted Eve and who was "really" the Negro.[1] So-called ethnologists, sociologists and historians offered alleged proof of the natural inferiority of the Negro and the propriety, indeed, the necessity, of his filling the God-ordained role of slave to the white man.[2] Laws and propaganda emanating from colleges, pulpits, politicians, and press continually and incessantly drummed out the concept of the inferiority of an entire people, year after year, generation and generation.

The poison was, too, deliberately and plentifully administered to the slave himself from childhood to the cemetery, so that he was ever aware that his most heinous crime, that for which there was no forgiveness, was to forget his "place," to become "uppity."

The branding was done early, and all at once. Suddenly, the white playmates from the big house were no longer chums. A

1 See Harry McNeill, "No 'Curse' on the Negro," in *The Negro World Digest*, 1940, I, pp. 40-42.

2 William Sumner Jenkins, *Pro-Slavery Thought in the Old South*, pp. 242-284.

fugitive slave declared [3] that he remembered two great misfortunes of his youth, one when he was very painfully scalded, the other when he observed this new contempt of his white friends. Moncure D. Conway, a native Virginian, is one of the very few writers who have commented upon this aspect of American slavery. His words are worth quoting: [4]

There is a cruel pang that comes to every slave's life, which has been very little considered. It is customary in nearly all households in the South for the white and black children connected with each to play together. The trial I have referred to comes when the Negroes who have hitherto been on this democratic footing with the young whites are presently deserted by their more fortunate companions, who enter upon school-life and the acquaintance of white boys, and, ceasing to associate with their swarthy comrades any longer, meet them in future with the air of the master. This is the dawn of the first bitter consciousness of being a slave; and nothing can be sadder than to see the poor little things wandering about companionless and comfortless.

One thing, perhaps, was more tragic; the elders' attempts to explain this mystery.

Of the many outrages which may be charged against American slavery surely none was more revealing than the incident which a distinguished Marylander, Henry White, never forgot.[5] This concerned a pretty young girl, slave in his father's household, who carried herself with a pride dangerous and incongruous in one of her station. It was observed that her greatest joy was the lovely hair that crowned her head, and so, to make the child realize her place she was punished in a peculiar way. In Mr. White's words: " This was the cutting off of the

3 "Autobiography of a Negro slave," MS. Slave Papers 2, no. 24, folder Ac342 [Jan. 23, 1847] Library of Congress, p. 2.

4 M. D. Conway, *Testimonies Concerning Slavery*, pp. 5-6.

5 Allan Nevins, *Thirty Years of American Diplomacy*, pp. 8-9. For a pioneer attempt to determine the psychological results of caste segregation upon Negro youngsters see Allison Davis and John Dollard, *Children of Bondage*, Washington, 1940.

hair of a mulatto girl, who was almost white, and whose hair did not resemble in the least the woolly hair of the negroes. She greatly prided herself on her resemblance in general to the 'white folks,' and it was a great humiliation that it should be cut off, which of course was the basis of this particular punishment."

The nuances of this extra-legal form of social control were numerous. Some of the many possibilities were mentioned by Judge Nash of the North Carolina Supreme Court in a decision [6] read June, 1852:

What acts in a slave towards a white person will amount to insolence it is manifestly impossible to define—it may consist in a look, the pointing of a finger, a refusal or neglect to step out of the way when a white person is seen to approach. But each of such acts violates the rules of propriety, and if tolerated, would destroy that subordination, upon which our social system rests.

One who was an expert on the humiliations incident to being a slave remarked,[7] " Does a slave look dissatisfied? It is said he has the devil in him ... Does he speak loudly when spoken to by the master? Then he is getting highminded, and should be taken down a button hole lower. Does he forget to pull off his hat at the approach of a white person? Then he is wanting in reverence ... Does he venture to vindicate his conduct when censured for it? Then he is guilty of impudence, one of the greatest crimes a slave can commit."

The goal, perhaps not consciously seen, but nevertheless present, on the part of the slaveholders, so far as both the Negro and the white were concerned, was to make slavery appear as an inseparable constituent of the whole way of life; to make slavery so acceptable that it would go unquestioned.[8] And if

6 Helen T. Catterall, ed., *Judicial Cases Concerning American Slavery and the Negro*, II, p. 168.

7 *Narrative of the Life of Frederick Douglass*, Boston, 1849, p. 79.

8 This idea, with, however, a much exaggerated statement as to the success of the effort, is in Bertram W. Doyle, *The Etiquette of Race Relations in the South*, p. 107. The slaveocracy directed its propaganda particularly at

this could not be reached, certainly the idea was to make those who did question or disturb the institution appear to be not merely enemies of slavery, but of society, of life itself.

The words of man were reinforced by those of God, the latter carefully selected, interpreted and censored. During the first decades of English slavery religious teaching was suspect, and this led to careful regulation of worship procedure. The hostility seems to have been due, in part, to conscience-qualms over enslaving Christians. In addition, there existed concern lest it lead to delusions about equality of all the images of God, and hasten the forming of close associations, common aspirations, and a common language.[9] Nothing could for long prevent the spread of a common language and the formation of close associations, but the master class could and did attempt to control religious instruction.

The aim of this instruction was to inculcate meekness and docility.[10] An example of a typical sermon is pertinent. We choose one [11] that was popular among clergymen of the Protestant Episcopal Church in Maryland and Virginia during the eighteenth and nineteenth centuries. The slaves here are assured that God has willed that they occupy their lowly position. They are told that unless they perform their allotted tasks well they will suffer eternally in Hell. Specifically, they are warned that the Lord is greatly offended when they are saucy, impudent, stubborn, or sullen. Nor are they to alter their behavior if the

the poorer whites. See W. G. Bean, "Anti-Jeffersonianism in the antebellum South," in *North Carolina Historical Review*, 1935, XII, pp. 103-24; James B. Ranck, *Albert Gallatin Brown*, p. 147; J. D. B. DeBow, *The Interest in Slavery of the Southern Non-Slaveholder, passim*.

9 H. Aptheker, "The Quakers and Negro slavery," in *The Journal of Negro History*, XXV, p. 333. See also, R. C. Strickland, *Religion and the State in Georgia*, pp. 179-82.

10 C. G. Parson, *Inside View of Slavery*, p. 275; *The Negro in Virginia* (by W. P. A.), p. 108; L. B. Washington, "The use of religion for social control in American slavery," master's thesis, Howard, 1939; H. P. Perkins, "Religion for slaves," *Church History*, X, pp. 228-45.

11 The Rev. William Meade, *Sermons Addressed to Masters and Servants*, pp. 95-135. Meade was Bishop of the Episcopal Church in Virginia.

owner is cross or mean or cruel; that is the Lord's concern, not theirs, and they are to leave the master's punishment to Him. One fact, particularly, the beatings and lashings (or, in the sermon's euphonious language, "correction") might make patience difficult. This is recognized, and explaining it away is done in a most complete and ingenious manner. The section devoted to this is lengthy, but inimitable, and exact quotation alone does it justice:

There is only one circumstance which may appear grievous that I shall now take notice of; and this is CORRECTION. Now, when *correction* is given you, you either deserve it, or you do not deserve it. But whether you deserve it or not, it is your duty, and Almighty God requires, that you bear it patiently. You may, perhaps, think that this is a hard doctrine; but if you consider it rightly, you must needs think otherwise of it. Suppose, then, that you deserve correction; you cannot but say that it is just and right you should meet with it. Suppose you do not, or at least you do not deserve so much or so severe a correction for the fault you have committed; you perhaps have escaped a great many more, and are at least paid for all. Or suppose you are quite innocent of what is laid to your charge, and suffer wrongfully in that particular thing; is it not possible you may have done some other bad which was never discovered, and that Almighty God, who saw you doing it, would not let you escape without punishment one time or another? And ought you not in such a case to give glory to Him, and be thankful that He would rather punish you in this life for your wickedness, than destroy your souls for it in the next life? But suppose that even this was not the case—a case hardly to be imagined—and that you have by no means, known or unknown, deserved the correction you suffered; there is this great comfort in it, that if you bear it patiently, and leave your cause in the hands of God, He will reward you for it in heaven, and the punishment you suffer unjustly here shall turn to your exceeding great glory hereafter.

After this one can well understand the inspiration of a resolution adopted by a Southern religious organization [12] in 1850

12 Alabama Baptist Association, quoted in Charles S. Davis, *The Cotton Kingdom in Alabama*, Montgomery, 1939, p. 89. For the anti-slavery stand

declaring that, " intelligent masters with the light of experience before them will regard the communication of sound religious instruction [to their slaves] as the truest economy and the most efficient police and as tending to the greatest utility, with regard to every interest involved."

Many of the slaves, however, constructed a different religion. Their God had cursed man-stealers, had led slaves out of bondage, had promised the earth as an inheritance for the humble, had prophesied that the first would be last and the last would be first. Their God had created all men of one blood, and had manifested no preferences among those into whom He had breathed life.

The slave's attitude seems very largely to have been that listening to, or, at least, attending the sermons of the white preacher (when the master required this) was merely another chore, another of the consequences of enslavement. Occasionally, indeed, a slave less politic than his fellows, or more seriously bothered by what he felt was a distortion of the Lord's Word, would dare publicly to express his feelings. Ex-Virginia slave, Beverly Jones, tells of one such case involving an aged Negro, " Uncle Silas," and the Reverend Mr. Johnson. The latter was [13]

a preachin' an' de slaves was sittin' dere sleepin' an' fannin' theyselves wid oak branches, an' Uncle Silas got up in de front row of de slaves' pew an' halted Reverend Johnson. " Is us slaves gonna be free in Heaven?" Uncle Silas asked. De preacher stopped an' looked at Uncle Silas like he wanta kill him 'cause no one ain't sposed to say nothing' 'ceptin' "Amen" whilst he was preachin'. Waited a minute he did, lookin' hard at Uncle Silas standing there but didnt give no answer.

" Is God gonna free us slaves when we git to Heaven?" Uncle Silas yelled. Old white preacher pult out his handkerchief an' wiped de sweat fum his face. " Jesus say come unto Me ye who are

of certain Southern religious groups, as the Methodists and Quakers, up to about 1800, see *post*, pp. 102-104.

13 *The Negro in Virginia*, p. 109.

free from sin an' I will give you salvation." " Gonna give us freedom 'long wid salvation?" ask Uncle Silas. " De Lawd gives and'
de Lawd takes away, an' he dat is widdout sin is gonna have life
everlastin'," preached de preacher. Den he wen' ahead preachin',
fast-like, widdout payin' no 'tention to Uncle Silas.

But Uncle Silas wouldn't sit down; stood dere de res' of de service, he did, an' dat was de las' time he come to church. Uncle Silas
died fo' nother preachin' time come roun'. Guess he foun' out
whether he gonna be free sooner dan he calculated to.

Frequent occurrences during the slave era were secret and
illegal religious assemblies of Negroes held at more or less irregular intervals in any secluded spot—'hush-harbor' meetings,
the Negroes called them. Here the slaves listened to one of
their own choosing, were not confined to a respectful "Amen"
every now and then, and were not left in doubt as to Jehovah's
opinion concerning slavery. They were assured that Heaven
harbored no overseers and no whips. Indeed, they were not infrequently urged to clear the earth itself of both these instruments of the Devil.

The last possibility is what the slaveholders particularly
dreaded and it was this that led them to be especially active in
ferreting out such meeting places and punishing the members
whom they could catch.[14]

Throughout the South's history there were two schools of
thought amongst its rulers as to the best method of maintaining
their position. One group, definitely the minority, which, in line
with modern usage, may be designated as the liberal school,
favored reforms and greater elasticity in the slave system; the
other group, of conservative or reactionary opinion, would tol-
erate no coddling, but urged an out and out policy of blood and
iron.

14 *Ibid.*, pp. 143 ff.; Austin Steward, *Twenty-two years a Slave, and Forty
Years a Freeman*, pp. 34-38. Many of the leaders of slave rebellions were
deeply religious men, often leaders of the. worshipping activities of their
comrades. Regulations against such activities will be given later.

The attitude of the former group was expressed [15] as early as 1790 by Congressman John Page of Virginia who argued for at least the commitment of a Quaker anti-slavery petition with these words, " Placing himself in the case of a slave, on hearing that Congress had refused to listen to the decent suggestions of a respectable part of the community, he should infer that the general government, from which great good was expected to every class, had shut their ears against the voice of humanity. If any thing could induce him to rebel, it must be a stroke like this, impressing on his mind all the horrors of despair." A similar attitude was expressed by Judge Brockenbrough, of the Virginia Supreme Court, in dissenting from the court's dismissal of a complaint brought against a master " for cruelly beating his own slave." The court held " that it has no jurisdiction over this offence," but Brockenbrough asked,[16] " is there no danger that oppression and tyranny, against which there is no redress, may drive them to despair?"

Late in the slave era there developed, particularly in Virginia and North Carolina, an organized reform movement aiming at the legalization of slave marriages, the prevention of severance of families, and the encouraging of Negro (free and slave) education.[17] This liberal wing, however, was not strong and its desires were easily shunted aside by the always dominant blood-and-iron group.

But it is to be noted that while no program of the type contemplated above was acceptable to the slaveocracy, it did, nevertheless, find it necessary to provide some elasticity. Thus, it did establish, in certain cases, minima in standards [18]—miserable

15 Richard Hildreth, *History of the United States*, IV, p. 181.

16 Helen T. Catterall, *op. cit.*, I, p. 150.

17 Broadside memorial, undated, to the legislature of North Carolina, in folder marked " Pam. 1 ", Historical Commission, Raleigh, N. C.; a similar memorial to the Virginia legislature is summarized in *The Liberator*, Febru-1, 1856. See also R. H. Taylor, " Humanizing the slave code of North Carolina," *North Carolina Historical Review*, 1925, II, pp. 323-31.

18 As occurred in South Carolina in 1740, and in Louisiana in 1795 following slave outbursts.

though they were—; it did maintain a hierarchy among the slaves themselves—personal servants, general domestic workers, drivers, and field workers; there did exist a fairly well-developed system of rewards; and it was possible for a particularly fortunate and extraordinarily persevering individual to buy his own freedom, granted, of course, the owner's permission and honesty.

The fostering of division among the slaves—the ancient divide and rule formula—was an important method of control. Carefully selected [19] slaves were the personal servants, male and female, who often were assigned to, and did serve, a particular member of the master's family throughout his or her life. Here, as was natural, there frequently developed a strong attachment, and it was very largely from this group that spies and traitors were obtained by the ruling class. Betrayal always brought substantial economic regard and invariably freedom—the greatest gift in the possession of the slaveholders.[20]

Positive assignments as spies were also not unknown. Thus, Frederick Douglass remarked: [21] " Slaveholders are known to have sent spies among their slaves to ascertain if possible their views and feelings in regard to their condition; hence the maxim established among them, that 'a still tongue makes a wise head'." Again, during considerable excitement in North Carolina over signs of restlessness among the slaves, and fear that David Walker's revolutionary pamphlet might have reached them, it was decided [22] " as the best means of ascertain-

19 See J. Winston Coleman, Jr., *Slavery Times in Kentucky*, pp. 48-51.

20 In the course of the narrative these facts will be substantiated. There is, of course, nothing extraordinary, or peculiar to the Negro people, in the frequency with which plots were betrayed. Note, for example, Herbert Paul's remark anent the fact that the informer, Nagle, made possible the proving of the charge of treason-felony in the Fenian trials of 1865-66— " one of those inevitable informers without whom no Irish conspiracy seems to be complete." *A History of England*, III, p. 18.

21 *Life and Times of Frederick Douglass*, Hartford, 1882, p. 70.

22 David Walker had been born free in North Carolina. The quotation is from a letter by L. D. Henry to Governor John Owen, dated Fayette, September 3, 1830, in Governor's Papers, no. 60, Historical Commission, Raleigh. See also, Clement Eaton, "A dangerous pamphlet in the old south," *The Journal of Southern History*, 1936, II, p. 330.

ing whether the pamphlet was here or not, to employ secret agents to pervade the black community . . . this plan has been sometime in operation." At times, masters themselves attempted by apparently innocent, matter-of-fact questioning to ascertain the sentiments of their slippery, dangerous, mysterious property.[23]

The domestic slaves generally were encouraged to hold themselves aloof from the field workers, and tended (though this was not universally true) to identify their own interests with those of the owners. The idea was expressed by Judge J. C. B. Lucas of St. Louis in a letter published in the Missouri *Gazette* of April 12, 1820, in these words: [24]

I confess that I do not entertain very serious apprehensions of slaves as domestics . . . they are usually treated with a degree of humanity, and not infrequently of paternal affection. The opportunities they have to observe the conduct of the master's family, to attend public worship, and the satisfaction they receive from enjoying in a reasonable degree the comforts of life, generally induces them to respect the rights of others and be harmless.

Former slaves emphasized this as important in weakening the slave class. Henry Bibb's testimony is [25]

that the domestic slaves are often found to be traitors to their own people, for the purpose of gaining favor with their masters; and they are encouraged and trained up by them to report every plot they know of being formed about stealing any thing, or running away, or any thing of the kind; and for which they are paid. This is one of the principal causes of the slaves being divided among themselves, and without which they could not be held in bondage one year, and perhaps not half that time.

Austin Steward similarly declared [26] that a domestic slave

23 Benjamin Drew, *A North-Side View of Slavery*, p. 340.

24 Quoted by Harrison Trexler, *Slavery in Missouri, 1804-1865*, p. 91.

25 *Narrative of the Life and Adventures of Henry Bibb*, p. 136.

26 A. Steward, *op. cit.*, p. 32. See also the interesting study, based on interviews with one hundred former slaves, by E. O. Settle, " Social attitudes

will for the sake of his master and mistress, frequently betray his fellow-slave . . . he is often rewarded by his master who knows it is for his interest to keep such ones about him . . . hence it is that insurrections and stampedes are so generally detected. Such slaves are always treated with more affability than others, for the slave-holder is well aware that he stands over a volcano.

An indication of the value slaveholders placed upon their favorite slaves appears in an interesting letter [27] from a Mrs. Martha L. Nelson of Mecklenburg County, Virginia, to Governor Henry Wise. The lady, writing in a period of panic due to Negro unrest, appealed to the Governor to pardon her domestic slave, Coleman, who had been sentenced to transportation upon conviction for a crime. The slave was devoted to her, said Mrs. Nelson, and " would inform on the negroes, as soon as any white person would, if he knew or suspected anything wrong was planing [sic] among them . . . I am almost a maniac from the loss of sleep, now in the dept [sic] of night I write, beseeching you to pardon my servant . . . such a servant ought not to be sent away particularly in these perilous times of insurrection."

Another device for weakening unity and solidarity among the slaves which was particularly important during the early years of the institution was the separation of slaves of similar family or tribe. Thus sympathies between the Negroes were less keen and association less familiar than might otherwise have been

during the slave regime: household servants versus field hands," in *Publication of the American Sociological Society*, 1934, XXVIII, pp. 95-99. It was, of course the rare Negro who betrayed his people. Note H. M. Henry's comment, " it was difficult to get one slave to inform against another. Mr. Seabrook, in a pamphlet on the management of slaves, published in 1834, says that this was one of the things that most interfered with the police control of the slaves."—*The Police Control of the Slave in South Carolina*, p. 17.

27 Mrs. Nelson to Governor Wise, dated Boydton, December 28, 1856. The plea was not granted. An earlier letter, of December 9, to the Governor, in which the lady declares that the $900 awarded her by the court for the slave is too little indicates another motive for her request. Executive Papers, Archives, Virginia State Library, Richmond.

true. Language differences were also in this way introduced which tended to make uprisings and plots more difficult.[28]

Occasional bright spots tended to serve as safety-valves letting off some of the steam accumulated by abuses, grievances, and oppressions. Holidays, bringing rest and recreation, were few and the days were long between them, but they were important emotional outlets. Frederick Douglass stressed the point. Speaking from painful and intimate personal knowledge he declared: [29] " These holidays were also sort of conductors or safety-valves, to carry off the explosive elements inseparable from the human mind when reduced to the condition of slavery. But for these the rigors of bondage would have become too severe for endurance, and the slave would have been forced up to dangerous desperation." He notes, too, that a slave who did not make the most of these holidays in the accepted style of hilarious carryings-on was suspect, and, " Not to be drunk during the holidays was disgraceful."

Monetary rewards or gratuities seem to have been fairly prevalent, particularly in the more northern of the slave states, and during the latter part of the era. Thus, in evidence presented before a North Carolina court in 1858 it was declared [30] to be customary for hired slaves to get twenty-five cents at the end of each week " as an inducement to good behavior." The next year Judge Manly of this state [31] " handed down a decision in which he implied that the system of rewards was necessary to preserve the system of slavery and that the gratuities might ' be developed to any desired extent without violating either the express law or general policy of the country'."

28 Robert E. Park, " The conflict and fusion of cultures with special reference to the Negro," in *Journal of Negro History*, 1919, IV, p. 117; E. F. Frazier, *The Negro Family in the United States*, p. 8.

29 *Life and Times of Frederick Douglass*, Hartford, 1882, pp. 165-67.

30 H. T. Catterall, *op. cit.*, II, p. 217.

31 Guion G. Johnson, *Ante-Bellum North Carolina*, p. 530. Of course, a " good " slave would normally be rewarded by being subjected to less cruelty, certainly less physical brutality, than one who did not thoroughly understand his " place."

From these gratuities and rewards, and from money received for " overtime " work, (especially among slaves, hired or owned, in border state factories), as well as from pennies accumulated by the occasional sale of vegetables or chickens and pigs, produced by " leisure-time " labor, (i. e., after twelve to fifteen hours of field or domestic work), Negroes were able to purchase their freedom. And thousands of Negroes did actually buy their way to freedom, among them several prominent persons, including Andrew Bryan, Lott Cary, Richard Allen (and his brother), Absalom Jones (who also purchased his wife's freedom), Denmark Vesey, Venture Smith, Gustavus Vassa, Fanny J. Coppin, Lunsford Lane, Peter Still, James Bradley, a brother of James W. C. Pennington, and a sister-in-law of Henry Highland Garnet.[32] This made possible a certain elasticity in the slave system, and by creating hope—even if limited—took the edge off desperation. It may have made the maintenance of the institution itself somewhat less difficult.

But all the preceding form merely the penumbra of the control system—the rather light touches, shadings, frills—essential to the entire picture, but not its focus. The central theme of the slaveocracy's policy was given in one sentence by an anonymous Virginian when terror produced frankness:[33] " In a word, if we will keep a ferocious monster in our country, we must keep him in chains."

The basis of the system, then, was the master's power, and this, for all practical purposes, was absolute and unconditional.

32 See article by H. Aptheker, " They bought their way to freedom," in *Opportunity*, June, 1940, pp. 180-82. See also, J. W. Coleman, Jr., *op. cit.*, p. 79, and W. M. Drake, ed., " The road to freedom," in *The Journal of Mississippi History*, III, pp. 44-45. It is to be noted as indicative of the prevalence of the practice, that Tennessee in 1833 recognized the right of a slave to make a contract for the purchase of his freedom—Catterall, *op. cit.*, II, p. 479. In addition, particularly meritorious service sometimes earned freedom by legislative act. Another method, service in the navy and army, was at times open, and brought liberty to several thousand slaves during the War of the Revolution.

33 " Letter from —— county to editor of a Fredericksburg paper," quoted in the New York *Commercial Advertiser*, September 30, 1800.

In the words of Judge Thomas Ruffin of the North Carolina Supreme Court, spoken in 1829: [34] " The power of the master must be absolute, to render the submission of the slave perfect ... As a principle of moral right, every person in his retirement must repudiate it. But in the actual condition of things it must be so."

A similar statement was made by the highest court of Virginia in 1827, and in 1851.[35] In the latter case there was, unfortunately for the master involved, a white man who not only had witnessed the deeds of the owner but also was willing to testify against him, a necessary condition for prosecution since Negro testimony was not accepted against a white person. This case was one of remarkable brutality, the master tying his slave to a tree and beating him with switches until tired. He then ordered another slave to " cob Sam with a shingle," and " applied fire to the body of the slave; about his back, belly and private parts," proceeded to wash him with hot water in which had been steeped pods of red pepper, kicked and stamped upon him, and finally choked the Negro with a rope, continuing the latter process of " correction " until death.

The defendant, Mr. Souther, maintained, however—and apparently with a straight face—that he did not intend to kill the slave (the proof of intent was necessary for conviction) and thought Sam " was feigning and pretending to be suffering or injured, when he was not." The decision of the Court read: " It is the policy of the law in respect to the relation of master and slave, and for the sake of securing proper subordination and obedience on the part of the slave, to protect the master from prosecution in all such cases, even if the whipping and punishishment be malicious, cruel, and excessive," but since here death ensued under circumstances sworn to by a white person and not denied by the defendant, it felt compelled to sentence Mr. Souther to five years' imprisonment.

34 Catterall, *op. cit.*, II, p. 57; G. G. Johnson, *op. cit.*, p. 503.

35 Catterall, *op. cit.*, I, p. 150, 223-24; *The Negro in Virginia*, p. 154.

Behind the owner, and his personal agents,[36] stood an elaborate and complex system of military control. In the cities were guards and police, for the countryside there were the ubiquitous patrols, armed men on horseback. Their duties, performed at intervals varying with the state of society at any given moment, included searching the hovels and hearts of the slaves for signs of disaffection, detaining and lashing Negroes found abroad without proper authorization, and searching out and disbanding secret assemblies of slaves, usually, or at least ostensibly, gathered for religious purposes. Practically all adult white men were liable for patrol service.[37]

Behind this were the state militias which, in the South, were " fairly efficient " armed bodies,[38] in sharp contrast to the condition in the North. Moreover, as a measure of additional precaution and as a result of the prestige of the military profession in the South, numerous and well-armed voluntary organiza-

36 Ability to control the slaves was a prime requisite for an overseer. Contracts between master and overseer usually stress this, and at times the latter commits himself to follow the detailed suggestions of the former. Thus, in the contract between the Alabama planter, William B. Gould, and his overseer, Ludwig Henderson, signed in 1837, the employes agreed "to inspect the cabins at different hours of the night as often as once a week," in order to check, as it is put nowadays, subversive activities—Charles Davis, *op. cit.*, p. 47.

37 For details, and as examples, see the South Carolina patrol act of 1721 conveniently summarized in H. M. Henry, *op. cit.*, p. 32; the North Carolina act of 1794 in G. G. Johnson, *op. cit.*, p. 516; and the Alabama act of 1819 in C. S. Davis, *op. cit.*, p. 97.

38 As described by William E. Dodd, *The Old South Struggles for Democracy*, p. 105. Note also the statement by Samuel A. Ashe, as concerns North Carolina, that " The constant possibility of insurrection required that attention should ever be given to the militia," *History of North Carolina*, II, p. 282. For details on militia organization in Virginia, see W. W. Hening, *Statutes at Large*, IV, pp. 197-204, act of 1727, passed, says the preamble, because of danger from abroad, Indians, and because "great dangers may likewise happen by the insurrection of negroes, and others." Hening's collection is filled with militia regulations; see IV, pp. 323, 395; V, pp. 24, 99 ff., 228; VI, pp. 112, 350; VII, 106 ff., 275, 384, 539; VIII, pp. 37, 189, 514; IX, pp. 291-97; XI, pp. 476 ff., XII, pp. 9 ff.

tions [39] abounded. Finally, but by no means of least importance, stood the armed might of the federal government, a large percentage of which was stationed within the South itself, and all of which was pledged, as the Constitution was then generally interpreted, to assist in suppressing servile unrest.[40]

The militarism characteristic of the slave South was commented upon by several contemporaries, and has not gone entirely unnoticed by historians. A famous British scientist, visiting the South at the end of the eighteenth century was so impressed that he remarked [41] of the white men, " The fact is, they are all soldiers." Another visitor from Great Britain, Captain Basil Hall, was struck [42] by the " military police . . . constantly

39 For a description of one such famous body see the anonymous article on the Richmond Light Infantry Blues in *Tyler's Quarterly Historical and Genealogical Magazine*, 1919, I, pp. 1-17. Reference is made here to use of this body for slave control purposes in 1829, and during the Turner Revolt (incorrectly dated 1830). The article first appeared in the October, 1841 issue of the *United States Military Magazine*, published in Philadelphia.

40 That it was so used, at various times, will appear in the course of the narrative. When, in 1842, the navy and army appropriation bills came before Congress, Southern members, including Calhoun and Benton, expressed concern whether Negroes, free or slave, were employed by these services. (This was in a period of strained relations with England, and it was feared that in case of war that no longer slaveholding nation might stir up insurrections in the United States—Hugh R. Fraser, *Democracy in the Making the Jackson-Tyler Era*, p. 138) Resolutions were therefore, passed calling upon the Secretary of the Navy, Mr. Upshur, and of the Army, Mr. Spencer, to provide the facts. Mr. Upshur reported that slaves were not in the navy, but that free Negroes were, though no record of their number was available. A regulation, however, forbade over one-twentieth of a ship's crew to be Negro, and it was thought "the number generally is very far within this proportion." Mr. Spencer reported no Negroes serving as soldiers, but one hundred and six slaves worked in the Quartermaster's department, eight in the commissary's, and five hundred and seventy Negroes (twenty-five free) in that of Engineering. In addition, twenty-eight slaves labored in various Southern arsenals—*Executive Documents*, 27 Cong., 2nd Sess., V, documents nos., 282, 286. See also Charles Elliott, *op. cit.*, II, p. 157; *The Friend of the African*, London, 1844, no. 9, p. 132; G. H. Barnes and D. L. Dumond, eds., *Letters of Theodore Dwight Weld* . . . , II, p. 886.

41 Francis Baily, *Journal of a Tour in . . North America . . 1796-97*, p. 99.

42 Anonymously edited collection, *Negro Slavery; or, a view of some of the more prominent features of that state of Society*, London, 1823, p. 424.

kept up" in Charleston. Governor Robert Y. Hayne of South Carolina remarked: "A state of military preparation must always be with us a state of perfect domestic security. A period of profound peace and consequent apathy may expose us to the danger of domestic insurrection." [43] This military preparation was commented upon by Fanny Kemble, while in Charleston in 1838. She noticed [44] particularly the nine o'clock curfew for Negroes and the imposing new guard house which, she thought, was "very large for so small a town."

Frederick Law Olmsted was moved to a very interesting series of comments by his observations in this same city of Charleston, as well as in other Southern communities during the last years of slavery. There, he wrote,[45] one sees

police machinery such as you never find in towns under free government: citadels, sentries, passports, grapeshotted cannon, and daily public whippings of the subjects for accidental infractions of police ceremonies. I happened myself to see more direct expression of tyranny in a single day and night in Charleston, than at Naples in a week; and I found that more than half the inhabitants of this town were subject to arrest, imprisonment, and barbarous punishment, if found in the streets without a passport after the evening "gunfire". Similar precautions and similar customs may be discovered in every large town in the South . . . There is . . . nearly everywhere, [in the South] always prepared to act, if not always in service, an armed force, with a military organization, which is invested with more arbitrary and cruel power than any police in Europe.

Herbert Levi Osgood noted the development of armed precautionary measures in the slave area as early as the first decade

43 Quoted by Harvey Wish, "American slave insurrections before 1861," in *The Journal of Negro History*, 1937, XXII, p. 306.

44 Margaret Armstrong, *op. cit.*, p. 211.

45 F. L. Olmsted, *A Journey in the Back Country*, p. 444; see also his comment on the little standing army maintained in Richmond after the Gabriel plot, in *A Journey in the Seaboard Slave States*, I, p. 22.

of the eighteenth century. He recorded [46] the establishment and maintenance of about eight watch-houses along the coast of South Carolina and declared, " One duty of the armed watchmen at these posts was to look out for slaves who were trying to escape by sea. The influence of slavery in developing the military spirit and institutions of the province is further evidenced by the creation of the patrol system " in 1704. Henry Adams and Rosser H. Taylor are other historians who have commented [47] upon the militarism so notable in the slave South, and of such basic importance in the continuance of the system.

Laws regulating and restricting nearly every conceivable activity of the slaves were another fundamental factor in their control. Thousands of such measures were passed and it is manifestly impractical to catalogue each, or even most, of them. It is proposed, however, to indicate, in general terms, the stipulations of these enactments, and then to give, in some detail, the important laws passed in various colonies early in the history of slavery (which served as models for later legislation), and those passed by several states during a period of considerable slave unrest, when batches of new laws always appeared.[48]

In general, then, it may be stated that slaves were forbidden to assemble without the permission and presence of responsible whites, were not to own or carry arms of any kind, were not to trade, buy, sell, or engage in any other economic activity without the permission of their masters, were not to be off the plantation grounds at any time or on the city streets after nine or ten in the evening without written permission, were not to practice or administer medicine, were not to lift their hands

46 H. L. Osgood, *The American Colonies in the Seventeenth Century*, II, p. 385. See also *ante*, pp. 44, 46.

47 H. Adams, *History of the United States during the First Administration of Thomas Jefferson*, I, p. 150; R. H. Taylor, " The gentry of antebellum South Carolina," in *The North Carolina Historical Review*, XVII, p. 122.

48 In the course of the narrative other laws passed as a result of, or important to an understanding of, various revolts will be mentioned.

against any white person,[49] were not to be taught to read or write, and were not permitted to testify in court in any case involving a white person.

Laws laying the groundwork for this elaborate legal system of repression were passed in several colonies in the seventeenth century. Virginia, for example, being seriously troubled by maroons, or outlying, belligerent slaves, passed a law in 1672 urging and rewarding the hunting down and killing of these fugitives. The same province enacted a law [50] in 1680 declaring assemblies among slaves illegal and prohibiting them from carrying any weapon. The House of Burgesses passed a similar bill eight years later, but this was rejected by the Council because, " The part of this Bill Restraining Negroes from Meeting in Considerable Numbers and Walking abroad, as also from bearing any Armes, Carrying of Clubbs, Staves, or Other Offensive Weapons, or Instruments, we are of Opinion is sufficiently provided for " by the 1680 enactment.[51] In 1682, moreover, there had been passed " an Additional Act for the better preventing Insurrections by Negroes " which repeated and reinforced that of 1680, and added the regulation that no slave from one plantation was to remain in another for more than four hours at any one time.[52] In June, 1694 Governor Andros issued a proclamation calling attention to the laws of 1680 and 1682, declaring that " diverse Negroes & slaves in Sundry parts & Countyes in this Collony have mett congregated & gott to-

49 It is, however, to be stated that in 1834 Judge Gaston declared for the Supreme Court of North Carolina that a slave had a right to defend himself if his life was in danger. If death for his attacker ensued the slave was guilty of manslaughter, not murder. How this could, in practice, be enforced it is difficult to understand. See G. G. Johnson, *op. cit.*, p. 503.

50 Hening, *op. cit.*, II, pp. 299, 481; Philip A. Bruce, *Economic History of Virginia in the 17th Century*, II, p. 115; H. Aptheker, *The Journal of Negro History*, 1939, XXIV, p. 168; Thomas J. Wertenbaker, *The First Americans, 1607-1690*, p. 234.

51 H. R. McIlwaine, ed., *Legislative Journals of the Council of Colonial Virginia*, I, p. 127.

52 H. R. McIlwaine, ed., *Executive Journals of the Council of Colonial Virginia*, II, p. 35.

gether, which meeting & gatherings together of such Negroes or slaves as aforesaid being of dangerous consequence," and ordering that this proclamation and the laws to which it referred were to be published and displayed in churches and Chapels of Ease and all meetings of Malitia or Musters." [53]

New York in 1684 declared that over four slaves should at no time and at no place meet together away from their master's service, and no slave was to carry arms. In 1702 the number permitted to meet together was dropped from four to three, and it was declared that a slave's evidence would be acceptable only " in Cases of Plotting or Confederacy among themselves." [54]

At about this time the slave control problem became serious in Kings County (Brooklyn) of this colony, finally compelling the Governor of New York and New Jersey, Lord Cornbury, to issue, in July, 1706, this proclamation [55] addressed to the Justices of the Peace :

Whereas, I am informed that several negroes in Kings County have assembled themselves in a riotous manner, which if not prevented may prove of ill consequence ; you and every one of you are therefor hereby required and commanded to take all proper methods for seizing and apprehending all such negroes in the said county, as shall be found to be assembled in such manner as aforesaid, or have run away or absconded from their masters or owners, whereby there may be reason to suspect them of ill practices or designs, and to secure them in safe custody, that their crimes and actions may be inquired into; and if any of them refuse to submit themselves, then to fire on them, kill, or destroy them, if they cannot otherwise be taken; and for so doing this shall be your sufficient warrant.

Other colonies, notably Maryland and South Carolina, in 1690, passed laws [56] severely punishing the instigation or the

53 York County Records, 1694-1697, pp. 22-23, Virginia State Library. Richmond; see also P. A. Bruce, *op. cit.*, II, p. 118.

54 Edwin V. Morgan, *Slavery in New York*, p. 12; A. Judd Northrup, *Slavery in New York*, pp. 260-61.

55 Stephen M. Ostrander, *A History of the City of Brooklyn, and Kings County*, I pp. 171-72.

56 Jeffrey R. Brackett, *The Negro in Maryland*, p. 92; H. M. Henry, *op. cit.*, p. 148.

practice of conspiracy or rebellion. In the same year (1750) that Parliament authorized the holding of slaves in Georgia it provided,[57] as precautionary measures, that for every four Negroes in the colony there was to be at least one white man-servant of militia age, and that Negroes were not to be employed in any trade except that of agriculture, nor were they to be apprenticed to artisans, with the exception of carpenters.

The years from 1792 to 1804 are rather arbitrarily selected as comprising the period of prolific law-making which, as previously remarked, it is proposed to study in some detail. This will complete, for the present, the picturing of the legal machinery of control under which American Negro slaves toiled. The period (marked by numerous slave plots here and in Latin America) is especially noteworthy for acts restricting or temporarily outlawing the slave trade, both domestic and foreign.

The federal government in 1794 and in 1800 passed laws aimed at the foreign slave trade. The first forbade citizens from equipping ships for such commerce and the second prohibited them from serving aboard them or from having any interest in their voyages.[58]

States also sought to regulate the slave-trade.[59] South Carolina, beginning in 1792, passed several laws against the impor-

---

57 L. C. Gray, *A History of Agriculture in the Southern United States* to 1860, I, p. 100. The restriction of Negroes to agricultural work was probably a reflection of the fear of the urbanization of slaves, something that recurs. See also Richard B. Morris, "Labor & mercantilism in the Revolutionary Era" in R. B. Morris, ed., *The Era of the American Revolution*, pp. 79-80. In 1698 because "the great number of negroes which of late have been imported into this Collony may endanger the saftey thereof," a law was passed in South Carolina encouraging the entrance of white servants. This was repeated ten times between 1714 and 1764—see W. E. B. Du Bois, *op. cit.*, pp. 9, 203, 209, 211, 215.

58 Du Bois, *op. cit.*, p. 84.

59 Joseph Brevard, *The Statute Law of South Carolina*, II, pp. 256-261; W. Littell, *The Statute Law of Kentucky*, I, p. 246; William Kilty, *The Laws of Maryland*, II, Chaps. LXVII, LXXV; Horatio Marbury and W. H. Crawford, *Digest of the Laws of Georgia*, pp. 440-441; DuBois, *op. cit.*, p. 73; Elizabeth Donnan, *Documents Illustrative of the History of the Slave Trade to America*, IV, p. 244.

tation of slaves, that of 1801 being the most severe ever enacted. Had this law remained on the books for any considerable length of time, and had it been enforced, it would have gone far to cripple the institution of slavery itself. It declared that no person might import more than two slaves, and these were to be for personal use only. No other importation of Negroes from any source or for any purpose whatever was to be permitted, with violation bringing a fine of one hundred dollars for each slave, and the loss of the Negro. This, however, was weakened the next year when the number of slaves one might import for his own use was made unlimited, and in 1803 the restriction to personal use was itself lifted. It was still illegal, however, to import slaves from the West Indies or South America, and even those brought in from the sister states of the Union had to come accompanied by a statement signed by two magistrates that the Negroes were " persons of good character and have not been concerned in any insurrection or rebellion." Kentucky in 1794 and Maryland in 1796 forbade slave importation except for the personal use of the importer, while a North Carolina act of 1795 prohibited the bringing in of West Indian slaves. Georgia in 1793 did the same but added East and West Florida to the forbidden zone, and in 1798 flatly forbade further importation of Negroes. In Baltimore slaves who had been imported from the French West Indies from 1792 to 1797 were declared, in the latter year, " to be dangerous to the peace and welfare of the city," and their masters were ordered to banish them or suffer seeing them arrested and sold by the city officials.

These years saw the passage of laws not merely for the purpose of restricting the number or regulating the origins of new slaves, but also many for the purpose of aiding in the holding of those already present. The new State of Kentucky enacted a whole series of control measures [60] in 1798 which provided machinery for the apprehending and securing of runaways, forbade meetings of slaves without the presence of whites, denied them the right to possess weapons, required them to have passes

[60] W. Littell, op. cit., II, pp. 5-6, 113-123.

when off plantations, and provided severe penalties for sedition.

South Carolina found it advisable in 1800 to enact a new and elaborate slave code, for, as the preamble stated,[61] " the laws heretofore enacted for the government of slaves, free negroes, mulattos, mestizos, have been found insufficient for the keeping them in due subordination." Here it was provided that all meetings at which slaves were present (even though whites were present, as required by law) were to be open, never closed or barred. Moreover, no slaves, even with whites present, were " to meet together and assemble, for the purpose of mental instruction, or religious worship, either before the rising of the sun, or after the going down of the same." Another regulation made it necessary for a magistrate and five freeholders to pass upon a document of manumission for the interesting reason that " it hath been a practice for many years past in this state, for persons to emancipate or set free their slaves, in cases where such slaves have been of bad or depraved characters, or from age or infirmity, incapable of gaining their livelihood by honest means." Finally, this State in the same year placed a fine of two dollars upon every white man each time he failed to perform the patrol duty required of him.

Delaware in 1798 passed a law [62] forbidding all Negroes (free or slave, except if latter were in attendance upon his master) from being present in any town at a time when voting was in progress. Georgia the next year enacted a measure [63] containing most interesting phrases. This provided that anyone guilty of " wilfully and maliciously " killing or dismembering or maiming any slave was to be subject to the same penalties as though the victim had been white, " except in cases of insurrection by such slave, and unless such maiming or dismembering [or killing] should happen by accident, in giving such slave moderate correction." Finally, so far as this period is concerned, both Virginia, in 1798, and South Carolina, in 1805,

61 J. Brevard, *op. cit.*, II, pp. 105, 253-55.

62 *Laws of the State of Delaware, 1798-1805*, III, pp. 9-11.

63 Marbury and Crawford, *op. cit.*, pp. 443-44.

observing that slaves were sometimes aided in their conspiracies or uprisings by free people, Negro and white, passed laws [64] making such assistance a capital offense.

This type of legislation by no means exhausts the laws aimed against the free Negroes in the slave area. These pariahs, these walking refutations of the entire slaveocratic ideology, were ever a source of concern. As proof of this may be cited the Richmond *Enquirer* of January 18, 1805, which referred to free Negroes as "possible chieftains of formidable conspiracies," or the *Virginia Argus* of the next year, January 17, 1806, which thought [65] " it may be proven that it is the free blacks who instil into the slaves ideas hostile to our peace." A striking illustration of this type of thinking occurred in the speech [66] of the blunt John Randolph of Virginia delivered in Washington at the formation meeting, in December, 1816, of the American Colonization Society. His remarks demonstrate not only the existence of fears and suspicions of the free Negroes but also the essential purpose of that Society, the forging of a firmer grip on the slave population by the removal of a disturbing element. Mr. Randolph said that

with a view to securing the support of all the citizens of the United States, it ought to be made known that the colonization scheme tended to secure the property of every master to, in, and over his slaves ; that it was a notorious fact that the free negroes were regarded by every slaveowner as one of the greatest sources of insecurity and unprofitableness of slave property ; that they excited discontent among their fellow beings ; [and] that they acted as channels of communication, not only between different slaves, but between slaves of different districts.

64 Thomas Cooper, *Statutes at Large of South Carolina*, V, p. 503 ; Samuel Shepherd, *The Statutes at Large of Virginia, 1792-1806, being a continuation of Hening*, II, p. 77.

65 Quoted by John H. Russell, *The Free Negro in Virginia, 1619-1865*, pp. 69, 135.

66 William C. Bruce, *John Randolph of Roanoke*, II, p. 247 ; see also, James Madison, "Answers to questions concerning slavery " addressed to Jedediah Morse, 1823, in Gaillard Hunt, ed., *The Writings of James Madison*, IX, p. 133 ; Harold Schoen, " The free Negro in the Republic of Texas," in *Southwestern Historical Quarterly*, 1937, XLI, pp. 101, 107.

As a rule, these people were deprived of important civil rights,[67] such as that of voting and of testifying in court against white persons; social rights,[68] such as regulations concerning miscegenation, regulating their presence on city streets after dark, and restricting their educational opportunities and their freedom of movement from state to state or county to county; economic rights,[69] by restricting trades or professions which they might pursue. Moreover, in order to cut down the growth of this type of population, it became, as the years passed, the policy of the states to make the act of manumission increasingly difficult,[70] and, indeed, just prior to the Civil War, some of the

[67] Virginia withdrew voting privileges from free Negroes in 1723, North Carolina as late as 1835. The State of Delaware enacted a law in 1799 which did permit free Negroes to testify against whites, except for the purpose of charging a white " with being the father or reputed father of any bastard child." This State was also an exception among Southern States in that there a Negro was assumed to be free until proven to be a slave—the contrary prevailed elsewhere. See H. T. Catterall, *op. cit.*, IV, p. 211.

[68] For data on miscegenation see W. W. Hening, *op. cit.*, I, pp. 146, 552; *The Negro in Virginia, op. cit.*, p. 112; *Laws of the State of Delaware 1806-1813*, pp. 109-113; *Acts passed by the General Assembly of the State of North Carolina at session of 1830-31*, pp. 9-11 (this act also forbade cohabiting between a free Negro and a slave); Carter G. Woodson, " The beginnings of miscegenation of the whites and blacks," *The Journal of Negro History*, III, pp. 335-353; for examples on curfew laws see Harold Schoen, *op. cit.*, p. 93; Bertram Doyle, *op. cit.*, p. 90; on education, see J. Russell, *op. cit.*, p. 140; on locomotion, see Lucius Q. C. Lamar, *A Compilation of the Laws of Georgia 1810-1819*, p. 814; S. Shepherd, *op. cit.*, II, pp. 300-301.

[69] For examples of economic restrictions see, Lamar, *op. cit.*, p. 814; *Laws of the State of Mississippi passed at the 14th Session of the General Assembly* (Jackson, 1830), p. 88; U. B. Phillips, " The public archives of Georgia," *Annual Report of the American Historical Association for the Year 1903*, I, pp. 467-68. For details on restrictions placed upon free Negroes see Victor H. Peterson, " The position of the free person of color in Mississippi, Louisiana, and Alabama before the Civil War," unpublished master's thesis, University of Chicago, 1939, pp. 10-14.

[70] Exceptions to this are the Virginia law of 1782, passed under the impetus given to liberal movements by the Revolution, and the laws in the border States of Maryland (1796), Kentucky (1794, 1800), and Tennessee (1801) during a period of serious questioning of the righteousness and wisdom of slavery. See Mary S. Locke, *op. cit.*, pp. 121-22; Littell, *op. cit.*, I, pp. 246-47, 387; Kilty, *op. cit.*, II, chap. LXVII. Otherwise one finds a

states passed laws for the purpose of enslaving Negroes already free.[71]

To summarize, then, one may say that the masters of the Southern states were not content to depend merely upon social inertia, or the power that their ownership of the means of production gave them in order to maintain their dominant position. On the contrary they called into play every trick, rule, regulation, and device that the human mind could invent to aid them; the attempted psychological, intellectual, and physical debasement of an entire people, the inculcating and glorifying of the most outrageous racial animosities buttressed by theological, historical, and anthropological theories, the dividing of the victims against themselves, the use of spies and the encouragement of traitors, the evolving of a rigid social code helpful for their purpose, the disdaining, tabooing, and finally repressing of all opposition thought and deed, the establishment of elaborate police and military systems, the enacting of innumerable laws of oppression and suppression; the developing, in short, of a social order within which the institution of Negro slavery became so deeply imbedded that it was true that to touch one was to move the other. This indissoluble linking of one with the other epitomizes the entire method of control, and was at once its strength and its weakness.

procession of steadily stiffer requirements for manumission—see Catterall, *op. cit.*, I, p. 72; II, pp. 4, 268. Louisiana in 1857, Georgia and Arkansas in 1859, and Alabama in 1860 totally forbade manumission—*Acts Passed by the Third Legislature of Louisiana at its Second Session* (New Orleans, 1857), p. 55; *Acts of the General Assembly of the State of Georgia, 1859* (Milledgeville, 1860), p. 68; *Acts of the Seventh Biennial Session of the General Assembly of Alabama, 1859-60* (Montgomery, 1860), p. 28; *Acts Passed at the 12th Session of the Gen. Ass. Ark. 1858-59* (Little Rock, 1859), p. 69.

71 This was done by permitting the sale of free Negroes, for various periods of time, convicted of "idleness or vagrancy," as in Florida and Georgia in 1859—*Acts of Gen. Ass. Fla., 9th Sess.* (Tallahassee, 1859), pp. 13-14; *Acts of the Gen. Ass. Ga. 1859* (Milledgeville, 1860), pp. 69-70.

CHAPTER IV
SOME PRECIPITANTS OF REBELLION

DESPITE the existence of this intricate machine for exploitation, the direct victims of it, the Negro slaves, persistently resisted its creators, and occasionally received assistance from the less direct victims, the poorer whites.[1] What were the factors that impelled the slaves towards their militant behavior?

Frederick Law Olmsted correctly remarked [2] that " any great event having the slightest bearing upon the question of emancipation is known to produce an 'unwholesome excitement' " among the slave population. It is, moreover, a fact that on numerous occasions unusual or striking events having no apparent connection with slavery were interpreted by the Negroes as though the connection was present. This played a part in precipitating some plots and uprisings.

Thus the arrival of Governor Alexander Spotswood in Virginia in 1730 set the slaves whispering that he had brought from the King an order " to sett all those slaves free that were Christians," and to free those who became Christians, but that their masters had suppressed this. While, at first, " no discovery could be made of any formed Design of their Rising " but merely " unlawful Meetings " and " loose Discourses " and these were soon stopped by " keeping the Militia to their Duty, by Imprisonment and severe Whipping of the most Suspected," within six weeks an actual conspiracy was uncovered. This centered in Norfolk and Princess Anne Counties and had reached the point where, on a Sunday, " whilst the People were at Church " some two hundred slaves gathered and proceeded " to

---

1 These under-privileged whites carred on their own struggle against the ruling groups within the South. The critical study of the internal condition of the South, getting away from the myth of a placid, contented, classless, united land, that has generally been pictured, is a distinctly modern phenomenon. That phase of it which involves the whites alone is beyond the scope of this study.

2 F. L. Olmsted, *A Journey in the Back Country*, pp. 474-75.

chuse from among themselves officers to Command their intended Insurrection." This time imprisonment and lashings were thought to be insufficient stimulants to docility and four of the leaders were executed. Thereafter it was provided that white men who went to worship the Prince of Peace were to take their guns with them.[3]

Similarly, " some hundreds " of slaves of East Jersey, near Somerville, planned a rebellion and flight to nearby Indians in 1734, and one of the considerations moving them was a belief that the King had issued orders freeing them, but that these had been kept secret by their owners.[4] One Negro, belonging to a Mr. Hall, who appears to have had a drink too many, could not resist, under such exhilarating circumstances, the pleasure of telling a white man of the above " fact," his further belief that " English-men were generally a pack of villains," and that he, the slave, " was as good a Man as himself, and that in a little Time he should be convinced of it." Complete details of the plot were soon uncovered, many slaves were arrested (on some of whom were found quantities of poison), some were whipped, others had their ears cut off, and two were condemned to hang, though since one—he of the loquacious mood—escaped, the gallows claimed but one Negro.

Note has already been taken of Governor Dinwiddie's remark in July, 1755 that the slaves of Virginia, learning of the French victories over the British, were becoming " very auda-

3 Lt. Gov. William Gooch to Lords of Trade, dated Williamsburgh, September 14, 1730 in Virginia Manuscripts from British Record Office, Sainsbury, IX, p. 496, Archives, Virginia State Library; same to the Bishop of London, Williamsburgh, May 28, 1731, in *The Virginia Magazine of History and Biography*, XXXII, pp. 322-23. Some of this material has been published by the present writer under the title " Negro History—A Cause for Optimism " in *Opportunity* (August, 1941), pp. 228-31.

4 New York *Gazette*, March 18-25, 1734 in William Nelson, ed., *Archives of the State of New Jersey*, 1st ser., IX, pp. 335-37, 340-42. See also, Henry S. Cooley, *A Study of Slavery in New Jersey*, pp. 42-43; Andrew D. Mellick, Jr., *The Story of an Old Farm*, p. 225. Mr. Mellick states that at least two slaves were executed. The sources do not substantiate this.

cious " since they believed that the former would " give them their freedom." [5]

The bitter and prolonged Congressional debates concerning the admission of Missouri into the Union, in the course of which men like King and Tallmadge expressed opposition to slavery, somehow reached the ears of certain of the slaves involved in the great Vesey conspiracy of 1822 in South Carolina. But it reached their ears in exaggerated form, or, as is perhaps more likely, they put into what they heard that which they wished to believe. In this way they became convinced that Congress had not merely heard speeches denunciatory of slavery but had actually passed an act of emancipation, by which their masters refused to abide. Mention of this is made in the official report [6] of the trials of the rebel Negroes, and it is also remarked upon by Joel R. Poinsett, who was in Charleston at the time and declared: [7] " The discussion of the Missouri question at Washington, among other evils, produced this plot. It was considered by this unfortunate and half instructed people as one of emancipation."

In the winter of 1825 a slave plot was uncovered and crushed in Edgecomb and, " it is believed, some of the adjacent counties " in North Carolina. Slave preachers were blamed and, it was stated,[8] they had told the Negroes " that the national government had set them free in October and that they were being unjustly held in servitude."

There was more basis for the belief in the imminence of freedom that moved slaves in Texas and disturbed their masters in 1828; for the constitution of the State of Coahuila-Texas of

5 *Ante*, p. 20.

6 Lionel H. Kennedy and Thomas Parker, *An Official Report of the Trial of Sundry Negroes Charged with an Attempt to Raise an Insurrection in the State of South Carolina*, p. 64.

7 Poinsett to James Monroe, dated Charleston, August 13, 1822, in Monroe Papers, Library of Congress.

8 MS. petition dated December 27, 1825 in Legislative Papers, Senate, Historical Commission Raleigh; quoted by G. G. Johnson, *Ante-Bellum North Carolina*, p. 515.

March, 1827, declared that no one was thereafter to be born a slave and outlawed (after six months) the introduction of any more slaves. A law, however, of May, 1828 recognized the legality of contracts made between masters and workers prior to arrival in Texas so that, by the use of life-time contracts, slavery for all practical purposes was legalized. Yet the slaves felt that the government had indeed freed them, and they became very difficult and " restless under the yoke." The owners had their own inimitable method of driving concern over legal questions from the minds of their chattels, so that, according to a contemporary investigator,[9] they " in the effort to retain them, are making that yoke even heavier; they extract their teeth, set on the dogs to tear them to pieces, the most lenient being he who but flogs his slaves until they are flayed."

Widespread unrest was characteristic of the slaves in the South in 1829. One of the factors moving the Negroes of Virginia was their belief that the recent elections of delegates to the Constitutional Convention, to be held in 1829-30, was for the purpose of deciding the question of their emancipation. Some had decided to rebel unless this decision were in their favor.[10]

According to a magistrate of police in Wilmington, North Carolina, unrest and plotting among Negroes of that neighborhood in the summer of 1830 were attributable not merely to the circulation among them of David Walker's seditious pamphlet.

9 The investigator, Don Manuel Mier y Terás, was sent into Texas by President Guadalupe Victoria of Mexico. The quotations are from his letter to the President dated June 30, 1828 in Alleine Howren, " Causes and origin of the decree of April 6, 1830," in *The Southwestern Historical Quarterly*, XVI, pp. 397-98.

10 Christian Tompkins to Governor John Floyd of Virginia, Mathews Court House, July 18, 1829, Executive Papers, Archives, Virginia State Library. In a rare and very interesting pamphlet, which the present writer has never seen mentioned, published in New York City early in 1829 (copyrighted February 23) a free Negro foretells the coming of a mulatto savior. He, who is described as a huge, bearded, and invincible man, was to come from Grenada's Island and destroy slavery. [Robert Alexander Young], *The Ethiopian Manifesto, Issued in Defense of the Black Man's Rights, in the Scale of Universal Freedom*, pp. 8-9.

In addition, the magistrate reported [11] that " a very general and extensive impression has been made on the minds of the negroes in this vicinity, that measures have been taken towards their emancipation on a certain & not distant day . . ." Again, one of the considerations stirring slaves of Elizabeth City in the same State in 1835 was the belief,[12] shared by free Negroes, that a liberator was on his way there from the North to lead them in the struggle for freedom.

The tremendous fan-fare of the " Tippecanoe and Tyler too " campaign of 1840, with each side denouncing the other as "Abolitionist," and vying in their alleged devotion to " liberty," developed dangerous illusions amongst the slaves of Perry County, Alabama. Many believed that they were to be freed, one maintaining that Van Buren was in the region of Montgomery with an army of liberation totalling two hundred thousand men, while another felt that deliverance would come through the hands of a British force.[13] Negroes told each other at their " hush-meetings " that the coming of freedom [14]

ain't no dream, nor no joke. De time's a'most yer. Der won't be no mo' whippin', no mo' oversee's, no mo' patrollers, no mo' hunt-

11 James F. McRae to Governor John Owen, dated Wilmington, August 7, 1830, in Governor's Letter Book, vol. XXVIII, pp. 218-219, Historical Commission, Raleigh.

12 Elizabeth City, N. C., *Herald*, October 3, 1835, in *The Liberator*, October 17, 1835; also extracts from the Richmond *Whig*. October 20, 1835, and the Tarborough, N. C. *Press*, October 17, 1835, kindly supplied the present writer by Dr. Clement Eaton of Lafayette College.

13 Extract from letter dated Perry County, Alabama, December 24, 1840 in *The Liberator*, January 22, 1841. Some of the Negroes involved in Nat Turner's Revolt of 1831 believed that the British would aid them—See letter from E. P. Guion to Judge Thomas Ruffin, dated Raleigh, August 28, 1831 in J. G. deRoulhac Hamilton, ed., *The Papers of Thomas Ruffin*, II, p. 45; W. S. Drewry, *The Southampton Insurrection*, p. 76. This may possibly have been due to the presence of English troops in southeastern Virginia during the War of 1812 to which many slaves fled. The rumor in 1840 may have originated as a result of the slaves learning of the emancipation of slaves in the British West Indies.

14 Kate E. R. Pickard, *The Kidnapped and the Ransomed*, pp. 159-61.

in' wid dogs; everybodys a gwine to be free, and de white mass'r's a gwine to pay 'em for der work. O, my brudders! de bressed time's a knockin' at de door!

More frequent patrolling, arrests, and lashings were needed to convince the slaves that they were wrong when they shouted, " The year of jubilee is come! We all's a gwine to be free!"

A letter [15] written from Clarksville, Georgia, February 2, 1844, contained the interesting remark that " the negroes in Georgia are already saying to each other that great men are trying to set them free and will succeed, and many other expressions of similar import."

Certain it is that one of the inspirations moving slaves in Texas and Tennessee, to plot insurrection in 1856 was their belief that Colonel Frémont, the Republican presidential candidate, would aid them. A Memphis newspaper reported,[16] in alluding to widespread evidences of unrest in that city, " that a lady a few days ago went into her kitchen, and gave some directions to the negro cook, who impudently replied with a sneer, "When Frémont's elected, you'll have to sling them pots yourself'." This hope gave encouragement to slaves convicted of conspiracy in Clarkville, Tennessee, even while they were receiving their punishment. Thus, a contemporary witness remarked,[17] " Certain slaves are so greatly imbued with this fable

15 John W. H. Underwood to Howell Cobb in U. B. Phillips, ed., " The Correspondence of Robert Toombs, Alexander H. Stephens, and Howell Cobb," *Annual Report of the American Historical Association*, 1911, II, p. 55; see also James G. Birney to Theodore D. Weld, dated near Danville, Ky., July 26, 1834 in G. H. Barnes & D. L. Dumond, eds., *Letters of T. D. Weld, A. G. Weld and Sarah Grimké*, I, p. 164.

16 Memphis *Visitor*, n. d., quoted in *The Liberator*, December 12, 1856.

17 Letter dated Clarkville, December 3, 1856, originally in the N. Y. *Times*, in *The Liberator*, December 19, 1856. Note Abraham Lincoln's remarks to John Hay, November 24, 1863: "When the Democrats of Tennessee continually asserted in their canvass of '56 that Frémont's election would free the negroes, though they did not believe it themselves, their slaves did; and as soon as the news of Frémont's defeat came to the plantations the dissappointment (sic) of the slaves flashed into insurrection." Carl Sandburg, *Abraham Lincoln The War Years*, II, p. 27.

that I have seen them smile when they were being whipped, and have heard them say that 'Frémont and his men can hear the blows they receive'." A vigilante committee in Harrison County, Texas, at the same period reported [18] that there "had been a good deal of loose talk [among the Negroes] about the late election—the prospects of Frémont's election, and the belief of some, that they would be free if Frémont was elected."

The next campaign led, as may be expected, to the development of similar ideas. Concrete examples of this occur less frequently than four years before, though at least one slave, in Georgia, following the success of Abraham Lincoln, announced, "Lincoln was elected now, and he was free." Severe whipping was necessary to convince him that his conclusion was rather premature.[19]

The presence of Spaniards in Florida who were hostile to the English and befriended their fugitive slaves was important in leading Negroes to gamble their lives in uprisings and attempts to reach that haven. This condition is well indicated in

18 Galveston *News*, December 4, 1856, quoted in the New Orleans *Daily Picayune*, December 8, 1856; see also N. Y. *Weekly Tribune*, December 20, 1856. A petition asking for arms from Carolina County, Virginia addressed to Governor Henry Wise, dated Port Royal, Dec. 26, 1856, and signed by several citizens including the well-known writer, George Fitzhugh, explained the request on grounds of evidence of slave insubordination since "the negroes of the South [had been] deluded by the nefarious conduct and representations of Northern fanatics in the late Presidential canvass." Executive Papers, Archives, Virginia State Library.

19 Correspondence dated Savannah, February 15, 1861 in the N. Y. *Daily Tribune*, February 20, 1861. The Boston *Atlas* of November 20, 1860, declared that the day before "Joseph W. Ribero, a native of Savannah, a carpenter, and, so far as is known, a worthy man" arrived in Boston with his family. Vigilantes, called "Regulators," "had severly whipped him, cut the hair and board from one side of his head and face, and put him immediately on a boat bound northward. His crime was telling a slave who, seeing him read a newspaper, had asked what was the news, that it was 'nothing but politics,' the North contending for freedom, and the South for slavery; and, when asked if Lincoln's election would free the slaves, replying that he did not know"—*Twenty-Eighth Annual Report of the American Anti-Slavery Society*, by the Executive Committee, for the year ending May 1, 1861, pp. 194-95.

an unsigned letter [20] dated "Carolina June 24, 1720" describing a recent " very wicked and barbarous plott of the designe of the negroes rising with a designe to destroy all the white people." Most of the rebels were captured, " and some burnt and hang'd and some banish'd," but fourteen at first eluded arrest. These " thought to gett to [St.] Augustine," and hoped the Creek Indians would aid, but the latter " would not joine them or be their pylots." Another fact mentioned in this letter may also have had some importance in precipitating the formation of this scheme: " I am to inform you that at the same tyme the negroes was playing the rogue we had a small war with the Vocamas a nation on Winea river not above 100 men . . .".

For many years after this Florida remained a magnet for America's slaves as will be observed in the course of the narrative. It may here be noted that the slaves who took part in the uprising at Stono, South Carolina in September, 1739, headed for the Edisto River whose mouth is directly north of St. Augustine, their ultimate goal. Contemporaries, indeed, felt [21] that this insurrection and others that immediately preceded and followed it were directly stimulated by agents of Spain (which, by 1739, was officially at war with England), but no conclusive evidence of this has been seen.

In 1729 and 1730 the regular armed forces of the French in Louisiana found it difficult to suppress hostile Indians. Governor Perier therefore decided to arm adult male slaves and use them against the Chonaches. In the latter year, however, certain of the Negroes, being armed, becoming aware of the dependence of the white man upon their assistance, and realizing that they and the Indians had a common foe, conspired to unite

20 Addressed to a Mr. Boone in London, in Public Records of South Carolina, vol. VIII, pp. 24-27, Historical Commission, Columbia, South Carolina.

21 " Report of Committee on failure of expedition against St. Augustine," dated July 2, 1741, in Council Journal, Vol. VII, pp. 424-25, Historical Commission, Columbia. See also Robert L. Meriwether, *The Expansion of South Carolina, 1729-1765*, pp. 26-28.

their forces against him.[22] The French learned of the plot in time and the usual story of lashings of all involved, and the executions of the leaders, was repeated.

Mention has already been made[23] of the signs of unrest noticed among slaves in Virginia and Maryland in the years 1755 and 1756 in the midst of and, as contemporaries felt, largely because of the derangements and excitements consequent upon the waging of the French and Indian War.

Much the same situation prevailed during the years of the American Revolution. Here it is likely that the spirit and philosophy of that movement were important in arousing organized displays of discontent amongst the Negroes[24] as well as the excitement and turmoil characteristic of warfare, especially revolutionary warfare.

Negroes in Boston conspiring for liberty in September, 1774, tried to get the English to help them. They contacted an Irishman and got him to write to Governor Gage offering to fight with him " provided he would arm them, and engage to liberate them if he conquered." It has been said that the Governor thought enough of the proposal to call it to the attention of a Colonel Percy of the Fifth Regiment and to detail a Lieutenant Small to look carefully into the matter. The fact that this affair was " kept pretty private " and that there was " little said " or written about it cuts off further information, but clearly the

22 E. Bunner, *History of Louisiana from its First Discovery and Settlement to the Present Time*, p. 92. Carter G. Woodson gives the main facts, but appears to confuse this plot with one that occurred in Louisiana in 1732, *The Negro in Our History*, p. 87.

23 *Ante*, p. 19.

24 A negative, but very interesting, piece of evidence concerning the infiltration of this philosophy among Negroes occurs in an advertisement of a slave girl for sale in the Boston *Continental Journal* of March 1, 1781. One of the recommendations stressed by the advertiser was the alleged fact that the girl "has no notion of Freedom." G. H. Moore, *Notes on the History of Slavery in Massachusetts*, p. 209. Positive evidence appears during the Revolution in the mass petitions for freedom of Negroes in several areas— see H. Aptheker, *The Negro in the American Revolution*, pp. 9-10.

strained situation in the colony was important in stirring up the slaves.[25]

Negroes involved in a considerable plot in North Carolina in 1775 were well acquainted with and, apparently, moved by the existing political conditions. Thus, they were aware of the fact that a large group of Loyalists was present in the frontier regions. They had planned, after a successful rebellion,[26] to head for " the back country where they were to be received with by a number of Persons there appointed and armed by the Government for their protection, and as a further reward they were to be settled in a free government of their own."

Some uneasiness prevailed in Bucks County, Pennsylvania, in July, 1776, because of the absence of the militia and evidence of slave discontent, exemplified in the statement [27] of one Samson, slave of Jeremiah Dungan, Jr., that " he would burn the houses and kill the Women and children of the Associators when they marched out."

In the spring of 1778 a slave named Tom, owned by a Mr. Henry Hogan in Albany, New York, was jailed because he had attempted to lead fellow slaves in an effort to obtain freedom and " join the Enemy." He was later released but a warrant for his arrest was again issued (with what result is unknown) in

25 Mrs. John Adams to her husband, dated Boston Garrison, September 22, 1774, in Charles F. Adams, ed., *Letters of Mrs. Adams, the wife of John Adams,* I, p. 24; Moore, *op. cit.,* p. 129. In 1768 a British Captain, John Wilson, was accused of inciting slave rebellion in Boston in order to drive the "Liberty Boys to the devil." The Captain hurriedly left the Province— Samuel A. Drake, *History and Antiquities of Boston,* p. 754. A rumor of similar content disturbed New London, Conn., in 1768—New London *Gazette,* December 2, 1768, cited by Lorenzo J. Greene, *The Negro in Colonial New England, 1620-1776* (Ph.D. thesis, Columbia University, 1941, read in ms.).

26 Colonel John Simpson, Chairman of Safety Committee in Pitt County, to Colonel Richard Cogdell, Chairman of Safety Committee in Craven County, dated Chatham, July 15, 1775, in William Saunders, ed., *The Colonial Records of North Carolina,* see also Henry T. King, *Sketches of Pitt County,* pp. 66-67; Samuel A. Ashe, *History of North Carolina,* I, pp. 435-36.

27 Samuel Hazard, ed., *Pennsylvania Archives,* First Series, IV, p. 792; William H. Egle, ed., *ibid.,* Second Series, XV, p. 368.

January, 1779, for he was [28] " endeavoring to Stir up the minds of the Negroes against their Masters and raising Insurrections among them." A slave woman belonging to Hendrick Van Schoonhaven betrayed a plot in July, 1780 among a number of Negroes in Albany County, New York to burn the Half Moon Settlement and flee to the British. An effort, apparently unsuccessful, was made to arrest two Loyalists, William Loucks and Frederick Coonradt, who were believed [29] to be implicated in the conspiracy. Again a fairly considerable slave plot of June, 1779 in Elizabeth Town, New Jersey, was blamed by the local populace upon the intrigues of Tories, a group particularly prominent in that community.[30]

During the seige of Savannah, Georgia, by a combined American and French force in 1779 the hard-pressed British armed the Negroes and permitted them to serve in the ranks, something they willingly did as they expected freedom to be their reward. The Revolutionists were defeated but Governor James Wright found it a difficult matter to disarm and re-enslave the Negroes. Precise details of these men are lacking, but the trouble certainly at least approached outright rebellion and it was [31] " a difficult matter " for the authorities to " reduce them to their proper obedience and position."

28 Victor H. Paltsits, ed., *Minutes of the Commissioners for Detecting and Defeating Conspiracies in the State of New York, Albany County Sessions,* 1778-1781, I, pp. 104, 304. In 1771 (the nearest date for which figures are available) there were about 3,800 Negroes in Albany County, according to George Howell and J. Tenney, *History of the County of Albany,* p. 303.

29 Paltsits, *op. cit.,* II, pp. 454-55. The slaves said they planned only to flee, not to rebel. Their fate is unknown.

30 Edwin F. Hatfield, *History of Elizabeth, New Jersey,* p. 476; Leonard Lundin, *Cockpit of the Revolution the War for Independence in New Jersey,* p. 11. It need hardly be said that in view of the bitterness between Whigs and Tories it was quite possible for either to falsify an account of the other's activities. The contemporary account seen by this writer does not implicate Tories—N. Y. *Packet and American Advertiser,* July 1, 1779 in W. A. Stryker, ed., *Archives of New Jersey,* Second Series, III, p. 490.

31 William B. Stevens, *A History of Georgia,* II, p. 317; F. D. Lee and J. L. Agnew, *Historical Record of the City of Savannah,* p. 65. (Last source kindly called to my attention by Miss Mary Granger, District Supervisor, Georgia Writers' Project, Savannah.)

It is highly possible that the outbreak of slave revolts in Louisiana in 1795 (then owned by Spain) was partly attributable to the war then raging between France and Spain, a conflict that greatly complicated the whole problem of social control of Negroes and whites, since many of the latter in Louisiana were French.[32]

The acquisition of Louisiana Territory by the United States in 1803 aroused fears that the non-American inhabitants of the area would express their discontent over the change in sovereignty by inciting slave troubles. This was, for example, expressed December 9, 1803 in a letter dated " Hunt's town " in Mississippi Territory : [33] "Altho' there is no danger to be apprehended from either government [France or Spain] it is supposed that the Spaniards, such as are opposed to the Americans taking possession of the country will be troublesome, as it is expected they will get the negroes to join them in doing private injuries; but such attempts can soon be stopped."

In the summer of 1804 a former officer in the Spanish service, John B. T. Palliet, at the moment a planter at Natchitoches, Orleans Territory, swore before Captain Edward Turner of the United States Army that when recently in the Spanish town of Nacogdoches he had seen a Crown decree granting freedom and land to all American fugitive slaves.[34] The officer and Governor Claiborne of Orleans were asked to patrol the border more effectively and this was done, while pressure was brought upon the Spanish officials to repudiate the decree. In October, 1804, nine slaves in Natchitoches broke into a planter's house, took lead, powder, and horses, and reached Spanish territory. Another slave was wounded by the patrol and, under questioning, implicated about thirty more Negroes in similar plans, and declared that two whites, one a Spaniard named Martinez, were

32 James A. Padgett, in *Louisiana Historical Quarterly*, XX, p. 590.

33 New York *Evening Post*, January 6, 1804.

34 As noted before (p. 30) a Spanish Royal decree of 1789 having special reference to Florida had granted land and freedom to fugitive slaves and had promptly caused trouble between Spain and the United States.

also involved. Slaves elsewhere in Orleans, particularly Pointe
Coupée, then became restless. Patrols were put on the alert, and
federal troops, who earlier in the year had been moved into
the newly-acquired region in large numbers, partly due to fears
of the slaves, were sent into the town of Natchitoches itself.
The Spaniards soon thereafter revoked the decree.[35] A final
piece of evidence of unrest appears in a letter written by Governor Claiborne to the Mayor of New Orleans on November 1,
1804. Here reference is made to the coming trials of slaves,
men and women, and the Governor declared [36] that if they were
convicted he would punish them " in such a manner and at such
places as may best serve to terrify those who may be inclined
to commit similar enormities."

Quite a few conspiracies marked the years of the War of 1812
and probably many of them, if not all, were evoked, at least in
part, because of the existence of the war itself. In only a few
cases, however, is there direct evidence of such a connection.
The possibility that the military activity and, particularly, the
withdrawal of bodies of armed men from a given area, would be
likely to encourage slave unrest was widely understood and, as
has been shown,[37] guarded against in at least Mississippi Territory, Maryland, Virginia, South Carolina, and Louisiana from
1812 to 1815.

In addition, two specific instances of unrest were ascribed to
the war by contemporaries. One involved the slaves of the Capital as the British advanced towards it in the summer of 1813.
John Graham noted this in a letter to James Monroe,[38] " We
have some intimation of proposed insurrections among the

35 See Isaac J. Cox, " The Louisiana-Texas Frontier," in *The South-
western Historical Quarterly*, XVII, pp. 37-40; I. J. Cox, *The West Florida
Controversy, 1798-1813*, p. 148; letter from Natchitoches, Oct. 27, 1804 in
N. Y. *Evening Post*, November 23, 1804.

36 V. A. Moody, " Slavery on Louisiana sugar plantations," in *The
Louisiana Historical Quarterly*, VII, p. 224.

37 *Ante*, pp. 23-24.

38 Dated Washington, July 18, 1813 in Monroe Papers, Library of Congress.

Blacks in case the Enemy come up—on this score, however, I feel no alarm." The diary entry of the son of the Vice-President is more full on the subject. After noting the reported proximity of the enemy, young Mr. Gerry wrote: [39]

As the militia are ordered off, I expect to patrole more frequently, and this is very necessary, for the blacks in some places refuse to work, and say they shall soon be free, and then the white people must look out. One Negro woman went so far as to steal her mistress's keys, and refused to return them, saying she would soon pay her for old and new. This was in the city, and the negro was confined. Should we be attacked, there will be great danger of the blacks rising, and to prevent this, patroles are very necessary, to keep them in awe. One other preventative at present is, the want of a leader.

In the summer of 1814 a free Negro betrayed a slave conspiracy in Fredericktown, Maryland. The affair was rumored to be very serious and great fear prevailed. [40] Because of this the local newspaper " thought it necessary to notice the affair," and proceeded to minimize it, declaring that but eight Negroes were imprisoned and that the seriousness of the matter had been greatly exaggerated. There had been among the slaves, the paper admitted, " some talk of arming themselves with knives, that when a larger number of militia was called out they were to attack the town, and had proceeded to nominate a captain and other officers for their company." The betrayal, however, and the arrests of the leading rebels, effectively removed all

39 Dated, Summer, 1813, in Claude G. Bowers, ed., *The Diary of Elbridge Gerry, Jr.*, pp. 198-99; see also, William B. Bryan, *A History of the National Capital*, II, p. 135.

40 Fredericktown *Herald*, August 20, 1814, in N. Y. *Eve. Post*, August 24, 1814; Richmond *Enquirer*, August 27, 1814. In addition, Benson J. Lossing told, without documentation other than reference to an unnamed " accomplished American scholar and professor," of the existence of secret societies of slaves in South Carolina in 1813 banded together for the purpose of rebelling once the English army arrived, which it did not do—*The Pictorial Field-Book of the War of 1812*, p. 690. There is a strikingly similar account in Lydia M. Child's " The Black Saxons," *The Liberator*, January 8, 1841.

danger, said the paper, and it concluded by urging the populace to remain calm.

The fighting incident to the revolt of the Anglo-Americans in Texas against Mexico, and the excitement this produced, were important in precipitating a slave conspiracy there in 1835. The rebelling whites were told that the Mexicans aimed to " put their slaves free and let them loose upon their families " and the spreading of this idea while creating fear among the slave-holders undoubtedly created hope and determination amongst some of their slaves. There is, moreover, evidence of active agitational work on the part of an unnamed free Negro at this same time. Early in October it was reported that a force of two thousand Mexicans were approaching the Brazos River and one week later came the report,[41] " The negroes on Brazos made an attempt to rise. Major Sutherland came on here [Goliad] for a few men to take back . . . near 100 had been taken up many whipd nearly to death some hung etc. R. H. Williams had nearly Kild one of his . . .". There followed a most interesting postscript: " The negroes above alluded to had devided [sic] all the cotton farms and they intended to ship the cotton to New Orleans and make the white men serve them in turn."

During the years of the Mexican War a few slave plots were reported but in only one case was any direct connection between that event and a conspiracy noted. This occurred in May, 1846 in Pensacola, Florida. A letter [42] from that city declared that

41 See contemporary letters in Eugene C. Barker, ed., *The Austin Papers, 1834-1837*, III, pp. 108, 162, 180; and Harold Schoen, " The free Negro in the Republic of Texas" in *The Southwestern Historical Quarterly*, 1937, XL, pp. 171-72. The General Council passed an ordinance in January 1836 forbidding the migration into Texas of free Negroes. In 1836 there were about 5,000 Negroes, 3,500 Mexicans, 14,000 Indians, and 30,000 Anglo-Americans in Texas—H. Yoakum, *History of Texas*, II, p. 197.

42 Dated May 9, 1846 to the Cincinnati *Citizen*, quoted in the *Liberator*, June 5, 1846. Solomon Northrup, at the time a slave in Louisiana, wrote: " During the Mexican war I well remember the extravagant hopes that were excited. The news of victory filled the great house with rejoicing, but pro-duced only sorrow and disappointment in the cabin." *Twelve Years a Slave*, p. 248.

the slaves had planned to rebel " as soon as a sufficient number of the white men went off to war." Arrests and great excitement followed: " Every body is armed, and some of the ladies are so frightened that they keep pistols loaded." And, since many Negroes were employed at the city's navy yard, its commander, Commodore Latimore, placed it under martial law.

During the Civil War there was much disaffection and unrest among the slaves,[43] frequently advancing to the form of conspiracy and rebellion. Unquestionably the conflict itself, particularly as its anti-slavery nature became more manifest, was of prime importance in bringing this about. Again, however, direct evidence of this relationship is available in only a few cases.

Thus, in May, 1861, a servile conspiracy, in which whites were supposed to be implicated, was uncovered in Arkansas. The plot was to have matured on July 4, and the Negroes had planned,[44] after killing their enslavers, to " march up the River to meet Mr. Linkum." In December of that year " numerous houses and barns " were burned by Negroes in Henry County, Kentucky, while in New Castle of the same State in the same month about three score slaves paraded the city " singing political songs, and shouting for Lincoln " [45] with no one daring to suppress this unique demonstration.

Early in 1862 seventeen Negroes, free and slave, were re-

43 Recent literature has thoroughly refuted the myth of Negro indifference or docility during the Civil War. See on this, W. E. B. DuBois, *Black Reconstruction*; W. H. Stephenson, "A quarter century of a Mississippi plantation," in *The Mississippi Valley Historical Review*, XXIII, pp. 355-74; J. C. Sitterson, " Magnolia plantation, 1852-1862 " in *ibid.*, XXV, pp. 207-09; H. Wish, " Slave disloyalty in the Confederacy" in *The Journal of Negro History*, XXIII, pp. 435-50; H. Aptheker, *The Negro in the Civil War*; Bell I. Wiley, *Southern Negroes, 1861-1865*; Clement Eaton, *Freedom of Thought in the Old South*, pp. 105-106 presents some additional material, though he repeats the idea about " peaceful and tractable " slaves.

44 B. I. Wiley, *op. cit.*, p. 82.

45 Frankfort, Ky., *Yeoman*, January 17, 1862, in the N. Y. *Daily Tribune*, January 23, 1862.

ported [46] to have been executed in Culpeper County, Virginia. Among them were found copies of the recently issued preliminary Emancipation Proclamation. The plot was believed to be widespread and there existed " the greatest consternation imaginable among the whites in that section."

A Confederate newspaper [47] in reporting a slave plot in Richmond indicated its belief that it was connected with intrigues by the enemy. Under the heading, " Serious Charge Against A Negro," a typically laconic account followed : "A Negro named Bob Richardson, well known in Richmond as a waiter in the saloons, has been committed to Castle Thunder upon the charge of being at the head of a servile plot which received its inspiration from the enemy, and which was broken in upon a few days ago by the detectives. He will receive his deserts right speedily." At about this time slaves burnt a considerable portion of Yazoo City, Mississippi, destroying the courthouse and fourteen homes. In noting this incident, the *Mississippian* remarked [48] that " it was with great difficulty that the negroes were kept from burning it when the enemy were there before."

The coming into prominence of a revolutionary philosophy,

46 The Washington *Republican*, October 20, 1862, in *ibid.*, October 21, 1862; also *The Liberator*, October 24, 1862. News of the Emancipation Proclamation spread like wildfire amongst the slaves, generally carried via their "grapevine telegraph" (i. e., the use of a code language), and by Union soldiers, particularly Negroes. See the message of General Rufus Saxton to his Negro troops in South Carolina, assigning them the task of spreading news of the Proclamation, in the N. Y. *Daily Tribune*, January 1, 1863.

47 The Richmond *Examiner*, June 13, 1864. In May, 1863, Governor Vance of North Carolina sent captured plans to President Davis, said to have originated among officers of the Union government, for a general slave revolt, to start August 1, 1863. This was called to the special attention of the Secretary of War, and sent to General Robert E. Lee, but, so far as is known, nothing came of them, and their authenticity is doubtful. Davis to Vance, Richmond, May 30, 1863, in D. Rowland, ed., *Jefferson Davis, Letters, Papers, Speeches*, V, p. 500.

48 Quoted by the Richmond *Sentinel* June 2, 1864, in Harvey Wish, *op. cit.*,, p. 444. Wish places the event in June, but the date of the Virginia newspaper's quotation makes it clear that the burning must have occurred earlier, probably in May.

or the occurrence of mass upheavals were other factors tending to produce slave unrest.

The probability that the radicalism current during the American Revolution played a part in provoking slave plots during that period has already been noted. Certainly, however, the event of a revolutionary nature that had more effect than any other in producing slave unrest within the present borders of the United States was the tremendous rebellion and prolonged struggles of the Negroes of San Domingo, beginning in the summer of 1791. Concerning this influence there is considerable evidence.

A white man of Richmond, Virginia, who filed a deposition in connection with plots in his state in 1793, reported what he had overheard while spying on a group of Negroes. He declared that,[49] " The one who seemed to be the chief speaker said, you see how the blacks has killed the whites in the French Island and took it a while ago." On November 25th of this year the commanding officer of the militia in Warwick County, Virginia, appealed to the Governor for an additional supply of arms and explained his plea by remarking [50] that " since the melancholy affair at Hispaniola, the Inhabitants of the lower country and especially this county have been repeatedly alarmed by some of their Slaves having attempted to raise an Insurrection, which was timely suppressed in this county by executing one of the principal advisors of the Insurrection."

At times slaves brought from the French Islands by refugees were themselves directly implicated in trouble. This was intimated in a news item from South Carolina in 1793: [51] " They write from Charleston (S. C.) that the NEGROES have become very insolent, in so much that the citizens are alarmed, and the militia keep a constant guard. It is said that the St.

49 William P. Palmer, and Samuel McRae, eds., *Calendar of Virginia State Papers*, VI, pp. 452-53.

50 *Ibid.*, VI, p. 651.

51 *The New York Journal & Patriotic Register*, October 16, 1793, quoted by Mary Treudley, " The United States and St. Domingo," in *The Journal of Race Development*, VII, p. 124.

Domingo negroes have sown these seeds of revolt, and that a magazine has been attempted to be broken open."

Similar sentiments were voiced from this same city a few years later. Serious and recurrent fires disturbed Charleston in the spring of 1796. Arson was suspected, and a group of plunderers was seized as the incendiaries. An inhabitant, however, wrote,[52] June 19, 1796:

Fresh alarms of a similar nature, so often repeated on the next day . . . gave a very serious Cast to the countenance of the citizens; yet tho' it was clear enough that in every instance it was design, there was a silence observed respecting it which I could not account for—People seemed afraid to inquire into it—some would whisper their opinion that the negroes of the place were the authors; others that the French negroes were, and that they certainly intended to make a St. Domingo business of it.

He further told of the arrest and confessions of " some Negroes," who implicated whites as confederates. In November, 1797, three slaves were executed and two banished for conspiring to burn the city,[53] and early in 1798 a " conspiracy of several French Negroes to fire the City, and to act here as they had formerly done at St. Domingo " was discovered.[24]

---

52 Letter dated "Charleston, Sunday morning, June 19" in New York *Minerva*, July 16, 1796. There was an extraordinary series of fires throughout the nation during the 1790's, often attributed to the slaves. This will be discussed in detail later. The Frenchman, Liancourt, noticed the Charleston fires of 1796 and attributed them to poor construction "and the heedlessness of the negroes"—Duke de la Rochefoucault Liancourt, *Travels Through the United States of North America, 1795, 1796, 1797*, translated by H. Newman, I, p. 579. A general movement for the erection of brick homes throughout the city followed, and a committee for this purpose under General Thomas Pinckney's chairmanship was formed in Charleston—N. Y. *Minerva*, July 1, 1796. The effort met difficulties, one of the causes being that wood was then believed to be healthier—Isaac Weld, Jr., *Travels Through the States of North America, 1795, 1796, 1797*, I, p. 156.

53 Charleston City *Gazette*, November 22, 1797, cited by H. M. Henry, *The Police Control of the Slave in South Carolina*, p. 150.

54 *St. George Chronicle and Grenada Gazette*, February 23, 1798, in M. Treudley, *op. cit.*, VII, p. 124. See also John H. Wolfe, *Jeffersonian Democracy in South Carolina*, p. 126.

In one of the numerous mob attacks against Negroes that have intermittently disgraced the United States, that in Philadelphia in 1804, the embattled black folk rallied in the struggle under the shout [55] of " show them San Domingo."

At least one of the leaders in the uprising at St. Charles and St. John the Baptist Parishes in Louisiana in January, 1811, was declared [56] to be a " free mulatto from St. Domingo," named Charles Deslondes, and employed as a driver on the plantation of Major André where the rebellion commenced.

Certain of the slaves involved in the Vesey conspiracy in South Carolina of 1822 counted upon aid from San Domingo (and, unique in the history of American slave revolts—to this writer's knowledge—from Africa) in maintaining control after an initial success in the uprising. Moreover, Vesey himself is reported to have written two letters to an unnamed individual (or individuals) in San Domingo in connection with his plans, but their contents were not disclosed.[57]

In December, 1829, slaves aboard the *Lafayette* bound for sale at New Orleans from Norfolk, revolted, " with the intention of regaining their liberty and making their escape to St. Domingo with the schooner. They stated that a similar effort was to be made on board the schr. Transport, from the same place . . . Some of the mutineers were severely wounded." They were, " after considerable difficulty " subdued, " and 25 of them were bolted down to the deck, until the arrival of the vessel at New Orleans." [58]

55 U. B. Phillips, ed., *Plantation and Frontier Documents*, II, p. 159; Edward Channing, *A History of the United States*, IV, p. 134.

56 Letter dated New Orleans, January 10, 1811, in N. Y. *Evening Post*, February 20, 1811; letter from André to Governor Claiborne, January 11, 1811, in Louisiana *Courier*, January 14, quoted in the Hartford *Connecticut Courant*, February 20, 1811. John S. Kendall states that the leaders generally were from Haiti, " Shadow over the city," *Louisiana Historical Quarterly*, XXII, p. 143.

57 Kennedy and Parker, *op. cit.*, pp. 40 n, 64.

58 N. Y. *Evening Post*, December 29, 1829, Niles' *Weekly Register*, Baltimore, January 9, 1830 (XXXVII, p. 328); Richmond *Enquirer*, January 28, 1830.

Another, and final, piece of evidence of the influence San Domingo exerted upon American slaves appears in the course of correspondence between Louisiana planters and officials in Washington directly after the Turner rebellion in Virginia. Late in September or early in October, 1831 a Mr. Nathan Morse had written [59] to the President " at the request of a number of Planters and Inhabitants of Louisiana, on the subject of their exposed situation having reference to the insurrectionary disposition of the colored people." The Commanding Officer of the United States Army, Major-General Alexander Macomb, replied :

In consequence of the representations made to the President, by the Governor of Louisiana (A. B. Roman), setting forth apprehensions of the authorities, and citizens of New Orleans, as to the disposition of the coloured population of that city, and along the coast, to rise upon the white inhabitants, and also that information had been received that the colored people in the (West Indian) Islands, had a correspondence with the Blacks of Louisiana, tending to further their insurrectionary dispositions, the Secretary of War addressed a letter to the Governor in reply, informing him that the Major General commanding the Army, would be directed to take measures, for complying with the wishes of the Governor. I lost no time in communicating to the Officer commanding the troops, at Baton Rouge . . . to call to his aid any of the Troops in the vicinity or on the Arkansas or Red Rivers . . . Two companies of Infantry, according to the request of the Governor, are now stationed in the City—Arms are provided for the Militia ; . . .

As to the means proper to adopt in case of necessity, it is believed that the Troops at Baton Rouge, are competent to all the purposes of suppressing any attempts of the Blacks . . . the troops, in case of need, from the Red and Arkansas Rivers, places at his [the commander's, Colonel Duncan A. Clinch] disposal ample means under any contingency. For reasons, which will naturally suggest themselves to you, it is desirable that the information here given, may not find its way into the public prints, but there is no

59 Mr. Morse's letter has not been found. The quotations are from a reply thereto by Major-General Macomb, dated October 12, 1831, in Personal Papers, Miscellaneous, M, Library of Congress MSS.

objection to its being [word illegible] imparted to those interested for their satisfaction.

In noting evidence of the influence of the servile rebellions in the West Indies upon American slaves one is not to overlook the fact that the local plots and uprisings were themselves contagious. It is exceedingly difficult, however, to put one's finger on specific proof of this connection. Nevertheless, as will be seen, the revolts tended to occur in bunches, or periods, and it is believed that reasons for this are the infectious quality of disaffection, the great excitement its discovery occasioned, the dislocation and turmoil its suppression meant, and the further acts of restriction and repression that invariably followed.

The French Revolution itself, the philosophy it expounded (its slogan, " Liberty, Equality, Fraternity " expressing precisely those things of which the Negro people, more than any other, were deprived) and, particularly, the bitter partisanship and widespread discussion it developed on this continent,[60] were influential in arousing ideas of rebellion among the slaves. The Marseillaise and Ca Ira were sung, newspapers were filled with reprints of revolutionary decrees passionate with paeons to liberty and truculent with denunciations of tyranny, and prominent Southerners addressed each other as " Citizen " Taylor, or " Citizen " Randolph. The French envoy, Genet, starting his tour of the United States from Charleston was given a hero's welcome, and that city's Democratic Club was recognized by the Jacobin Club of Paris as an affiliated branch. The same city's council, moreover, decided that " His Honor " and " Esquire " were aristocratic titles which should no longer mar its journal, and the countryside, in the South as elsewhere, was

60 See Charles Warren, *Jacobin and Junto*, pp. 87 ff.; R. Hildreth, *The History of the United States of America*, IV, pp. 475, 503; J. B. McMaster, *A History of the People of the United States*, II, p. 176; W. C. Bruce, *John Randolph of Roanoke*, I, pp. 140-41; J. H. Wolfe, *op. cit.*, pp. 72-79. As indicative of the effect of revolutionary philosophy on the slaves may be mentioned the fact that several conspiracies placed July 4 as the date for the outbreak. Very probably the physical characteristics of the celebrations on that day—gatherings, speeches, parades, drunkenness—of which the slaves were, of course, aware, may also have moved them to select this day.

often ablaze with the burning effigies of anti-Revolutionists like Fisher Ames, William L. Smith, and William Pitt, with Benedict Arnold added for good measure.

In Spanish Louisiana the turmoil was great, and "the fever of the French Revolution stirred up sedition among the numerous French creoles . . . and insubordination among the slaves." When, in 1793, Spain declared war upon France, only severe measures of repression directed against both the white and the Negro population prevented revolution.[61]

That the slaves in the United States itself were also aware of the implications of the French event appears in the fact that those involved in the Gabriel conspiracy of 1800 in Virginia had intended not to harm Frenchmen. The slaves, moreover, knew of the strained relations between the United States and France, particularly from 1797 to 1799, and this led them to hope for assistance from France once their own rebellion was well under way.[62] Indeed, two white Frenchmen, never named, were declared to be directly implicated in the formation of the plot.[63]

In addition to Frenchmen, the slaves involved in the Gabriel

61 The quotation is from Arthur P. Whitaker, *The Spanish-American Frontier 1783-1795*, p. 186; see also pp. 22, 176, and his *The Mississippi Question 1796-1803*, pp. 41-42; E. W. Lyon, *Louisiana in French Diplomacy 1795-1804*, p. 67. There were several slave plots in Louisiana in the 1790's.

62 *Calendar of Virginia State Papers*, IX, pp. 147, 151, 152, 165. One slave witness at the rebels' trials declared that "poor white women" were also to be spared.

63 *Ibid.*, pp. 141, 164. A slave, John Scott, a leader in Norfolk, was reported (in the Federalist newspaper, N. Y. *Commercial Advertiser*, September 30, 1800) found with a letter addressed to "Alexander Biddenhurst or Widdenhurst in Philadelphia." The former is the name of the Frenchman in Arna Bontemps' beautiful novelization of the conspiracy, *Black Thunder*. Yet James Monroe, Governor of Virginia, in reply to the questioning of Lt. Gov. Drayton of South Carolina, wrote, Oct. 21, 1800, "If white men were engaged in it, it is a fact of which we have no proof." (S. M. Hamilton, ed., *The Writings of James Monroe*, III, p. 218). It may, however, be remarked that nothing would have been more embarrassing to the Republican, Mr. Monroe, in this election year of 1800, than the acknowledged implication of Frenchmen in a revolt of slaves. The Federalists, as shall be shown, did use the plot for political purposes.

Plot had planned to exempt Methodists and Quakers from harm. The former group had, moreover, been declared to be the real instigators of the plot rather than the French.[64] Both these groups because of their equalitarian and emancipationist leanings had aroused considerable fear and hostility among the slaveholders. The Methodist Church in particular was felt to be dangerous for it had grown mightily in the generation following the American Revolution, and was predominantly Southern (especially strong in Virginia and North Carolina), and to a considerable extent Negro, so that, in 1796, about twenty per cent of all Methodists were Negroes.[65]

Complaints that Methodists instilled dangerous notions of equality and liberty in the minds of the slaves were frequent.[66] At times, too, came concrete charges that they actively developed insubordination, as for example in a letter [67] from the

64 *Calendar of Virginia State Papers*, IX, pp. 151, 165. The Philadelphia *Aurora*, September 29, 1800, denied, on behalf of the Methodists, that they were responsible for the conspiracy.

65 Wesley M. Gewehr, *The Great Awakening in Virginia*, pp. 170, 235, 246-49; Charles Wesley, *Richard Allen*, p. 49; Thomas P. Abernethy, *From Frontier to Plantation in Tennessee*, p. 212; L. C. Matlack, *The Antislavery Struggle and Triumph in the Methodist Episcopal Church*, p. 54; G. G. Johnson, *op. cit.*, p. 334: " ... in the East, especially in Fayetteville and Wilmington, N. C. the Negroes were the first to accept the faith. In fact, Henry Evans, a free Negro, shoemaker by trade, was responsible for having introduced Methodism into Fayetteville."

66 Carter G. Woodson, *The History of the Negro Church*, p. 72; same author's, *The Negro in Our History*, p. 147.

67 Executive Papers, Archives, State Library, Richmond, quoted by James H. Johnston, "The participation of white men in Virginia Negro insurrections," in *The Journal of Negro History*, XVI, pp. 158-60. A similar complaint was made June 5, 1792. See also Luther P. Jackson, "Religious development of the Negro in Virginia from 1760 to 1860," *ibid.*, XVI, pp. 172-73. Violence at times flared up against them as the threatened mobbing of Bishop Coke in Virginia in 1785, and the burning of a Methodist school in Abington, Maryland in 1796—Gewehr, *op. cit.*, p. 245; Liancourt, *op. cit.*, II, p. 345. In the spring of 1820 certain Methodist Ministers in Missouri were accused of fomenting rebellion. A spokesman for the group, Mr. McAlister, denied the charge, declaring that the "Methodist Church would no sooner countenance such conduct than they would any gross immorality." *Missouri Gazette*, May 24, 1820, in H. A. Trexler, *Slavery in Missouri*, p. 114.

sheriff of Culpeper County, Virginia, to the Governor, dated September 5, 1789. The writer declared that while the duty of the patrols was to break up meetings of slaves, they had found its performance actively, and even forcibly, hindered by groups of Methodists. These people " are determined to encorige our Negroes to Wrong & the other day they sent to the Capt. of the Patterolers that on Friday night they wood have a meeting & if they came there & offered to tuch a Negroe that they wood protect the Negroes & if they said a word wood beat them."

Quakers, too, were the objects of bitter attacks. Thus, in May, 1796, the Grand Jury of Chowan County in northeastern North Carolina presented [68] " that the county is reduced to a situation of great peril and danger in consequence of the proceedings of . . . Quakers . . . minds of the slaves are not only greatly corrupted, and alienated from the service of their masters . . . but runaways are protected . . . Arsons are committed, without a possibility of discovery." It went on to remark that while the growth of anti-slavery feeling in the North, and the West Indian rebellions, were also disturbing, still the " quakers and their abettors [were] the authors of the common mischief, in this quarter of the state." Resolute measures of repression were needed "in order to prevent that common appeal to arms, in their own defence, which at present appears to be almost, if not altogether necessary." The Quakers replied by declaring that unrest was inherent in the existence of slavery, and not their creation, and concluded by urging more lenient manumission laws.[69]

68 N. Y. *Minerva and Mercantile Evening Advertiser*, June 11, 1796, quoted in part by S. B. Weeks, *Southern Quakers and Slavery*, p. 222.

69 N. Y. *Minerva*, January 29, 1797. In November, 1796, North Carolina passed regulations requiring all emancipated slaves to give bond of £200 for good behavior while in the State, and permitting manumission for meritorious services only. Virginia tightened her manumission law in 1805 (requiring freed Negroes to leave State). Both had made the act of manumission easy in 1782, with Quakers and Methodists prominent in agitation for this, and while these laws remained manumissions were very frequent, especially by those two groups, perhaps in part stimulated by the low prices slaves brought during the 1790's. See, S. Weeks, *op. cit.*, p. 219; Gewehr, *op. cit.*, p. 249; G. G. Johnson, *op. cit.*, p. 460; John H. Russell, *The Free Negro in Virginia*, pp. 57, 60-61, 78, 140.

With the thorough commercialization of slavery, however, and its strengthening grip upon the South (largely due to Whitney's and Bore's inventions in cotton (1793) and sugar (1795), the industrial revolution, and the annexation of Louisiana Territory, and the intense fear caused by the many plots that occurred from about 1791 to 1802, and the restrictive measures these fostered, both groups made adjustments. The Quakers [70] solved the problem of their philosophy's inconsistency with their surrounding social order very largely by moving away from that order (the few remaining tended to play down or repudiate its anti-slavery background), while the Methodists [71] solved same problem by modifying and changing their attitude and regulations as concerns slavery.

The progressive and revolutionary movement, however, which more than any other was considered responsible for the creation of organized expressions of discontent on the part of

70 H. Aptheker, "The Quakers and Negro slavery" in *The Journal of Negro History*, 1940, XXV, pp. 341, 358-59.

71 The Methodists from 1780-1784 forbade preachers from holding slaves, but exemptions and exceptions weakened this. A plan for gradual emancipation of all slaves held by Methodists was adopted in 1784 but suspended the next year. After this only the buying and selling of slaves were forbidden to church officials, and the laity was *advised* against these practices. In 1800 tame antislavery petitions were ordered to be presented to the State legislatures, but in 1804, the Carolinas, Tennessee, and Georgia were exempted from all slave regulations, and in 1808 the General Conference voted to permit each annual conference to make its own regulations concerning the buying and selling of slaves (the owning of slaves was no longer even considered). See *Journal Of the Reverend Francis Asbury*, I, pp. 374, 482; II, pp. 246, 326, 367; III, pp. 10, 11; Herbert Asbury, *A Methodist Saint*, p. 152; L. C. Matlack, *op. cit.*, pp. 63-64; C. B. Swaney, *Episcopal Methodism and Slavery*, Chap. I; W. B. Posey, *The Development of Methodism in the Old Southwest*, pp. 94-95. It is pertinent to note that while the Baptist General Committee of Virginia denounced slavery in 1789, it resolved in 1793 "that the subject be dismissed from this committee as believing it belongs to the legislative body"—Gewehr, *op. cit.*, p. 241. Of course, certain individual Methodists heroically continued their anti-slavery work, even into the 1850's, as Adam Crooks and Jesse McBride of North Carolina (driven out in 1851), and Jarvis C. Bacon in Virginia (arrested several times)—G. G. Johnson, *op. cit.*, p. 577; Clement Eaton, *Freedom of Thought in the Old South*, pp. 133, 135, 138.

the slaves was that which had as its aim the abolition of the practice of human enslavement itself. It is simple to find any number of statements intimating or boldly affirming that the Abolitionists were responsible for slave unrest generally, or for some specific plot, but it is far from simple to find substantiation for these assertions.

The fashionable viewpoint of the slaveocracy was expressed in the Senate of the United States on January 10, 1861, by Jefferson Davis. Declaring that he found the speculations as to whether "our servants" would rebel or not "exceedingly offensive," he went on to assert:[72] "Governments have tampered with slaves; bad men have gone among the ignorant and credulous people, and incited them to murder and arson; but of themselves—moving by themselves—I say history does not chronicle a case of negro insurrection." Several years earlier a committee of the Senate of South Carolina had similarly remarked, in connection with the Negro:[73] "The animal predominating largely over the intellectual being, he has no aspiration for liberty, and would never dream of revolt, or of elevating his social status, but for the machinations of those who, professing themselves his friends, are in fact his worst enemies. Unfortunately for him these machinations have been in some instances, to a certain extent successful . . ."

A leading authority on the history of the American Negro, Carter G. Woodson, while making by no means so sweeping a statement as Jefferson Davis (curious association!) does say[74] that beginning about 1830 when "intelligent Negroes" made "so many attempts to organize servile insurrections" they were "encouraged by abolitionists."

72 Dunbar Rowland, *op. cit.*, V, p. 30.

73 *Senate of South Carolina. December 9, 1844—Report of the Committee on Federal Relations on the second and third resolutions introduced into the Senate, in reference to the message of the Governor, on the subject of Mr. Hoar's agency in this State, under the resolutions of the legislature of Massachusetts*, pp. 6-7.

74 C. G. Woodson, *The Education of the Negro Prior to 1861*, p. 2.

Specific insurrections and plots were often directly ascribed to the same source. Thus one writer asserted [75] (and let it go at that) that Denmark Vesey and some of his comrades in conspiracy had visited the North and had been " infected " by the propaganda of the Abolitionists.

Any number of contemporary and later commentators on the Turner rebellion have maintained that Abolitionist propaganda was responsible for its occurrence. This was the opinion of Virginia's Governor, John Floyd, which he expressed briefly in his message [76] to the legislature on December 6, 1831, and in detail in a letter to the Governor of South Carolina.

Here it appears that when Floyd accused Abolitionists in his legislative message, he was using the word in a very broad sense to include all people who definitely opposed slavery and desired its speedy demise, and not especially followers of any particular school of antislavery thought. Governor Floyd wrote: [77]

I will notice this affair in my annual message, but shall only give a very careless history of it, as it appears to the public.

I am fully persuaded, the spirit of insubordination which has, and still manifests itself in Virginia, had its origin among, and eminated (sic) from the Yankee population, upon their first arrival amongst us, but most especially the Yankee pedlars and traders.

The course has been by no means a direct one—they began first, by making them religious—their conversations were of that character—telling the blacks, God was no respecter of persons—the black man was as good as the white—that all men were born free and equal—that they cannot serve two masters—that the white people rebelled against England to obtain freedom, so have the blacks a right to do.

75 Mrs. St. Julien Ravenal, *Charleston the Place and the People,* p. 437. According to Kennedy and Parker, *op. cit.,* p. 61, one of the conspirators had been North and there imbibed anti-slavery ideas. See also Joseph C. Carroll, *Slave Insurrections in the United States,* p. 96.

76 Printed in *Niles' Weekly Register,* XLI, p. 350 (Jan. 7, 1832).

77 John Floyd to James Hamilton, Jr., November 19, 1831, in Papers of John Floyd, Library of Congress.

He added that local white ministers and religious ladies taught the Negroes how to read so that the Bible's wonders might be opened to them, but the slaves, he asserted, read the productions of David Walker and William Lloyd Garrison as well, and this, together with the urgings of the Negro preachers produced the Turner rebellion.

Mrs. Lawrence Lewis, a niece of George Washington, in a letter dated Alexandria, Virginia, October 17, 1831 told her friend, Harrison Gray Otis, the Mayor of Boston, that [78] " to the Editor of the 'Liberator' . . . we owe in *greatest measure* this calamity." Again, W. Gilmore Simms, in reviewing a book by Harriet Martineau, indicated [79] his belief that actual underground organizational and agitational work on the part of the Abolitionists caused the uprising. He quoted, in part and not quite correctly, a statement by Miss Martineau to the effect that the revolt happened before the " abolition movement began," objected to this and declared : " Our author confounds cause with effect. She should have said that the Southampton insurrection broke out before the secret workings of the abolitionists had been generally detected or suspected."

Albert Bushnell Hart felt [80] that the Walker pamphlet " may possibly have influenced " Turner. This very guarded statement is cited by Hilary A. Herbert to substantiate his definite and unqualified assertion [81] that northern agitators were responsible for the revolt. It is possible that Professor Hart made his statement on the basis of the opinion of Benjamin Lundy [82] who believed that Nat Turner " had probably seen " the pamphlet and

78 Samuel E. Morison, *The Life and Letters of Harrison Gray Otis*, II, p. 260.

79 " The Morals of Slavery " in *The Pro-Slavery Argument*, by Harper, Hammond, Simms, and Dew, p. 223. Miss Martineau's statement is in her *Society in America*, 4th edit., I, p. 378.

80 *Slavery and Abolition 1831-1841*, pp. 217-18.

81 *The Abolition Crusade and its Consequences*, p. 60.

82 [Thomas Earle], *Life, Travels and Opinions of Benjamin Lundy*, pp. 237, 247, 249.

thought it " probable . . . that the conspiracies [that of Turner and those which immediately followed] were instigated chiefly by the aforementioned pamphlet of David Walker, if in fact they owed their origin to any publication whatever." Several later writers have adopted the attitude of Herbert [83] or Hart.[84]

Others, fewer, deny that there is discernible any causative connection between this agitation and the outbreak of the revolt. First in this group is William Lloyd Garrison himself, who persistently and truthfully denied having advised the Negroes to use force, and declared,[85] " We have not a single white or black subscriber south of the Potomac." As James Ford Rhodes aptly put it : " The assertion that slavery is a damning crime is one thing; the actual incitement of slaves to insurrection is another." [86]

One may, of course, safely say that Walker's pamphlet "possibly" influenced Turner. It is also possible that some work on Napoleon influenced him and he decided that [87] " I was ordained for some great purpose in the hands of the Almighty." There is as much evidence for the one as for the other. The fact is that never has there been presented an iota of clear evidence going to show a causal relation between any anti-slavery literature and Turner's action. Both were, of course, characteristic of the spirit of the times and possessed a kinship in origin—hatred of slavery—but no other relationship has been demonstrated.[88]

83 W. S. Drewry, *The Southampton Insurrection,* p. 150; R. A. Brock in *Collections of the Virginia Historical Society,* new series, VI, p. 24 n.; Arthur Y. Lloyd, *The Slavery Controversy,* pp. 106, 111. Dr. Lloyd, who is about as objective in the " controversy " and as scientific concerning the Negro as John C. Calhoun was, blames the Abolitionists for an " increase " in the crime of rape among Negroes in the nineteenth century, as he blames the "inciting" of the Negroes by radicals for an allegedly similar phenomenon that he sees in the present century. His proof for these assertions is characteristic of the work; that is to say, it does not exist.

84 C. G. Woodson, *Education of the Negro,* p. 163.

85 *The Liberator,* September 24, 1831; See Morison, *op. cit.,* II, p. 261.

86 *History of the United States from the Compromise of 1850,* I, p. 57.

87 Thomas R. Gray, *The Confessions of Nat Turner, the Leader of the Late Insurrection in Southampton, Virginia,* p. 9.

88 See Jesse Macy, *The Anti-Slavery Crusade,* p. 59; Gilbert H. Barnes,

A somewhat similar state of affairs prevailed concerning the widespread conspiracies of 1835. Southern newspapers and letter writers were free and easy with generalized accusations [89] hurled against the Abolitionists as the originators and prime movers of the trouble. And in this case the charge was dignified by being repeated by the President of the United States. Part of Andrew Jackson's seventh annual message reads as follows: [90]

I must also invite your attention to the painful excitement produced in the South by attempts to circulate through the mails inflammatory appeals addressed to the passions of the slaves, in prints and in various sorts of publications, calculated to stimulate them to insurrection and to produce all the horrors of servile war ... It is fortunate for the country that the good sense, the generous feeling, and the deep-rooted attachment of the people of the nonslaveholding States to the Union and to their fellow-citizens of the same blood in the South have given so strong and impressive a tone to the sentiments entertained against the proceedings of the misguided persons who have engaged in these unconstitutional and wicked attempts, and especially against the emissaries from foreign parts [91] who have dared to interfere in this matter, as to authorize the hope that those attempts will no longer be persisted in.

The Anti-Slavery Impulse 1830-1844, p. 51. Nat Turner in his rather full *Confessions* made no mention of being influenced by Abolitionism, or by any particular individual. Evidence on the influence of Walker's pamphlet on other plots will be presented later.

89 For Mississippi see *A Memoir of S. S. Prentiss*, edited by his brother, I, p. 162; for North Carolina, the Elizabeth City *Herald*, October 3, 1835; for Georgia, the Macon *Messenger*, n. d., in *The Liberator*, December 12, 1835; for Louisiana, *Niles' Weekly Register*, XLIX, p. 331 (Jan. 16, 1836); for Virginia, the Norfolk *Beacon*, August 10, 1835, in *The Friend of the African*, London, 1844, no. 9, pp. 130-131.

90 Delivered December 7, 1835, in James D. Richardson, *Messages and Papers of the Presidents*, III, p. 1394.

91 Jackson is here probably referring particularly to the noted English Abolitionist, George Thompson, whose lectures in America had recently created great interest. The latter according to Claude G. Bowers, "proposed that the slaves should arise and cut their masters' throats" — *The Party Battles of the Jackson Period*, p. 434. Arthur Y. Lloyd says

These contemporary charges have been reiterated by some later writers,[92] but again it must be stated that while it is clear whites were involved in these 1835 plots, no proof, indeed, no good evidence, is known to exist tying up the Abolitionist movement or any bona fide member of that movement with those conspiracies. It is to the point to note that the Governor of Mississippi himself in his proclamation calling [93] upon all citizens and state officers to aid in suppressing the insurrectionary movements disturbing the State did not refer to the suspected whites as Abolitionists. Rather he called them (and in some cases, in this particular plot, accurately called them) " lawless base villainous whitemen."

The Abolitionists themselves denied any part in the plots. The remarks of Angelina E. Grimké made in her famous "Appeal to the Christian Women of the South " [94] may be referred

the same thing—*op. cit.*, p. 115, and cites James Schouler. Schouler, however, merely says that Thompson used " imprudent language "—*History of the United States under the Constitution*, IV, pp. 217-18. The fact is that George Thompson did not advocate servile rebellion and never said what these writers claim he did. It is of interest to note the denunciation of lynch law that was so prevalent at this time in the South made in a speech delivered January 27, 1837 by a young Illinois politician named Abraham Lincoln — See John G. Nicolay and John Hay, eds., *Complete Works of Abraham Lincoln*, I, p. 10.

92 A. Y. Lloyd, *op. cit.*, p. 122. Arthur Styron, in the most amazing three pages of what is supposed to be American history that this writer has ever seen (*The Cast-Iron Man John C. Calhoun and American Democracy*, pp. 204-206) states—and does nothing more—not only that Abolitionists were involved, but that they had great sums of " Massachusetts money " with them, and that one carried a letter from a resident of that State—no signature or date is mentioned—urging on the rebellion. Another, writes Mr. Styron, sold " to a trader for a small sum of money " his own wife, who had, apparently, become an encumbrance. It is decidedly unfortunate that the ingenious Mr. Styron suffers his imagination to be restricted within the confines of an even nominally historical work.

93 Proclamation of Governor H. G. Runnels, July 3, 1835, State Archives, Jackson, Mississippi—copy supplied present writer by Dr. Clement Eaton.

94 *The Anti-Slavery Examiner*, Boston, September, 1836, I, p. 33. It is believed that anyone examining the Abolitionist literature itself during this period will recognize the justice of Miss Grimké's remarks. It is, however,

to as an apt summary of their views. She declared that she knew
the material mailed to prominent white people in the South by
the American Anti-Slavery Society contained no appeal to the
slaves (to whom they were not sent) to rebel. Moreover,

With regard to those white men, who, it was said, did try to raise
an insurrection in Mississippi a year ago, and who were stated to
be Abolitionists, none of them were ever proved to be members of
Anti-Slavery Societies, and it must remain a matter of great doubt
whether, even they were guilty of the crime alledged (sic) against
them, because when any community is thrown into such a panic
as to inflict Lynch law upon accused persons, they cannot be supposed to be capable of judging with calmness and impartiality.

That paragraph is an admirable epitome of the evidence concerning this subject.[95]
Later outbreaks were also specifically attributed to the direct
interference of Abolitionists. This was true especially of the vast
disturbances of 1856 and 1860. In September, 1856, " northern
incendiaries " were blamed [96] for unrest in Clark County, Mississippi, and in Elba, Florida. In both places the accused were
forced to flee for their lives. Later this year a man described [97]
as an " Ohio abolitionist " named Davidson was declared to be
implicated in a servile plot in Lavaca County, Texas, and suffered one hundred lashes.
A southern newspaper [98] editorializing early in 1857 when
the unrest appeared to have passed its peak felt that the phe-

true that people reading that literature, but rejecting the pacifism and non-
resistant philosophy explicit therein, might be moved to direct, militant
action.

95 Note the conclusion of Charles S. Sydnor: " Such white leaders were,
of course, sometimes called abolitionists, but little or no evidence was ever
presented to prove that they were connected with the abolition movement "
—Slavery in Mississippi, p. 251.

96 Richmond Daily Dispatch, September 30, 1856, citing local newspapers.

97 Maysville, Ky. Eagle, December 13, 1856, cited by Harvey Wish, " The
slave insurrection panic of 1856," in The Journal of Southern History, 1939,
V, p. 208.

98 New Orleans Daily Picayune, January 2, 1857; see also the Savannah
Republican, December 19, 1856.

nomenon was due to the machinations of "northern seducers," while the British consul in Richmond, a popular novelist, G. P. R. James, believed [99] the wide diffusion of the disorders and the implication of whites indicated that the movement had been planned in the North. As a final instance of this viewpoint may be mentioned a letter from Charles Dimmock, Superintendent of the Richmond Armory, to the Governor of Virginia. He made, at considerable length, suggestions for strengthening the military prowess of the State, and asked [100] "pardon for this seeming officiousness" on the ground of the great dangers arising from the slave population. His concern was heightened, said the official, "when I regard the hellish designs of those who are working upon the passions and ignorances of our slaves—stimulating them to deeds of horror, abortive as they must be for good to any...".

The year 1860 almost exactly paralleled, as concerns trouble with slaves, that of 1856, and once again Abolitionists were held largely responsible. Yet here, as before, the investigator is forced to conclude that the evidence of this complicity, or of the character and political or philosophical affiliations of the whites involved, are far from satisfactory.

Again many Southern publications rang with the familiar charges against "Northern incendiaries" and Abolitionists [101] and, particularly favored by the politicians, "Black Republicans." The latter are well exemplified by the remarks of the influential Senator from Texas, Louis T. Wigfall. Declaring [102] that Abraham Lincoln himself was a professional Abolitionist organizer and agitator [103] the Senator went on to warn: "We

99 Laura W. White, "The South as seen by British consuls," in *The Journal of Southern History*, I, p. 44.

100 Dated December 15, 1856, Executive Papers, Virginia State Library.

101 Austin, Texas *State Gazette*, July 28, 1860; [John Townsend] *The Doom of Slavery in the Union: its Safety out of it, passim*; extracts in *28th Annual Report of the American Anti-Slavery Society*, pp. 200-203.

102 In the Senate, December 12, 1860, *Congressional Globe*, 36th Cong., 2nd Sess., 73-74.

103 As reported in that paragon of truth, the New York *Herald*, September 21, 1860.

say to those States [in the North] that you shall not . . . permit men to go there and excite your citizens to make John Brown raids or bring fire and strychnine within the limits of the State to which I owe my allegiance. You shall not publish newspapers and pamphlets to excite our slaves to insurrection . . . We will have peace . . . [or] withdraw from the Union." Becoming more specific in his charges—but unfortunately not in his proof —the Senator told of the many towns and cities that, said he, had been destroyed by the slave-created fires, and the quantities of poison found among the Negroes, and then, in a most interesting passage, stated: "An association called 'The Mystic Red' was entered into by members of the Methodist Church North [104] and the John-Brown men; and their purpose was to carry out the irrepressible conflict, to burn our towns, burn up the stores of our merchants, burn up the mills, to bring free-soil northern capital in, and thus get possession of Texas . . .".

Once again the implicated organizations denied the truth of these accusations.[105] One who personally, and whose Party generally had been and was again to be accused, while not deigning to dignify the charges against himself by noting them, did, as the leader of the Republican Party, disavow [106] any connection between that organization and slave conspiracies, and denied that it desired to see the forming or the maturing of such conspiracies.

104 Ministers of this Church had been persecuted in Texas in the spring of 1859—see N. Y. *Tribune*, May 7, 1859. This paper felt that a desire to check the growing anti-slavery feeling in this religious body, as well as among the Germans of western Texas, was important in explaining the campaign of terror conducted by a large part of the press of that State— editorial in issue of September 15, 1860.

105 *28th Annual Report of the American Anti-Slavery Society*, pp. 200-214; N. Y. *Tribune*, September 15, 1860.

106 Cooper Institute address of Abraham Lincoln, February 27, 1860, in Nicolay and Hay, *op. cit.*, I, pp. 607-608. We do not mean to deny that there existed Negro and white people who believed in the justice of slave outbreaks, and even some who attempted to provoke them. These will be considered as they appear in the course of the narrative. For a detailed study of this subject see H. Aptheker, " Militant Abolitionism," in *The Journal of Negro History*, XXVI, pp. 438-484.

CHAPTER V
FURTHER CAUSES OF REBELLION

THREE factors other than those already mentioned appear to have had some influence in promoting slave unrest. A relative increase in the number of Negroes as compared with that of the whites accentuated the danger arising from the former; industrialization and urbanization were phenomena that made the control of slaves more difficult; and, perhaps most important, economic depression, bringing increased hardships, sharpened tempers, forced liquidations of estates (including the human beings involved), and more widespread leasing of slaves, induced rebelliousness.

It has been shown that the presence of large numbers of Negroes, free and slave, evoked expressions of fear and impelled measures of precaution on the part of the masters from the seventeenth through the nineteenth centuries. In our discussion of the plots and uprisings we shall examine the relative population figures. Here it is sufficient for us to notice that areas of dense Negro population, particularly areas showing a recent accession, were very frequently the centers of unrest. While no causal relationship between these phenomena can be *demonstrated,* yet contemporary observers believed that such a relationship did exist, and the later investigator finds reasons for concurrence in that conclusion.

The easier acquisition of knowledge,[1] the greater possibility of association, and the greater confidence and assurance that city life and mechanical and industrial pursuits developed, as

1 For example, the Richmond *Daily Dispatch*, August 24, 1858, reported the recent arrests in the city of ninety Negroes for the " crime " of attempting to learn how to read. It urged severe punishment and said, " Scarcely a week passes, that instruments of writing, prepared by negroes, are not taken from servants [slaves] in the streets, by the police." See also, James Stirling, *Letters from the Slave States*, p. 295; Carter G. Woodson, *The Education of the Negro Prior to 1861*, pp. 81-84, 128, 208, 217; J. Redpath, *The Roving Editor*, p. 160; B. I. Wiley, *Southern Negroes, 1861-65*, pp. 278-79.

compared with country life and agrarian activities, were widely recognized as dangers associated with the growth of a large urban slave population.

A work published as early as 1779 emphasized [2] these facts, mentioning not only the greater ease of association and acquisition of knowledge, but also the belief that urban slaves might acquire with comparative facility dangerous quantities of arms and ammunition. Following the Vesey plot of 1822, which originated and centered in Charleston, and which was inspired largely by mechanical workers, many suggestions for more effective slave control were offered. Among these the following is noteworthy: [3] " The great fundamental principle should be that the slave should be kept as much as possible to agricultural labors. These so employed are found to be the most orderly and obedient of slaves ... There should be no black mechanics or artisans, at least in the cities."

This idea was constantly emphasized between 1850 and 1860, while urbanization and industrialization made some progress in the South, opposition of the non-slaveholding whites to Bourbon control became acute, [4] and slave unrest, notably in cities, grew quite dangerous.

2 [Alexander Hewatt], *An Historical Account of the Rise and Progress of the Colonies of South Carolina and Georgia*, II, p. 97.

3 Article in S. C. *State Gazette*, during fall of 1822, quoted by Henry, *Police Control of the Slave*, p. 101. This same consideration was one of the factors moving Great Britain and the United States in the last years of the eighteenth century in attempting to keep the Negroes of St. Domingo confined to agricultural pursuits—see C. R. King, ed., *The Life and Correspondence of Rufus King*, II, pp. 499-500, 557.

4 For evidence of this opposition as provoked by the institution of slavery, see: New Orleans *Courier*, Oct. 25, 1850; Mobile *Mercury*, n. d., in N. Y. *Daily Tribune*, Jan. 8, 1861; Olmsted, *Back Country*, p. 180; Olmsted, *Seaboard Slave States*, II, pp. 149-50; J. H. Aughey, *The Iron Furnace*, pp. 39, 228; A. C. Cole, *The Whig Party in the South*, p. 72; G. G. Johnson, *Ante-Bellum North Carolina*, p. 577; L. M. Sears, *John Slidell*, p. 174; R. W. Shugg, *Origins of Class Struggle in Louisiana*, pp. 145-46; Stirling, *op. cit.*, p. 326; Redpath, *op. cit.*, p. 22; J. A. Flisch, " The common people of the old south," in *Ann. Rep't. Amer. Hist. Assoc.*, 1908, I, pp. 133-42; K. Bruce, *Virginia Iron Manufacture in the Slave Era*, p. 225; C. H. Wesley, *Negro Labor in the U. S.*, p. 71.

Frederick Law Olmsted referred [5] several times to the danger from proletarian slaves and asserted that this was the one objection he had heard urged against diversification and industrialization in the South. His own observations had convinced him that " slave-mechanics, manufacturers' hands, stevedores, [and] servants " were " more insubordinate than the general mass."

Other observers, like James Redpath, Henry J. Raymond [6] of the New York *Times,* and the Englishman, William Chambers, testified [7] to this danger. Still another visitor, in 1859 and 1860 declared that while it was not too difficult to keep the plantation slaves in profound ignorance, the task was much more imposing with those in the cities. " This has alarmed their masters, and they are sending them off, as fast as possible, to the plantations, where, as in a tomb, no sight or sound of knowledge can reach them." Flight, too, was easier for urban slaves, particularly those working in ports or on railroads. This, he said,[8] was an important explanation for the fact that slaves working on New Orleans wharves were being replaced by German and Irish workers. " 'The cities', said a gentleman to me, 'is no place for the niggers. They get stronge notions into their heads, and grow discontented. They ought, every one of them, to be sent back on to the plantations'."

Another consideration linking the development of an industrial life with slave discontent is indicated by a conversation between James Redpath and an aged Negro. The latter remarked [9]

5 Olmsted, *Seaboard,* I, p. 282; II, pp. 239-40; *Back Country,* p. 376. There were, of course, objections other than those indicated by Olmsted, such as a scarcity of fluid capital.

6 Redpath, *op. cit.,* p. 16; H. J. Raymond, *Disunion and Slavery,* p. 33.

7 W. Chambers, *American Slavery and Colour,* pp. 154-55.

8 John S. C. Abbott, *South and North; or, impressions during a trip to Cuba and the South,* pp. 124, 175. See also Herman Schluter, *Lincoln, Labor and Slavery,* pp. 94-95.

9 Redpath, *op. cit.,* p. 127. As improved marketing facilities and world-wide industrial expansion widened the demand for slave produce and so led to increased demands upon the workers (whose further importation had been illegalized), the soil which bore this produce became less and less fertile, again necessitating increased labor by a given number of workers on a given

that since railroad lines had been introduced the slaves had
been forced to work harder than ever before. What was the
explanation? " Why," said the slave, " you see it is so much
easier to carry off the produce and sell it now; 'cause they take
it away so easy; and so the slaves are druv more and more to
raise it."

He who prepares a table of the outstanding periods of slave
rebellion and another of the years of economic depression will be
struck by their great similarity. Again, as in the case of population trends—which were largely affected by economic conditions—this conjunction of events will be shown in the course of
the description of the plots and uprisings themselves. And,
again as in the former case, it is not possible to *prove* a causal
connection between suffering occasioned by depression and outbreaks against enslavement, but it does appear reasonable to
suggest that such a relationship existed.

Some evidence of the disastrous effect of economic depres-
sions within a slave society upon the workers—slaves—is pertinent. It is, moreover, necessary to present this evidence in some
detail, for the romanticists, who have described the Old South,
have pictured a closed, self-sustaining, idyllic, almost social-
istic [10] society immune to such annoying things as business
cycles; yet business cycles have a way of affecting all profit-
seeking, private ownership, world-dependent industries such as
the tobacco, rice, cotton, hemp, sugar, and slave raising busi-
nesses of the ante-bellum South.

area of land to raise the same amount of goods; or the shipment of these
people to richer land—so long as the latter was available.

10 Note George Fitzhugh: " slavery is a form, and the very best form,
of socialism." Slavery " is a beautiful example of communism, where each
one receives not according to his labor, but according to his wants." *Sociology
for the South*, pp. 28, 29. Professor R. S. Cotterill, too, has written that the
slave " was assured of an income proportioned to his necessities and not to
his productiveness "—*The Old South*, p. 269. See also Sterling A. Brown,
" Unhistoric History," in *The Journal of Negro History*, 1930, XV, pp. 134-
161; Howard W. Odum, *An American Epoch southern portraiture in the
national picture*, Chap. III.

In response to a query James Madison declared [11] in 1819: " The general condition of slaves must be influenced by various causes. Among these are 1. the ordinary price of food, on which the quality and quantity allowed them will more or less depend." This indicates that slaves would be made aware of periods of economic distress in a very real manner, namely, in the kind and amount of food they received.

Precise evidence of this is not easy to discover, but some examples are available. Thus, remarks made during the severe depression [12] of the 1790's by George Washington, a very efficient business man, are pertinent. " It is demonstratively clear," he wrote,[13] " that on this Estate (Mount Vernon) I have more working negroes by a full moiety, than can now be employed to any advantage in the farming system . . . Something must [be done] or I shall be ruined; for all the money (in addition to what I raise by crops, and rents) that have been *received* for Lands, sold within the last four years, to the amount of Fifty thousand dollars, has scarcely been able to keep me afloat." One of Washington's prospective land buyers during this critical time, the Englishman, Richard Parkinson, declared,[14] " It is well known that General Washington did not in some seasons raise so much from his land as would keep his people, [slaves] with the addition of a very numerous fishery."

An escaped slave, who had worn his chains in eastern Virginia during approximately these same years, wrote: [15]

11 Letter to Robert Walsh, March 2, 1819, in Gaillard Hunt, ed.,, *The Writings of James Madison*, VIII, p. 426.

12 On general economic conditions at this period see, A. O. Craven, *Soil Exhaustion in Virginia and Maryland*, pp. 82-84, 110, 119; L. C. Gray, *History of Agriculture in the Southern States*, II, pp. 616-17, 911; G. P. Garrison, ed., "A memorandum of M. Austin's Journey," in *Amer. Hist. Rev.*, V, pp. 525-26. Actual famine existed, at least in Virginia—see, Landon Carter to Washington, Sept. 28, 1796, in *William and Mary Coll. Quart.* (1) XX, p. 283; N. Y. *Minerva and Mercantile Evening Advertiser*, May 28, 1796.

13 In August, 1799, W. C. Ford, ed., *The Writings of George Washington*, XIV, p. 196.

14 R. Parkinson, *The Experienced Farmer's Tour in America*, II, pp. 424-25.

15 Charles Ball, *Slavery in the United States*, p. 44.

I am convinced, that in nine cases out of ten, the hardships and sufferings of the colored population of lower Virginia is attributable to poverty and distress of its owners. In many instances, an estate scarcely yields enough food to feed and clothe the slaves in a comfortable manner without allowing anything for the support of the master and family.

The attempt to avoid war by embargo and non-importation, and the War of 1812 itself, by shattering the foreign market for cotton and tobacco (and, in the latter case, by actual invasion and consequent devastation) brought severe economic crisis to the South. In the course of noting and describing this, brief, but pointed, references to the slave population were made. Thus, a gentleman wrote [16] from Charleston, December 24, 1811:

The supply of coarse Negro cloths for the immediate use of the present season has fallen short about one third—not a single piece can now be had; indeed all that was remaining on hand from last year's importation had been bought up in the course of the summer by speculators and has been sold at a very large advance. Many planters are now buying blankets and cutting them up to make clothes for their negroes. What the situation of slave owners would be, should the non-importation continue for twelve months longer, can easily be imagined, and must excite the well-grounded apprehension of every reflecting citizen—The wretched situation of a large proportion of our slaves is sufficient to harrow up the feelings of the most flinty heart . . .

John Randolph, whose opposition to Madison's war policy may have made him unduly lachrymose, lamented, in the summer of 1814, the ruin of his own crops, and stated,[17] " I fear a famine next summer . . . The poor slaves, I fear, will suffer dreadfully." A few months later he affirmed that " The searching miseries of war penetrate even into the hovel of the shivering negro whose tattered blanket and short allowance of salt bear witness to the glories of that administration under which his master is content to live."

16 In the New York *Evening Post*, January 6, 1812.

17 Statements dated July 31, 1814, January 7, 1815, quoted by William C. Bruce, *John Randolph*, I, pp. 412, 419.

In connection with Madison's statement of 1819 that the price of articles determined the quantity and quality given the slaves, may be noted a rather long letter from a Mr. E. Jackson, dated Savannah, Georgia, January 9, 1814, to the Connecticut Senator, David Daggett. Mr. Jackson declared [18] that the last cotton crop was very bad, perhaps one-fourth the usual amount, due to drought early in the season, excessive rains later, a hurricane thrown in to destroy the Seaboard cotton, and an unusually early frost as an additional guarantee of a poor year. He noted a fairly good rice crop but added that the embargo made its sale impossible. And, he pointed out, " To add to our misfortunes every article used by the planters is extravagantly high."

The period from 1819 to 1832 was similar to that of the 1790's. Natural disasters aggravated the distress brought on by the economic system. In 1826 a severe drought hit the Old South, particularly Virginia and North Carolina. A letter from Richmond dated May 23 stated that wells had dried up and that " The growing crops of rye, oats, clover, &c is much injured in the fields." A later letter declared,[19] " We do not suppose there was ever known in this section of country, a Summer season so dry as the present . . . The high prices of provisions, of all kinds, consequent on this state of things, added to the scarcity of fruit, has caused much distress among many poor people . . .".

The southwest was visited by a drought in 1827 which " blasted the hopes of the planters " of Alabama, Mississippi, and Louisiana. Not only were their commodity crops affected, but, in addition, their corn was disastrously hit so that [20] " it is certain that there will be a scarcity of that indispensable grain." Excessive rains early in the season of 1829 in Louisiana dam-

18 Quoted by W. F. Galpin in *Georgia Historical Quarterly*, VIII, pp. 325-26. The last embargo was passed December 17, 1813, and repealed April 14, 1814—J. B. McMaster, *A History of the People of the United States*, IV, p. 230.

19 In N. Y. *Evening Post*, May 30, July 19, 1826.

20 Item dated Huntsville, Alabama, September 7, *ibid.*, October 5, 1827.

aged crops, and, said [21] a resident, " These may really be called hard times." A communication from Opelousas in that State, dated August 12, 1829, declared [22] that crops were very poor and corn scarce: " Our situation is critical in the extreme." Similar conditions were at this time reported [23] as prevailing in South Carolina. The next year again a " distressing drought " plagued much of the Old South.[24]

Speaking just before an upswing in the business cycle—one whose trough had spread over a period of some dozen years— Robert Hayne, Senator from South Carolina, alleged [25] "the very grass " to be growing in the streets of Charleston. " If," said he, " we fly from the city to the country, what do we behold? Fields abandoned; agriculture drooping; our slaves, like their masters, working harder, and faring worse; the planter striving with unavailing efforts to avert the ruin which is before him."

A very clear statement of the relationship between economic depression and the condition of the slaves appears in the remarks of a New Orleans editor in 1837, the year of repudiation in Mississippi. Referring to the planters, he wrote: [26]

They are now left without provisions, and the means of living and using their industry for the present year. In this dilemma, planters, whose crops have been from 100 to 700 bales, find themselves forced to sacrifice many of their slaves, in order to get the common neces-

21 Item dated St. Martinsville, July 18, in *ibid.*, August 14, 1829.

. 22 *Ibid.*, September 16, 1829.

23 Savannah *Georgian*, September 26, 1829.

24 Huntsville, Ala., *Southern Advocate*, September 4, 25, 1830. See also Joseph C. Robert, *The Tobacco Kingdom*, p. 142.

25 Speech of January 16, 1832, *Register of Debates*, VIII, part 1, 80-81. See also the speeches of W. H. Brodaax of Dinwiddie, January 19, and of Thomas Marshall of Fanquier, January 14, 20, 1832, before the Virginia House of Delegates, printed in pamphlet form in Richmond, 1832. These speeches and others delivered at the same historic session are bound in one volume, *Virginia Slavery Debate of 1832*, in the Virginia State Library, Richmond. See also John Randolph's letter of November 15, 1831, in H. A. Garland, *Life of John Randolph*, II, p. 345.

26 Quoted by Olmsted, *Seaboard, op. cit.*, II, p. 374.

saries of life, for the support of themselves and the rest of their negroes. In many places, heavy planters compel their slaves to fish for the means of subsistence, rather than sell them at such ruinous rates. There are at this moment, thousands of slaves in Mississippi, that know not where the next morsel is to come from. The master must be ruined, to save the wretches from being starved.

The early forties were bad years, one Mississippi planter, Dr. M. W. Philips, telling his diary,[27] March 25, 1840: " The times seem so hard, that no one could think would be worse; the ablest men in the land cannot raise money; a vast number broke; many are running off their negroes. *The State is bankrupt . . .*". One of these able men was Andrew Jackson who at this time was in sore financial distress and, largely the fault of his adopted son, heavily in debt. He owned a rather large plantation — some eleven hundred acres — in Coahoma County, Mississippi, and learned [28] early in 1841 that the slaves there " were shivering and starving—provisions out and no shoes."

In 1855 near famine conditions prevailed in much of the South with, apparently, Georgia, Alabama, and Louisiana most seriously affected. People offered to work for a peck of corn a day and were turned down, others lived for days at a time " on boiled weeds, called pepper grass," while occasionally the bodies of individuals who had starved to death — including slaves — were discovered.[29] The next year a drought " destructive to a degree almost without precedent " afflicted portions of the slave

27 F. L. Riley, ed., "Diary of a Mississippi planter," in *Mississippi Historical Society Publications*, X, pp. 317-18.

28 Marquis James, *Andrew Jackson Portrait of a President*, p. 454.

29 Olmsted, *Seaboard. op. cit.*, II, pp. 371-75, quoting local newspapers— nationally circulating papers avoided printing this news. Note the comments by James L. Watkins: " 1854—Backward Spring, unseasonable rains, and early frosts in the South . . . Great drought in cotton States. 1857 . . . Remarkable frosts in April greatly damage the crops."—" Production and price of cotton for one hundred years," United States Department of Agriculture, *Miscellaneous Series Bulletin No. 9*, p. 13. See complaints concerning the weather, insects and plant diseases in July and August 1856 in U. B. Phillips, and J. D. Glunt, eds., *Florida Plantation Records*, pp. 163-67.

area, especially in Virginia and Texas. Thus, a letter from Huntsville in the later state dated July 22, 1856 declared: [30]

Our prospects in this country are of the gloomiest character. For twelve weeks not a drop of rain has fallen within ten miles of this place. Corn crops have failed entirely. Cotton is nearly gone . . . The grass is drying out, and the cattle is suffering to a great extent . . . general consternation prevails throughout the country.

Depression directly caused another form of suffering for it increased the practice of leasing or selling of slaves. These, particularly the latter, were usually among the most dreaded fates that could befall a slave. The hardships and heartaches incident to sale of human beings—notably forced sales, when considerations of family ties had even less weight than usual—are too well known and too patent to require any extended discussion. Leasing was also generally distasteful to slaves. A South Carolina judge in 1839 stated [31] as an accepted fact that, " Hired slaves are commonly treated more harshly, or with less care and attention, than those in possession of their owner."

In the terribly difficult year of 1796 Thomas Jefferson, himself, sold in the open market a dozen of his slaves, and George Washington, too, despite scruples, was seriously considering the leasing of some of his slaves. [32] An English traveller in Virginia at about that time commented [33] upon the " worn out " appearance of the State and upon the practice of leasing of slaves indulged in by masters who were " overstocked." As for

30 Richmond *Daily Dispatch*, July 31, August 7, September 12, 1856.

31 H. T. Catterall, *op. cit.*, II, p. 374. Note also the statement: " The practice of hiring out slaves was responsible for much of the ill-treatment of Negroes in Virginia," in *The Negro in Virginia*, p. 152, also p. 55. Where skilled slaves hired themselves out and were able to earn and keep money over and above that demanded by their owners, they, of course, preferred that arrangement, but it was exceptional and generally frowned upon. See J. C. Robert, *op. cit.*, p. 203.

32 *The Negro in Virginia*, p. 38; Washington's letters to Tobias Lear, March 13, 1796, and to David Stuart, marked private, February 7, 1796 in *Letters and Recollections of George Washington*, pp. 103, 193.

33 W[illiam] Strickland, *Observations on the Agriculture of the United States of America*, pp. 22, 32.

outright sales during economic distress the comment of the South Carolina Republican, Wade Hampton, during the embargo-induced stagnation is typical of the situation: [34] " there remains nothing between the hammer of the sheriff's auctioneer and their [planters'] property—and indeed sales of this description have multiplied to an astonishing degree, in every part of the state."

In attempting to ascertain the causes of slave rebellions, an effort has been made to show that when depression came to the ante-bellum South the slaves felt this in worsened conditions.

What, however, were the ordinary circumstances under which the field slaves—the vast majority—lived? For, as a New York *Times* book-reviewer once quaintly confessed,[35] "the Negroes, being slaves . . . had a grievance." Opinions as to the extent of this grievance—or, even, as to its existence—have and do differ.[36] But to understand the sources from which well up the desperation needed by any people who risk death to alter, by force, their status, an investigation of that status is required.

Here is a typical day in cotton-picking time, described [37] by a resident of Mississippi and a partisan of slavery:

The hands are regularly roused, by a large bell or horn, about the first dawn of day, or earlier so that they are ready to enter the field as soon as there is sufficient light to distinguish the bolls. As the dews are extremely heavy and cool, each hand is provided with a blanket coat or wrapper, which is kept close around him until the dew is partially evaporated by the sun . . . The hands remain in the field until it is too dark to distinguish the cotton, having brought their meals with them. For the purpose of collecting the cotton, each hand is furnished with a large basket, and two coarse bags about the size of a pillow case, with a strong strap to suspend them from the neck or shoulders. The basket is left at the end of the row, and both bags taken along; when one bag is as full as it

34 Statement made March 15, 1808, quoted by John H. Wolfe, *Jeffersonian Democracy in South Carolina*, p. 222.

35 R. L. Duffus, N. Y. *Sunday Times*, Book section, Feb. 13, 1938, p. 4.

36 See E. B. Greene, *Provincial America 1690-1740*, p. 240.

37 J. H. Ingraham, *The Southwest by a Yankee*, II, pp. 285-86.

can well be crammed, it is laid down in the row, and the hand begins to fill the second in the same way. As soon as the second is full, he returns to the basket, taking the other bag as he passes it, and empties both into the basket, treading it down well, to make it contain his whole day's work. The same process is repeated until night; when the basket is taken upon his head and carried to the scaffold-yard, to be weighed. There the overseer meets all hands at the scales, with the lamp, slate, and whip [the latter to be used on those whose work is considered insufficient or unsatisfactory].

That was the working-day, from sun-up to sun-down, or from " dark to dark," six days a week, with minor variations depending upon the season, crop, and location. "Apparently the gangs were at leisure on Sundays," wrote the editors of a Florida slaveholder's records,[38] " except for some slight special tasks such as loading a wagon with cotton bales. Likewise no work at night was recorded, except for the boiling of syrup in emergencies occasioned by the frosting of the sugar-cane, and except sometimes the making of rope to serve as plowlines—which latter may have been in penalty for misdeeds." It should be noted that this refers only to work performed for the master and does not consider the labor often found necessary by slaves for themselves such as, at times, cooking, tailoring, shoe-mending, furniture repairing, or the tending of personal gardens occasionally permitted the Negroes as a supplementary source of nourishment.

When the day's work was done they went back to what? Said a Polish poet,[39] Julian Ursyn Niemcewicz, who visited Washington's Mount Vernon estate for two weeks in 1798: " We entered some negroes' huts for their habitations cannot be called houses. They are far more miserable than the poorest of the cottages of our peasants. The husband and wife sleep on a miserable bed, the children on the floor." More revealing is what may be called a slum-clearance project discussed two generations later by a Mississippi planter who apparently consid-

38 U. B. Phillips and J. D. Glunt, eds., *op. cit.*, pp. 31-32.
39 *The Negro in Virginia*, p. 67. See also Robert Sutcliff, *Travels in Some Parts of North America*, p. 51.

ered himself particularly enlightened. He regretted [40] the fact that " Planters do not always reflect that there is more sickness, and consequently greater loss of life, from the decaying logs of negro houses, open floors, leaky roofs, and crowded rooms than all other causes combined," and urged them to bear this in mind and do as he did : " There being upward of 150 negroes on the plantation, I provide for them 24 houses made of hewn post oak, covered with cypress, 16 by 18, with close plank floors and good chimneys, and elevated two feet from the ground." That is, about six people lived in a " house "—a room—sixteen by eighteen feet, and this was proudly held up as a model for others to emulate!

Clothes were either homespun of short-staple cheap cotton, or bought from New England firms as a special " Negro cloth," being a very coarse mixture of cotton and hemp, or imported from England, the material in this case being osnaburgh, again exceedingly coarse. The cloth [41] " was jus' like needles when it was new. Never did have to scratch our back. Jus' wiggle yo' shoulders an' yo' back was scratched." The men's outfit consisted of canvas trousers, and a cotton shirt, women's of a cotton " shift " and a heavier dress over it. Children, when wearing anything, wore a single " tow " shirt, or a guano bag. Grown-ups, too, occasionally wore nothing but guano bags.

Corn meal was the basic food, this mixed with water and fried on the flat edge of a hoe—hoe-cake—was the main dish. Rations were roughly apportioned according to the productivity of the field workers—the full, three-quarter, and half hands, as they were divided—with the most efficient getting the largest portion.

Thus, a North Carolina plantation journal shows that fullhands received very much more than the others, often called

40 Charles S. Sydnor, *Slavery in Mississippi*, p. 39, quoting *DeBow's Review*, X, p. 623.

41 *The Negro in Virginia*, pp. 69-70. See also, Sutcliff, *op. cit.*, p. 98; " Diary of the Hon. Jonathan Mason," *Proceedings of the Massachusetts Historical Society*, 2nd series, II, p. 22.

" idlers," so that in one case two " workers " received 104 pecks of meal annually, while six " idlers " in the same family were given 196 pecks. Another combination of two " workers " and five " idlers " saw the former get 105 pecks and the latter 126 pecks; in still another case both two " workers " and four " idlers " got the same amount of meal, 104 pecks, or two pecks a week for two people in one case and for four people in the other.[42] A Florida plantation record of 1847 shows a somewhat similar situation. The average weekly ration of meal for men was about three pecks, but slaves whose names are preceded by " Old " received from one to two pecks, about what the women received. These supplies were meant to be used for the feeding of the children too.

Pork or herring or molasses, was also not infrequently part of the rations with, again, relative productivity being a most important determinant of the quantity allowed. Further variations in the food allowance were caused by economic conditions, as already demonstrated, and by " the season and ... the amount of work being done." [43]

An indication of the importance of the latter item, which is tied in with the question of economic conditions, appears in the following conversation, reported [44] by a Southern magazine:

[42] Rosser H. Taylor, " Feeding slaves," in *The Journal of Negro History*, 1924, IX, pp. 139-43; R. H. Taylor, " Slaveholding in North Carolina: an economic view," *James Sprunt Historical Publications*, XVIII, p. 90; Phillips and Glunt, eds., *op. cit.*, p. 333. Olmsted declared that women, generally, were classed as light hands and provided accordingly—*Seaboard*, *op. cit.*, II, p. 351. See also John R. Williams, ed., *Philip Vickers Fithian Journal and Letters 1767-1774*, p. 69.

[43] Dorothy S. Magoffin, "A Georgia planter and his plantations 1837-1861 " in *North Carolina Historical Review*, XV, p. 373; note the appeal of John Taylor of Carolina County, Virginia, president of the Agricultural Society of Virginia for some variety in the slaves' diets: " Bread alone ought never to be considered a sufficient diet for slaves except as a punishment ... Give our slaves ... in addition to bread, salt meat and vegetables, and ... we shall be astonished to discover upon trial, that this great comfort to them is a profit to the master."—*The Negro in Virginia*, p. 69.

[44] G. G. Johnson, *op. cit.*, p. 522 quoting *Farmers' Journal*, May, 1853.

They say, Toney, that the Doctor is a hard man to live with. He wants a great deal done, said one slave to another.

Yes, replied Toney, but he gives plenty of good fat pork, which helps mightily. Where they ain't no work, they ain't no eating.

A final and very important source for arriving at some conception of the field hand's general standard of living at various periods is provided by the estimates made, usually by slaveholders themselves, as to the cost of the upkeep of the chattels. An anonymous work, published in 1775, declared [45] that the cost of slave labor was about one-third " that of English labourers." In another place the author, referring specifically to South Carolina, made these reckonings: "A negro costs 2/13s per annum, to which if we add 2/10s the interest of his prime cost, the total is only 5/3s and as the common calculation is, that one English labourer does as much work as two negroes, a labourer to the planter costs 10/6s a year, where as to an English farmer he costs from £20 to £25." While all these figures were of interest to the proprietor, only the first directly concerned the slave, and this showed that the planter spent 2/13s each year in order to keep his human machine operating. Twenty years later a wealthy South Carolinian estimated " the expense for a negro, including duty, board, clothing, and medicines . . . [at] . . . from twelve to thirteen dollars " per year.[46]

The Vesey plot of 1822 moved General Thomas Pinckney to publish his ideas concerning slavery. In the course of doing this he wrote,[47] " The average annual expense of plantation slaves in the lower country of South-Carolina, extracted from the account of several executors and attornies, for four successive years, amounts to $35 per head." This figure included not

45 Harry J. Carman and Rexford J. Tugwell, eds., *American Husbandry*, pp. 219, 302.

46 Duke de la Rochefoucault Liancourt, *Travels Through the United States of North America*, I, p. 596.

47 "Achates" [Thomas Pinckney] *Reflections Occasioned by the Late Disturbances in Charleston*, p. 29. The upkeep of town slaves, said the author, cost more. The districts of Beaufort, Charleston, and Georgetown comprised the low country of South Carolina.

merely food and clothing, but taxes, overseer's wages, medi-
cinal costs, "ploughs, tools, nails, locks, hinges, fish-hooks,
pipes, salt, etc., etc." A statistician has come to the conclusion [48]
that the yearly cost of medical care, feeding, and clothing adult
slaves working in cotton fields in 1822 came to $23.10. James
Madison, writing the next year and referring to his own Virginia, stated that [49] " the annual expense of food & raiment in
rearing a [slave] child, may be stated at about 8, 9, or 10 dollars; and the age at which it begins to be gainful to its owner,
about 9 or 10 years."

A report submitted to Congress in 1836 having to do with
cotton production, prepared by Levi Woodbury, Secretary of
the Treasury, declared in reference to prime field hands, that
" capital in field hands, and in other lands, stock, labor &c to
feed and clothe them," all taken together cost one hundred dollars a year, while for other slaves, as those " more youthful, or
more aged, or infirm females," the maintenance charges plus
the other indicated costs came to thirty dollars annually.[50]

The yearly cost of maintaining a slave child, age not specified,
entered into a Maryland court case in 1841. The estimates mentioned,[51] witnesses differing from five to twenty dollars as the
approximate figures, varied little from that suggested by James
Madison as accurate in 1823 for Virginia.

Forty-eight sugar planters of the Parish of St. Mary in
Louisiana told [52] the Secretary of the Treasury in 1845 that

48 James L. Watkins, *op. cit.*, pp. 41-42. This same source places the annual
cost of feeding an adult slave in Virginia in 1849 at $22.00.

49 "Answers to questions concerning slavery, addressed to Jedediah Morse "
in Gaillard Hunt, *op. cit.*, IX, p. 133.

50 Report of Levi Woodbury, " Cultivation, manufacture and foreign trade
of cotton," March 4, 1836, *Executive Documents*, House of Representatives,
24th Cong., 1st Sess., Doc. No. 146, pp. 18-21.

51 H. T. Catterall, *op. cit.*, IV, p. 96 n.

52 Report of the Secretary of Treasury, *Executive Documents*, House of
Representatives, 29th Cong., 1st Sess., December 3, 1845, Doc. No. 6, pp.
708, 748. These estimates, leaving out the three dollars for medical costs,
were given by F. L. Olmsted (*Seaboard*, II, p. 347), but incorrectly stated
to have been made in 1846.

the cost of supplying their prime field hands with food, medical treatment and clothing was thirty-three dollars, and for the other slaves, eighteen dollars a year. Frederick Law Olmsted cited a South Carolina planter as asserting in 1846 that food and clothing for a " full-tasked hand " cost fifteen dollars annually, and his own observations made ten years later led him to declare,[53] " In fact, under favorable circumstances, on the large plantations the slave's allowance does not equal in quantity or quality that which we furnish the rogues in our penitentiaries."

A Southern work of 1854, J. D. B. DeBow's *Resources of the South,* contains [54] a table furnished by a cotton planter who was annoyed by the alleged fact that the expenses of raising cotton were " generally greatly underrated." He proposed to provide the true facts. This gentleman maintained that upon " a well improved and properly organized plantation," the expense of feeding one hundred slaves " as deduced from fifteen years' experience " was found to be seven hundred and fifty dollars a year, or seven dollars and fifty cents per slave per annum, that is, about two cents per day. In this sum were included the costs of the " hospital and the overseer's table." Other expenses, clothing, bedding, sacks for gathering cotton, " and so forth," were estimated at the same sum.

The upkeep of urban slaves, as previously mentioned, cost more.[55] Thus, during the 1850's slaves employed in a cotton factory at Jackson, Mississippi, were allowed twenty cents a day for board (white workers at the same establishment received thirty cents) while those engaged in railroad work in the same state were boarded at fifteen cents a day.

These conditions of living were by no means the last of the " grievance " the Negroes bore as slaves. For to keep human

53 *Ibid.,* II, pp. 352, 363; Olmsted was a resident of New York.

54 I, p. 150; see also J. B. McMaster, *op. cit.,* VII, p. 240, F. L. Olmsted, *Back Country, op. cit.,* p. 52. For other estimates on cost of slave upkeep, see, J. Winston Coleman, Jr., *Slavery Times in Kentucky,* p. 66; Ralph B. Flanders, *Plantation Slavery in Georgia,* p. 103; L. C. Gray, *op. cit.,* II, p. 727.

55 Charles S. Sydnor, *op. cit.,* p. 36.

beings within a status situation entailing those conditions, physical repression—cruelty in its usual sense—was often necessary, so often indeed that one is correct, it is believed, in declaring that cruelty was characteristic of the institution of American Negro slavery.

Many, perhaps most, writers on this subject have denied this and assert, on the contrary, that [56] " kindliness [was] the rule " under the system. Those holding this view tend to base it upon a theoretical proposition which they appear to believe is self-evident and need merely be stated to have its truth immediately and universally recognized. A recent repetition of this idea urges the reader to bear in mind that " owners of slaves were hardly likely to be cruel or careless with expensive pieces of their own property," just as most people do not abuse their horses or automobiles.[57]

When one takes into consideration the estimate of the Negro that is characteristic of most if not all writers of this type of thinking, the particular sleight of hand in this legerdemain becomes more comprehensible. For, of course, the fatal error in the above proposition is the assumption that one may accurately compare any two pieces of property, even if they be so far apart and so distinct as is an automobile or a horse from a human being.[58]

There are, however, fundamental differences. Basic is the reasoning faculty which leads men, unlike automobiles, to compare, plan, hope, yearn, desire, hate, fear, which leads them to seek pleasure and shun pain, to spin dreams and build philosophies and struggle and gladly die for them. Human beings, in

56 U. B. Phillips, *American Negro Slavery*, p. 306.

57 Stewart Mitchell, *Horatio Seymour*, p. 103.

58 A less fundamental consideration is the fact that society does find it necessary to maintain societies for the prevention of cruelty to animals and even to children. A slave society would probably not be less productive than a free society of the perverse and insane people whose existence calls these societies into being. There was, it may be noted, little protection for slaves held by irresponsible or insane individuals. The notorious case of John Randolph is well known. See also H. T. Catterall, *op. cit.*, II, p. 336; III, p. 337.

fine, or, at least, many human beings, do possess the glorious urge to improve themselves and their environment. And people who are beaten, branded, sold, degraded, denied a thousand and one privileges they see enjoyed by others will be discontented, will be unhappy, and will plan, or, at least, think of bettering their lot.

This was the slaveholders' nightmare. This it was that led them to erect theologic, economic, social and ethnologic justifications for their system, that led them to build a most elaborate machine of physical repression and terrorization. For, and here was another crucial difference, most slaves were owned as investments, not as ornaments or commodities of consumption, as are most automobiles. Slaves were instruments of production, were means by which men who owned land were able to produce tobacco and rice and sugar and cotton to be sold and to return them a profit. Their existence had no meaning other than this for the employers. Profit must be gotten from these workers—whom the bosses owned—no matter what blood and sweat and tears this entailed, and the more profit the better.

When one combines the differences, then, he finds the slaves to have been not inanimate ornaments or instruments of pleasure, but thinking, living commercial investments, rational machines of production. It may be said, therefore, that cruelty was an innate, inextricable part of American Negro slavery, for these peculiar machines, possessed of the unique quality of human beings—reason—had to be maltreated, had to be made to suffer physical cruelty, had to be chained and lashed and beaten into producing for a profit. The latter was the reason for their existence and incorrigibility, protest, disobedience, discontent, rebelliousness were bad in themselves, and disastrous as examples. Instead of the slave's value preventing cruelty, it was exactly because of that value, and that greater value he could produce—when forced—that cruelty existed.[59]

59 Note the letter from Theodore D. Weld to J. F. Robinson, dated Buffalo, May 1, 1836: "That slavery in itself is cruelty—atrocious cruelty; that in the system cruelty is the rule, not the exception; that those who hold human beings as property will inflict upon them greater cruelties than they do upon

So much for an attempt at a theoretical refutation of the idea that ownership necessarily operated against and all but excluded physical cruelty as a phenomenon incident to American slavery. When one leaves the field of theory and enters the realm of actuality he finds that there is an abundance of excellent evidence establishing the pervasive character of this cruelty. Its absence, not presence, is exceptional.

It is manifestly impossible here to offer the thousands of instances of this that fill diaries, journals, newspapers, travellers' reports, and court records. One may, however, offer certain examples which, in their nature, or in their manner of reporting, indicate the existence of widespread and often horrible cruelty. Without presenting this—the nerve-racking and body-searing reality of enslavement—one has neglected what undoubtedly was a major factor in provoking the state of desperation that leads men and women to contemplate and undertake insurrection.

A Maryland slave named Tony, back in 1656, fled, was captured by dogs, waited for his wounds to heal, fled again, and was again captured.[60] Tony then staged a sit-down strike letting it be known that he would not work as a slave. His master, Symon Overzee, proceeded to demonstrate the treatment that incorrigible rational instruments of production might expect.

---

their brutes, I know from years of personal observation in the midst of southern slavery."—Barnes and Dumond, eds., *op. cit.*, I, p. 297. And observe the remark of a prominent native of Virginia, Moncure D. Conway: "So far from a man's interest in his slave as property being a guarantee against the laceration of that slave, such laceration may be, and frequently is, the only means of retaining him as property. 'Breaking their spirit' is a phrase as frequently used with regard to slaves as to horses."—*Testimonies Concerning Slavery*, p. 10. For a famous description of life under one such "breaker" see *The Autobiography of Frederick Douglass*, pp. 135 ff.

60 Bernard C. Steiner, ed., *Archives of Maryland*, XLI, pp. 190-191, 205-206. Mrs. Catterall's reference to this case (*op. cit.*, I, p. 54 n.) is incorrectly given. In October, 1669 the Virginia Assembly passed an act "about the casuall killing of slaves," whose preamble read: "Whereas ... the obstinacy of many of them by other than violent means cannot be supprest," and which provided that those killing slaves under such circumstances were not to be punished—William W. Hening, *The Statutes at Large of Virginia*, II, p. 270.

Tony was severely lashed, but this did not alter his determination. He was then hung by his wrists and Mr. Overzee poured hot lard over him. Three hours later Tony died. This procedure was irregular and, something over a year later, the murderer was tried before the provincial court. The facts were presented to this honorable body which, learning of Tony's behavior, announced, " The Prisoner acquitted by Proclamation." Similarly, during approximately the same period, the Reverend Samuel Gray, in Virginia, branded and flogged one of his slaves, who had run away, and killed him. The reverend gentleman was not punished, for, as he remarked,[61] " such accidents will happen every now and then."

The Reverend Charles Wesley (brother of the better-known John) was in South Carolina in the summer of 1736 and, while noting some specific instances of cruelty, remarked [62] in disgust, " It were needless to recount all the shocking instances of diabolical cruelty, which these men, as they call themselves, daily practice upon their fellow-creatures." The Reverend George Whitefield, who lived in various parts of the South in the spring and summer of 1738, and from 1739 to 1741, sent an open letter [63] in 1739 to the inhabitants of the southern colonies lamenting " the miseries of the poor negroes " that he had seen, their excessive labor, poor provisions, " not to mention what numbers have been given up to the inhuman usage of cruel taskmasters, who, by their unrelenting scourges have plowed their backs, and made long furrows, and at length brought them even to death." Still another religious leader, the great Quaker, John Woolman, who travelled through much of the south in 1746 and in 1757, recorded [64] similar impressions.

61 Philip A. Bruce, *Institutional History of Virginia in the Seventeenth Century*, I, p. 213. See also, L. B. Wright and M. Tinling, eds., *The Secret Diary of William Byrd*.

62 John Whitehead, *The Life of the Reverend John Wesley*, p. 86.

63 Quoted by Charles Elliot, *Sinfulness of American Slavery*, II, pp. 176-77. For a striking illustration of the type of back Whitefield was referring to, see Frederick Bancroft, *Slave-Trading in the Old South*, facing p. 108.

64 *The Journal of John Woolman,* with an introduction by John G. Whittier, pp. 72, 109-115. See also the observations made in South Carolina and Georgia

The well known journal of the tutor employed by the wealthy Carter family at their plantation in Westmoreland County, Virginia, contains some biting observations on the treatment of the slaves, even of those owned by his employer. He made note at considerable length of the disciplinary measures found most useful by a Mr. Martin, the overseer for a neighbor, George Lee. Mr. Martin, as a man of experience, declared that " whipping of any kind " was of little use for the slaves " will laugh at your greatest Severity." [65] He had, however, invented two types of punishment that

by several experiments had proved their success.—For Sulleness, [sic] Obstinacy, or Idleness, says he, Take a Negro, strip him, tie him fast to a post; take then a sharp Curry-Comb, & curry him severly til he is well scraped; & call a Boy with some dry Hay, and make the Boy rub him down several Minutes, then salt him, & unlose him. He will attend to his Business, (said the inhuman Infidel) afterwards!—But savage Cruelty does not exceed His next diabolical invention—To get a Secret from a Negro, says he, take the following Method—Lay upon your Floor a large thick plank, having a peg about eighteen Inches long, of hard wood, & very Sharp, on the upper end, fixed fast in the plank—then strip the Negro, tie the cord to a staple in the Ceiling, so as that his foot may just rest on the sharpened Peg then turn him briskly round, and you would laugh (said our informer) at the Dexterity of the Negro, while he was relieving his feet on the sharpened Peg!—I need say nothing of these seeing there is a righteous God who will take vengeance on such Inventions!

Indications that punishment frequently extended to the point of killing recur. Thus a communication in a Charleston, South Carolina, newspaper in 1806 remarked how frequent Negro

in 1791 by William Savery (Jonathan Evans, ed., "A Journal of the life, travels and religious labours of William Savery," in *The Friends' Library*, edited by W. & T. Evans, pp. 330-331) ; and in Georgia two years later by Thomas Scattergood (*ibid.*, VIII, Phila., 1844, p. 41).

65 Entry of December 23, 1773, in John R. Williams, ed., *op. cit.*, p. 69. See also, John S. Bassett, *The Southern Plantation Overseer*, pp. 6, 125, 147, 264; C. S. Sydnor, *op. cit.*, pp. 70, 72; present work, *ante*, pp. 66-67, 82.

homicides were, and the Kershaw grand jury in the same state complained [66] " that the existing laws to prevent the murder of slaves were inadequate." Eight years later the Charleston grand jury presented [67]

as a most serious evil the many instances of negro homicide, which have been committed within the city for many years. The parties exercising unlimited control, as masters and mistresses, in the indulgence of their malignant and cruel passions, in the barbarous treatment of a slave, using them worse than beasts of burden and thereby bringing on the community, the State and the city the contumely and opprobrium of the civilized world.

Early in 1810 a North Carolinian, who signed himself " E. Post," wrote a revealing letter which the Raleigh *Star* published under the heading "A Caution to Slave Drivers." Here appeared the sentence: [68] "Although there is no danger of a man's being hurt for killing a negro, it might be well for some people to know how to punish, without killing them." Five years later a man named John R. Cooke was actually convicted, in North Carolina, of killing a slave, under the most atrocious conditions, and was sentenced to hang. The Governor pardoned him. A native of Raleigh reported: [69]

Some thought, as this was the first instance in which a white man had ever been convicted for killing a negro, it would be impolitic to hang him so unexpectedly. And others believed that it would be

66 Charleston *Times*, June 2, 1806; Charleston *Courier*, December 7, 1808, quoted by H. M. Henry, *The Police Control of the Slave in South Carolina*, p. 67.

67 Charleston *City Gazette*, January 22, April 24, 1816, quoted by Theodore D. Jervey, *Robert Y. Hayne*, p. 68. See also the remarks of Dr. William Langley made in December, 1816 and printed in the Camden, S. C. *Gazette*, quoted by Thomas J. Kirkland and Robert M. Kennedy, *Historic Camden*, part two, p. 187.

68 Quoted in the N. Y. *Evening Post*, May 11, 1810. He later retracted the force of this original statement—see G. G. Johnson, *op. cit.*, p. 412.

69 Item dated Raleigh, October 27, in the N. Y. *Evening Post*, November 2, 1815. For a comment on conditions in this state somewhat earlier, see, Charles W. Janson, *The Stranger in America*, pp. 374-78.

wrong in all respects, to hang a white man for killing a negro. But whatever might have been the motives of his Excellency, we hear no dissatisfaction expressed by any at this act of clemency; yet we think it may be well to caution the unwary against the repetition of the too common practice of whipping negroes to death as.... executive interposition may not be expected in all cases.

A Major in the United States Army, Amos Stoddard, who was in Louisiana (Orleans Territory) for about five years, from 1804 to 1809, expressed his surprise at the debilitated condition of the slaves, and went on :[70]

Their masters and overseers affect to believe, that their want of industry arises from laziness, and a perverse disposition. Hence cruel and even unusual punishments are daily inflicted on these wretched creatures, enfeebled, oppressed with hunger, labor, and the lash. The scenes of misery and distress constantly witnessed along the coast of the Delta, the wounds and lacerations occasioned by demoralized masters and overseers, most of whom exhibit a strange compound of ignorance and depravity, torture the feelings of the passing stranger, and wring blood from his heart. Good God! why sleeps thy vengence!

Some idea of the conditions that provoked this outburst may be gained by looking into the plantation journal of a rather well-to-do Florida planter, George Noble Jones. He owned about seventy slaves who labored on two plantations, one under a Mr. Evans, called Chemonie, the other, under a Mr. Moxley, called El Destino. Here are a few typical references : [71]

Mr. Moxley, August 31, 1854: "the hands dont pick Cotton well yet. they is a few of them that pick Verry well the balance dont so I have bin pushing them up a Little and Esaw and Little Dick has runaway on the Strength of it."

The same, September 8, 1854: "Boy Jack and di has runaway. for picking for about 85 to 95 [pounds] I maid Prince [a Negro

70 Amos Stoddard, *Sketches, Historical and Descriptive of Louisiana*, p. 332.

71 U. B. Phillips and J. D. Glunt, eds., *op. cit.*, pp. 95-98, 108, 110-112.

driver] give them both about 30 [lashes] apeas yesterday and they lef. but I have Jack in jail. Di is out yet tho I think I shall git her to night."

Mr. Evans, September 9, 1854, reported the capture of the fugitives and added: "I am getting on verry well with my business and hav Caught the two boys that run off and gave them a light Flogging and put them to work. the Cause of Esaws and Little Dicks Runing away was this, Jacob and England and Nathan had made a plot to leave if I should attempt to Flog them for picking Cotton [i. e., for failing to pick the required amount of cotton] and persuaded those two boys into it. So I gave Jacob and England and Nathan a Flogging apeace. they acknowledge they had done wrong so I let them off Lightly."

A month later Mr. Moxley was again complaining of flight, and added that he caught a runaway, Venus: "I caut her, and Aberdeen [Venus' brother] caut oup a ax to Strike me, and prince prevented it. I have don nothing with him yet but I intend to git Mr. Evans and give him a basting."

Planter Jones asked Mr. Evans his opinion of Moxley's overseering. Said Evans: " I don't think that Mr. Moxley treats the negroes on Eldestino Cruely When they don't deserv it... they is but one thing I see in Mr. Moxleys Management that I don't Like and it is this, I think when he Flogs he puts it on in two Large doses. I think moderate Floggings the best. When Ever I See that I have Convinced a negro I always turn him loose. I always punish according to the Crime, if it a Large one I give him a genteel Floging with a strop, about 75 Lashes I think is a good Whipping. When picking Cotton I never put on more than 20 stripes and Verry frequently not more than 10 or 15. I find I get along with this as well as if I was to give them Larger Whippings."

Yes, a Mississippian told Edwin Lawrence Godkin two years later,[72] " He knew how it was that I wouldn't like to take a feller's breeches off, lay him down, and give him two hundred right away ... But if I was living there I'd soon get accustomed to it, and see the necessity of it." Necessity—that was it.

72 Rollo Ogden, ed., *Life and Letters of Edwin Lawrence Godkin*, I, p. 143.

Said the British consul in Charleston,[73] " The cry of self-preservation is always on the lips of a Carolinian when he is about to justify an outrage connected with slavery." The cry was frequent for " the frightful atrocities of slave holding must be seen to be described. . . My next door neighbor, a lawyer of the first distincton, and a member of the *Southern Aristocracy,* told me himself that he flogged all his own negroes, men and women, when they misbehaved . . . It is literally no more to kill a slave than to shoot a dog." These were almost the precise words of an overseer in Alabama who told [74] Olmsted he felt not the slightest qualms about beating a slave—indeed—" Why, sir, I wouldn't mind killing a nigger more than I would a dog."

To summarize, it may be declared that many factors appear to have been of consequence in bringing on slave rebellions within the area of the present United States. Excitement of almost any kind, but especially that which more or less directly affected the slaves, such as the prevalence of slogans and propaganda about liberty and equality, or the knowledge of some not too distant haven or ally offering emancipation, tended to increase slave disaffection. A disproportionate growth of the Negro population as compared with the white also tended to increase the slaves' boldness, and move them to attempts to gain in action what seems never to have been totally absent from their dreams—freedom. Industrialization and urbanization were other forces producing similar results. Economic depression seems to have been even more important in evoking protest. Yet, the fundamental factor provoking rebellion against slavery was that social system itself, the degradation, exploitation, oppression, and brutality which it created, and with which, indeed, it was synonymous.

73 Robert Bunch to J. G. Bergne, Charleston, January 11, 1854, in Laura W. White, " The South in the 1850's as seen by British consuls," *The Journal of Southern History,* I, p. 33. Emphases in original.

74 Olmsted, *Back Country,* p. 82 ; see also, pp. 56, 62, 79.

CHAPTER VI

INDIVIDUAL ACTS OF RESISTANCE

In considering the subject of slave insurrections it is proper to bear in mind that it forms but one method used by the Negroes in fighting against enslavement. There were several others which must be considered.

As has already been observed, it was often possible for the slave, by great perseverance and labor, to purchase his own freedom and, this being accomplished, the freedom of those dear to him. It is not possible to say how many Negroes were thus emancipated, but it is probable that thousands actually ransomed themselves or those they loved.[1]

Another method by which an indeterminate number, but again probably thousands, gained their freedom was by serving in the Army and Navy of the Republic during the War for Independence.[2]

Flight was a major factor in the battle against bondage. Slaves fled wherever havens of liberation appeared, to the Spaniards, Mexicans Dutch, Canadians, French; to the armies of Britain and France; and, of course, to the army of Lincoln; to mountains, forests, and swamps in the South (often establishing camps therein) ;[3] and, along the routes of the Underground Railroad. The figures here again must be only guesses, but it is probable that hundreds of thousands in the course of slavery *succeeded* in gaining liberty by flight. Estimates for the Underground Railroad alone have been summarized by W. B.

1 H. Aptheker, " They bought their way to freedom," in *Opportunity*, June. 1940, pp. 180-182.

2 H. Aptheker, *The Negro in the American Revolution*, pp. 27-42; *The Negro in Virginia*, pp. 20-22.

3 At times maroon activity reached the point of rebellion. This will be noticed later. On the subject see H. Aptheker, " Maroons within the present limits of the U. S.," *The Journal of Negro History*, XXIV, pp. 167-184.

Hesseltine as follows :[4] " Between 1830 and 1860 as many as 2,000 slaves a year passed into the land of the free along the routes of the Underground Railroad." When people were willing to pay as high as three hundred dollars for one bloodhound, the loss of runaway slaves had indeed become a serious problem.[5]

Sabotage, shamming illness, " stealing," suicide and self-mutilation, and strikes were other devices which plagued slave-holders. The carelessness and deliberate destructiveness of the slaves, resulting in broken fences, spoiled tools, and neglected animals, were common phenomena.[6]

Pretending illness was probably even more common, certainly more frequently complained of,[7] than sabotage. It was as often mentioned as was the slaves' habit of " stealing," as the masters put it, " taking," as the slaves put it. To the slaves only

4 *A History of the South*, p. 258. The census reports on this subject (and indeed as a whole, but particularly for the South, prior to the Civil War) were utterly unreliable. See W. H. Siebert, *The Underground Railroad*, p. 26; S. Mitchell, *Horatio Seymour*, p. 482; F. L. Olmsted, *A Journey to the Seaboard Slave States*, II, p. 150.

5 Olmsted, *op. cit.*, I, p. 182. The possibility and actuality of flight was undoubtedly an important safety-valve and cut down rebellions. This point was made by Horace Mann in the House of Representatives, Feb. 15, 1850; by Harriet Beecher Stowe in *Dred*, II, p. 302; and Siebert, *op. cit.*, p. 340. Fleeing was so common that a Louisiana physician, Dr. Cartwright, ascribed it to a disease peculiar to Negroes which he called " drapetomania "—*The Negro in Virginia*, p. 128.

6 J. S. Buckingham, *The Slave States of America*, I, p. 402; W. Strickland, *Observations on the Agriculture of the United States*, p. 33; U. B. Phillips and J. D. Glunt, eds., *Florida Plantation Records*, p. 394; U. B. Phillips, *A History of Transportation in the Eastern Cotton Belt*, p. 25; B. I. Wiley, *Southern Negroes*, 1861-65, pp. 51-52; Karl Marx, *Capital* (N. Y., 1929), I, p. 191 n.; *The Negro in Virginia*, p. 62. See also, " Day to day resistance to slavery," by R. A. Bauer and A. H. Bauer, in *The Journal of Negro History* (1942), XXVII, pp. 388-419.

7 [J. H. Ingraham], *The Southwest by a Yankee*, II, p. 123; D. S. Magoffin, "A Georgia planter," in *North Carolina Hist. Rev.*, XV, p. 372; J. C. Robert, *The Tobacco Kingdom*, p. 205; U. B. Phillips, *American Negro Slavery*, pp. 263-64; Phillips and Glunt, eds., *op. cit.*, p. 34; Olmsted, *op. cit.*, I, pp. 111-12, 208; Wiley, *op. cit.*, p. 250; L. B. Wright and M. Tinling, eds., *Secret Diary of William Byrd*, pp. 290, 295, 468, 501.

appropriating the possession of a fellow slave, or a non-slave-holder, was " stealing," helping oneself to sorely-needed meat or milk belonging to the master was but taking that which one's labor produced.[8]

Strikes were by no means unknown under slavery. The method most commonly pursued was for the Negroes to flee to outlying swamps or forests, and to send back word that only if their demands—perhaps for better food or clothes, or fewer beatings, shorter hours, or even a new overseer—were met (or, at least, discussed) would they willingly return. It is interesting to observe that during the Civil War the slaves added a new demand, the payment of money wages, and at times won, thus lifting themselves by their own boot-straps from chattels to wage workers.[9]

Self-mutilation was another method which at times appealed to slaves as a method of shortening their own misery, and hurting their oppressors.[10] Notices of acts of self-destruction also occur.[11] Because of the possibility of imitation, planters tended to keep news of suicides from the other Negroes. On at least one occasion, in 1807 in Charleston, mass suicides occurred; in

8 R. Parkinson, *Experienced Farmer's Tour*, II, pp. 432-33; Olmsted, *op. cit.*, I, p. 130; W. Meade, *Sermons*, p. 215; S. Ferrall, *A Ramble of Six Thousand Miles*, p. 203. Each of these sources not only refers to the existence of the " taking," but to the presence of a well-thought out justification for it. This practice and philosophy exist today—see A. Davis and B. B. and M. R. Gardner, *Deep South*, p. 396. See also W. H. Stephenson in *The Mississippi Valley Hist. Rev.*, XXIII, pp. 355-74.

9 U. B. Phillips, *American Negro Slavery*, pp. 303-04; Magoffin, *op. cit.*, pp. 365, 374; Wiley, *op. cit.*, pp. 74-75; J. C. Sitterson, " Magnolia plantation," in *Miss. Valley Hist. Rev.*, XXV, pp. 207-09.

10 Olmsted, *op. cit.*, I, p. 208; F. Bremer, *Homes of the New World*, III, p. 339; Richmond *Daily Dispatch*, July 2, 1856, reported that three men, to prevent being sold, had cut off three fingers from each hand.

11 *The Liberator* (Boston), June 6, 1835, October 6, 1837, quoting local papers; *Documents 21-89, House of Delegates, 1852, Virginia*, Document # 46 lists several poison cases; [A. Hewatt], *An Historical Account of ... South Carolina and Georgia*, II, p. 93; C. G. Woodson, *The Negro in Our History*, p. 92; *Virginia Mag. Hist. and Biog.*, XXIV, p. 412.

this case two boatloads of newly-arrived Negroes starved themselves to death.[12]

Individual attempts at assassination or property damage by
gun, knife, club, axe, poison, or fire were so numerous that
undertaking an enumeration of all would be a well-nigh impossible task. Some specific references to the last two devices
will be given in order to present an idea of how prevalent they
were.

In 1751 South Carolina enacted a law providing the death
penalty, without benefit of clergy, for slaves found guilty of attempting to poison white people. The preamble related that the
frequency with which this had occurred was the reason for legislative action. The law provided a reward of four pounds to any
Negro whose information concerning a slave's attempt to poison
his master led to conviction.[13] A decade later the Charleston
Gazette [14] complained that " The negroes have again begun the
hellish practice of poisoning." In 1770, Georgia passed an act
similar to South Carolina's, providing death for poison attempts, the preamble explaining its origin in the words,[15]
" whereas, the detestable crime of poisoning hath frequently
been committed by slaves." A slave informer in such a case was
to receive twenty shillings each year until death and, upon the
day he received this money, was to be excused from labor. Typical examples of this type of activity on the part of the slaves are
the convictions in Maryland in 1755 of five slaves for conspir-

12 C. W. Elliott, *Winfield Scott*, p. 18. A Southern physician, Dr. E. N.
Pendleton, " stated that abortion and miscarriage were four times as frequent
among the Negroes as among the whites; that ' all country practitioners are
aware of the frequent complaints of planters from this subject; ' that while
the planters believed the Negroes used drugs he was not certain of this
personally."—*Southern Medical Reports*, New Orleans, 1849, in J. J. Spengler,
" Population theory in the ante-bellum South," in *Journal of Southern
History*, II, p. 379 n.

13 T. Cooper, *Statutes at Large of S. C.*, VII, p. 422; H. Henry, *op. cit.*,
p. 17.

14 Dated Jan. 17, 1761, in D. D. Wallace, *The History of South Carolina*,
I, p. 374.

15 H. Marbury and W. H. Crawford, *Digest of the Laws of Georgia*, p. 430.

ing to poison four different masters, and the convictions of two slaves in Virginia in 1803 for the same offense.[16]

Arson was more frequent and appears, indeed, to have been one of the greatest dangers to ante-bellum Southern society. While slaves generally would have had difficulty in getting hold of guns or knives,[17] or poison, they had little trouble in creating fire. The subject merits detailed treatment, more detailed than it can be given here. Mention, however, may be made of some of the evidences of the widespread character of this means of personal revenge.

Contemporary letters indicate that the prevalence of incendiarism in the slave area affected the policy of insurance companies. Thus, an official of the American Fire Insurance Company of Philadelphia told [18] a gentleman in Savannah, February 17, 1820, " I have received your letter of the 7th instant respecting the insurance of your house and furniture, in Savannah. In answer thereto, I am to inform you, that this company, for the present, decline making insurances in any of the slave states." Another pertinent letter is that written by a business man in Richmond, August 28, 1831, at the height of the panic following the Turner outbreak, to a New York firm,[19] " If they [the slaves] attempt any harm in town, they would most likely resort to *fire* to aid them: and goods destroyed by such a fire would not be paid for by insurers. For this reason, we should not, just

16 H. T. Catterall, ed., *Judicial Cases Concerning American Slavery and the Negro*, IV, pp. 39-40; N. Y. *Evening Post*, September 15, 1803. Poison cases are frequently mentioned in Mrs. Catterall's monumental work—see the indexes. See also Carl Bridenbaugh, *Cities in the Wilderness*, p. 379.

17 This difficulty did not hold true for slaves working in cane fields, for each had to have a cane-knife, a murderous weapon whose blade was fifteen inches long, three inches wide in the middle, and was kept very sharp.

18 Savannah *Republican*, March 2, 1820, in N. Y. *Evening Post*, March 15, 1820. Savannah was frequently beset by incendiarism and this was often ascribed to the slaves. See *ibid.*, April 5, 15, 1809; April 2, 1814; December 26, 29, 1817; May 4, 8, November 30, 1818; September 29, 1819; March 10, 20, May 21, 1820; January 2, 23, 1821; February 19, April 3, 1823.

19 N. Y. *Evening Post*, September 2, 1831.

at this time, care to have goods sent us on which we might have to make advances."

Notice has already been taken of the fact that incendiarism (probably the offense of slaves) moved outstanding citizens of Charleston, South Carolina in the 1790's to organize a committee for the purpose of seeing to it that brick or stone instead of wood was used in buildings. The same menace accounted for another architectural feature which was particularly noted in Virginia homes early in the nineteenth century. This was a fire-escape, described as follows: [20]

As a security from fire, or to favor escape from it, a ladder is fixed on the roof, reaching from a garret window to the ridge, and down the other side:—It is an expedient in many houses, and denotes extraordinary fear, or extraordinary danger. I was informed that the carelessness of the negroes rendered such precautions necessary.

A Maryland slave woman was executed in 1766 because she had burned down her master's home, tobacco house, and outhouses. The prosecutor in the course of his argument declared,[21] " I must not Omitt to mention that there have been two other Tobacco Houses full of Tobacco burnt in this County this Winter."

The possibility of arson by slaves was prominently mentioned in advocating curfew laws, and in establishing night watches. Thus, a citizen of Edenton, North Carolina in 1807 urged the enactment of a curfew regulation and the selection of " a sufficient number of vigilant and trusty men " to enforce its observance. Were this done, said he, order and peace would reign and one might sleep " undisturbed by the . . . distressing apprehensions of fire and other casualties." After two attempts at arson

20 Morris Birkbeck, *Notes on a Journey in America*, p. 15, entry dated May 6, 1817. The entry of May 4 (p. 14) read, "There are along the [James] river the ruins of many houses, which I was told had been accidentally burnt by the negroes, whose carelessness is productive of infinite mischief."

21 H. T. Catterall, *op. cit.*, IV, p. 45. For other cases in Maryland at about the same time see also pp. 38, 43, 44. See also the comment of Newton D. Mereness, *Maryland as a Proprietary Province*, p. 132.

in Plymouth, North Carolina, a patrol was organized which walked the streets at night and cried out the hour. This was done, too, at the same time, 1808, in Edenton, so that, wrote "Mentor," "our wives and children surrounded by desperadoes, *white and black*" might repose more easily.[22]

In March and April, 1814, the city of Norfolk, Virginia, was plagued by incendiarism. Several fires a day created panic in a community already tense with fear of a foreign enemy. Said the Norfolk *Herald* on April 8: [23]

There are now four negroes in the jail of this Borough who have been committed as incendiaries! Where is this evil to stop, and when can the citizens consider his property secure? A dreadful example must be made, as the only means of preventing a repetition of this horrid crime. The danger to be apprehended to our town from an attack of the enemy is safety to what is to be apprehended from the lurking incendiary. We are always prepared for an open and declared enemy; but no measures can be taken to guard our property against the fell designs of the incendiary.

From January 31, 1850 to May 30, 1851 there were reported at least seven *convictions* of slaves for arson in Virginia, while one New Orleans newspaper, the *Daily True Delta*, from November 26, 1850 to January 15, 1851, reported slave-set burnings of at least seven nearby sugar houses.[24] There are other

22 *The Edenton Gazette and North Carolina Advertiser*, November 18, 1807; October 5, 10, 1808; G. G. Johnson, *Ante-Bellum North Carolina*, pp. 128-29, 134.

23 Quoted in N. Y. *Evening Post*, April 15, 1814; see also *ibid.*, April 5, May 23, 1814. It is possible that this represented the result of organized conspiracy rather than acts of individual terrorism. Several slaves burned a hemp factory in Nashville, Tenn., in January, 1815—*ibid.*, January 31, 1815. Observe, too, J. S. Buckingham's comment (*op. cit.*, II, p. 50) after a hotel in Augusta, Georgia was destroyed in 1839 by a slave-created fire, "it is a very usual mode of revenge with the slaves to burn down the houses of their oppressors."

24 *Document # 46, House of Delegates, 1852*, Virginia; V. A. Moody, "Slavery on Louisiana sugar plantations," in *The Louisiana Historical Quarterly*, VII, p. 230.

evidences of the frequency of this phenomenon during the decade of crisis,[25] and it continued through the years of civil warfare, in one of which, 1864, the official residence of Jefferson Davis himself was damaged by a slave-created fire.[26]

Members of the hated patrol were at times especially selected by the slaves to suffer the destruction of their property by fire. Thus, serious slave disaffection troubled eastern North Carolina in 1830. Many inhabitants of four counties in this region—Bladen, Sampson, Duplin, and New Hanover—urged [27] the legislature to have the county militia take over patrol work, " as patrols are of no use on account of the danger they subject themselves to." And the citizens cited as examples the cases of two patrolmen who " had their dwelling houses and other houses burnt down," while another had " his fodder stack burnt."

25 Correspondence concerning and court records of arson trials may be found in the MS. Executive Papers, Archives, Virginia State Library, especially for December, 1859, and January, November, December, 1860. See also *The Liberator*, September 22, 1854; Milledgeville, Ga., *Federal Union*, March 20, 1855, in U. B. Phillips, ed., *Plantation and Frontier Documents*, II, p. 125; New Orleans *Daily Picayune*, November 25, 30, December 2, 1856; H. T. Catterall, ed., *op. cit.*, III, pp. 59, 115, 196, 200, 235, 336, 347, 619; V, pp. 197, 202, 215, 287; J. C. Roberts, *op. cit.*, pp. 206, 210. Two interesting comments on particular cases came from southern sources; one from the Richmond *Enquirer* (cited in *The Liberator*, January 19, 1855) reporting the hanging of a slave convicted of arson: " From the first to the last, he exhibited not the slightest sensibility, but yielded to the awful penalty with as much coolness and composure as if assigned an ordinary duty of everyday life." The other came from a Mississippi court record of 1857, concerning a slave convicted of burning his master's gin and cotton house. The master asked " him why he burned the gin-house, and he replied ... because he wished to be hung."—H. T. Catterall, *op. cit.*, III, p. 347.

26 References are again restricted only to fires set by one or two slaves, not those involving many and rising to the point of insurrecton. Isabella D. Martin and M. L. Avary, eds., *A Diary from Dixie*, pp. 145, 281-82; Richmond *Examiner*, January 21, 1864; J. B. Jones, *A Rebel War Clerk's Diary*, II, pp. 132-33; H. T. Catterall, ed., *op. cit.*, II, p. 252.

27 MSS. in Legislative Papers, Senate, December 14, 1830, and petition of December 24, 1830, Historical Commission, Raleigh; G. G. Johnson, *op. cit.*, pp. 515, 517.

The Norfolk *Beacon* of September 21, 1852, described another such case. It explained that the slaves of Princess Anne County, Virginia, had excited alarm, and that an extra patrol had been ordered out.

On Sunday night last, this patrol made a descent upon a church where a large number of negroes had congregated for the purpose of holding a meeting, and dispersed them. In a short time, the fodder stacks of one of the party who lived near were discovered on fire. The patrol immediately started for the fire, but before reaching the scene it was discovered that the stacks of other neighbors had shared a like fate, all having no doubt been fired by the negroes for revenge. A strict watch is now kept over them, and most rigid means adopted to make every one know and keep his place.

A letter from Berryville, Virginia early in 1860 contained reference to this same practice.[28]

Let me detail to you [wrote a Mr. Larue to Governor John Letcher] what a negro woman told her young master on the night that his fathers stack-yard was burnt. The sd young man a Son of Col. Josiah W. Ware was summoned by the Captain of the patrol to attend on the following Saturday night. Col. Wares negro woman said to her young master Marster Charley if you go on the patrol to night masters stack yard will be burnt this night and Sir Col. Wares stack yard was burnt.

28 C. C. Larue to Governor Letcher, Berryville, January 17, 1860, in MS. Executive Papers, Archives, Virginia State Library. There is evidence to show that occasionally slaves were paid by white people, desiring the destruction of a building, to accomplish this for them. In the collection of petitions in the Virginia archives is one (A5196) dated December 15, 1810, from many residents of Petersburg, urging that a slave named Emanuel be freed, for he had disclosed that a white man, Matthew Murray, had tried to get his aid in burning the city. The record of a slave, Jim, of Buckingham County, Virginia, convicted December 4, 1811, shows that the influence of one named William Cobbs, probably a white man, was great in bringing the slave to commit the act. On this ground, though the jury brought in a verdict of guilty it recommended mercy.—Executive Papers. A fire in Winton, North Carolina was set by a Negro who had been paid to do that by a white man —Richmond *Enquirer*, April 13, 1830.

In addition to the above, numerous references may be found in widely scattered sources [29] to devastation by fires deliberately created by individual slaves in protest against their oppression and as a means of revenge against their exploiters.

29 As examples, see, Carl Bridenbaugh, *op. cit.*, p. 69; Catterall, *op. cit.*, I, p. 84; III, pp. 423-24; Moncure Conway, *Testimonies Concerning Slavery*, London, 1864, p. 6; D. P. Corey, *The History of Malden, Massachusetts*, p. 521 n.; Lorenzo J. Greene, *op. cit.*, pp. 186-88; Susie M. Ames, *Studies of the Eastern Shore in the 17th Century*, p. 175. W. E. B. DuBois, *The Philadelphia Negro*, p. 237; Edwin Olson, *Negro Slavery in New York, 1626-1827*, unpublished doctor's dissertation, New York University, 1938, pp. 26, 97; W. H. Stephenson, *Isaac Franklin*, p. 111; "Miscellaneous Colonial documents," in *The Virginia Magazine of History and Biography*, XVI, p. 95; Thomas J. Wertenbaker, *The First Americans 1607-1690*, p. 216; *Minutes of the Provincial Council of Pennsylvania*, IV, p. 259; Carter G. Woodson, *op. cit.*, p. 92; U. B. Phillips, in *Annual Report of the American Historical Association for 1903*, I, p. 462; Boston *Weekly News-Letter*, January 18-25, 1739; N. Y. *Evening Post*, March 1, 1804; December 23, 1836; *The Liberator*, May 26, 1837; May 19, 1843; September 6, 1844.

CHAPTER VII

EXAGGERATION, DISTORTION, CENSORSHIP

THE unearthing of the history of Negro slave rebellions is peculiarly subject to difficulties arising from exaggeration, distortion, and censorship. Evidence showing the character and scope of these difficulties is, therefore, necessary to an understanding of that history.

It has already been shown that, in the 1790's, Federalists made use of fears of slave revolts, or reports of their occurrence, to further their party's fortunes. Similarly, the Gabriel plot, occurring in the presidential campaign year of 1800, and showing that the slaves had been influenced by the Democratic ideas associated with the French Revolution and Thomas Jefferson, was used by the Federalists in appeals to Southern voters. Thus, the Philadelphia *Gazette of the United States,* on September 13, declared:

The insurrection of the Negroes in the southern states, which *appears to be organized on the true French plan,* must be decisive with every reflecting man in those States of the election of Mr. Adams and Gen. Pinckney.

The military skill and approved bravery of the General, must be peculiarly valuable to his countrymen at this moment. *He is not one who shrinks from danger.*[1] He has met it, and, when occasion requires he will meet it with firmness in its most horrid form.

We congratulate our fellow citizens of South Carolina on the possession of this Gallant Soldier at this Important Crisis. To him they may look with confidence for every aid which courage and talents can supply.

The Republicans denied that the French had had anything at all to do with the plot,[2] and the *Aurora* even proved to its

[1] This italicized sentence was undoubtedly intended as a slur upon Jefferson for his alleged cowardice when revolutionary Governor of Virginia.

[2] Hartford *American Mercury,* October 16, 1800.

own satisfaction that the scheme was organized on the British and not the French plan. It arrived [3] at this mainly by saying that the Alien Act kept whites out of the South, which made possible a Negro conspiracy,[4] and that that act was passed because the British wanted to hold the Irish at home.[5]

At about the same time Federalist newspapers published letters purportedly from South Carolina telling of great alarm there in consequence of a rebellion comprising, according to varying estimates, anywhere from seven hundred to six thousand Negroes.[6] These, according to the Republican press,[7] were forgeries, and the entire story was labelled " *wholly false.*" That appears to be the fact, for nothing [8] has been found to substantiate the stories, told in considerable detail, of rebellion in South Carolina in 1800.

3 Philadelphia *Aurora*, September 23, 25, 26, 1800.

4 On the other hand a Federalist member of the Virginia House of Delegates, George Keith Taylor, argued in favor of the Alien measure in December, 1798, for " he claimed that the Alien Law was particularly calculated for the protection of the Southern States, because French aliens had already attempted to incite the slaves to insurrection "—Henry H. Simms, *Life of John Taylor*, p. 79.

5 William Cobbett, at the moment an arch-conservative, was persuaded that part of the French plan to revolutionize the world depended upon the United Irishmen in conjunction with free Negroes, slaves, and " Jacobin" slaveholders. The conviction was announced to the world May, 1798, but, with peculiar restraint, Mr. Cobbett added, " I do not take it upon me to say that these preparatory steps have been taken...." *Porcupine's Works*, VIII, pp. 199, 224-25.

6 See the letter from William Vans Murray to John Quincy Adams, dated The Hague, December 9, 1800, reporting the " news " in recently received American papers, in W. C. Ford, ed., " Letters of William Vans Murray to John Quincy Adams, 1797-1803," *Annual Report of the American Historical Association for 1912*, p. 663.

7 Hartford *American Mercury*, October 16, 1800.

8 The only item possibly hinting at trouble is an ordinance passed in July, 1800 by the city of Charleston requiring all hired slaves to wear an identifying badge, and the master of a hired slave to pay a fee of ten dollars a year. If the slave were discovered without the tag he was to be whipped and his master was to be fined ten dollars—Charleston *City Gazette*, July 18, 1800.

A similar flavor pervades a letter sent from Charleston by a native of Massachusetts to friends in Salem in 1808, when sectional and political feeling was quite intense. Wrote the Federalist: [9]

> I am quite tired of this Jacobinical place. They talk a great deal about hanging and driving (poor devils! fit only for slave drivers) the people of Massachusetts into Nova Scotia. They talk big of patriotism, the rights of man, &c. in this region of slavery! There has not been a night this week, without alarms of fires and murders; and the panic has become so great, they were last night obliged to order three detachments of Infantry, and part of the horse from several companies, to guard the city; and should the embargo continue another year, I believe that the poor will stir up such commotions, that they will find the whole militia, instead of detachments, necessary for that purpose. I can only say, God of his infinite mercy grant that my dear native Massachusetts may always be as unlike as possible this country of Jacobinism and slavery.

This letter aroused discussion, protest, and agitation, but the specific remarks about servile unrest were not denied. Yet, in the absence of other confirmatory evidence, it is dangerous to accept the statement from this prejudiced correspondent at its face value.

Again, in 1810, a Federalist newspaper, the Philadelphia *Gazette,* reported a slave rebellion in the neighborhood of Richmond, Virginia, giving the names of the victims in several families and stating that the uprising had been suppressed by militia. A Boston paper of the same leanings, the Columbian *Centenel,* referred to this report but admitted that papers and letters from Richmond were " entirely silent on the event." The Republican *General Advertiser* (Aurora) of Philadelphia, however, denied in toto the story, and said the members of the families concerned were amazed to learn, prematurely, of their deaths. " For what purpose such a rumor was circulated, we

9 Charleston *City Gazette*, February 17, 1808, in John H. Wolfe, *Jeffersonian Democracy in South Carolina*, p. 233.

cannot conceive—at least, any honest or useful purpose." [10] In this case, however, there does exist proof, which will appear later, of the existence of a slave conspiracy in Virginia at the time, though the account of an actual outbreak seems to have had no basis in fact.

It has been shown that distortion and exaggeration, for political motives, played a part in the panic over the extensive slave conspiracies of 1856 and 1860, both coming in years of terrific excitement; the latter in the months just preceding and following, a presidential election whose result would touch off a counter-revolutionary effort on the part of the slaveocracy. The sensational accounts of amazing quantities of poison being found among Texas slaves, and of the total destruction by incendiaries of town after town in the same State are particularly questionable—though the result in swinging black bodies is certain.

It is not denied that conspiracies and outbreaks did occur but it is affirmed, as was affirmed by anti-secession papers, and anti-secession leaders, like General Sam Houston [11] himself, and even by an occasional Breckenridge paper,[12] that often those that did occur were grossly exaggerated, and that probably some were created out of whole cloth in order, by mass hysteria, to forge unity around the Southern extremists, and to attach the stigma of midnight assassin to all opponents of that clique.

Ulterior motives, other than that of political advantage, occasionally led to false alarms. In some cases monetary gain seems to have been sought by people anxious to buy slaves at reduced prices that immediately followed considerable alarms.[13]

10 Philadelphia *General Advertiser (Aurora)*, July 2, 1810; Boston *Columbia Centinel*, July 4, 1810.

11 See *Principia*, N. Y., November 10, 1860, quoting the Louisville *Democrat*; N. Y. *Tribune*, editorial, September 15, 1860; *Brownlow's Knoxville Whig*, November 7, 1860; Clement Eaton, *op. cit.*, pp. 103-104.

12 Memphis *Daily Avalanche*, December 10, 1860, quoted by C. Eaton, *op. cit.*, p. 105.

13 Thus, early in 1832 in North Carolina was formed the Nash County Humane and Slave Protecting Society whose purposes were three-fold: 1. to

Another alleged motive appears in a letter from a member of the Virginia Senate, John James Maund, to Colonel Robert Carter, dated Richmond, November 9, 1793 : [14]

You must, I doubt not, sir, have heard of the fancied negro insurrections of which so much has been said in Virginia. They orginate in the minds of the worse of men for the worst of purposes, namely that of arresting the gentle arm of humanity, which either is, or may be outstretched for the relief of the slaves and with a design of procuring a repeal of the laws authorizing their manumission. But in this they will fail, as I know of no more virtuous body of men in the world than that of which I have the happiness to be a member, and whose opinions I well know on the subject.

Reprehensible motives of an unspecified nature were held responsible by a North Carolina newspaper for a farcical occurrence in that State in 1802, following the discovery of a serious plot. The rumor spread in Windsor that the town of Winton had been demolished by slaves, and at the same time the folks of Winton heard the same story about Windsor. Each town sent a messenger to the other to learn the exact extent of the damage, and the couriers met on the road to learn the truth! Said the Raleigh *Register* of July 6: "Altho' a vigilance on all occasions is truly laudable and praise-worthy, yet it would be highly commendable to trace the authors of such false reports

detect and suppress sources of disaffection; 2. to scrutinize the slaves' conduct and keep in touch with slaveholders throughout the State; 3. to prevent "the indiscriminate and unceremonious sacrifice of slaves by the white population acting under the influence of excitements, regardless of the truth or falsity of any reported insurrection—fabricated or circulated to lessen the prices of slaves or for any other purpose"—Tarborough *Free Press*, January 31, 1832, in R. H. Taylor, "Slave conspiracies in North Carolina," *North Carolina Historical Review*, 1928, V, p. 33. During the Turner excitement four white men were jailed in North Carolina for maliciously circulating false rumors of slave uprisings—N. Y. *Evening Post*, October 29, 1831.

14 In *William and Mary College Quarterly*, XX (1), p. 275. The evidence of conspiracy in 1793 in Virginia is, however, very good, as will appear. In 1805 the State of Virginia tightened her liberal manumission act of 1782 by requiring freed Negroes to leave the State—H. T. Catterall, *op. cit.*, I, p. 73.

and severely punish those who, from base and unprincipled motives, should dare to invent them." [15]

Mystery, indeed, surrounds the reasons for the invention of
a report of rebellion amongst slaves in Nashville, Tennessee in
1836. A letter [16] written on the stationery of a business firm,
J. and R. Yeatman and Company, of that city and mailed to
Philadelphia, told in stirring detail of burning buildings, rebelling slaves, and fleeing masters, though nothing of the kind
occurred and the letter was proven to be a hoax.

A South Carolina lady, however, who raised the cry, "the
negroes have risen—we shall all be killed" and created much
commotion had a plain motive. A friends of hers, with her
knowledge and consent, shot and killed her husband. The dear
lady, after the event, ascribed it to a slave revolt, and even named
a specific Negro as the one responsible for her spouse's demise.
But the court acquitted Edom, and found [17] Mrs. Green "guilty
of being an accessory before the fact."

Fear itself, of course, created exaggeration so that the figures
concerning the number of rebels or victims given in first reports were usually greater than those finally given. Indeed, at
times, entire communities were reported as wiped out, and days
went by before the rumors were shown to be false. This was the
case, for example, in the stories of the destruction of Wilmington, North Carolina, following the Turner outbreak.[18]

With the exceptions noted above, however, it was a practice
of the rulers of the South to censor news of slave unrest. Specific admissions and evidences of this are numerous and will
appear in the course of the narrative. Some instances may be

15 See G. G. Johnson, *op. cit.*, p. 510.

16 N. Y. *Courier and Inquirer*, February 19, 1836, in *The Liberator*,
February 29, 1836.

17 H. Catterall, ed., *op. cit.*, II, p. 362. The lady was convicted in 1836.

18 W. B. Lewis to Martin Van Buren, dated Washington, Sept. 17, 1831:
"It is said that Wilmington, No Carolina, has been burnt by the blacks,
and 18 persons killed. Much confidence is reposed in this information—a
few days will test its correctness."—Van Buren Papers, Lib. of Cong. See
also, Niles' *Weekly Register*, Sept. 17, 24, 1831, XLI, 35, 67.

presented here, in order to show the problem facing the investigator.[19]

The editor of the influential Richmond *Enquirer,* for example, had promised at first to carry full accounts of the slave upheavals shaking the West Indies coincident with the French Revolution, and to print the proclamations and statements of the Negro leaders.[20]

A brief experience revealed, however, that such a promise was not in harmony with the feelings and sentiments of Virginia, which had already decided upon a policy of studied silence upon the subjects of negroes and negro slavery. Accordingly his promises were never kept, and he expressed the wish that no one would demand the reason.

Again, a Charleston paper in reporting the arguments of State Senator Barnwell against reopening the slave trade in 1803 stated that these included the assertion that it would lower the prices of cotton and of slaves. Moreover, " The Hon. member adduced in support of his opinion various other arguments,

19 G. G. Johnson aptly characterizes the attitude of the press generally when she writes: " In North Carolina, as elsewhere in the United States and especially in the South, the opinion prevailed that the chief significance of local news was the opinion of the well-born concerning it. An editor deliberately withheld local news if he thought that he might offend the delicate sensibilities of the gentry by publishing it "—*op. cit.,* p. 781. Note also the remarks in F. A. Kemble's *Journal of a Residence on a Georgian Plantation,* pp. 300-301 : " He [her husband] told me too, what interested me very much, of a conspiracy among Mr. C——'s slaves some years ago. I cannot tell you about it now ... It is wonderful to me that such attempts are not being made the whole time among these people to regain their liberty ; probably because many are made ineffectually, and never known beyond the limits of the plantation where they take place." The Mr. C referred to was the wealthy John Couper who owned " Hopeton " and " Cannon's Point " plantations in Georgia, and is referred to by R. B. Flanders as a " model planter." — *Plantation Slavery In Georgia,* pp. 101-103. See M. Armstrong, *Fanny Kemble,* p. 244.

20 C. H. Ambler, *Thomas Ritchie,* pp. 136-37. It is to be noted, however, that the bi-weekly paper, the Fredericksburg *Virginia Herald,* was filled with reports and official announcements concerning these events. See the issues of 1802-1804, *passim.*

still more cogent and impressive, which from reasons very obvious we decline making public." As Phillips stated,[21] " It may be surmised that the suppressed remarks dealt with the danger of slave revolts."

James Monroe, Governor of Virginia during the Gabriel conspiracy in the summer of 1800, told[22] the Speakers of the General Assembly, in detailing his precautionary measures, that during the first twenty-four hours he had " endeavored to give the affair as little importance as the measures necessary for defence would permit," and that he had " hoped it would even pass unnoticed by the community." The extent of the plot, and particularly the fact that the rebel leaders were not immediately captured, made the desired secrecy impossible.

The Governor of Mississippi Territory, William C. C. Claiborne, while informing[23] the leading planters of this momentous event in Virginia and urging the adoption of special precautionary measures, did not fail to advise them against discussing the occurrence. He strongly adverted to

the impolicy of unnecessarily alarming *them* [the slaves] by informations upon a *subject* which mild and wise Treatment may happily long keep from their Views and wishes.

Violent assaults upon the overseers of Mr. Lintots and Mr. Moores slaves, and the severally wounding one or both, I believe may be *judiciously* urged as the motive for the extraordinary Circumspection in the present Moment, and to Completely enforce the Law against the Slaves retaining any kind of Weapons.

21 Charleston *Courier*, Dec. 26, 1803; U. B. Phillips, *American Negro Slavery*, pp. 136-37. It is amusing to observe that papers during the War of 1812 often reported the flight of slaves by using anything but the words slaves and Negroes, occasionally substituting therefor even stars and dashes —Richmond *Enquirer*, July 13, 1813.

22 Monroe's account is dated Dec. 5, 1800, in S. M. Hamilton, ed., *The Writings of James Monroe*, III, p. 236.

23 D. Rowland, ed., *Mississippi Territorial Archives*, I, pp. 311-12. The letter, dated Nov. 18, 1800, was printed and sent to about one hundred slaveholders.

A North Carolinian who had been informed of this plot by a private source wrote to his brother three weeks after the day of its discovery,[24] " Tho' nothing of this has transpired in the papers, it comes in a way that cannot be doubted." The Charleston press noticed the event but once, eight weeks after its occurrence, and that was for the purpose of recording,[25] in about seventy-five words, the executions of several of the rebels, never mentioning that Negroes were the subject of the story.

A Norfolk, Virginia, newspaper [26] finally broke its silence concerning a slave conspiracy within its own borders after, as it stated, its ramifications had been disclosed and the leaders punished. And while its account of unrest in North Carolina at about the same time was more full, since the scene of the action was more distant, even here one notes sentences like: " The particulars, we are constrained to observe, must be withheld for the present, from motives of precaution. It may not, however, be improper to remark that too much vigilance cannot be used in our own neighborhood."

Censorship even reached government bodies, as, for example, when the Virginia Council on December 20, 1808 advised the Governor, John Tyler, against informing the legislature, even in closed session, of a current slave conspiracy, since he had already ordered the adoption of precautionary measures.[27] A secret session of the legislature convened for the purpose of imparting such alarming news would " probably increase the spirit of insurrection among the slaves." The Council's advice was followed.

In 1830, however, the North Carolina legislature was secretly convened in order to devise means of subduing the dangerous

24 Letter by Charles W. Harris, dated Halifax, September 18, 1800, in H. M. Wagstaff, ed., " The Harris Letters," *The James Sprunt Historical Publications*, XIV, p. 32.

25 Charleston *City Gazette*, October 22, 1800.

26 Norfolk *Herald*, May 13, June 10, 1802, in the Fredericksburg *Virginia Herald*, May 18, June 15, 1802; and the N. Y. *Evening Post*, June 18, 1802.

27 Executive Papers, Virginia State Library. The Governor was the future President's father.

disaffection of the Negro population. This, according to one contemporary,[28] plus the fact that the newspapers " afford no clue " as to the truth of the matter, tended to heighten, rather than allay, the fear of the public, which had vague forebodings of trouble over which to brood but no clear knowledge of the state of affairs. In this case greater publicity was advised, but the time-honored technique of secrecy was followed.

In any number of cases one finds admissions from Southern newspapers that their coverage of this feature of current events was something other than complete, even if the matters were not of local origin. One sees such words or phrases as " we dislike to allude," [29] " we have refrained," [30] " we forbear," [31] ject. As already noted, even these hints were sometimes absent and there was complete silence, so far as the press of the region was concerned.[33] Thus, one must depend frequently upon government archives, personal letters (sometimes published in distant newspapers), journals, diaries, and court records in an attempt to piece together the story.

Typical is the diary entry of Edmund Ruffin under date of September 5, 1860. Mr. Ruffin, while on a train en route from Louisville to Frankfort, Kentucky, struck up a conversation

28 Calvin Jones to Governor John Owen, dated Wake Forest, December 28, 1830, in Governor's Papers, vol. 60, North Carolina Historical Commission.

29 Augusta, Ga., *Dispatch*, quoted in *The Liberator*, August 24, 1860.

30 New Orleans, *Daily Picayune*, December 7, 9, 1856.

31 Easton, Md., *Gazette*, in *The Genius of Universal Emancipation*, Washington, July, 1830, p. 52.

taking particular notice of, or discussing the " delicate " [32] sub-

32 " Delicate " was a favorite word. See item dated New Orleans, October 7, in N. Y. *Eve. Post*, November 7, 1826; New Orleans *Daily Picayune*, December 23, 24, 1856; Milledgeville, Ga., *Federal Union*, December 23, 1856, in U. B. Phillips, *Plantation and Frontier Documents, op. cit.*, II, p. 116.

33 See the report of the Georgetown, S. C. plot of 1829 (corroborated from other sources) in the N. Y. *Eve. Post*, August 28, 1829 (quoting the New Haven *Advertiser*, and based upon a letter received by a resident of Connecticut from a friend in Georgetown) preceded by the remark that it " is news to us. The Southern papers do not notice the circumstance."

with Mr. J. J. Hooper, editor of a pro-Breckenridge paper, the
Montgomery, Alabama, *Mail*. Talk turned, as it inevitably did,
to the slaves, and the evidences of unrest that were, at the moment, so widespread. Wrote the diarist: [34]

He told me of much that has not entered the newspapers in
which indeed there has been very little said, either of statement
or comment, of the abolition and incendiary doings in the south.
[Here follows a short clipping from the Petersburg, Virginia, *Express* on current plots.] Mr. Hooper tells me that like discoveries
have been made in different parts of Alabama—& that the infur-
iated inhabitants have in sundry cases executed summary vengeance (or justice, if not mistaken), on the detected culprits, white
& black.

During the Civil War, as one would expect, and as an authority has written,[35] the Confederate Government " tended to
. . . suppress and minimize reports of misconduct and insubordination " among the slave population. An inkling of what,
concretely, this meant may be gained from the letter [36] of a lady
in Charleston, South Carolina, dated November 23, 1861. This
declared that the greatest fear of the inhabitants was of slave
rebellion.

No general insurrection has taken place, though several revolts
have been attempted; two quite recently, and in these cases whole
families were murdered before the slaves were subdued. Then came
retaliation of the most fearful character. . . This news is suppressed
as far as possible, and kept entirely from the papers, for the negroes

34 MS. Diary of Edmund Ruffin, IV, Library of Congress.

35 B. I. Wiley, *op. cit.*, p. 62.

36 Printed in the Philadelphia *Inquirer*, November 30, 1861 and *The
Liberator*, December 20, 1861. The authenticity of this letter is not certain.
Some corroboration of trouble in South Carolina in 1861 will be offered later,
but the statement about the wiping out of several families has not been seen
elsewhere, and it is difficult to believe that that would have been the case
were the report completely accurate. The reputation of the Philadelphia
Inquirer for truthfulness was not enviable — See C. Sandburg, *Abraham
Lincoln, The War Years*, III, pp. 42-3.

hear what is published if they do not read it, and such examples might produce disastrous consequences.

Faced with these difficulties and uncertainties the present writer has attempted to exercise caution in handling reports of conspiracies and rebellions. An attempt has also been made to make the coverage of the subject as intensive and extensive as possible for it was observed early in the course of the investigation that pertinent material appeared in the most unexpected and widely-scattered sources. Yet, it is highly probable that all plots, and quite possibly even all actual outbreaks, that did occur, and that are, somewhere, on record, have *not* been uncovered. And the subject is of such a nature that it appears almost certain that some, perhaps many, occurred and were never recorded. The narration that follows is not, then, offered, as definitive, in the sense of being complete and subject to no alterations and additions, but an attempt has been made to make it as full and as accurate as the subject appears to permit.

CHAPTER VIII

EARLY PLOTS AND REBELLIONS

A SLAVE state offered the following definition of the term slave insurrection:[1] " By ' insurrection of slaves ' is meant an assemblage of three or more, with arms, with intent to obtain their liberty by force." Were one to follow this definition literally the number of slave insurrections and conspiracies within the present borders of the United States would be huge, certainly reaching several hundreds.

In this study, however, the tests for insurrection or conspiracy are more severe. The elements of the definition herein subscribed to are: a minimum of ten slaves involved; freedom as the apparent aim of the disaffected slaves; contemporary references labelling the event as an uprising, plot, insurrection, or the equivalent of these terms. The study, moreover, excludes, with a few exceptions, the scores of outbreaks and plots that occurred upon domestic or foreign slave-traders.[2]

Observing such restrictions, the author has found records of approximately two hundred and fifty revolts and conspiracies in the history of American Negro slavery.[3] Two additional facts of particular interest appear from the study. These are, first, that occasionally the plans or aspirations of the rebels were actually *reported* as going beyond a desire for personal freedom

1 In an act passed February 12, 1858—*General Laws of the 7th Legislature of the State of Texas*, p. 175.

2 For material on revolts aboard boats see Harvey Wish, " Slave insurrections before 1861," in *The Journal of Negro History* (1937), XXII, pp. 300-306; Elizabeth Donnan, ed., *Documents Illustrative of the History of the Slave Trade to America, passim.*

3 There are, in addition, a few references to undated plots, besides that mentioned by Kemble—*ante*, p. 156. See a communication by R. R. Hoes in *The New York Genealogical and Biographical Record* (1890), XXI, pp. 162-63; Benjamin Drew, *A North-Side View of Slavery*, p. 239; Philip A. Bruce, *Institutional History of Virginia in the 17th Century*, I, pp. 625-26; J. B. O'Neall and J. A. Chapman, *The Annals of Newberry* [*S. C.*], part 2, p. 501; J. A. Redpath, *The Roving Editor*, pp. 269-83.

and envisioning, in addition, a property redistribution; and, second, that white people were frequently implicated—or believed to be implicated—with the slaves in the plans or efforts to overthrow the master class by force.

The first settlement within the present borders of the United States to contain Negro slaves was the locale of the first slave revolt.[4] A Spanish colonizer, Lucas Vasquez de Ayllon, founded, in the summer of 1526, a community whose probable location was at or near the mouth of the Pedee River in what is now South Carolina. The settlement consisted of about five hundred Spaniards and one hundred Negro slaves. Trouble soon beset it. Illness caused numerous deaths, carrying off, in October, Ayllon himself. Internal dissension arose, and the Indians grew increasingly suspicious and hostile. Finally, probably in November, several of the slaves rebelled, and fled to the Indians. The next month what was left of the adventurers, some one hundred and fifty souls, returned to Haiti, leaving the rebel Negroes with their Indian friends—as the first permanent inhabitants,[5] other than the Indians, in what was to be the United States.

Negro slave plots are not reported in English America until the latter part of the seventeenth century, and those that did occur in that century were generally centered in Virginia. It was moreover, not until the early years of the eighteenth century that the uprisings and conspiracies appear to have been of considerable importance or frequent occurrence. This is probably due to the fact that there were few Negroes in the prescribed limits until about 1680, Virginia itself having but three hundred in 1649, and only two thousand in 1670, about five per cent of the colony's population.[6] It was not until 1660 that

4 Woodbury Lowery, *The Spanish Settlements Within the Present Limits of the United States, 1513-1561*, pp. 165-67; J. C. Carroll, *op. cit.*, p. 13.

5 Unless one accepts the conclusions of Leo Wiener, that Negroes were in the New World long before Columbus—*Africa and the Discovery of America, passim.*

6 L. C. Gray, *History of Agriculture in the Southern United States to 1860*, p. 1025, table 39.

the latter government actually declared them to be slaves.[7] Staple crop production was largely confined in the seventeenth century to tobacco raising in Virginia and even this was mainly handled by white indentured servants until approximately 1675. It was not until the third decade of the next century that other staple crops, rice and indigo, became important, and led to the spread of the plantation system to the Carolinas.[8]

By 1715 one-third of the population of Virginia, the Carolinas, and Maryland (Georgia had no slavery—legally—until 1750) were slaves, i. e., 46,700 out of 123,510.[9] Within five years Negro importation became important in Louisiana also, so that from 1720 to 1731 about seven thousand slaves had been brought into that area although due to abominable conditions there were less than thirty-five hundred alive in the latter year.[10] By 1754 when the plantation system, based principally on crops of rice, tobacco, and indigo, (cotton and sugar became important about forty-five years later) was well established, over thirty-six per cent of the population of the five southern English colonies, Georgia, South Carolina, North Carolina, Virginia, and Maryland, were Negro slaves, i. e., 222,000 out of 609,000.[11]

So far as is known, the first serious conspiracy involving Negro slaves in English America [12] occurred in Virginia in 1663,

7 W. W. Hening, *Statutes at Large of Virginia*, I, p. 540, II, p. 26; H. T. Catterall, ed., *Judicial Cases Concerning the Negro and American Slavery*, I, p. 50.

8 L. C. Gray, *op. cit.*, I, pp. 308-309; P. A. Bruce, *Economic History of Virginia in the 17th Century*, II, p. 57; U. B. Phillips, *American Negro Slavery*, p. 75.

9 L. Gray, *op. cit.*, II, p. 1025.

10 *Ibid.*, I, p. 335.

11 As note 9. Figures in text on Maryland (I, p. 348), do not agree with those in this table.

12 Reference here is made only to that part of English America that was to form the United States. There had been a formidable rebellion of Negro slaves in the ill-fated Puritan settlement called Old Providence on the coast of Nicaragua—see W. N. Sainsbury, ed., *Calendar of State Papers, 1574-*

during a period of " suffering, poverty and discontent." [13] Information concerning this event is scanty. It is, however, clear that indentured white servants and Negro slaves in Gloucester County had jointly conspired to rebel, overthrow their masters, and secure their freedom. A man by the name of Berkenhead, probably a white indentured servant, betrayed the plot, and this soon led to the display of several bloody heads from local chimney tops.

The informer was given his freedom and a reward of five thousand pounds of tobacco, a treatment which, it was hoped, would encourage future betrayals. The legislature " resolved that the 13th of September be annually kept holy, being the day those villains intended to put the plot into execution." [14]

Considerable open discontent flared among the slaves of Virginia in 1672. This does not seem to have been an organized rebellion, but, as appears from an act passed that year by the Assembly, an attempt of fugitive slaves to form small armed groups in various sections of the colony and to harrass neigh-

---

1660, pp. 229, 271, 295; A. P. Newton, *The Colonizing Activities of the English Puritans*, p. 261. There is evidence of a local uprising in Virginia as early as 1644, for the entry in the Council's minutes for September 3 reads: " Concerning the riotous & rebellious conduct of Mrs. *Wormleys* negroes; " while for September 10 appear the words: "Persons apprehended for rebellion (Perhaps Mrs. *Wormleys* Servants Sept. 3d)." H. R. McIlwaine, *Minutes of the Council and General Court of Colonial Virginia 1622-1632, 1670-1676*, p. 502. In the spring of 1657 Indians aided by some Negro slaves created havoc in Hartford, Connecticut by burning down several buildings—see petition of Mrs. Elinor Howell to the Connecticut General Assembly, dated May 5, 1663, in " The Wyllys Papers," *Collections of the Connecticut Historical Society*, XXI, pp. 137-38. I am indebted to Dr. Lorenzo J. Greene for bringing this item to my attention.

13 Thomas J. Wertenbaker, *The Planters of Colonial Virginia*, p. 96, see also, pp. 33, 49, 91-99. This author points out that exiled Puritans and Oliverians were among the indentured servants who rebelled. See also, William E. Dodd, *The Old South*, pp. 156, 182, 195.

14 Hening, *op. cit.*, I, p. 204; Phillips, *op. cit.*, p. 472. J. C. Carroll, *op. cit.*, p. 13, says the traitor was a Negro slave, but the evidence tends to indicate that he was an indentured servant, probably white. In an earlier work, the present writer made the same mistake—*Negro Slave Revolts in the United States, 1526-1860*, pp. 17-18.

boring plantations, at the same time creating bases to which others might flee. In the words of the enactment,[15]

Forasmuch as it hath beene manifested to this grand assembly that many negroes have lately beene, and now are out in rebellion in sundry parts of this country, and that noe means have yet beene found for the apprehension and suppression of them from whom many mischiefes of very dangerous consequences may arise to the country if either other negroes, Indians or servants should happen to fly forth and joyne with them.

the House of Burgesses therefore urged their capture by force, and announced that no punishment would fall upon any who might kill these outlaws.

What appears to have been a large-scale conspiracy disturbed the Northern Neck region of Virginia in 1687. The extermination of the white people was planned, but the scheme was uncovered, the leaders arrested, and executed. According to a contemporary living in Westmoreland County the plot was entered into during the mass funerals which slaves were permitted to hold. As a result the Council banned public slave funerals.[16]

The next year a Maryland slave, Sam, belonging to Richard Metcalfe, was tried as the leader behind conspiracies aimed at rebellion. The only detail that has been recorded is the fact that

15 Hening, op. cit., II, p. 299; P. A. Bruce, Economic History. op. cit., II, p. 115. In June, 1680 provision was again made for the hunting down and killing of maroons in Virginia—Hening, op. cit., II, p. 481.

16 H. McIlwaine, ed., Executive Journals, Council of the Colony of Virginia, I, pp. 85-87; John Burke, The History of Virginia, II, p. 300; P. A. Bruce, Institutional History, I, p. 672; James C. Ballagh, A History of Slavery in Virginia, p. 79; U. B. Phillips, op. cit., p. 472; J. C. Carroll, op. cit., p. 14. Burke, Ballagh, and Carroll declared that in this year the Negroes formed about one-half the population. Figures are not available for the year, but this percentage appears to be much too high. As shown, in 1670 they formed but 5% of the population, while in 1715 (as Ballagh, p. 12, himself correctly states) there were 23,000 Negroes and 72,500 whites in Virginia. The peninsula jutting into Chesapeake Bay and bounded by the Potomac on the north and the Rappahannock on the south is the Northern Neck.

this Negro was convicted of having " several times endeavored to promote a Negro Insurrection in this Colony." For this he was severely beaten and forced to wear, for life, " a strong iron collar affixed about his neck " with death the penalty for its removal.[17]

There are rather vague indications of trouble in the 1690's in several of the colonies. In 1690 a mysterious Mr. Isaac Morrill of New Jersey came to Newbury, Massachusetts and is supposed to have attempted to get the few Negro, and probably more numerous Indian, slaves to flee to the French in Canada and then join the latter in an attack upon the English.[18] At least one Negro, James, a slave of a Mr. Dole, and one Indian, Joseph, slave of a Mr. Moody, as well as another Jerseyman, George Major, were implicated, but their fate is not known.

A slave by the name of Mingoe, who had fled from his master in Middlesex County, Virginia, gathered an unspecified number of followers and ravaged plantations, particularly in Rappahannock County. These Negroes, according to an item of November 9, 1691,[19] not only appropriated cattle and hogs, but, what was more disturbing, had recently taken " two guns, a Carbyne & other things." What became of them is not recorded.

A strongly-worded proclamation issued three years later by Governor Andros of Virginia, condemned the remissness with which the acts to prevent servile rebellion had generally been enforced,[20] " in consequence of which, negroes had run together in certain parts of the Colony, causing assemblages so dangerous as to threaten the peace of the whole community." He de-

17 *William and Mary College Quarterly Historical Magazine*, X, p. 177.

18 This is based upon an account in Joshua Coffin, *A Sketch of the History of Newbury, Newburyport, and West Newbury from 1636 to 1845*, pp. 153-54. No contemporary account has been seen.

19 MS. Order Book, Middlesex County, 1680-1694, pp. 526-27 (Va. St. Lib.) ; P. A. Bruce, *Economic History*, II, p. 116.

20 MS. Record of York County, 1694-1697, pp. 22-23; Bruce, *ibid.*, II, p. 118. Similar trouble is reported from Accomack County in 1694—See Susie M. Ames, *op. cit.*, p. 99.

manded strict enforcement of precautionary measures, and ordered that his proclamation be read in churches, at militia meetings and all large public gatherings. Other hints of concern during these same years come from Maryland and South Carolina.[21]

Evidences of unrest of apparently a minor nature come from South Carolina and New York in 1702. On September 9 of that year there appeared before the Commons House of Assembly of the former Colony " Capt Wm Davis and Capt wilkinson [who] Informed this House of a negro man of mr John williamson's who is now in Irons at his masters House for threatning that he with other negroes would Rise and Cutt off the Inhabitants of this Province." The slave was ordered brought before the House, but further information concerning him is not available. The House did, however, on that same day reprimand the constables of Charles Town for alleged negligence in their control of the slaves. It demanded, too, that a Mr. William Harvey of that city be checked from " Suffering Caballs of negroes at his house on ye Neck called ye Rat Trap," and recommended,[22] finally, that the Governor issue a proclamation " to enforce the act for the better ordering of Slaves to be more punctually observed."   The preamble to an act passed by New York in November, 1702, indicates that all was not docility amongst the slaves. This "Act for Regulateing of Slaves," which contained provisions against permitting the assemblage of slaves or accepting their testimony in court, was enacted in [23]

21 Jeffrey R. Brackett, *The Negro in Maryland*, p. 92; H. M. Henry, *The Police Control of the Slave in South Carolina*, p. 148.

22 A. S. Salley, ed., *Journals of the Commons House of Assembly of South Carolina for 1702*, pp. 99-100. A plot of Indian slaves had been crushed in South Carolina in 1700. The nearest date for which approximate population figures are available is 1708, at which time there were 9,580 people in South Carolina, 2,900 being Negroes—Verner W. Crane, *The Southern Frontier*, p. 113. In May, 1702 the Council of Virginia authorized the Governor to levy forces for slave or servant insurrection as well as for war—W. P. Palmer, ed., *Calendar of Virginia State Papers*, I, p. 79.

23 A. J. Northrup, *Slavery in New York*, Albany, 1900, pp. 260-61. J. T. Scharf has declared that the rebellion of the poorer classes in Maryland in

" as much as the Number of slaves in the Citty of New York and Albany, and also in other Towns within this Province, doth daily increase, and that they have been found oftentimes guilty of Confederating together in running away, or other ill practices."

Early in 1708 a small group of slaves in Newton, Long Island, rebelled and killed seven whites. Four slaves, including an Indian and a woman, were executed, the men being hanged and the woman burned. As a result of this event, in October, 1708, a new regulation aimed at " preventing the Conspiracy of Slaves " was passed allowing Justices to sentence rebels to be executed in any way or manner they might think most likely to secure public tranquillity.[24]

As the early years of the eighteenth century pass on, and the sociological and economic changes occur that have previously been noted, slave rebellions and conspiracies become more numerous and more serious. Thus, a plot of this nature was discovered early in 1709 in Surry, James City, and Isle of Wight Counties, Virginia, involving Indian as well as Negro slaves. A special court of investigation was appointed by the Governor in Council to look into this matter. On March 24 this court returned with the results of [25]

ye Examination of Sevll Negroes and Indian slaves concerned in a Late Dangerous Conspiracy, formed and carried on by greate num-

1705 was participated in by some Negro slaves, but substantiation of this elsewhere has not been seen—*History of Maryland*, I, p. 375.

24 E. B. O'Callaghan, ed., *Documents Relative to the Colonial History of the State of New York*, V, p. 39—Lord Cornbury to Board of Trade, dated February 10, 1707/8. Probably because of the manner of dating customary at the time, this outbreak has occasionally been erroneously placed in 1707, as by William Dunlap, *History of the New Netherlands*, II, pp. clv-clvi; Stephen M. Ostrander, *A History of the City of Brooklyn*, I, p. 171. The evidence of trouble with slaves in Kings County, New York in 1706 has previously been presented, *ante*, p. 72.

25 *C. V. S. P.*, I, p. 129. On March 21, 1709, Lt. Gov. Jenings had issued a proclamation " to prevent negro slaves assembling together "—C. Headlam, ed., *Calendar of State Papers, Colonial Series 1710–June 1711*, p. 238; H. R. McIlwaine, ed., *op. cit.*, III, pp. 234-35.

bers of ye said negroes and Indian slaves for making their Escape by force from ye Service of their masters, and for ye Destroying and cutting off Such of her Majesties Subjects as Should oppose their Design.

By the time this report had been submitted an unspecified number of slaves had already been " punished [in what way is not stated] and Discharged," but three others, Scipio, Salvadore, and Tom Shaw, believed to be " the Principal Contrivers and most remarkable in ye aforesaid Conspiracy " were still in confinement. Their ultimate fate is not known. Another leader, named Peter and owned by a Mr. Samuel Thompson, eluded capture.

Peter remained free at least one year, for in April, 1710, a reward of ten pounds was offered for his capture, alive, and five pounds for his dead body.[26] This notice was issued in the midst of another serious conspiracy, in Surry and James City Counties, involving only Negro slaves. The plot was betrayed by Will, slave of Robert Ruffin of Surry, an act which led the legislature to purchase, for forty pounds, his freedom, as both " a reward of his fidelity and for encouragement of such services." [27]

Lieutenant-Governor Jening's report to the Lords of Trade, written in April, 1710,[28] is the best available evidence on this episode :

There hath of late been very happily discovered an intended insurrection of the negroes, which was to have been put in execution in Surry and James City Countys on Easter Day ; but the chief

26 H. R. McIlwaine, ed., *op. cit.*, III, p. 236.

27 W. W. Hening, *op. cit.*, III, pp. 537-38.

28 In Headlam, ed., *op. cit.*, p. 83, Jening's letter is dated April 24, but in the bound volumes at the Virginia State Library entitled Virginia Manuscripts from the British Record Office, Sainsbury, VIII, p. 142, it is dated April 4. The latter source will, hereafter, be cited as Sainsbury. See Louis B. Wright and Marion Tinling, eds., *The Secret Diary of William Byrd*, pp. 167, 168.

conspirators having been seasonable apprehended, their design is broke. There are two of them tryed this General Court, found guilty, and will be executed, and I hope their fate will strike such terror in the other negroes as will keep them from forming such designs for the future, without being obliged to make an example of any more of them.

In June the two rebels were executed, an event which the Lords of Trade hoped would " serve as an example to deter any attempt of the like nature for the future." [29]

In the spring of 1711, the inhabitants of South Carolina were kept " in great terror and fear " by the activities of " several Negroes [who] keep out, armed, and robbing and plundering houses and plantations." These insurgents were led by a slave named Sebastian, and their activities appear to have been checked when he was finally tracked down and killed by an Indian hunter.[30]

29 Jenings to Lords of Trade, June 10, 1710; and Lords of Trade to Colonel Spotswood, August 28, 1710, in Sainsbury, VIII, pp. 153, 235; Headlam, *op. cit.*, p. 115. Philip A. Bruce in *A History of Virginia*, I, p. 301, says this plot was suppressed "without loss of life;" by this he must have meant the loss of the life of any white person. He also erroneously states that it was uncovered after Spotswood succeeded Jenings. Herbert L. Osgood has pointed out that Governor Spotswood's recommendation, in October, 1710, for a stronger militia "may have been suggested by recent disturbances among the slaves in three of the counties"—*The American Colonies in the Eighteenth Century*, II, p. 218.

30 [Edwin C. Holland], *A Refutation of the Calumnies...*, p. 63; David D. Wallace, *The History of South Carolina*, I, p. 372. On May 15, 1711, Governor Gibbes said to the South Carolina Assembly (Holland, *op. cit.*, pp. 28-29) : "And, Gentlemen, I desire you will consider the great quantities of negroes that are dayly brought into this government, and the small number of whites that comes amongst us, and how many are lately dead and gone off. How insolent and mischievous the negroes are become, and to consider the Negro Act already made, doth not reach up to some of the crimes they have lately been guilty of; therefore it might be convenient by some additional clause of said Negro Act to appoint either by gibbets, or some such like way, that, after executed, they may remain more exemplary, than any punishment hitherto hath been inflicted on them." The Governor went on to suggest the possibility that better food and clothing might also improve the behavior of the slaves.

A conspiracy was formed by Negro slaves in New York City on the first day of 1712, the plotters " tying themselves to secrecy by Sucking ye blood of each Others hand," and reassuring themselves by accepting a charm from a free Negro. Early in April, probably on the morning of the seventh, about twenty-five or thirty of these slaves, including two Indians, set fire to a building and, armed with a few guns, clubs, and knives, waited for the whites to approach. Several did, and were then attacked by the slaves who killed about nine men and seriously wounded five or six others.[31]

The alarm soon spread and soldiers hastened to the scene from the fort. In about twenty-four hours most of the rebels were captured. About six, however, were not, for [32] " one shot first his wife and then himself and some who had hid themselves in Town when they went to Apprehend them Cut their own throats." A newspaper correspondent, who had stated that the outbreak " has put us into no small consternation the whole Town being under Arms," later reported,[33] " we have about seventy Negro's in Custody, and 'tis fear'd that most of the Negro's here (who are very numerous) [34] knew of the late conspiracy to murder the Christians."

31 A good contemporary description will be found in the Boston *Weekly News-Letter*, April 7-14, 1712.

32 Letter by the Reverend John Sharpe, dated New York, June 23, 1712, in *The New York Genealogical and Biographical Record*, XXI, pp. 162-63.

33 Boston *Weekly News-Letter*, April 7-14, 14-21, 1712.

34 Population figures are unreliable and conflicting. Carl Bridenbaugh (*op. cit.*, p. 200) declares there were 750 Negroes in New York City in 1700, and about 1,600 in 1720; according to Northrup (*op. cit.*, p. 268) there were 1775 slaves and 10,551 whites in the City in 1712, but those figures are probably too high. Olsen (*op. cit.*, p. 106) places the approximate number at 1,100 slaves and 5,000 whites. It is certain, however, that the Negroes did form a substantial part of the total population. Later writers have pointed out that the English in 1712 were distraught over the failure of a campaign against the French in Canada in the fall of 1711, evidences of hostility on the part of the Iroquois, and fears of an attack upon them by the French, and have intimated that this may have had a causal relationship with the uprising. See Mary L. Booth, *History of the City of New York*, I, pp. 291-92; Martha J. Lamb, *History of the City of New York*, I, p. 495.

Twenty-seven slaves were condemned, but six, including a pregnant woman, were pardoned. Twenty-one, then, were executed and since the law of 1708 permitted any kind of punishment for this offense, the Governor was able to describe the modes of execution as follows: [35] " some were burnt others hanged, one broke on the wheele, and one hung a live in chains in the town, so that there has been the most exemplary punishment inflicted that could be possibly thought of . . .".

This outbreak moved the legislators of New York to enact in December, 1712, still another law " for preventing, Suppressing and punishing the Conspiracy and Insurrection of Negroes and other Slaves." The same event was also important in leading to a measure adopted by Massachusetts in 1713 forbidding further importation of slaves, and a Pennsylvania act of August, 1712, placing a high duty on Negroes, thus effectually discouraging their importation.[36]

Sometime in 1713 a slave plot was betrayed and crushed in South Carolina. According to a missionary working among the slaves and Indians, the prime mover in this conspiracy was a Negro recently imported from Martinique, but the reverend gentleman maintained [37] that those whom he had converted had taken no part in the subversive activity. An entry in the House

35 Governor Robert Hunter to Lords of Trade, June 23, 1712, in E. B. O'Callaghan, ed., *op. cit.*, V, pp. 341-42. At least two writers have erroneously referred to this event as a mere hoax, comparable, they write, to the plot in New York of 1741—Dunlap, *op. cit.*, I, p. 277; Michael Kraus, " Social classes and customs," in Alexander C. Flick, *History of the State of New York*, II, p. 408.

36 Northrup, *op. cit.*, p. 269; A. W. Lauber, *Indian Slavery*, p. 290; C. P. Keith, ed., *Chronicles of Pennsylvania*, II, p. 505; N. Y. *Weekly Tribune*, September 22, 1855. W. E. B. DuBois states that one of the causes " in all probability " of the Pennsylvania act of 1712 was the opposition of white workers to slave competition—*The Philadelphia Negro*, pp. 14-15.

37 Letter from the Reverend Francis Le Jau, January 22, 1714, in Edgar L. Pennington, " The Reverend Francis Le Jau's work among Indians and Negro slaves," in *The Journal of Southern History*, I, p. 458.

journal of the Colony dated May 11, 1715 gives the only other piece of evidence that has been seen concerning this: [38]

> The House being informed by Capt. David Davis, that a negro man of his had been and was the chief instrument in discovering a dangerous plot & conspiracy designed among the Negroes in Goose Creek quarters, about two years ago for which he was promised a reward ... Ordered That the said Negro man, by name Job, have the sum of five pounds allowed and paid him ...

The next slave conspiracy of which any record has been found is the serious one in South Carolina in 1720. The colony at this time had a considerable slave population,[39] and was suffering from an acute economic depression, accentuated by a drought and by difficulties with Indians.[40] These factors, plus the lure of freedom held out by the Spaniards in Florida,[41] were probably important in accounting for the slaves' schemes to rebel.

38 MS. Journals of the Commons House of the Assembly, Historical Commission, Columbia, South Carolina, IV, p. 409.

39 In a manuscript entitled "Queries relating to Carolina written by J. Boone and J. Barnwell" in 1720 (Public Records of South Carolina, Historical Commission, Columbia, S. C.) the colony's population is put at 9,000 whites and 12,000 Negroes. Reference here is made, too, to economic distress and Indian danger, and to the fact that within the last five years the number of whites had decreased. "Yet the number of Blacks that time have very much increased for the Pitch & Tar Trade prodigiously Increasing have occasioned ye Inhabitants to buy Blacks to the great indangering of this Province." These facts reached the Lords Commissioners for Trade and Plantations, for in a representation to the King dated September 8, 1721 they were repeated together with a proposal urging the propriety of "encouraging the entertainment of more white servants for the future."—E. B. O'Callaghan, op. cit., V, p. 610. See also R. L. Meriwether, op. cit., p. 5.

40 The depression lasted from 1715 to 1720. A food shortage faced Charles Town in 1715, while in 1717 a planter wrote, "We are ready to eat up one another for want of provisions, and what we can get is very bad." In October, 1719, Governor Johnson asked the Assembly to seriously consider "the very great rates of all provisions in Charles Town." That year a revolt occurred among the white people. See C. Bridenbaugh, op. cit., pp. 178, 197; L. C. Gray, op. cit., I, p. 176; V. Crane, op. cit., p. 184; H. L. Osgood, op. cit., IV, p. 114.

41 Ante, pp. 23-24, 30.

An anonymous letter addressed to a Mr. Boone in London, and dated "Carolina June 24, 1720" is the fullest contemporary account of this conspiracy. It reads as follows: [42]

I am now to acquaint you that very lately we have had a very wicked and barbarous plott of the designe of the negroes rising with a designe to destroy all the white people in the country and then to take the town [Charles Town] in full body but it pleased God it was discovered and many of them taken prisoners and some burnt some hang'd and some banish'd.

I think it proper for you to tell Mr. Percivall at home that his slaves was the principal rogues and 'tis my opinion his only way will be to sell them out singly or else I am doubtful his interest in slaves will come to little for want of strict management. work does not agree with them. 14 of them are now at the Savanna towne[43] and sent for [by?] white and Indians and will be executed as soon as they come down they thought to gett to [St.] Augustine and would have got a creek fellow to have been their pylott but the Savanna garrison tooke the negroes up half starved and the Creeke Indians would not join them or be their pylott...

A report sent to the King in 1721 further demonstrates the gravity of this plot and also seems to hint at others of which apparently no record survives. This report after referring to the recent quick growth of the Negro population in South Carolina

42 MS. Public Records of South Carolina, VIII, pp. 24-27. Abstracts from or references to this letter are in *Collections of the South-Carolina Historical Society 1857*, I, p. 252; Edward McCrady, *History of South Carolina under the Royal Government 1719-1776*, p. 5; U. B. Phillips, *op. cit.*, p. 473; C. Headlam, *Calendar of State Papers, March 1720 to December 1721*, p. 57; D. D. Wallace, *op. cit.*, I, p. 372; Joshua Coffin (*An Account of some of the Principal Slave Insurrections*, p. 11) refers to an actual uprising in May, 1720 in Charles Town, and presents many details. This is followed by Benjamin Brawley, *A Social History of the American Negro*, p. 40, and by J. C. Carroll, *op. cit.*, p. 17, but no contemporary account resembling this has been seen. Coffin is unreliable in several other instances and it is probable he is in error here.

43 This Savannah Town, the Indian trading center of the colony (which developed into Augusta, Ga.) was about 110 miles north-west of Charles Town. See Charles M. Andrews, *The Colonial Period of American History*, III, p. 206; V. Crane, *op. cit.*, p. 21, and map at end of that volume.

declares [44] that the " black slaves . . . have lately attempted and were very near succeeding in a *new* [my emphasis] revolution, which would probably have been attended by the utter extirpation of all your Majesty's subjects in this province . . .".

A slave plot was unearthed and crushed in 1722 in Virginia. In a report on this event to the Council of Trade and Plantations in London, Lieutenant-Governor Drysdale asserted that the conspiracy had covered " two or three counties." On November 2 three of the leaders, Cooper Will, slave of Gabriel Throckmorton, and two Sams, one the property of Elizabeth Burwell, the other of Elizabeth Richardson, were found guilty of " unlawfully Assembling meeting and Congregating themselves with other slaves and Communicating contriving and Conspiring among themselves and with the said other Slaves to kill murder & destroy very many " of the King's subjects. They were therefore sentenced to three years' imprisonment, or, if their masters gave " such Security as the Government shall Approve," they were to be turned over to their owners for sale and transportation out of the Colony.[45]

Drysdale's letter, already referred to, written some six weeks after this legal proceeding, on December 20, 1722, added,

Divers of the ringleaders have been taken upp and tryed, others are continued over in prison, till next Genll. Court, in expectation of further proofe: the design of these slaves was to cutt off their masters, and possess themselves of the country; but as this would have been as impractical in the attempt as it was foolish in the contrivance, I can forsee no other consequence of this conspiracy than the stirring up the next Assembly to make more severe laws for the keeping of their slaves in greater subjection. . .

44 Representation of the Lords Commissioners for Trade and Plantations to King, September 8, 1721, in E. O'Callaghan, ed., *op. cit.*, V, p. 610.

45 Drysdale's letter is in C. Headlam, ed., *Calendar of State Papers, colonial series*, 1722-1723, p. 192; a manuscript copy of the November court proceedings is in the collection of the Virginia Historical Society, Richmond, photostat in writer's possession. J. Coffin, *op. cit.*, p. 11, and, following him, J. Carroll, *op. cit.*, p. 17, refer to a plot of two hundred Negroes in October, 1722 near the mouth of the Rappahannock River in Virginia, but where Coffin got his information is unknown. The cited evidence is all, of a contemporary nature, that has been seen for the plot of 1722.

Slaves of Middlesex and Gloucester Counties, Virginia, were discovered in the spring of 1723 to be scheming to gain their freedom. By a resolution of the House of Burgesses, adopted May 17, 1723, seven of the Negroes were sentenced to sale and transportation out of the Colony.[46] In his message to the General Assembly this year, Governor Drysdale remarked :[47]

Your laws seem very deficient in the due punishing any intended Insurrection of your Slaves, you have had a Late Experience of ye Lameness of them; I am persuaded you are too well acquainted with the Cruel dispositions of those Creatures, when they have it in their power to destroy or destress, to let Slipp this faire opportunity of making more proper Laws against them. . . .

The Virginia legislature agreed and that year passed additional regulations, since, as it said, those in existence were " found insufficient to restrain their tumultuous and unlawful meetings, or to punish the secret plots and conspiracies carried on amongst them . . .". These, among other things, provided death without benefit of clergy for conspiracy, forbade all meetings of slaves except if licensed, and enacted other restrictive measures. Free Negroes, moreover, were this year deprived of the franchise.[48]

A dozen years later the Lords Commissioners of Trade got around to asking why the last regulation was passed. Governor Gooch's reply throws further light on the nature of this plot: [49]

46 Record of General Court proceeding dated April 26, 1723 in manuscripts of the Virginia Historical Society, photostat in writer's possession; U. B. Phillips, *op. cit.*, pp. 472-73; *Catalogue of the Manuscripts in the Collection of the Virginia Historical Society*, pp. 93, 103.

47 Reprinted in *The Virginia Historical Register and Literary Note Book*, IV, p. 63.

48 Hening, *op. cit.*, IV, pp. 126 ff. Free Negroes were also hit by a higher tax rate and forbidden to possess arms. Manumission was to be granted only for meritorious service and by a license issued by the Governor and Council —John H. Russell, *The Free Negro in Virginia*, p. 52.

49 Quoted by H. A. Wyndham, *The Atlantic and Slavery*, p. 297, citing British Public Record office, CO/5/1324.

It is to be noted, as I am well informed, that just before the meeting of that Assembly, there had been a conspiracy discovered amongst the negroes to cutt off the English, wherein the free negroes and mulattos were much suspected to have been concerned (which will forever be the case) and tho' there could be no legal proof, so as to convict them, yet such was the insolence of the free negroes at that time, that the next Assembly thought it necessary, not only to make the meeting of slaves very penal, but to fix a perpetual brand upon free negroes and mulattos by excluding them from that great priviledge of a Freeman, well knowing they always did, and ever will adhere to and favour the slaves ... and to preserve a decent distinction between them and their betters ...

From 1721 to 1723 there occurred a number of fires—reaching greatest frequency during the spring and summer of the latter year—in Boston and in New Haven, for which the Negro slaves were held to be responsible. In addition to considerable property damage several people suffered injuries. At least one Negro was executed in Boston, on July 4, 1723, after having been found guilty of " maliciously setting on Fire a Dwelling House in this Town, in the dead of Night, when the Inhabitants were asleep in their Beds." Another Negro was arrested in October for a similar deed, in New Haven, and reportedly confessed his guilt, but his punishment was not reported. The Governor of Massachusetts offered a reward of fifty pounds for the arrest of those responsible, while the Boston Council passed a regulation for the punishment by lashing of any slaves who gathered together in groups of two or more, unless in the service of their owners.[50]

Before the end of the decade the activities of outlying belligerent fugitive slaves became important enough to attract widespread attention in Louisiana and Virginia. A case [51] involving an Indian slave of the former region who had, in 1727,

50 Boston *Weekly News-Letter*, April 4-11, May 2-9, 9-16, July 4-11, August 8-15, October 10-18, November 14-21, 1723. See also J. Coffin, *op. cit.*, p. 12, and J. Carroll, *op. cit.*, pp. 18-19. There were about 2,000 Negroes in Boston in 1720—Bridenbaugh, *op. cit.*, pp. 200, 368.

51 H. T. Catterall, *op. cit.*, III, p. 401.

" marooned because he was afraid to return after failing to find an ox that had gone astray," revealed the existence of an outlaw village called des Natanapallé. There, at the moment, about fifteen other slaves, Negro and Indian, lived and protected themselves from recapture with " eleven guns and some ammunition " which they possessed. An additional case that same year revealed the existence of another such community of maroons in the same territory.

An indeterminate number of Virginia slaves ran off into the Blue Ridge Mountains in 1729, and took along with them guns, ammunition, and agricultural implements. Their settlement, whose continued existence would have been a most disturbing factor to the entire institution of slavery, was attacked by a strong body of armed white men, and, after a pitched battle, the remaining Negroes were led back into bondage. Lieutenant-Governor Gooch, reporting this incident to the Lords of Trade, on June 29, 1729, assured them that the militia was being trained to " prevent this for the future." [52]

The next year conspiracies were uncovered and crushed in Virginia, South Carolina, and Louisiana. A precipitating factor, so far as Virginia was concerned, was the rumor that spread with amazing rapidity among the Negroes that the newly-arrived Colonel Spotswood had come empowered by the King to free all slaves that had been baptized. The colony's authorities observed many gatherings and meetings of slaves with " loose Discourses " on the topic of liberty. This was indeed a dangerous situation, for, as Lieutenant-Governor Gooch remarked,[53] their idea concerning Spotswood was " a Notion,

52 Sainsbury, IX, p. 462; P. A. Bruce, *History of Virginia*, I, p. 322. J. Coffin, *op. cit.*, p. 13, mentioned and gave details concerning an alleged plot among slaves in Savannah, George in 1728, and some later writers have followed his account. The date mentioned by Coffin, however, precedes by four years the founding of Georgia, and by over twenty years the introduction of slavery within that colony. It is possible that Coffin had reference to Savannah Town, in what was then South Carolina (see *ante*, p. 175, note 43), but no information of the nature he gave has been seen for that settlement.

53 Gooch to the Bishop of London, dated Williamsburgh, May 28, 1731, in *The Virginia Magazine of History and Biography*, XXXII pp. 322-23.

in their Circumstances, sufficient to incite them to Rebellion, were they Masters of a more peaceable Disposition than generally they have."

The leaders in these " Discourses" were arrested and suffered "severe Whipping" which it was hoped would rid them of their peculiar " notion," but six weeks later, " about two hundred" slaves of Norfolk and Princess Anne Counties, according to the above official, " had the assurance to assemble on a Sunday whilst the People were at Church, and to chuse from among themselves officers to Command their intended Insurrection, which was to have been put in Execution very soon after; But this Plot being happily discovered, the Ringleaders were brought to a Tryal and four of them, on clear Evidence Convicted, were executed." The Governor closed his remarks with the " hope" that the slaves would now " rest contented with their condition."

In addition to hoping, the Lieutenant-Governor issued a proclamation referring to the fact that though laws forbidding the assemblying of slaves were in effect, yet [54] " Divers Meetings of great numbers of Slaves have of late been held in Several parts of this Colony whereby they have had opportunity of framing Conspiracys against the Public Peace of this Colony and the lives and properties of his Majesties good Subjects." It was, therefore, ordered that the aforesaid laws be more strictly enforced, and commanded that, hereafter, worshippers carry arms with them to church.

A letter written in Charles Town on August 20, 1730, is the single available contemporary account of that year's plot in South Carolina: [55]

54 Dated October 28, 1730, in *ibid.*, XXXVI, pp. 345-46.

55 Published in the Boston *Weekly News-Letter*, October 15-22, 1730, and in the Boston *Gazette*, October 19-26, 1730. The plot is mentioned by E. C. Holland, *op. cit.*, pp. 68-69, but he cites no sources. His account was followed by Coffin, *op. cit.*, p. 13; Carroll, *op. cit.*, p. 20; Harvey Wish, *op. cit.*, p. 308; and D. D. Wallace, *op. cit.*, I, p. 372. Whether the writer of the above letter did "find out the whole Affair" or not is unknown. According to Holland, who probably had access to materials destroyed during the Civil War, the

I shall give an Account of a bloody Tragedy which was to have been executed here last Saturday night (the 15th Inst.) by the Negroes, who had conspired to Rise and destroy us, and had almost bro't it to pass: but it pleased God to appear for us, and confound their Councils. For some of them propos'd that the Negroes of every Plantation should destroy their own Masters; but others were for Rising in a Body, and giving the blow at once on surprise; and thus they differ'd. They soon made a great Body at the back of the Town, and had a great Dance, and expected the Country Negroes to come & join them; and had not an overruling Providence discovered their Intrigues, we had been all in blood...The Chief of them, with some others, is apprehended and in Irons, in order to a Tryal; and we are in Hopes to find out the whole Affair.

In New Orleans one day in 1730 a woman slave received " a violent blow from a French soldier for refusing to obey him," and, in her anger, shouted " that the French should not long insult negroes." This remark aroused suspicion, the woman was brought before the Governor and sent, by him, to prison. Investigators were not, however, " able to draw anything out of her " and it was decided to charge the director of the public plantations with the task of discovering what, if anything, lay behind the woman's defiant cry. He soon reported a widespread conspiracy to destroy the slaveholders had been developed. Shortly eight of the leaders, including one, Samba, who had been a confidant of the director, were arrested—individually, however, and without one knowing of the other's fate, and without arousing any untoward excitement.

The next day, reported the director,[56]

leaders were executed. A fact possibly throwing some light on a specific provocation of the Negroes in this instance is the existence of a fearful epidemic of influenza in South Carolina in 1729 which was "particularly fatal to the blacks." See St. Julien Ravenal Childs, "Kitchenphysick, medical and surgical care of slaves on an eighteenth century rice plantation," in *The Mississippi Valley Historical Review*, XX, p. 119.

56 LaPage Du Pratz, *The History of Louisiana, and of the Western Parts of Virginia and Carolina*, pp. 77-78. This was first published, in French, in 1750—see Lyle Saxon, *Old Louisiana*, pp. 64-66. DuPratz lived in Louisiana, as a planter, for sixteen years, and was, as is stated in the preface, " director

they were put to the torture of burning matches; which, though several times repeated, could not bring them to make any confession. In the meantime I learnt that Samba had in his own country been at the head of the revolt by which the French lost Fort Arguin; and when it was recovered again by M. Perier de Salvert, one of the principal articles of the peace was, that this negro should be condemned to slavery in America: that Samba, on his passage, had laid a scheme to murder the crew, in order to become master of the ship; but that being discovered, he was put in irons, in which he continued till he landed in Louisiana.

These facts were read to Samba by an official, who ended by threatening to torture him again, upon which he confessed his complicity in a plot as charged by the director. The other Negroes, being confronted with this confession, did likewise, " after which the eight negroes were condemned to be broke alive on the wheel, and the woman to be hanged before their eyes; which was accordingly done, and prevented the conspiracy from taking effect."

There is some evidence, though it is not firsthand, and is in some respects confusing, of another plot in Louisiana amongst the slaves in 1732, possibly acting with Indian allies, after the French had defeated the Natchez tribe. In this case a woman was hanged and four men were broken on the wheel. Their heads were then stuck on poles at the upper and lower ends of New Orleans as grim and stark inducements to docility.[57]

Considerable slave difficulty beset the rulers of South Carolina in the early 1730's. Rumors of trouble moved the Council

of the public plantations, both when they belonged to the company, and afterwards when they fell to the crown." As has been noted this plot came in the midst of serious trouble with the Natchez Indians. Population figures, and the very great death rate during this period among the slaves, have also been previously referred to—ante, p. 164.

57 The clearest account is in Francois-Xavier Martin, The History of Louisiana, I, pp. 293-96. The details given by E. Bunner, History of Louisiana, p. 97, differ, and the plot is put in 1734. Carter G. Woodson appears to consider that there was but one plot and that was in 1730, but this does not seem, to the present writer, to be correct—The Negro in Our History, p. 87.

to recommend special care during the Christmas holidays in 1732.[58] Its Journal entry of February 26, 1733 noted the fact that there had recently occurred many mysterious and large-scale meetings of slaves—some running into the hundreds—several " robberies and insolences " had been reported, and, in brief, a conspiracy was feared. As a result the colony's militia and Charles Town's guard were particularly warned to be on the alert and twelve slaves were ordered arrested and questioned, though no record of their disposition appears to be available.[59]

Later this year the lower House of the Colony, " on reading a letter from Capt. Charles Russell to the Honble Thomas Broughton Esqr. relating to Several Run away Negroes who are near the Congerees, & have robbed several of the Inhabitants thereabouts," asked [60] the Governor to offer a reward of twenty pounds a head, alive, and ten pounds, dead, for each of these rebels, which was done. In November, 1733, reference was made to the flight of slaves to St. Augustine. The masters were urged to do their utmost to get these slaves back, for that would tend to halt the steady flight of these unique pieces of property. In March, 1734, a reward was urged for the white servant and slaves who had caught and killed a well-known leader of a destructive band of slave outlaws.[61]

58 MS. Council Journal, South Carolina, V, p. 340, Historical Commission, Columbia, S. C.

59 D. D. Wallace, op. cit., I, p. 372, mistakingly puts this in 1734.

60 MS. Council Journal, V, pp. 487, 494.

61 Ibid., V, pp. 595, 668. The shooting of runaway slaves is mentioned in 1731 and 1732 (V, pp. 161, 384). And an entry of June 6, 1735 (VI, p. 143) reads: "sevl. slave have made their Escapes ... and very probably are sheldered (sic) and Protected by the Tuscarora Indians in North Carolina Government, which has a very evil tendency ... " Some pertinent material occurs in the MS. Journals of the Commons House of the Assembly of the same colony at this time. Thus on February 12, 1734 it was declared that twenty-five pounds "ought to be paid " to Edward Keating "for his expense and attendance in taking up several negroes according to the Govrs. Letters to him " (IX, p. 71), and there are several references to Negroes being killed or executed, for reasons unspecified, during the same period—IX, pp. 74, 79, 82, 91, 99, 110, 369.

Occasion has already presented itself for a consideration of the fairly extensive slave plot which occurred in New Jersey in 1734. In addition, two sources of a secondary nature refer to plots in Pennsylvania in 1734 and in South Carolina in 1736, but as no confirmation whatsoever has been seen for either statement it seems likely that both are erroneous.[62]

A remark made by a Philadelphia judge in September, 1737, indicates the existence of trouble with the slaves of that city. The official was giving his reason for refusing a master's request that his slave, who had been convicted of deliberately burning down a house, should be pardoned. "A Complyance," said the judge,[63] with this wish, " cannot but be attended with many ill consequences, more especially as the insolent Behaviour of the Negroes in and about the city, which has of late been so much taken notice of, requires a strict hand to be kept over them, & shows the Necessity of some further Regulations than our laws have yet provided."

Much more serious trouble, however, began this year in South Carolina, and continued to flare forth at frequent intervals for about four years. As has been pointed out, the proximity of Spaniards whose hostility to the English made them friendly to the slaves of the British, served to encourage their hopes for liberty and thus aroused efforts to realize them. This was especially true after a royal decree of October, 1733 announced that all fugitive slaves reaching Florida were to be permitted to reside there as free people. In 1738 Negroes liberated in this way were established in a fort about three miles north of St. Augustine, and when, in November of that year, a single batch of over twenty fugitives arrived at this settlement, an official seized the occasion to let his sovereign's traditional

62 J. Coffin, op. cit., p. 14; Appendix to diary, kept in 1780, by the Hessian officer, Captain Johann Hinrichs, in Bernhard A. Uhlendorf, ed., The Seige of Charleston with an Account of the Province of South Carolina, pp. 323, 331. The account contains circumstantial details.

63 Minutes of the Provincial Council of Pennsylvania, from the Organization to the Termination of the Proprietary Government, IV, p. 259.

enemies know that any others would also be welcomed and liberated.[64] In 1739 warfare between the two powers was actually declared and this, too, of course, reached the ears of the slaves of the English and increased their unrest.

In addition, the whites of South Carolina were heavily outnumbered by the slaves during the 1730's so that, for example, in 1734, the ratio was three to one. Again, in 1737, it was estimated that the colony could muster no more than 5,000 fighting men while it contained about 22,000 slaves, and in 1739 there were but 9,000 whites to a total of 35,000 slaves in the province. The trend, moreover, continued adverse to the masters' safety, for while the number of slaves in 1740 had reached about 40,000, the number of whites had declined to some 5,000.[65]

As a final factor that may well have been of great importance in stimulating unrest is to be mentioned the fact that actual famine conditions prevailed in the Southern colonies in the year 1737. The outstanding authority on southern agriculture has remarked [66] that while Virginia and Maryland faced " extraordinary scarcity " at that time, yet " conditions were much worse in South Carolina " and " a number of Negroes died of want."

Three slaves were arrested early in 1737 as the leaders of a " Conspiracy against the Peace of this Government," but

64 See Wilbur H. Siebert, " Slavery and white servitude in East Florida, 1726-1776," in *The Florida Historical Society Quarterly*, X, pp. 3-4; Robert L. Meriwether, *The Expansion of South Carolina 1729-1765*, p. 26.

65 Ruth Scarborough, *The Opposition to Slavery in Georgia Prior to 1860*, pp. 4, 12-13. As early as 1709 there were, in the city of Charles Town itself, as many Negroes as whites. " Disorders caused by the growing number of Negro slaves led to the establishment in 1734 of slave patrols in St. Philip's Parish," consisting of two squads each of nine mounted men which took turns covering the district Saturday night and all day on Sundays and holidays.—C. Bridenbaugh, *op. cit.*, pp. 249, 377. From 1729 to 1737 about 16,000 slaves were brought from Africa to South Carolina. Note, too, should be made of disastrous epidemics which swept the province in 1738 and 1739. See Meriwether, *op. cit.*, pp. 24, 26.

66 L. C. Gray, *op. cit.*, I, p. 176.

their disposition is not on record.[67] Throughout this year
and the next, attempts by slaves, singly or in groups, to get into
St. Augustine continued and were complained of frequently.
Indeed, the evidence seems to indicate that the prevailing conditions approached a state of actual warfare, of guerilla type,
with, as an official committee reported, assassinations recurrent,
great alarm prevalent, and conspiracies uncovered, including
one in Charles Town itself in 1738. The slaves seem to have
been particularly active during the month of November of that
year, and even inhabitants of Georgia were disturbed—some
killed—by South Carolina slaves fighting their way down into
the Promised Land.[68]

This turmoil of discontent probably reached its climax in
1739, when several plots and uprisings rocked the province of
South Carolina. A journal entry of a Georgian for February
8 opens the story for this year: [69]

But what we heard told us by several newly come from Carolina,
was not to be disregarded, viz. that a Conspiracy was formed by the
Negroes in Carolina, to rise and forcibly make their Way out of
the Province, to put themselves under the Protection of the
Spaniards, that this was first discovered at Winnyaw, which is at
the most Northern Part of the Province; from whence, as they
were to bend their course South, it argued, that the other Parts of
the Province must be privy to it, and that the Rising was to be

67 MS. Journals of the Commons House of Assembly, February 24, 1737,
X, p. 434.

68 Report of Committee on Failure of Expedition against St. Augustine,
dated July 2, 1741, in MS. Council Journal, VII, pp. 424-25; see *ibid.*, pp.
135, 137, 141-44, 146-47, 168; C. Bridenbaugh, *op. cit.*, p. 380; A. D. Candler,
ed., *Colonial Records of Georgia*, XVIII, p. 135; R. B. Flanders, *Plantation
Slavery in Georgia*, p. 24.

69 " Stephen's Journal" [Stephen was Secretary to the Trustees of
Georgia] in A. D. Candler, ed., *op. cit.*, IV, pp. 275, 277. A conspiracy at
" Winyar " is also mentioned by one of the founders of Georgia, Benjamin
Martyn, in his "Account showing the progress of the colony of Georgia, in
America," in *Collections of the Georgia Historical Society*, II, pp. 301-302.
The region here referred to is probably that around Winyah Bay, near
the present Georgetown.

universal; whereupon the whole Province were all on their Guard...

On February 20 this same source referred to another conspiracy among the numerous slaves of two planters, Montaigut, and de Beaufain, located " on the Banks of the Savannah within the District of Purysburgh, a little below that Town." [70]

A news item of early March reported that a group composed of " several Negroes " and two whites, supposed to be a Spaniard and an Irishman, had killed one white man and wounded three others in this troubled Province. They were, however,[71] " beat off by People coming and firing on them from the Neighbourhood; but they all made their Escape and are gone clear as yet." On March 15 a bill aimed at preventing slave insurrections was submitted to the legislature, and it was enacted on April 11, 1739.[72] But the greatest uprising of the year was yet to occur.

On a Sunday evening, September 9, 1739, about a score of slaves at Stono, South Carolina (some twenty miles south-west of Charleston) led by one named Jemmy, rebelled,[73] killed the

70 *Ibid.*, pp. 283-84.

71 Boston *Weekly News-Letter*, May 24-31, 1739.

72 MS. Council Journal, VII, pp. 189, 217.

73 This account is based upon the available contemporary sources, from which all quotations are taken. These are: a letter from William Bull to the Duke of Newcastle, dated Charles Town, October 5, 1739 in *Collections of the South Carolina Historical Society*, II, p. 270; " Stephens Journal," *op. cit.*, entry of September 13, 1739, pp. 412-413; an anonymous "Account of the Negroes Insurrection in South Carolina" in A. D. Candler, W. J. Northen, L. L. Knight, eds., *Colonial Records of the State of Georgia*, XXII, part 2, pp. 233-34 (this source states that many of the slaves involved had been brought from the Portuguese colony of Angola and were Catholics, thus being especially attracted to the Spaniards); MS. Council Journal, VII, pp. 424-25; letter dated South Carolina, September 28, 1739 in the Boston *Weekly News-Letter*, November 1-8, 1739. The name Jemmy for the slave rebel leader is mentioned in Candler, Northen, Knight, eds., *op. cit.*, p. 233. According to David Ramsay (who erroneously dated the event as 1740) the leader of the Negroes in their pitched battle was named Cato—*The History of South-Carolina*, I, p. 112 n. His account, which appears largely fanciful

two guards (a Mr. Bathurst and Mr. Gibbs) of a warehouse or magazine (belonging to a Mr. Hutchenson) and appropriated " a pretty many small Arms and Powder," and headed, at a slow pace, south, apparently aiming to reach St. Augustine. On the way they killed all in their path, with the exception of an inn-keeper by the name of Wallace who, they felt, " was a good Man and kind to his Slaves," and burned several buildings—six or seven—so that " the Country there about was full of flames."

Other Negroes " joyned them," until something like seventy-five or eighty slaves were gathered, " they called out Liberty, marched on with Colours displayed, and two Drums beating." Colonel Bull, Lieutenant-Governor of the Province, chanced to be riding near their line of march, saw them, and immediately spread the alarm.

Guards were posted at all ferries and roads, and the militia was assembled and set out in pursuit. The Negroes, whose activities had delayed them, and who had been marching and fighting for ten or twelve hours, rested some ten miles south of Stono. Here they were met and attacked by a detachment of militia of approximately their own number, but probably better armed. "An engagement [ensued] wherein one fought for Liberty & Life the other for their Country & every thing that was Dear to them." The Negroes, though they " behaved boldly " were defeated. In the opening exchange of gunfire the militiamen " bro't down 14 on the Spot; and pursuing after them, within ten Days kill'd twenty odd more, and took about 40; who were immediately some shot, some hang'd, and some Gibbeted alive. A number came in and were seized and discharged; and some are out yet, but we hope will soon be taken."

(see D. D. Wallace, *op. cit.*, I, p. 373) is followed, almost word for word by Edward McCrady, *History of South Carolina under the Royal Government 1719-1776*, p. 185, except that here McCrady gives the correct date, though his earlier account, *Slavery in the Province of South Carolina*, p. 156 followed Ramsay even as concerns the wrong date.

Certainly the search and pursuit were maintained for some of these rebels were captured months later.[74] The number of casualties resulting from this uprising are not precisely known but probably about twenty-five whites and twice that number of slaves were killed in the course of the uprising and its suppression.[75]

Early in June, 1740, another major conspiracy was crushed in South Carolina, this time in and around Charles Town itself.[76] A traitor [77] had given the slaveholders advance warning of about twenty-four hours, so that an armed force was prepared and in readiness for any trouble. On the day set for the outbreak, from one hundred and fifty to two hundred slaves did " get together in Defiance: But as they were unprovided with Arms, and there was no Corn on the Ground ripe, for their Subsistence" their disposition and subsequent capture were not difficult. At least fifty of the Negroes were caught and hanged, in batches of ten a day, in order " to intimidate the other negroes."

74 Thus, for example, on November 11, 1739, two Indian slaves, Simon and Titus, who had been of service in suppressing the rebellion and aiding in the capture of the rebels received 25 and 50 pounds respectively. On March 20, 1740, three Negro slaves who had " Lately apprehended" two of the rebels (both were executed) received rewards, as did another Negro slave "who lately took one of the slaves that was concerned in the Insurrection at Stono," as late as August 13, 1740. MS. Council Journal, VII, pp. 265, 273, 343, 390.

75 This is based upon the contemporary accounts cited in note 72. There is not much variation as to these figures in secondary accounts, Coffin, *op. cit.*, p. 14; E. McCrady, *Slavery in the Province of South Carolina*, p. 657; D. D. Wallace, *op. cit.*, I, p. 373; though H. Henry's figure of forty-four as the total number, Negro and white, killed, is certainly too low—*op. cit.*, pp. 149-50.

76 Contemporary accounts are in " Stephens Journal," dated June 11, 1740, *op. cit.*, p. 592; [Benjamin Martyn] "An impartial inquiry into the state and utility of the Province of Georgia," London, 1741, in *Collections of the Georgia Historical Society*, I, pp. 172-73; Boston *Weekly News-Letter,* July 3-10, 1740.

77 His name was Peter, slave of a Major Cords. For his services he received "a suit of Cloaths hat, shoes & stockings & £20 in cash"—MS. Council Journal, August 13, 1740, VII, p. 343.

Later this same year a terrific fire devastated Charles Town destroying hundreds of buildings and necessitating an appeal to the other colonies for assistance. First reports ascribed the origin of this calamity to the slaves, but this was later denied, and it was decided that the fire had been caused " by some Accident." [78] However this may be, several fires that broke out in the same community the next year were definitely ascribed to the Negroes. A woman was condemned to die for the crime of arson in July, a man was burnt to death in August as punishment for having set fire to a house with the " evil intent of burning down the remaining Part of the Town," and two slaves were held guilty of setting fire, in December, to the city's magazine.[79]

In the midst of this rebellious activity and in order to combat the unrest, the Province of South Carolina in 1739 and 1740 passed rather vague laws requiring better food and clothing for slaves, and providing that they should not be worked over four-

78 Boston *Weekly News-Letter*, January 15-22, 1741; April 30–May 6, 1741; Bridenbaugh, *op. cit.*, p. 372, mentions the fire but does not note the charge of arson.

79 Boston *Weekly News-Letter*, September 24–October 1, 1741; MS. Council Journal, January 13, 1742, VIII, p. 406. In the cited newspaper. issue of August 27–September 3, 1741, appeared this sentence: " By private letters from Charlestown in South-Carolina we are inform'd, that the Town is in much Confusion, not only on account of the insolence of the Spaniards. but also from Apprehensions of Domestick Treachery, the Town having been several times alarm'd by Fire which too visibly appears to be wilfully occasion'd by their Blacks." Also to be noted is the following very interesting charge made by the Charles Town, S. C., Grand Jury on March 17, 1741: " We present as a Public Grievance a certain book or Journal sign'd by Hugh Brian, directed to ye Honble, the Speaker, and the rest of the members of the Commons house of Assembly in Charles Town, wch we have perused and find in general, contains sundry enthusiastic Prophecys, of the destruction of Charles Town, and deliverance of the Negroes from their Servitude. and that by the Influence of ye said Hugh Brian, great bodys of Negroes have assembled together on pretence of religious worship, contrary to ye Laws, and destructive of ye Peace . . ." Other whites, named Jonathan Brian, William Gilbert, and Robert Ogle, were also declared to possess opinions inimical to the security of a slave society. Mr. Brian's work was suppressed, but what punishment, if any, was meted out to the individuals is not known.—MS. Council Journal, VIII, p. 13.

teen hours a day in winter and fifteen hours in summer. On the other hand, bounties for the scalps of runaway slaves were offered, and, as a preventative measure, the Colony also placed a tariff on imported slaves and earmarked the revenue so obtained [80] for a subsidy with which to encourage the settling of Protestant white people. Slaves sold very slowly in 1740, and South Carolina imported none until 1744, when the slave traders of Bristol, England, complained, and the lucrative business once more began. It was very largely the object lesson of this rebellious activity that led the leaders of the border colony of Georgia, men like Oglethorpe, Stephens, Martyn, and Egmont, to institute and to maintain, until 1750, a ban against slavery.[81]

During these years of excitement in South Carolina other colonies were not free of a like danger. Thus, in the spring of 1738, several slaves broke out of a jail in Prince George's County, Maryland, united themselves with a group of outlying Negroes and proceeded to wage a small-scale guerrilla war. The Council of the Colony decided that the magistrates of the affected area had not exerted themselves sufficiently and so instructed the sheriff to put down the trouble, empowering him to use, if necessary, the entire strength of the County.[82] The next year this Council was presented with the depositions of several citizens of this County " relating to a most wicked and dangerous Conspiracy having been formed by them the slaves to destroy his Majestys Subjects within this Province, and to possess themselves of the whole Country." This deposition said a " con-

80 E. McCrady, op. cit., p. 657; Edward Channing, History of the United States, II, p. 391; D. D. Wallace, The Life of Henry Laurens, pp. 82-83; D. Wallace, History of S. C., I, p. 372; Elizabeth Donnan, Documents Illustrative of the History of the Slave Trade, IV, pp. 296-97.

81 A. D. Candler, ed., op. cit., I, p. 50; R. Scarborough, op. cit., pp. 9, 12, 37, 73.

82 J. R. Brackett, The Negro in Maryland, p. 76 n., citing Council records for May 5, 1738.

siderable number " of slaves were implicated. A letter from the leader of the province's lower house, Stephen Bordley, is more explicit. He, writing from Annapolis in Anne Arundel County on January 30, 1739, asserted that about 200 slaves were directly implicated, that they had agreed upon a leader, " a Clever Sensible fellow between 40 & 50 years old," and planned to capture the town's magazine and the Capitol, and establish their own government. Should they then be faced by overwhelming force they intended " to settle back in the Woods."

On the Sunday appointed for the revolt a terrific storm occurred, and the event was postponed for two weeks. At this point a slave belonging to a Mr. Brookes betrayed the plot, and immediate measures of repression were taken, including the execution of at least one of the leading rebels.[83]

Slaves in New York City were accused in 1740 of conspiring to kill their masters by poisoning the water supply. As a result of this, according to one authority,[84] most New Yorkers thereafter for quite some time bought spring water from vendors who carried it about the streets. This fact indicates how strong was the suspicion and fear of the approximately two thousand slaves among the ten thousand white inhabitants of the city.

The fear and the suspicion had full play, with tragic results, the next year. The hysteria of 1741 in the City of New York has been treated by some historians as arising from a complete hoax, or an unaccountable mob delusion, while others have dealt with it as resulting from a real and considerable slave con-

83 See H. T. Catterall, ed., *op. cit.*, *IV*, p. 35; W. H. Browne, ed., *Archives of Maryland*, XXVIII, pp. 188-190; Stephen Bordley to Matt Harris, Annapolis, January 30, 1739, in Stephen Bordley's Letterbook, original in possession of Maryland Historical Society, photostat in author's possession. The date of this letter is incorrectly given as 1740 by Charles A. Barker in *The Background of the Revolution in Maryland*, pp. 34-35 n. See also J. R. Brackett, *op. cit.*, pp. 93-94.

84 C. Bridenbaugh, *op. cit.*, p. 374. No contemporary account of this has been seen.

spiracy.[85] It seems fairly certain that neither of these views altogether coincides with the facts.

It does appear clear that discontent among the poor, Negro and white, was rife.[86] On the other hand, the existence of a plot was doubted by contemporaries, and the severity of the punishment was decried by some among them.[87] The fullest firsthand account of the event was written by Daniel Horsmanden whose position as Recorder made him prosecutor of the alleged conspirators, and it was produced in part in order to justify the city's proceedings. Horsmanden certainly exaggerated the seriousness of the disaffection. Indeed, by his own account, the star witness against the conspirators, a white woman named Mary Burton, was a bold liar, so that even the court, finally, disregarded her wild stories. And the methods by which confessions were extracted, that is, by promises of rewards, or by the use of torture, cast grave doubts as to their reliability.

The period was one, however, of distress for the inhabitants of the city. An unpopular war against Spain was then in progress, the winter of 1740-41 had been unusually severe, being remembered for years as the " hard winter," and suffering

85 The fullest secondary account is that by Walter F. Prince, *New York 'Negro Plot' of 1741* (typewritten copy in the New York Public Library, published in the *Saturday Chronicle* of New Haven, Conn., June 28–August 23, 1902). See also A. J. Northrup, *op. cit.*, pp. 275-77; Anonymous, " Negro plot in New York," in *The National Magazine, A Monthly Magazine of American History*, 1893, XVIII, pp. 128-131; William Dunlap, *op. cit.*, I, pp. 321-351; Mary L. Booth, *op. cit.*, I, pp. 321-351; J. C. Carroll, *op. cit.*, pp. 26-31.

86 For contemporary accounts, see Daniel Horsmanden, *The New-York Conspiracy*; E. B. O'Callaghan, *op. cit.*, VI, pp. 186-87, 196-99, 202; *The Letters and Papers of Cadwallader Colden*, N. Y., 1937, 9 vols., VIII, pp. 265-66, 270-72, 288-89; Boston *Weekly News-Letter*, May 7-14, June 4-11, 18-25, July 2-9, 16-23, 23-30, August 6-13, September 3-10, 1741.

87 See the preface to the above cited work by Horsmanden, and, especially the very interesting anonymous letter from Massachusetts written in July, 1741, to Cadwallader Colden in his *Letters, loc. cit.*, pp. 270-72, where the hysteria is compared to the Salem witchcraft panic. The same comparison has been made by later writers, as Charles and Mary Beard, *Rise of American Civilization*, I, p. 81.

among the poor—slave and free—was intense. The price of wheat was very high, leading, early in the spring of 1741, to a " general Combination of the Bakers not to bake until the Price fell, which Occasioned some Disturbance and reduced some notwithstanding their Riches to a Want of Bread." [88]

Fires moreover were exceedingly frequent, particularly during March and April, and of suspicious origins, affecting not only private houses, but the Governor's house, the Secretary's office, the King's Chapel, and the barracks of the soldiers. Many contemporaries were convinced that some, at least, were set by Negro slaves and white accomplices. And some of the testimony offered at the trials concerning disaffection rings true.[89] Indeed, the Governor of the Province declared on June 20,[90] " if the truth were ever known, there are not many innocent Negromen, and it is thought that some Negroes of the County are accomplices and were to act their part there." This last idea probably arose from the fact that late in April several suspicious fires occurred in Hackensack, New Jersey, for which at least two slaves were executed, by burning, on the fifth of May.[91]

Concerning the terrible results, in human terms, of the mass hysteria there can be no doubt. About one hundred and fifty slaves and twenty-five whites, including seventeen soldiers,

88 New-York *Journal*, April 20, 1741, quoted by Bridenbaugh, *op. cit.*, p. 358.

89 Thus one of the slaves arrested, Cuffee, "used to say, that a great many people had too much, and others too little; that his old master has a great deal of money, but that in a short time, he should have less, and that he (Cuffee) should have more." Horsmanden, *op. cit.*, p. 39.

90 Lieutenant-Governor George Clarke to the Duke of Newcastle, dated New-York, June 20, 1741, in E. B. O'Callaghan, ed., *op. cit.*, VI, p. 196.

91 *Proceeds of the New Jersey Historical Society for 1874*, p. 179; William Nelson, ed., *Archives of the State of New Jersey*, 1st series, XII, pp. 88, 91-92, 98-99; Boston *Weekly News-Letter*, May 7-14, 1741; Henry S. Cooley, *A Study of Slavery in New Jersey*, p. 43; W. F. Prince notes (*op. cit.*, p. 83) that slaves were arrested in New York City again in 1742 for incendiarism, and one was executed. The Boston *Gazette*, September 28–October 5, 1741, reported slave-created fires in Charlestown, Massachusetts—cited by L. J. Greene, *op. cit.*, p. 195.

were arrested. Four whites, an inn-keeper, John Hughson, his
wife, Sarah, a woman of unsavory reputation and various
names, though usually referred to as Margaret Kerry, and a
man held to be a Spanish priest,[92] John Ury, were executed. Of
the slaves arrested, thirteen were burned alive, eighteen were
hanged (two in chains), and seventy banished. Seven slaves
who had been indicted were never found.[93]

An entry in the journal of the Council of South Carolina for
April 13, 1744, indicates concern over the problem of slave control, for on that day the government accepted an offer of the
Notchee Indians " to assist . . . in Case of any Insurrection, or
rebellion of the Negroes." Occasion to make use of this came
in less than three months. On July 5 the Governor, James Glen,
having received a letter from a Captain Richard Wright asking
for " the assistance of some Notchee Indians, in order to apprehend some runaway Negroes, who had sheltered themselves in
the Woods, and being armed, had committed disorders in the
neighbourhood," notified the Council that he had written to the
Chief of the Notchees asking his aid in destroying these rebel
slaves, whose continued existence was a very dangerous example for their brethren in subjection.[94]

There exist two tantalizingly incomplete references to slave
conspiracies during 1747, though one is more definite than the
other. The first has reference to South Carolina again, and occurs in a letter from a distinguished native of that region,

92 Lt.-Gov. Clarke, in a letter to the Lords of Trade, August 24, 1741
(O'Callaghan, ed., *op. cit.*, VI, pp. 198-99, 202) said the entire episode was
a Popish plot. Ury denied he was a Catholic priest, claiming to be a non-
juring Anglican clergyman. A New York law of 1700 provided for the
hanging of any Catholic priest voluntarily entering the Province. John Ury
was executed August 29, going to his death calmly, and maintaining his
innocence to the end. Boston *Weekly News-Letter*, September 3-10, 1741;
M. J. Lamb, *op. cit.*, I, p. 444. See Ray A. Billington, *The Protestant Crusade
1800-1860*, p. 14.

93 These are the figures given by Horsmanden in an appendix to his work.
Some variations of these figures, none important, are given elsewhere.

94 MS. Council Journal, XI, pp. 183, 383.

Henry Laurens, dated London, March 21, 1748, and addressed to James Cowles. Mr. Laurens tells [95] his friend of the recent arrival of a boat from South Carolina bringing reports from that area up to January 27, 1748. There was nothing of particular importance among them according to him, except " confirmation of the Account of a most horrid Insurrection intended by the Negroes there which was provedentially [sic] discover'd before any mischief done."

The second has reference to New York,[96] but is of a much more negative nature. This occurs in a letter which the famous Cadwallader Colden wrote to his wife from New York City on April 18, 1747. He remarked, " There has been a new rumor of the rising of the Negroes but upon enquiry no foundation can be found for it."

So far as available records go the next generation is one during which there was a marked decline of organized rebellious activity on the part of the Negro slaves. Precisely why this is so the present writer is not certain. It may, however, be noted that acute economic depression or especially exciting events (with the exception of the French and Indian war, which had some effect on the slaves, but which was largely confined to the north and the west—away from the slave area) are generally lacking during these years. It is possible, too, that the rather strenuous activity indulged in during the previous twenty-five or thirty years and the ruthlessness and efficiency with which it was suppressed had an exhausting and cautioning effect upon the slaves. It is an observable tendency in the history of these rebellions as a whole that they seem to come in spasms and spurts, with what may be termed breathing spells or rest periods, of varying lengths, intervening.

Complete quiet, however, did not prevail. The evidence concerning unrest among Virginia and Maryland slaves in 1755-56, during the French and Indian War, and especially after news of the defeat of the English at Monongahela had penetrated to the interior, has previously been presented.[97]

There are reports, fragmentary and unsatisfactory, as is so often the case, of fairly considerable disaffection from 1759 to 1761 in South Carolina. According to one careful historian [98] a " serious attempt at revolt " occurred in the former year. In this connection there may be added significance to a message of February 7, 1760, which the Governor sent to this Province's House of Assembly. He referred to the presence of smallpox in the city and cited this to support his desire that the members return to their homes where, he went on,[99] " your presence will at this time be particularly useful to cause a due execution of the Laws, and preserve the internal quiet of the Country from any attempts of Negroes, or other Persons to disturb it . . ."

The complaint of a South Carolina paper early in 1761 that the slaves " have again begun the hellish practice of poisoning " seems to indicate organized efforts at revenge on the part of the Negroes. This same year the Province adopted special police measures and, as in 1740, offered a bounty for the purpose of attracting white settlers.[100]

Maroons became troublesome in South Carolina again in 1765, and at least one considerable settlement of these rebels was broken up by the militia. During the end of the year reports

97 *Ante*, pp. 19, 20. In 1756, according to Lieutenant-Governor Dinwiddie's letter to Lord Loudon of August 9, there were 120,156 Negroes and 173,316 whites in Virginia. R. A. Brock, ed., *The Official Records of Robert Dinwiddie*, II, p. 474. In Maryland there were 44,539 Negro slaves in 1755, equalling 30% of the total population—Charles A. Barker, *op. cit.*, p. 3.

98 William A. Schaper, *Sectionalism and Representation in South Carolina*, p. 310. J. Coffin, *op. cit.*, mentions a plot in Charles Town in the summer of 1759. This was the period of the Cherokee War in South Carolina, which may have induced restlessness among the slaves. The South Carolina *Gazette*, May 31, 1760, remarked: " Good Reasons have been suggested to us, for not inserting in this Paper any Account of Insurrections, especially at this time."—See R. L. Meriwether, *op. cit.*, p. 226 n.

99 MS. Journals of the Commons House of Assembly, XXXIII, p. 59.

100 D. Wallace, *op. cit.*, I, p. 374. The newspaper is the Charles Town *Gazette*, Jan. 17, 1761.

of large-scale plots recurred. On December 17, the Lieutenant-Governor, William Bull, told the London Board of Trade that he

a few days ago received intimation that some plots are forming and some attem[pt]s of insurrection to be made during these Holydays, [i. e. Christmas] at which Time Slaves are allowed some days of festivity and exemption from labour. I shall therefore take proper measures to prevent the execution of such designs by giving necessary directions to the militia and patrols to be alert on their duty on that season.[101]

These, indeed, were not the only precautionary measures taken, for Indians friendly to the whites were brought into eastern South Carolina to terrorize the slaves, and the white settlers in the up country and even in North Carolina were asked to be ready, at a moment's notice, to march into the lower section of South Carolina. These measures seem to have effectively checked any contemplated uprising.[102]

Late in 1767 Negroes of the neighborhood of Alexandria, Virginia, put into practice a plan for rebellion. How many were involved is not known, but several overseers died from the effects of poison administered to them by slaves. The contemporary press reported,[103] " that some of the negroes have been taken up, four of them were executed about three weeks ago,

101 D. Wallace, *op. cit.*, I, p. 374; E. Donnan, *op. cit.*, IV, p. 415. On January 1, 1766, as Lt.-Gov. Bull pointed out, a new high duty on slaves was to go into effect. Because of this over 8,000 slaves had been brought into South Carolina in the single year 1765, over twice the ordinary number, so that there was more than a " prudent number." In 1769 there were 80,000 Negroes and 45,000 whites in South Carolina.

102 D. Wallace, *op. cit.*, I, p. 374; and see letter from Lord Montagu to the Earl of Hillsborough, dated Charles Town, April 19, 1769, in W. Clark, ed., *State Records of North Carolina*, XI, pp. 225-26. As this indicates, the concern lasted through January, 1766. See also D. Wallace, *Laurens*, p. 120. In January, 1766 over one hundred slaves fled to a maroon settlement in Colleton County swamp—Journals of the Commons House of Assembly, Jan. 14, 1766; Meriwether, *op. cit.*, p. 24.

103 Boston *Chronicle*, January 11-18, 1768; *The Annual Register*, London, 1768, pp. 69-70; Helen Hill, *George Mason*, p. 271.

after which their heads were cut off, and fixed on the chimnies of the courthouse; and it was expected that four more would soon meet the same fate." It is probable that a few of the executed slaves belonged to the eminent George Mason of Virginia.

The next year during which trouble arose because of the concerted efforts of rebellious Negroes, is 1771, and the affected area is Georgia.[104] On December 4 the Council of the Colony was told by Governor James Habersham [105]

that he had received information that a great number of fugitive Negroes had Committed many Robberies and insults between this town [Savannah] and Ebenezer and that their Numbers (which) were now Considerable might be expected to increase daily: that it appeared absolutely necessary to fall upon Some Spirited measures to take and dispirse (sic) them to prevent further Inconvenience...

The Council decided it would be best

to engage some Indians to go out that way hunting, in order to discover the Camp of the Negroes and when they had so done...to order Capt Wylly with part of the Company of the Militia under his Command to go in Search of and apprehend them and to empower him to give a Small Reward to the said Militia if any Extra-

104 In 1768 a British Captain, named John Wilson, was accused in Boston of attempting to incite slave rebellion with the aim, according to one source, of driving the " Liberty Boys to death." He was arrested but the indictment was quashed and Wilson left the Province.—G. H. Moore, *Notes on the History of Slavery in Massachusetts*, p. 129. A letter dated Charles Town, August 16, 1768 (in the Boston *Chronicle*, October 3-10, 1768) concerning the Regulator events in South Carolina, asserts that the Regulators had fought a pitched battle with a large group of " banditti " described as a " numerous collection of outcast mulattoes, mustees and free negroes." In the work compiled and written by the Savannah unit of the Federal Writers' Project in Georgia, entitled *Savannah* (p. 50) reference is made to a slave insurrection in that city in 1768. This, however, is an error, as the writers had in mind the slave unrest in this city during the American Revolution, which will be noticed later. This information was kindly furnished the present writer by Miss Mary Granger, District Supervisor of the Georgia Writers' Project, letter dated Savannah, August 8, 1940.

105 A. D. Candler, ed., *op. cit.*, XII, pp. 146-47.

ordinary duty should be required of them on this necessary Service the Expense of which to be defray'd by the Treasurer...

It further advised that the city of Savannah itself be most carefully patrolled during the coming Christmas holidays, though what particular information made this suggestion especially pertinent does not appear.

Similar trouble in no less dangerous form was reported again within six months. Among the presentments of the Savannah Grand Jury in June, 1772, brought to the attention of the Governor and the Council was one reporting [106]

That a Number of fugitive Slaves have Assembled themselves on or near the borders of the River Savannah & are frequently committing Depredations on the Inhabitants in that Neighbourhood with Impunity...the said fugitive Slaves did lately Set fire to a Dwelling house near Black Creek in which a White Child was Burnt to death & also that some Slaves had lately Stopt a boat belonging to Jno Stirk upon the River & taken several articles of Value therefrom, also that some Slaves being at a Camp near Augustins Creek being Surprized by one Fendin a White Man did fire at the said Fendin.

It was decided

to direct the Officer Commanding the Company of Militia belonging to the first North West Division to send out Patrols of Men.... In Quest of the said fugitive Slaves on the Main or on the Islands in the River within the patrol Division of the said Compy & also that his Honor [the Governor] will order the Commander of the Scout boat to goe up the river Savannah and Search the Creeks & Secret places on the River & Islands as farr as Abercorn Creek in Order to discover & take any of the said fugitive Slaves or their boats.

In the year 1772 a Negro conspiracy was uncovered in the area around Perth Amboy, New Jersey, a center of the slave trade. The outbreak of actual violence was " prevented by due

106 *Ibid.*, XII, pp. 325-26.

precautionary measures," and just how serious this plot was is not clear. It is of interest to note that the fear this aroused stimulated at least one individual living in the affected region to advocate, at this early date, the shipment of all the slaves to Africa at the expense of their owners.[107]

The conspiracy of slaves in September, 1774, to liberate themselves by offering to fight with the British against the Bostonians on condition that, if successful, freedom was to be theirs, has already been mentioned, as has the fact that censorship cuts off further information.[108] It is to be noted that this conspiracy, coming in the midst of fierce debates in which the concepts of " natural rights," " liberty " and " equality " largely figured, stimulated thinking on the subject of Negro slavery itself, just as the New Jersey plot two years before had done. A Massachusetts commentator, Abigail, the wife of John Adams, went further than did he of New Jersey, for she wrote: [109] " I wish most sincerely there was not a slave in the province it always appeared a most iniquitous scheme to me to fight ourselves for what we are daily robbing and plundering from those who have as good a right to freedom as we have. You know my mind on this subject."

In November, 1774, several slaves, men and women, in St. Andrew's Parish, Georgia, possibly stimulated by the excitement that was at the moment running through all the colonies, rebelled and before being subdued killed four whites and wounded three others. Other than the fact that two of the slaves were burned alive for their part in this outbreak, the punishment meted out to the rebels as a whole is not recorded.[110]

107 William A. Whitehead, *Contributions to the Early History of Perth Amboy and Adjoining Country*, p. 320. In 1750 two slaves (convicted of murder, and of attempted murder) were burned alive in Perth Amboy.— Leonard Lundin, *Cockpit of the Revolution*, p. 44.

108 *Ante*, p. 87.

109 Mrs. John Adams to her husband, dated Boston, September 22, 1774, in Charles F. Adams, ed., *Letters of Mrs. Adams*, I, p. 24.

110 Savannah *Georgia Gazette*, December 7, 1774, in U. B. Phillips, ed., *Plantation and Frontier Documents*, II, pp. 118-119.

During the first year of actual hostilities of the American Revolution there occurred what appears to have been a serious plot in Beaufort, Pitt, and Craven Counties, North Carolina. Contemporary reference to or accounts of this are generally few and meagre, but there is one exception. A full and interesting description of the event was written in the midst of the excitement by one of the participants in the drive to crush the unrest.[111]

On July 8 a slave of a Mr. Dayner and another belonging to a Captain Thomas Respess told the latter that on that very evening " an insurrection of the negroes against the whole people " was scheduled to occur.

We immediately sent off an Express to Tarborough to alarm the inhabitants there, we then proceeded to business and appointed upwards of one hundred men as patrolers and passed a resolve that any negroes that should be destroyed. . . should be paid for by a tax on the negroes in this county.We then separated to sound the alarm through this county and apprehend the suspected heads. By night we had in custody and in goal(sic) near forty under proper guard.

The following day " the committee sett and proceeded to examine into the affair and find it a deep laid Horrid Tragick Plan laid for destroying the inhabitants of this province without respect of persons, age or sex." It was discovered that a white man, a Northern boat captain named Johnson who had recently

111 Letter from John Simpson, chairman of the Pitt County Committee of Correspondence to Richard Cogdell, chairman of the Craven County Committee, July 15, 1775, in William Saunders, ed., *Colonial Records of North Carolina*, X, p. 94, and in Henry T. King, *Sketches of Pitt County*, pp. 65-67. James S. Bassett has written, in *Slavery and Servitude in the Colony of North Carolina*, p. 62, that the alarm at this time was " entirely unfounded " and cited the above work edited by W. Saunders. But not only does the quoted contemporary letter appear in that collection, but the editor himself in his preface (*op. cit.*, X, p. xxiii) wrote, " the people were aware of the efforts to excite the negroes to insurrection, and had taken such precautions in the premises that when an extended insurrection was attempted . . . it was promptly suppressed before any mischief was done." The account by Francis-Xavier Martin in *The History of North Carolina*, II, pp. 353-54 is good. See also S. A. Ashe, *History of North Carolina*, I, p. 435.

landed for a supply of naval stores, and a slave named Merrick, of Bath, in Beaufort County, had " propagated the contagion ... There were five negroes ... whipt this day by order."

On July 10 the committee

ordered several to be severely whipt and sentenced several to receive 80 lashes each to have both Ears crap'd which was executed in the presence of the Committee and a great number of spectators. In the afternoon we received by express from Coll. Blount... of... negroes being in arms on the line of Craven and Pitt and prayed assistance of arms and ammunition which we readily granted. We posted guards upon the roads for several miles that night.

As often happened in these cases, exaggerated rumors of hundreds of armed slaves advancing every which way did fly about, one of them started by a slave woman who intended to kill her master and put the blame on one of these phantom bodies. Arms and ammunition were, however, found in the possession of several of the slaves; and that some, at least, were killed by the patrollers appears in Mr. Simpson's remark about one of his neighbors, that " had he been at Martinborough he would have received pay for his negroes." [112]

The end of this letter written one week after the plot's exposure shows that the work of repression was still going on, for it reads:

We keep taking up examining and scourging more or less every day; From which-ever part of the County they come they all confess nearly the same thing, viz., that they were one and all on the night of the 8th instant to fall on and destroy the family where they lived, then to proceed from House to House (Burning as they went) until they arrived in the back country where they were to be received with by a number of Persons there appointed and armed by the Government for their protection and as a further reward they were to be settled in a free government of their own.

112 On April 23, 1783, the State of North Carolina agreed to pay to William Bryan of Craven County, fifty pounds, " for a negro man slave killed in suppressing of Rebel Slaves." It appears probable, though by no means certain, that this has reference to the events of 1775. W. Clark, ed., *The State Records of North Carolina*, XIX, p. 258.

During this same year alarms were aroused because of the alleged concerted activities of slaves in the Provinces of New York, South Carolina, and Virginia, but none seems to have been important. One, that in Virginia, where Governor Dunmore justified his seizure of powder before a delegation of irate citizens led by Patrick Henry on the ground that he had information of a projected Negro insurrection, was almost certainly spurious.[113]

There were hints, rather than actual accounts, of disturbances among the slaves in Georgia, Pennsylvania, and New Jersey in 1776. There is, for example, indirect evidence that Colonel Stephen Bull of Georgia had written to Henry Laurens of South Carolina telling him of Negro unrest and plans for the execution of leading agitators among them. This is evident since the reply of Laurens, dated Charles Town, March 16, 1776, refers to the receipt of such a communication, and declares: [114]

Now for the grand we may say awful business contained in your Letter, it is an awful business notwithstanding it has the Sanction of Law, to put even fugitives & Rebellious Slaves to death—the prospect is horrible—We think the Council of Safety in Georgia ought to give that encouragement which is necessary to induce proper persons to seize & if nothing else will do to destroy all those Rebellious Negroes upon Tybee Island or wherever they may be found...

Reference has already been made to the evidence of alarm among the inhabitants of Bucks County, Pennsylvania, in the

113 James Sullivan, ed., *Minutes of the Albany Committee of Correspondence, 1775-1778*, I, pp. 24, 87; D. Wallace, *Laurens*, p. 120 n.; see also, Peter Force, ed., *American Archives*, 4th Series, II, p. 180; C. H. VanTyne, *The War of Independence*, p. 199. The problem of slave control at the end of 1775, especially after Dunmore's proclamation of November 7, promising freedom to slaves of rebels able to bear arms if they came to his army, was very serious. But the danger here was more from wholesale flight than from rebellion. This problem, never satisfactorily resolved, was acute throughout the slave area during all the years of the Revolution. See H. Aptheker, *The Negro in the American Revolution*.

114 In *South Carolina Historical and Genealogical Magazine*, IV, p. 205.

summer of this year,[115] and the arrest of one slave, Samson, considered to be the chief disturber of the masters' security. During the same season, as appears from another of those tantalizingly incomplete letters—this from Samuel Tucker to John Hancock, President of the Continental Congress, dated Trenton, New Jersey, July 5, 1776—like troubles, apparently of a more serious nature, bothered Pennsylvania's northern neighbor. Mr. Tucker told [116] Mr. Hancock of various difficulties besetting the American cause in his region, and among these appeared this sentence, " The story of the negroes may be depended upon, so far at least as to their arming and attempting to form themselves, particularly in Somerset county."

Henry Laurens, whose correspondence has already been twice called upon to furnish information about Negro uprisings, was once again the recipient of a letter on this subject in 1778. The informant this time is the Marquis de Lafayette, writing on March 11, from Albany, New York. Lafayette tells Mr. Laurens that [117] demoralization has filtered into his army's ranks for the soldiers had gone without pay for a long time. He adds that he had recently received an anonymous letter detailing a plot in which slaves and soldiers were involved, " to burn the city of albany, the stores, magazines, batteaux as soon as the rivers would open . . . that many officers and gentlemen were

115 *Ante*, p. 88.

116 Peter Force, ed., *American Archives*, Fifth Series, I, p. 16. According to E. B. Greene and V. D. Harrington, *American Population before the Federal Census of 1790*, p. 108, there were, in 1772, 3,313 Negroes and 67,710 whites in New Jersey. But Leonard Lundin, *op. cit.*, p. 44, states that there were some 10,000 Negroes, and 120,000 whites in 1776 in New Jersey. The same year, 1776, the Shrewsbury, N. J., Committee of Observation confiscated all arms in the possession of Negroes, free and slave, and restricted the movements of the latter—*ibid.*, p. 44; while the Albany, N. Y. Committee of Correspondence ordered that any male Negro slaves within the Manor of Renssalaerwyck found abroad without a pass after 6 P. M. were to " receive Corporal punishment "—J. Sullivan, ed., *op. cit.*, I, p. 585.

117 *The South Carolina Historical and Genealogical Magazine*, VIII, p. 7. See *ante*, p. 88. According to George Howell and J. Tenney, *History of the County of Albany*, p. 303, there were 3,877 Negroes in the area in 1771.

to be assassinated by their own nigroes etc etc etc," but he had not been able to uncover anything definite.

Further evidence of unrest among the approximately four thousand slaves in Albany County, New York from 1778 to 1780 has been referred to earlier. Sufficient reference has also already been made to like difficulties in New Jersey and Georgia in 1779.[118]

In the decade of the eighties there were a few reports of slave conspiracies, but the activities of maroons seem to have been more important. A passage in a letter of July 21, 1781 from a Colonel Wooding of Halifax County, Virginia, to another officer asking for arms is pertinent. He remarked [119] that there were some good guns in the possession of private individuals but they " secrete them and Say they will do it for their own Defence against insurrections of Slaves or Tories—Reasons that seem to carry weight (with me at least) ...". In a letter of May 2, 1782 from Accomack County, Virginia, reference is made [120] " to a conspiracy of tories, British and negroes," but details are lacking. There are indications [121] of a " dangerous insurrection " having been planned by slaves of Cumberland County, in the same State in the spring of 1786, but early disclosure seems to have effectively blocked any actual uprising at that time.

118 *Ante*, p. 89. In addition is to be noted a report of July, 1779, from Shrewsbury, Monmouth County, New Jersey, of a raid by whites and fifty Negroes against *Revolutionists, resulting in the loss of eighty head of cattle, twenty horses, and the capture of two male prisoners by the raiders.— William Nelson, ed., *Archives of New Jersey*, 2nd ser., III, p. 504. There was much guerilla warfare and a strong Loyalist group in Monmouth County. L. Lundin, *op. cit.*, p. 116.

119 *C. V. S. P.*, II, p. 233. Note also a petition from citizens of Botetourt County, Virginia, urging the execution of a slave, Jack convicted in April, 1780, of " enlisting several negroes to raise in arms and join Lord Cornwallis " —*ibid.*, I, p. 477.

120 Colonel George Corbin to Colonel Davies, *ibid.*, III, p. 149.

121 W. J. Moulson to Governor Patrick Henry, dated Cumberland County, May 6, 1786, in *ibid.*, IV, p. 132.

The Spanish province of Louisiana was seriously troubled from 1782 to 1784 by numerous " rebellious maroons and negroes," under the leadership of one called St. Malo. An expedition succeeded in capturing about twenty-five of these people, men and women, and their punishments varied from hanging to branding and receiving hundreds of lashes.[122]

Fuller information is available concerning like conduct in Virginia during approximately the same period. It is known, for example, that a slave, Bill, of Prince William County, was sentenced to death in May, 1781, having been convicted (peculiarly enough for one in his status) of the crime of treason,[123] " in aiding abetting, and felloniously and traitorously waging & levying war against the Commonwealth, in conjunction with divers enemies of the same, in an armed vessel." A letter of September 10, of this year, from a resident of Accomack County, seems to have reference to the same sort of thing for which Bill was hanged: [124]

We have had most alarming times this Summer all along shore, from a sett of Barges manned mostly by our own negroes who have run off — These fellows are really dangerous to an individual singled out for their vengeance whose property lay exposed — They burnt several houses.

On August 30, 1782 Edmund Randolph wrote [125] James Madison of the alarming activities of a group of whites and fugitive slaves numbering about fifty men whose attacks on plantations within his native City County, Virginia, was a serious menace to life and property. A communication written four

122 Roscoe R. Hill, ed., *Descriptive Catalogue of the Documents Relating to the History of the United States in the Papeles Procedentes de Cuba Deposited in the Archivo General de Indias at Seville*, p. 137; L. Porteus, " Index to Spanish Judicial Records," in *The Louisiana Historical Quarterly*, XX, pp. 840-865.

123 *C. V. S. P.*, II, p. 90.

124 Levin Joynes to Colonel Davies, *ibid.*, II, p. 411.

125 M. D. Conway, *Omitted Chapters of History disclosed in the Life and Papers of Edmund Randolph*, pp. 50-51.

days later and dated "Point of Fork," in the same State, declared [126] that "Runaway negroes joined by a few white men have of late been doing mischief in the neighborhood."

The British had combatted the revolutionists' siege of Savannah with the aid of a numerous body of Negro slaves who served under the inspiration of a promised freedom. The final defeat of the English in this war crushed the hopes of these Negroes. They fled, with their arms, called themselves soldiers of the King of England, and with a stockaded village half a mile long and over four hundred feet wide in the Bell Isle Swamp some twenty miles north of Savannah as their base, carried on a guerrilla warfare for years along the Savannah River. Finally, in 1786, militia from Georgia and South Carolina, together with Indian allies, successfully attacked the Negro settlement with resulting heavy casualties. Other camps of desperate fugitive slaves in Georgia were also attacked and reportedly destroyed during the following year.[127] And in the legislative message delivered that year, 1787, by Governor Thomas Pinckney of South Carolina, reference was made [128] to the serious depredations of a group of armed maroons in the southern part of the State.

126 Captain John Peyton to Colonel Davies, September 3, 1782, *C. V. S. P.*, III, p. 287. Columbia in Goochland County was known as Point of the Fork. See Rochefoucault-Liancourt, *op. cit.*, II, p. 48; I. Weld, *op. cit.*, I, p. 197.

127 According to Harry E. Wildes (*Anthony Wayne*, p. 288), when Savannah was entered by the American Army in July, 1782, "slaves abandoned by the British refused to work again." W. B. Stevens, *A History of Georgia*, II, pp. 376-78; Allan Nevins, *The American States During and After the Revolution 1775-1789*, p. 450; C. G. Woodson, *The Negro in Our History*, p. 123; U. B. Phillips, *American Negro Slavery*, p. 510.

128 C. C. Pinckney, *Life of General Thomas Pinckney*, p. 95; D. D. Wallace, *History of South Carolina*, II, p. 415.

CHAPTER IX

1791-1809

THE dozen years following 1790 formed a period of more intense and widespread slave discontent than any that had preceded (with the possible exception of the much shorter period from 1737 to 1741). Some of the factors that help explain this phenomenon have already been examined—such as the revolutionary philosophy then prevalent abroad and at home, the great Negro uprisings in the nearby West Indies, and the severe depression that gripped the South, especially North Carolina, Virginia, and Louisiana, for practically the entire period.

Some further particulars may be noted as possibly of importance in the same connection. For example, the defeat of St. Clair by the Indians in November, 1791, caused great alarm in western Virginia, while provocation by the whites started the Cherokees south of the Ohio on the warpath in the summer of 1793,[1] both events necessitating the absence of large bodies of militia from areas of considerable concentration of slaves. Again, in 1793 and 1794 the slogan of liberty or death rang through western North Carolina and Virginia as part of the Whiskey Insurrection,[2] the excitement and implications of which may possibly have reached the slaves.

It has been remarked that a concomitant of depression during these years was a disproportionate population growth so that the number of Negroes increased more rapidly than the number of whites. This may be exemplified by the condition in the two States, Virginia and North Carolina, most disturbed by slave unrest.

In North Carolina the Negro population increased by 32 per cent (41.6 per cent for the free Negroes) from 1790 to 1800, while the white population showed a growth of but 17 per cent.

1 Richard Hildreth, *The History of the United States of America*, IV, pp. 445-46.

2 John B. McMaster, *A History of the People of the United States*, II, p. 198.

The bulk of this disproportion centered in the eastern portion of the State.[3] Similarly in Virginia, during the decade, the white population grew by 16.2 per cent, the slave population by 17.8 per cent, and, alarming indeed, the free Negro population by 56.4 per cent. The figures for the two eastern sections (Tidewater and Piedmont) sharpen this trend. Thus, in the Tidewater area the white population increased by but 1.2 per cent, the slaves over 6 per cent, and the free Negroes by 55.8 per cent. Indeed, out of thirty Tidewater counties comparable for the period, nineteen actually lost in white population, while but ten, and those very slightly, in slave population. In the Piedmont the whites advanced 11.4 per cent, the slaves 28.4 per cent, and the free Negroes 43.2 per cent.[4]

Slave uprisings occurred in lower Louisiana in 1791 and again in 1792, but details are not known.[5] The latter year witnessed serious trouble in Virginia during May, June, and July, in Norfolk, Portsmouth, Hampton, and the county just across the Chesapeake Bay, Northampton,[6] which appears to have been the center of the unrest, as well as alarm in at least

3 R. H. Taylor, " Slaveholding in North Carolina: an economic view," in *James Sprunt Historical Publications*, XVIII, pp. 19, 28.

4 Figures calculated from " The Census—A tabular statement of the free white, free colored, slave, and total population in each county ... 1790 ... 1850," in *Documents Containing Statistics of Virginia*, ordered to be printed by the State Convention sitting in the City of Richmond 1850-1851, Richmond, 1851, no pagination. A. O. Craven, *Soil Exhaustion as a Factor in the Agricultural History of Virginia and Maryland 1606-1860*, p. 119, says twenty-three out of forty Tidewater counties lost in white population from 1790 to 1800. But not all counties were comparable, some being formed after 1790, and some having areas taken from them. Thus, for example, the city of Richmond is given with Henrico County in 1790, but separately in 1800.

5 R. R. Hill, ed., *op. cit.*, p. 100: " 1792 New Orleans. Sobre levantamiento de negros," p. 402, reference to letter from Estevan Miro, Governor of Louisiana to Luis de las Casas, Captain-General of Cuba, 1791," negro insurrection at Punta Cortada."

6 In 1790 Northampton had 3,181 whites, 3,244 slaves, 464 free Negroes; Norfolk Borough (including Norfolk and Portsmouth) had 8928 whites, 5345 slaves, 251 free Negroes; Hampton was included in Elizabeth City which had 1556 whites, 1876 slaves, 18 free Negroes. See note 4.

two western counties, Greenbrier and Kanawha (now in West Virginia, and in the neighborhood of Newbern, North Carolina.

On May 5, 1792, the Northampton County militia lieutenant, Smith Snead, received a letter signed by six local residents assuring him that " a variety of circumstances " made it clear that a revolt was impending and urging him to get arms. Accordingly, he wrote the same day to Governor Henry Lee for " one hundred weight of powder and four hundred of Lead." [7] A letter dated Petersburg, Virginia, May 17, 1792, gives one a more concrete idea of the " circumstances " reported to exist: [8]

Several alarming accounts have been received in town, of a very dangerous Insurrection among the Negroes in the Eastern shore of Virginia ;—Reports state, That about two weeks ago, the Negroes in that part of the State, to the amount of about 900, assembled in different parts, armed with muskets, spears, clubs &c and committed several outrages upon the inhabitants. A favorite servant of Colonel Savage, who had joined them, met his master on the road, took his horse and some money from him, and treated him in an insolent manner.   Celeb, a negro, the property of Mr. Simkins, was to command this banditti ; he was also a favorite servant of his master and had long lived with him in the capacity of overseer.   A barrel of musket balls, about 300 spears, some guns, powder, provisions, &c have already been discovered and taken ; the spears, it is said, were made by a negro blacksmith on the Eastern shore.   A considerable number of the slaves have been taken up, and it is expected will be hanged.

It appears from a letter which has been lately discovered in Norfolk from one of the Negroes on the Eastern shore that they had concerted a plan with the Negroes from Norfolk and Portsmouth to commit some violent outrages in and about those towns. Six hundred of them were to cross the bay, at a certain time in the night, and were to be joined by the Negroes, in that Neighborhood ; then they meant to blow up the magazine in Norfolk, and massacre the inhabitants.

7 *C.V.S.P.*, V, pp. 534-35.

8 Published in *The Boston Gazette and the Country Journal*, June 18, 1792.

On May 9, a Mr. H. Guy of Northampton had written to the militia captain of Norfolk, Thomas Newton, Jr., concerning evidence gotten from ringleaders about a plot in that city. The next day Mr. Newton wrote to the Governor asking for arms, and remarking,[9] " From circumstances, I apprehend there has been a general communication in the lower parts of the County, tho' we cannot fix anything hereabouts." The same day the harrassed Governor received a letter from Portsmouth pleading for arms and adding that the conduct of the slaves in that neighborhood " has long since warranted the suspicion . . . The fears of the people of the county are greatly agitated from bodies of negroes collecting among them in numbers not less than 300 and dispercing again." Next week the Governor again heard from Northampton and learned that about ten slaves had been arrested, but that " the proof [was] insufficient to convict them." Three, however, were banished, and " some of them whip'd, and the rest discharged," which it was thought " has had a good effect, for we experience a very different behaviour among them." Yet it was cautiously added, " how long it will continue God only knows " and the strengthening of the militia was recommended. A letter detailing similar activities, but concerning sixteen slaves, was sent the same day from Hampton to Richmond.

Two days later, on May 19, 1792, the Governor heard jointly from Mr. Newton and the Mayor of Norfolk. They asked for two hundred stands of arms, and commented,[10] " we have generally a number of strangers here, whose interest it will be to take up arms as well as the [slave] inhabitants," probably referring to the Negroes brought by the West Indian refugees.

On May 21 Mr. Snead of Northampton was again writing, this time rather cheerfully. He now felt that not many slaves were implicated and thought it worthwhile to add, " no white person was concerned with them." He stated, however, that his

9 *C.V.S.P.*, V, pp. 542, 546-47.

10 *Ibid.*, V, p. 552. Fears of slaves and a call for aid from Kanawha, then troubled by Indians, are mentioned on this same page.

idea that the disaffection was not widespread, " by no means is a general opinion, a large majority think differently." The patrol was therefore increased and sent out " as often as possible," encountering no particular difficulty until July 8 when a member of it was attacked by six slaves. Five of these were captured, tried with amazing speed, so that by July 9 three of them had been condemned and executed. It was hoped that this would " be a sufficient terror, and teach them wisdom." [11]

A communication from Newbern, North Carolina dated July 26, 1792, though confident in tone, still indicates that the unrest and terror had reached that area: [12]

> The negroes in this town and neighbourhood, have stirred a rumour of their having in contemplation to rise against their masters and to procure themselves their liberty; the inhabitants have been alarmed and keep a strict watch to prevent their procuring arms; should it become serious, which I don't think, the worst that could befal (sic) us, would be their setting the town on fire. It is very absurd of the blacks, to suppose they could accomplish their views, and from the precautions that are taken to guard against a surprise, little danger is to be apprehended.

And a letter from Richmond, Virginia, dated November 19, told of that ever-recurring phenomenon under slavery, the visitation of armed, outlawed fugitive slaves, this one in Charles City County, and resulting in the killing of an armed overseer, followed by the capture, with the aid of dogs, of about ten of the maroons.[13]

On the night of July 20, 1793, a certain Mr. Randolph of Richmond was awakened by voices: [14]

11 *Ibid.*, V, pp. 555, 625. Fears in the Counties of Greenbrier and Mathews are expressed on page 585.

12 The Boston *Gazette*, September 3, 1792.

13 *Ibid.*, December 17, 1792. Concerning the events of 1792, U. B. Phillips wrote only this: "At Norfolk in 1792 some negroes were arrested on suspicion of conspiracy but were promptly discharged for lack of evidence" *op. cit.*, pp. 473-474.

14 *C. V. S. P.*, VI, pp. 452-53.

I arose & went softly to my window, when I discovered two ne-groes close to the wall of my house under me; the one spoke to the other telling him that the blacks were to kill the white people soon in this place. The other asked how soon; the other replied there must be a day set. He said when; & the other answered, between this and the 15th day of October. The other said, you wont kill them; his reply was, Ill be dammed if we don't on the 15th of October.

Soon a third joined them and the slaves were, verbally, dividing the houses amongst them. One " who seemed to be the chief speaker said, you see how the blacks has killed the whites in the French Island and took it a while ago."

This deposition and " a copy of a letter found in York Town signed ' Secret Keeper, Richmond '," aroused the fears of five aldermen of Petersburg so that, on August 17, they asked the Governor for arms. A similar appeal, dated August 21, came from Portsmouth. Two days later the Governor directed the militia in Richmond itself to be on the alert, while James Wood, the Lieutenant-Governor, received a request for arms, dated September 10, from Elizabeth City, the writer declaring, " I am satisfied this county is in Danger, and I hope you will use your best endeavour to aid us with arms." The eminent John Mar-shall, himself, sent a letter he had received from Powhatan, to the Governor, describing the absconding of Negro drivers, the whipping of numerous slaves, and affirming,[15] " takeing all matters into consideration, I can't help thinking that the in-tended Rising is true."

The commanding officer of the militia of Warwick County forwarded a plea for arms on November 25, and declared,[16] " since the melancholy affair at Hispaniola, the Inhabitants of the lower country and especially this county have been repeat-edly alarmed by some of their Slaves having attempted to raise

15 *Ibid.*, VI, pp. 488-89, 490, 493, 494, 524, 547.

16 *Ibid.*, VI, p. 651. This evidence indicates that the Virginia State Senator, John J. Maund, was mistaken in ascribing the reports of slave unrest at this time entirely to the designs of malicious people, as previously noted. *Ante*, p. 96.

an Insurrection, which was timely suppressed in this county by executing one of the principal advisors of the Insurrection."

Evidence of organized disaffection in Charleston, South Carolina in 1793 has been noted.[17] In addition several fires in Albany, New York during the month of November of the same year, which caused damages totalling a quarter of a million dollars, were set by slaves. Three of them, a man and two women, were executed for this early in 1794.[18]

In the spring of 1795 two conspiracies, one of which, at least, was quite serious, were uncovered and suppressed in Pointe Coupée and St. Landry Parishes, Louisiana. Of the latter nothing more than its existence [19] is known, while the information concerning the Pointe Coupée episode is incomplete and rather uncertain.[20]

From the available evidence the facts concerning this plot appear to be as follows. Slaves in Pointe Coupée Parish [21] planned to rebel and kill their masters, but some disagreement among the leaders as to when to begin the actual attack led to the conspiracy's disclosure. The regular forces and militia units of the Spanish government were immediately pressed into serv-

17 *Ante*, p. 96.

18 G. Howell and J. Tenney, *op. cit.*, p. 302; E. Olson, *Negro Slavery in New York, 1626-1827*, pp. 98-99.

19 Among the letters to the Baron de Carondolet, Governor of Louisiana, noted by R. Hill (*op. cit.*, p. 16) is one referring to a "projected uprising of negro slaves" in May, 1795, near Opelousas, which is in St. Landry Parish, adjoining Ponte Coupée on the west.

20 U. B. Phillips (*op. cit.*, p. 474) gives thirty-six words to the Pointe Coupée event, and what he says is either wrong or highly doubtful. He, also, puts the plot in 1796. Though he gives no references, this was probably gotten from C. C. Robin who is his *Voyages*, as quoted by J. A. Robertson, *Louisiana Under the Rule of Spain, France, and the United States, 1785-1807*, I, p. 229, so dates it. J. C. Carroll, *op. cit.*, p. 44, follows Phillips.

21 In 1785 (the nearest date, so far as is known, for which figures are available) the parish had 482 whites, 1035 slaves, and 4 free Negroes, as given in *Appendix to an Account of Louisiana, being an Abstract of Documents in the Offices of the Departments of State and of Treasury*, Washington, n. d., p. lxxxiv.

ice for the purpose of apprehending the insurgents. Some of the Negroes resisted capture and in the ensuing struggle about twenty-five of them were killed. Approximately the same number were executed, and the bodies of several of the rebels were left hanging in various parts of the Parish as demonstrations of the fate awaiting slaves who should emulate them. It appears that a few whites—probably three—were implicated in this effort, and they were banished from the colony.[22]

Carondolet issued a decree in June, 1795 for the purpose [23] " of keeping them [the slaves] in that state of content and subordination which would alienate them from the wish of acquiring a freedom which has cost so much blood to those of St. Domingo." For this he ordered that each slave was to get a barrel of corn in the ear each month and *either* some waste land for his own use *or* a linen shirt and trousers in summer and coat and trousers in winter. He was to work from sun-up to sundown with a total of two and one-half hours for resting and eating. He was to rest on Sunday, except during harvest, when he was to be paid about thirty cents for each Sunday's work. Not all was " amelioration," however, for a new code detailing methods of punishment, organizing a police system, and stating when the killing of a slave would be proper, was also enacted.

22 See the account of Dr. Paul Alliot, who lived in the region at the time, written in 1804, in J. A. Robertson, *op. cit.*, I, pp. 119-121 ; Francis-Xavier Martin, *The History of Louisiana*, II, p. 127 ; E. Bunner, *History of Louisana,* p. 164. Charles Gayarré's account in *History of Louisiana*, III, pp. 354-55; is fairly similar, but he adds that the slaves intended to spare the white females in order " to gratify" their " lust," a statement without documentation, and for which the present writer has seen no corroboration. Bearing in mind Gayarré's vicious anti-Negro prejudice, the statement carries little weight. It is, however, followed by A. Phelps, *Louisiana*, pp. 171-72, and A. Fortier, *A History of Louisiana*, II, p. 164. It is to be observed, however, that the small number of female slaves in Louisiana was an important complaint of the males. This was aggravated by the very common practice among wealthy whites of keeping Negro concubines.—J. Robertson, *op. cit.*, I, pp. 183-84; A. P. Whitaker, *The Mississipi Question*, p. 162.

23 As note 21, pp. lxxvii-lxxxiii; reprinted with some verbal changes in *Louisiana Historical Quarterly*, XX, pp. 593 ff.

And, as a final precautionary step, the slave trade was forbidden, a prohibition that lasted for four years.

The neighborhood of Wilmington, North Carolina, was harrassed in June and July, 1795, by a [24] " number of runaway Negroes, who in the daytime secrete themselves in the swamps and woods ... at night committed various depredations on the neighboring plantations." They killed at least one white man, an overseer, and severely wounded another. About five of these maroons, according to a report of July 3, including the leader, known as the " General of the Swamps," were killed by hunting parties. It was hoped that " these well-timed severities " would " totally break up their nest of miscreants—At all events, this town has nothing to apprehend as the citizens keep a strong and vigilant night guard." On July 14 the capture and execution of four more maroons were reported. Three days later it was believed that only one leader and a " few deluded followers " were still at large.

Mention has already been made of the presentment of the Chowan County, North Carolina grand jury in May, 1796 denouncing the Quakers as responsible for the slave unrest declared to be shockingly prevalent, and citing as proof of this the frequency with which the crime of arson was committed in the area. Note has also been taken of similar troubles in Albany, New York in 1793 and in Charleston, South Carolina from 1796 to 1798.[25] These were, however, by no means the only regions hit by incendiarism during the decade, which was often blamed upon the slaves.[26]

In December, 1794 a reward of $5,850 was offered for the discovery of the incendiaries held responsible for a disastrous

24 Wilmington *Chronicle* (photostat, Library of Congress), July 3, 10, 17, 1795; Charleston *City Gazette*, July 18, 23, 1795; R. H. Taylor, " Slave conspiracies in North Carolina," in the *North Carolina Historical Review*, V, pp. 23-24.

25 *Ante*, pp. 96, 103.

26 Sometimes " Jacobins " were blamed. J. B. McMaster, *op. cit.*, II, pp. 538-39, is the only standard historian who pays any attention to these fires. He refers only to those of 1796, and misses the fact that slaves were blamed.

fire in Augusta, Georgia.[27] Charleston was swept by fire in November, 1795, as well as later, and in this case large rewards were offered for the apprehension of the guilty persons, the Governor promising pardon for those confessing, and declaring a day of fasting.[28] In 1796 fires alarmed not only Charleston, but New York City, Newark and Elizabeth in New Jersey, Savannah, and Baltimore, with contemporaries generally convinced that slaves were the agents.[29] A serious fire in Fredericksburg, Virginia, in April, 1799 was declared to be the work of incendiaries,[30] while James T. Callender, writing to Thomas Jefferson on September 29, 1800 from the Richmond jail, then overcrowded by the slave followers of Gabriel, declared,[31] " It has come out that the fire in Richmond within these two years, was the work of negroes."

The excitement throughout the nation, particularly in 1796, because of these recurrent mysterious fires, was extraordinary, one contemporary declaring it was greater than that aroused by the yellow fever epidemics of the same era. It is impossible to confidently express an opinion as to the real cause of these fires, or any of them, but it is pertinent to note the fact that they were generally [32] ascribed to the deliberate working out of plots amongst the slaves.

27 Philadelphia *Gazette of the United States*, January 17, 1795.

28 Charleston *City Gazette*, November 4, 1795. Note the item in the issue of November 12, 1795, where a Captain William Cunningham of Charleston is scolded for permitting a dance of Negroes to last past ten o'clock in the evening, "at this critical time more particularly."

29 Hartford *Connecticut Courant*, January 2, February 20, 1797; N. Y. *Minerva*, August 4, 12, 26, November 21, and all December, 1796; William Priest, *Travels in the United States*, pp. viii, 171; Joseph Atkinson, *The History of Newark*, p. 171.

30 Fredericksburg *Virginia Herald*, April 9, 1799.

31 Published in S. M. Hamilton, ed., *The Writings of James Monroe*, III, pp. 209-210 n.

32 There were exceptions, of course, as the letter from "a citizen but no alarmist" in the N. Y. *Minerva*, December 19, 1796, blaming poor construction for the fires.

In addition to the foregoing there were two rather small, and apparently spontaneous, outbreaks in Virginia during these years. The former slave, Austin Steward, told [33] of the resistance of a group of slaves to search by a patrol in Prince William County in about 1797. He stated that four whites were killed and one wounded, while six slaves died and two suffered wounds. This caused great " alarm and perfect consternation." And late in 1799 there was an uprising among a group of Negroes in Southampton County who were being transported to Georgia. Accounts agree that two whites were killed, but the fact as to the number of slaves executed is not clear, estimates ranging from four to ten.[34]

Probably the most fateful year in the history of American Negro slave revolts is that of 1800, for it was then that Nat Turner and John Brown were born, that Denmark Vesey bought his freedom, and it was then that the great conspiracy named after Gabriel, slave of Thomas H. Prosser [35] of Henrico County, Virginia, occurred.

This Gabriel, the chosen leader of the rebellious slaves, was a twenty-four year old giant of six feet two inches, " a fellow of courage and intellect above his rank in life," who had intended " to purchase a piece of silk for a flag, on which they

33 A. Steward, *Twenty-Two Years a Slave*, pp. 34-38. Note also the proclamation issued in September, 1797, by the Louisiana Governor, described by R. R. Hill, *op. cit.*, p. xv n., as " Una Proclamation sobre los Negros Simmarones de."

34 *C. V. S. P.*, IX, pp. 51-52; Charleston *City Gazette*, December 21, 1799; U. B. Phillips, *American Negro Slavery*, pp. 188-189.

35 According to contemporary sources this Mr. Prosser was a young man who had " fallen heir some time ago, to a plantation within six miles " of Richmond, and " had behaved with great barbarity to his slaves." He also owned a tavern.—J. T. Callender to Thomas Jefferson, dated Richmond Jail, September 13, 1800, in Papers of Jefferson, Library of Congress; and William Mosby to Governor James Monroe, dated Henrico County, November 10, 1800, in *Journal of the Senate of the Commonwealth of Virginia begun December 1, 1800*, Richmond, 1800, p. 26.

would have written 'death or liberty'." Another leader was Jack Bowler, four years older and three inches taller than Gabriel, who felt that " we had as much right to fight for our liberty as any men." Gabriel's wife, Nanny, was active, too, as were his brothers, Solomon and Martin. The former conducted the sword making, and the latter bitterly opposed all suggestion of delaying the outbreak, declaring,[36] " Before he would any longer bear what he had borne, he would turn out and fight with his stick."

The conspiracy was well-formed by the spring of 1800,[37] and there is a hint that wind of it early reached Governor Monroe, for in a letter to Thomas Jefferson, dated April 22, he referred [38] to " fears of a negro insurrection." Crude swords and bayonets as well as about 500 bullets were made by the slaves through the spring, and each Sunday Gabriel entered Richmond, impressing the city's features upon his mind and paying particular attention to the location of arms and ammunition.[39]

Yet, as Callender wrote,[40] it was " kept with incredible Secrecy for several months," and the next notice of apprehensions of revolt appears in a letter of August 9 from Mr. J. Grammer of Petersburg to Mr. Augustine Davis of Richmond. This letter was given to the distinguished Dr. James McClurg, who in-

36 The information in this paragraph is based upon Callender's letter to Jefferson of September 13, 1800, already cited; the Senate Journal also cited above, p. 28; and the testimony at the rebels' trials, in *C. V. S. P.*, IX, pp. 151, 160, 165. In a letter dated September 26, 1800 from John Randolph to Joseph H. Nicholson, Gabriel is referred to as a blacksmith, quoted in W. C. Bruce, *John Randolph*, II, p. 250.

37 *C. V. S. P.*, IX, pp. 141, 151.

38 The quoted words are from "Calendar of the correspondence of Thomas Jefferson," *Bulletin of the Bureau of Rolls and Library of the Department of State*, VIII, p. 405. A careful search was made for this letter in the Library of Congress, but it was not found. The card cataloguing it is now marked " missing."

39 *Journal of the Senate of Virginia, 1800*, pp. 26-27.

40 In his already cited letter to Jefferson, September 13, 1800.

formed the military authorities and the Governor.[41] The next
disclosure came during the afternoon of the day, Saturday,
August 30, set for the rebellion and was made by Mr. Mosby
Sheppard, whose slaves,[42] Tom and Pharoah, had told him of
the plot.

Monroe, seeing that speed was necessary and secrecy impossible, acted quickly and openly. He appointed three aides for
himself, asked for and received the use of the federal armory
at Manchester, posted cannon at the capitol, called into service
well over six hundred and fifty men, and gave notice of the plot
to every militia commander in the State.[43]

" But," as a contemporary declared,[44]

upon that very evening just about Sunset, there came on the most
terrible thunder accompanied with an enormous rain, that I ever
witnessed in this State. Between Prosser's and Richmond, there
is a place called Brook Swamp which runs across the high road,
and over which there was a [ms. torn] bridge. By this, the africans were of necessity to pass, and the rain had made the passage
impracticable.

Nevertheless about one thousand slaves, some mounted,
armed with clubs, scythes, home-made bayonets, and a few
guns, did appear at an agreed-upon rendezvous six miles outside the City, but, as already noted, attack was not possible, and

41 *C. V. S. P.*, IX, p. 128.

42 Legally they were the slaves of Mr. Sheppard's wife and son. The
legislature directed Monroe to purchase them and give them their freedom
because, " Sound policy dictates that rewards should be held out to those
who have rendered essential service to our country." Monroe did this, paying
$500 for each of the informers.—J. P. Guild, *Black Laws of Virginia*, p. 70;
Register of Certificates & Warrants issued for slaves executed 1783-1814, in
Virginia State Library, accession no. 195.

43 S. M. Hamilton, ed., *op. cit.*, III, pp. 237, 242; Jefferson to General
Dearborne, April 21, 1802, Papers of Thomas Jefferson, Library of Congress.

44 Callender to Jefferson, September 13, 1800, Jefferson MSS.; John
Randolph in his letter to J. H. Nicholson, of September 26, 1800 (W. C.
Bruce, *op. cit.*, II, pp. 250-51) also refers to this great storm and to the
existence of a stone bridge that had become impassable.

the slaves disbanded.[45] As a matter of fact even defensive measures, though attempted, could not be executed.[46]

The next few days the mobilized might of an aroused slave
State went into action and scores of Negroes were arrested.
Gabriel had attempted to escape via a schooner, *Mary,* but when
in Norfolk on September 25, he was recognized and betrayed
by two Negroes, captured, and brought back, in chains, to Richmond.[47] He was quickly convicted and sentenced to hang, but
the execution was postponed until October 7, in the hope that
he would talk. James Monroe personally interviewed him, but
reported,[48] " From what he said to me, he seemed to have made
up his mind to die, and to have resolved to say but little on the
subject of the conspiracy."

Along with Gabriel fifteen other rebels were hanged on the
seventh of October. Twenty-one were reported to have been
executed prior to this, and four more were scheduled to die after
October 7. A precise number of those executed cannot be given
with certainty, but it appears likely that at least thirty-five Negroes were hanged, four condemned slaves escaped from prison
(and no reference to their recapture has been seen), while one
committed suicide in prison.[49]

45 S. Hamilton, ed., *op. cit.,* III, p. 234; *C.V.S.P.,* IX, p. 141. It is to be
noted that about one thousand slaves actually gathered together on this
unprecedentedly stormy night. This is, of course, not indentical with the number
involved in the plot, even within the immediate neighborhood. This erroneous
identification is made by almost every handler of the story, as J. C. Ballagh,
A History of Slavery in Virginia, p. 92; R. R. Howison, *A History of
Virginia,* II, p. 390; B. Brawley, *op. cit.,* pp. 86-90; H. Wish, *op. cit.,* p. 310,
J. C. Carroll's account, *op. cit.,* pp. 48-54, is good.

46 *Journal of the Senate, 1800,* p. 26.

47 Fredericksburg *Virginia Herald,* October 3, 1800.

48 S. M. Mamilton, ed., *op. cit.,* III, p. 213.

49 The sources for this are, the Richmond *Examiner,* October 17, 1800;
N. Y. *Spectator,* October 7, 1800; Fredericksburg *Virginia Herald,* September 19, 1800; *C.V.S.P.,* IX, p. 160; *Journal of the House of Delegates of
Virginia, 1800-1801,* Richmond, 1801, p. 42. U. B. Phillips (*op. cit.,* p. 475)
says twenty-five Negroes were executed and cites manuscript vouchers in the
Virginia State Library. An examination of these vouchers, however, shows
that payment for convicted slaves was made by Virginia to thirty different

These Negroes, who were conscious revolutionists, behaved
nobly. A resident of Richmond declared,[50] in a letter of September 20, 1800, " Of those who have been executed, no one
has betrayed his cause. They have uniformly met death with
fortitude." An eminent eye-witness of the rebels' conduct while
in custody, John Randolph, six days later, stated,[51] " The accused have exhibited a spirit, which, if it becomes general, must
deluge the Southern country in blood. They manifested a sense
of their rights, and contempt of danger, and a thirst for revenge
which portend the most unhappy consequences." Monroe's
laconic comment concerning his interview with Gabriel a short
time before the latter's execution, has already been quoted.

Such testimony adds credibility to the story told by an Englishman who visited Virginia in 1804. On the afternoon of September 25 of that year, as he tells the tale,[52]

I passed by a field [near Richmond] in which several poor
slaves had lately been executed, on the charge of having an
intention to rise against their masters. A lawyer who was present
at their trials at Richmond, informed me that on one of them
being asked, what he had to say to the court in his defence, he
replied, in a manly tone of voice: " I have nothing more to offer

owners, two (Thomas Prosser and Dabney Williamson) being paid three
different times, and several being paid much more than the average, which
ran to about $350. Thus, Nat Wilkerson was paid $750, William Young,
$700, Charles Carter, $900, and William Benton and Roger Gregory each
$666.67, indicating that probably more than one of their slaves were exe-
cuted. The figure, then, of thirty-five executed appears to be conservative.—
See Register of Certs. & Warrants issued for slaves executed, 1783-1814,
Accession # 195, Archives, Va. St. Lib. Altogether, merely in *executed*
slaves the Gabriel plot cost the State of Virginia $14,242.31, plus one hundred
pounds paid to a Mr. Michael Ocletree. Other exenses, as for slaves banished,
rewards, costs of guards and militia, would bring the plot's expense to about
$25,000 (Auditor's Papers, Box 187, Archives, Va. St. Lib.), no small item
when it is remembered that the total planned budget of the State for the
fiscal year 1801-1802 was $377,703—*Journal of the House of Delegates of
Virginia, 1801-1802*, Richmond, 1802, p. 58.

50 Richmond *Virginia Argus*, October 14, 1800.

51 Randolph to Nicholson, September 26, 1800, in W. Bruce, *op. cit.*, II,
pp. 250-51.

52 Robert Sutcliff, *Travels in Some Parts of North America*, p. 50.

than what General Washington would have had to offer, had he been taken by the British and put to trial by them. I have adventured my life in endeavouring to obtain the liberty of my countrymen, and am a willing sacrifice to their cause: and I beg, as a favour, that I may be immediately led to execution. I know that you have pre-determined to shed my blood, why then all this mockery of a trial?"

The character of the rebels and their aim caused conscience-searching on the part of the one-time rebel who was at the moment Governor. He wrote to another who had played a leading role in a bloody revolution, written an immortal manifesto of rebellion and was at the moment the key-figure in a bloodless revolution—the Presidential campaign of 1800; [53] James Monroe wrote to Thomas Jefferson asking his advice about the execution of the Negro leaders. Mr. Jefferson replied: [54] " The other states & the world at large will forever condemn us if we indulge a principle of revenge, or go one step beyond absolute necessity. They cannot lose sight of the rights of the two parties, & the object of the unsuccessful one." Ten of the condemned slaves were reprieved and banished.

As has been previously mentioned (and this again is an indication of the attitude of the slaves), Methodists, Quakers, and Frenchmen were to be spared by the rebels. [55] It is also very

53 The political implications of the Gabriel plot have been noticed, *ante*, pp. 44n., 150.

54 Monroe to Jefferson, Richmond, September 15, 1800, in S. M. Hamilton, ed., *op. cit.*, III, pp. 208-209; Jefferson to Monroe, September 20, 1800, in P. L. Ford, ed., *The Writings of Thomas Jefferson*, VII, pp. 457-58.

55 *Ante*, pp. 101-102. At the trials one Negro said that poor white women were also not to be harmed (*C. V. S. P.*, IX, p. 152), while another said young women generally were to be spared (*ibid.*, IX, p. 171), intimating that this did not have the purest motives. This was mentioned but once, and implicitly contradicted many times, yet many writers on the plot (although not citing, and probably not knowing of this source) have made rape one of the certain and prime purposes of the slaves, certainly a flagrant instance of distortion.—Howison, *op. cit.*, II, p. 391; Ballagh, *op. cit.*, p. 92; George Morgan, *The Life of James Monroe*, pp. 228-29. It may be mentioned as an interesting fact that so far as the evidence shows there is no case of rape or attempted rape in the history of American Negro slave revolts.

interesting to observe that the Negroes expected or, at least, hoped that the poorer whites would aid them in their effort to destroy the system of slavery.[56] The Negroes had been aware, too, of the strained relations between the United States and France, which from 1797 to 1799, had brought the two nations to the thoroughly modern stage of undeclared war, leading the slaves to hope for French assistance. And the very recent reductions in the Federal army, following improvement in those relations, were also noticed and used as an argument against postponement of the uprising. It had been planned, too, to recruit allies from among the Catawba Indians.[57]

It is difficult to say just how many slaves were involved in this conspiracy. One witness at the trials said two thousand, another six thousand, and a third ten thousand. The Governor of Mississippi Territory said fifty thousand.[58] Monroe, himself, asserted:[59]

56 *C.V.S.P.*, IX, pp. 141, 164; *Journal of the Senate of Virginia, 1800*, pp. 27, 32. The alleged implication of two Frenchmen in the plot, and Monroe's denial that any whites were involved have been noted, *ante*, p. 101. The material in the Senate Journal was reprinted in the Richmond *Recorder*, April 2, 6, 9, 13, 1803.

57 *C.V.S.P.*, IX, pp. 147, 151, 152, 160. The army reduction is referred to by J. S. Bassett, *The Federalist System, 1789-1801*, 284; J. B. McMaster, *op. cit.*, II, p. 482. Other specific factors which may have had some bearing on the outbreak are the facts that Gabriel was told by the overseer of a Mr. Gregory (probably Roger Gregory mentioned *ante*, note 49) that slaves elsewhere were in rebellion; and that his master, Mr. Prosser, left his home on August 7 for a trip, of unknown duration, to Amherst, some one hundred miles westward.—*Journal of the Senate of Virginia, 1800-1801*, pp. 27, 29.

58 *C.V.S.P.*, IX, pp. 141, 164, 165; W. C. C. Claiborne's circular letter of November 16, 1800, in Dunbar Rowland, ed., *The Mississippi Territorial Archives, 1798-1803*, I, p. 311.

59 James Monroe to the Speakers of the General Assembly, December 5, 1800, in S. M. Hamilton, ed., *op. cit.*, III, p. 239. For the location of Point of Fork, see *ante*, p. 208 n. The census of 1800 was very faulty (see *Niles' Weekly Register*, I, p. 291) but its figures are the best available. According to it there were 346,968 slaves in Virginia in 1800. The areas specifically mentioned by Monroe contained about 40,000 slaves. For source see *ante*, p. 210, note 4.

It was distinctly seen that it embraced most of the slaves in this city [Richmond] and neighbourhood, and that the combination extended to several of the adjacent counties, Hanover, Caroline, Louisa, Chesterfield, and to the neighbourhood of the Point of the Fork; and there was good cause to believe that the knowledge of such a project pervaded other parts, if not the whole of the State.

Although Monroe was of the opinion that the plot did not extend beyond the borders of his State,[60] there were repercussions elsewhere. There were rumors of rebelliousness in North Carolina, but what foundation in fact these may have had is unclear.[61] It is, however, a fact that at the trials of the Virginia rebels, a slave did testify that he had asked Gabriel whether he or Jack Bowler was versed in the art of war, and that Gabriel had replied in the negative, but had declared that " a man from North Carolina, who was at the siege [sic] of York town " was to be with them and provide the necessary technical knowledge.[62]

Many free Negroes were ordered out of Massachusetts because " suspicions of the designs of the Negroes are entertained and we regret to say there is too much cause." [63] The precautionary measures and statements issuing from the executive of the Territory of Mississippi have already been noticed, as have also the rumors, certainly grossly exaggerated, of serious disturbances in South Carolina.[64]

The latter reports reached the notice of William Vans Murray, United States Minister to Batavia, and one of the envoys extraordinary to the French Republic. His observations are of

60 James Monroe to Lt.-Gov. John Drayton of South Carolina, October 21, 1800, in S. Hamilton, ed., op. cit., III, pp. 216-18.

61 S. A. Ashe, op. cit., II, pp. 185-86; T. W. Higginson, " Gabriel's plot," in The Atlantic Monthly, 1862, X, p. 343.

62 Journal of the Senate of Virginia, 1800-1801, op. cit., p. 26.

63 Philadelphia Gazette of the United States, September 23, 1800; G. H. Moore, op. cit., pp. 231-36.

64 Ante, p. 151.

such interest as to merit extensive quotation. He wrote [65] to
John Quincy Adams that if these reports were true, and the rebellion was serious

the South will be assisted by the East, if need be.   A young South
Carolinian who was with me when I had the papers observed, that
he had long expected this misfortune (66) and had often wondered that they had not risen before. Certainly there are motives
sufficiently obvious, independent of the contagion of Jacobinism, to
account for an insurrection of the slaves; but I doubt not that the
eternal clamour about liberty in V[irginia] and S[outh] C[aro-
lina] both, has matured the event which has happened.   There are
good things in most species of adversity.   You may not possibly
know that a year ago, if not later, a separation from the Union was
much talked of by some of the leaders of the opposition in Virginia; and their arsenal replenished from Europe.   Their rigid
collection of extra taxes gave reason for fear they had some plan
on foot.   These ideas I had last spring from a man who made it his
business to know in passing through Virginia, and who had talked
with several leaders of the fed[eral]party.[67]

65 Dated The Hague, December 9, 1800, in "Letters of William Vans
Murray to John Quincy Adams" edited by W. C. Ford, *Annual Report
of the American Historical Association for 1912.*

66 See speeches in Congress of the South Carolinians, John Rutledge and
Robert G. Harper, January 2, 4, 1800.

67 K. Bruce (*Virginia Iron Manufacture in the Slave Era*, p. 112) denies
that Virginia rearmed because of a plan of secession. This was due, she thinks,
to a threatening foreign situation, and Federalist war propaganda. P. Davidson ("Virginia and the Alien and Sedition laws," *Amer. Hist. Rev.*, XXXVI,
pp. 336-42) takes the same position but adds that attacks by privateers, and
fear of Indians were other factors. U. Phillips (*The Course of the South
to Secession*, p. 69 n.) thinks Davidson's article is conclusive. That article,
however, makes no mention of this important contemporary statement by
Murray, and it is, I believe, still a moot question whether disunion sentiments
were not a factor in Virginia's arming. And it is clear that fear of, and the
necessity of suppressing, slave disturbances were important causes of the
arming. The frequent calls for arms mentioned in this work indicate that,
and the calls continued, and so did Virginia's militarist program, that is, it
was from Dec. 1800 through 1802 that the program was pushed both in
state and private factories (see Bruce, *op. cit.*, p. 113) after fear of Indians,
France, and privateers was gone, but when fear of slaves was acute, and
plots frequent.

Beginning in November of this same year slave unrest was once more reported from Virginia. This seems to have originated in Petersburg, but by December the trouble had spread to Norfolk, Richmond, and throughout Nottoway County. Dozens of slaves were arrested during these months and in January, 1801.[68]

By that time Governor Monroe was once more receiving warnings from varied correspondents, including one from the Mayor of Petersburg and another from an individual who subscribed himself a " faithful servant." On the seventh of January Monroe ordered 50 pounds of grape shot and 75 pounds of powder sent to Petersburg, and on the same day two slaves of Nottoway County were convicted of conspiring to rebel. They had planned to annihilate the whites for, as they saw it, " if the white people were destroyed they would be free." Both were hanged nine days later.[69]

A letter dated January 18, 1802 from a Negro named Frank Goode and addressed to someone named Roling Pointer, of Powhatan, was intercepted, found to refer to a conspiracy and to contain the terrifying sentence: [70] "Our travelling friend has got ten thousand in readiness to the night." Fears were expressed in Williamsburg and Nansemond, and two slaves were executed in Brunswick on February 12. Two more were hanged in Halifax in April, and the same month witnessed the arrests of many slaves in Princess Anne and in Norfolk. Two were sentenced to hang in the latter city, but only one, Jeremiah, was executed, for the other, Ned, said to be weak-minded, was [71] reprieved

68 *C. V. S. P.*, IX, p. 173; N. Y. *Eve. Post*, Dec. 1, 1801; Boston *Columbian Centinel*, Dec. 9, 1801.

69 Journal of the Senate of Virginia, 1801-1802, p. 57 ff.; *C. V. S. P.*, IX, pp. 267, 270-72. The Ms. material concerning this is the Virginia State Archives, and in some cases spelling and punctuation—nothing else—differ from that in the printed versions.

70 *C. V. S. P.*, IX, p. 274.

71 *Ibid.*, IX, pp. 279, 293-96; Ms. Council Journal, 1801-1803, pp. 187, 238-42, 251; T. Wertenbaker, *Norfolk*, p. 140. In the Executive Papers, Va. State Lib. is a letter from Jeremiah, dated May 2, 1802, protesting his innocence. John Cowper wrote to Monroe from Norfolk, June 1, 1802,

and banished. Similarly, in Hanover County, one slave was hanged and another banished, while on April 3, according to a militia officer, " four unknown men made an attack with bricks upon the sentinel at the Capitol, and were fired on." [72]

Suppression went on into the months of June and July. Thus, a letter of June 5 from Richmond refers to the fact that " convicted slaves confined in the Penitentiary house [had] become so numerous as to render their maintenance burthensome and their safe keeping inconvenient." [73] On June 15 a Mr. Mathews of Norfolk told the Governor that many exaggerated reports were abroad, but that unquestionably disaffection still existed and asked that more arms be forwarded. With this appeal was enclosed an interesting letter from a slave written on June 7, which read as follows: [74]

White pepil be-ware of your lives, their is a plan now forming and intend to put in execution this harvest time — they are to commence and use their Sithes as weapons until they can get possession of other weapons; their is a great many weapons hid for the purpose, and be you all assured If you do not look out in time that many of you will be put to death. the sceam is to kill all before them, men, women, and children. their has been expresses going In Every direction for some days to see all the negroes they could this holladay, to make the arrangements and conclud what time it was to commence and at what plasis they are to assemble. watch they conduc of your Negroes and you will see an alteration. I am confident of the leaders and can not give

concerning him: " I am informed that he protested his own innocence of the crime for which he suffered, but on being pressed a few minutes before his death, to declare whether he had any knowledge of any conspiracy or not intended by the slaves, he refused an answer, and nothing would extract an answer." *C.V.S.P.*, IX, p. 302 f. For newspaper accounts see Richmond *Virginia Gazette*, June 2, 1802; N. Y. *Eve. Post*, June 18–July 10, 1802; N. Y. *Herald*, Jan. 20, and May to July, 1802; N. Y. *Spectator*, Jan. 16, May 12–June 19, 1802.

72 *C.V.S.P.*, IX, pp. 298-99. Petitions, dated May 19, and May 31, 1802, asking for reprieves for the two Hanover slaves, Tom and Glascow, are in the Executive Papers.

73 George Goosley to Governor Monroe, *C.V.S.P.*, IX, p. 305.

74 *Ibid.*, IX, p. 309.

you my name. I am also a greater friend to some of the Whites, and wish to preserve their lives. I am a favorite Servant of my Master and Mistis, and love them dearly.

Governor Monroe, upon the advice of four State Senators, commuted the death sentence of Ben,[75] a slave of King and Queen County, in June to sale and banishment out of the State. Another slave, John of Halifax County, also convicted of conspiracy, was less fortunate and died by hanging on the thirteenth of June. In this case Monroe's generally merciful hand was moved to sign the execution order by a petition subscribed to by sixty-three citizens urging he do this, for they believed,[76] " that the said John is one of the most criminal and dangerous of the order, not doubting, from general character, but that he has by himself and his agents been the means of poisoning many persons." On the first of July, Abram, a slave of Halifax County, was sentenced to die for his part in the plot, while two days later Arthur, slave of a Mr. Farrar of Henrico County, received for the second time a reprieve of his death sentence, to last for two weeks. There is no record of this being renewed, or the sentence being altered, so it is probable that he was finally hanged.[77]

75 Executive Papers, dated June 20, 1802.

76 Executive Papers, dated June 13, 1802; also MS. Council Journal, 1801-1803, p. 254. This Council Journal, under date of February 20, notes death sentences against three slaves in Southampton for murder, and of a slave of Lunenberg County, convicted as a poisoner (pp. 191-92), and on March 27 (p. 206) the reprieve for one month of another convicted poisoner, this one from Mecklenburg County. Whether these slaves were members of an organized conspiracy or not is unknown.

77 MS. Council Journal, 1801-1803, July 3, 1802, p. 262; C.V.S.P., IX, pp. 309-310. It is not possible to state just how many slaves were executed for insurrectionary activity in Virginia in 1802. The State, which recompensed the owner of executed slaves (if he was a citizen of the State and if the slave died as a result of the legal operation of the government's apparatus) paid for thirty-seven executed slaves during this year. But how many of them suffered because of their conspiratorial activities is not stated. This number, however, was nearly three times greater than the average number annually executed during the years from 1783 to 1814 inclusive. MS. Register of Certificates and Warrants for slaves executed, 1783-1814, Va. St. Lib. Accession # 195.

Fears in Virginia were accentuated when, in May, conspiracies were reported from eastern North Carolina. These were, at the time, attributed largely to the agitation of an outlawed Negro, Tom Copper, who had been a fugitive for months and who had " a camp in one of the swamps " in the region of Elizabeth City.[78]

Concerning these plots a later historian, using only local newspapers, reported the arrest of but fourteen slaves and the execution of one, while in a more recent work, the author, again depending solely upon the local press, reported the execution of five slaves, and the arrest, lashing, branding, and cropping of an unspecified number in Camden, Bertie, Currituck, Martin, Halifax, and Pasquotank Counties.[79]

Local papers, however, are far from trustworthy sources, and rarely give complete information concerning slave rebellions, and in this case a contemporary spoke accurately when he asserted [80] that " the North-Carolina papers speak reluctantly " about the trouble. It is a fact that stories of wholesale havoc and destruction allegedly caused by slaves at this time and reported elsewhere were undoubtedly false, but the truth is probably somewhere between these exaggerations and the minimizations of the North Carolina papers.

In addition to the counties above mentioned, Hertford, Wake, Washington, Warren, and Charlotte, if no others, were also disturbed by reported conspiracies. And, " a gentleman who last week passed through the lower counties of North Carolina " stated that " an attempt to liberate those [slaves] in Elizabeth City jail was made last week, by six stout negroes, mounted on horseback; four of the fellows were taken, the other two made their escape." The finding of arms and ammunition and swords and pikes was several times reported. It appears conservative to say that about fifteen slaves were executed,

78 Raleigh *Register*, June 1, 1802; N. Y. *Herald*, June 2, 1802.

79 R. H. Taylor, *op. cit.*, p. 31 ; G. G. Johnson, *Ante-Bellum North Carolina*, pp. 510-513.

80 Boston *Columbia Centinel*, June 23, 1802.

several scores were arrested, and dozens tortured one way or another in North Carolina during the year.[81]

The last trouble of 1802 is referred to by an English visitor, Charles W. Janson, and occurred in the northwestern county of Madison, Virginia, which for an area so located had a large Negro population.[82] A Mr. Alexander Hunton was alarmed by the language of a slave he was whipping, began an investigation, and

From what was collected there was every reason to believe that the negroes were planning an insurrection; and Mr. Hunton privately requested every white inhabitant to meet him, well-armed, on the same evening, at a certain time and place. A negro was lying in the gaol under sentence of death for murdering a white man, and we supposed that a rescue, if nothing more, would be attempted. With the insurrection at Richmond present to every mind, our fears were wrought up to a high degree of alarm. I attended with my gun, and a large supply of ball cartridges, with which I was supplied, with other inhabitants, by the corporation of Norfolk, a few months before, on a similar occasion.

Many slaves were arrested and chained, but all denied the existence of a conspiracy. Janson believed them, but the judge did not " and ordered them all to be severely flogged, which sentence was executed by the white men in turns." This Englishman and a friend were alarmed a few days later by the singing of some slaves at night, " conceiving that it was the negro

81 See letters dated June 5 and 10, 1802, in *C. V. S. P.*, IX, pp. 307-308; and correspondence from the affected regions in the Fredericksburg *Virginia Herald*, May 18, 1802; Richmond *Virginia Gazette*, June 2, 1802; N. Y. *Spectator*, May 22, 26, 1802; N. Y. *American Citizen and General Advertiser,* June 25, 1802; N. Y. *Herald*, June 2, July 14, 1802. During the excitement slaveholders accompanied the militia and restrained lynching mobs. By an act of 1786, passed because "many persons by cruel treatment of their slaves cause them to commit crimes," owners were not to be paid two-thirds the slave's value.—G. G. Johnson, *op. cit.*, pp. 498, 512; Raleigh *Register*, May 25, June 1, July 6, 27, 1802.

82 C. W. Janson, *The Stranger in America*, pp. 395-98; see also, p. 361. Madison was formed in 1792 from the western part of Culpeper. In 1800 it had 4,836 whites, 3,436 slaves and 50 free Negroes. For source see *ante*, p. 210, note 4.

war song." Armed, they hurried to other white men, who, how-ever, reassured them, "but they greatly commended our ac-tivity, and thus we became more respected by our neighbours."

A striking feature of the Virginia conspiracies of 1802 is that evidence of white participation is fairly good. Thus, a Mr. John B. Scott, while informing the Governor on April 23 of the trial and execution of slaves in Halifax, stated, "I have just received information that three white persons are con-cerned in the plot; and they have arms and ammunition con-cealed under their houses, and were to give aid when the ne-groes should begin." One slave witness, Lewis, twice declared that whites, "that is, the common run of poor white people" were involved.[83] At least one fairly prominent white man, James Hall Mumford, acting Justice of the Peace of Nottoway County, in a formal petition signed by many citizens and dated January 17, 1802, requesting his removal, was accused [84] " of encour[ag]ing the late insurrection of the Slaves of this County."

Finally, what is supposed to have been a recruiting speech delivered by Arthur, slave of Mr. William Farrar of Henrico County, has survived and makes fascinating reading: [85]

83 *C.V.S.P.*, IX, pp. 294, 299, 301.

84 Executive Papers; mention is made of this petition in the MS. Council Journal, January 16, 1802, p. 169, but no record of the action taken, if any, was seen. One need surely not take seriously the accusation in the Richmond *Recorder* (edited by Henry Pace and James T. Callender) of November 2, 1802, to the effect that that paper's political and commercial rival, Meri-wether Lewis (editor of the Richmond *Examiner*) had incited insurrection among his own Negroes, in order to win the favor of the women slaves in his "seraglio!"

85 In Executive Papers, under date of May 17, 1802. Also, in less complete form, in *C.V.S.P.*, IX, p. 301, and quoted by J. H. Johnston, "The participation of white men in Virginia slave insurrection," *The Journal of Negro History*, 1931, XVI, p. 161. In the Executive Papers there is a petition dated June 12, 1802, from Arthur to Governor Monroe, denying his guilt and declaring that the slave whose testimony against him was most important, Lewis, gave such testimony only after being severely whipped. Attached are statements from four white people affirming their belief in Arthur's innocence. For the known facts as to his disposition, see *ante*, p. 230.

Black men if you have now a mind to join with me now is your time for freedom. All clever men who will keep secret these words I give to you is life. I have taken it on myself to let the country be at liberty this lies upon my mind for a long time. Mind men I have told you a great deal I have joined with both black and white which is the common man or poor white people, mulattoes will Join with me to help free the country, although they are free already. I have got 8 or 10 white men to lead me in the fight on the magazine, they will be before me and hand out guns, powder, pistols, shot and other things that will answer the purpose... black men I mean to lose my life in this way if they will take it.

Some of the results of this decade of turmoil—such as new laws and regulations for slave control, and an impetus to militarism in the South have previously been discussed.[86] Others are also apparent.

In the midst of this decade of unprecedented slave disturbances (plus economic depression and the world-wide sweep of humanitarian and radical philosophies) there developed a very considerable anti-slavery sentiment, and these disturbances, bringing home to him who could see, the iniquities of human bondage and its danger to the masters, are not to be overlooked in attempting to explain this anti-slavery development.

Thus in the area north of Mason and Dixon's Line during this period many states passed anti-slavery laws so that by 1802 all Northern states (except New Jersey whose act came in 1804) had enacted measures for the gradual emancipation of all Negroes. To the conventional reasons therefor, i. e., unprofitableness of slavery in commerce and diversified, small-scale farming, and the relative numerical insignificance of the slaves, is to be added the fact that these Northern states witnessed the very ugly activities of the slaves to the south of them, both on the islands and the continent, plus the fact that

86 Other results, as an impetus to the colonization movement, and a drift away from the radicalism implicit in Jeffersonianism, particularly as exemplified in the Declaration of Independence, will be noted at length later, since it is not merely the unrest of these ten years that help account for these phenomena.

several of them tasted, or believed they tasted, samples of that same ugliness in the fires destroying their own or their neighbors' homes.

The economic stagnation in the lower South and the acute depression in lower Louisiana, eastern North Carolina, and eastern Virginia, together with the fact that the staples, cotton and sugar, that were to form the dominant types of economy in the South did not become important until the end of the nineties, fostered doubts about slavery. These doubts were most evident in those areas where its hold was least extensive, as Kentucky, eastern Tennessee, and the western parts of Virginia and North Carolina.[87] When to this is added the fact, as James Monroe rather mildly put it,[88] " that the publick danger proceding from this description of people [slaves] is daily increasing," the explanation for the vigor of this doubt (allowing and explaining, for example, the existence of such anti-slavery groups as the Quakers and the Methodists) becomes clearer.

A result of these uprisings coincident with this increased questioning was, naturally, a greater severity in the regulating and policing of the slave population, As a contemporary remarked,[89] " in a word, if we will keep a ferocious monster in our country, we must keep him in chains." The forging of the chains has been observed, but the word to notice in that sentence is "if." That word loomed large indeed during this decade, for slavery appeared to pay few dividends, and possessing slaves made one's devotion to fashionable " liberal " principles suspect,

87 See T. P. Abernethy, *From Frontier to Plantation in Tennessee*, p. 143 n.; S. B. Weeks, *Southern Quakers and Slavery*, p. 235 n.; G. G. Van Deusen, *The Life of Henry Clay*, pp. 20, 21 ; deed of manumission, July 28, 1797, signed by William Scott of Harrison County, Kentucky, in manuscript room, N. Y. Public Library, miscellaneous folder on slavery; G. Johnson, *op. cit.*, pp. 460, 561, 594; St. George Tucker, *A Dissertation on Slavery*, p. 70; J. H. Russell, *The Free Negro in Virginia*, Baltimore, 1893, pp. 61, 78; L. P. Jackson, in *The Journal of Negro History*, XV, pp. 281-87; H. M. Henry, *op. cit.*, p. 177; W. C. Bruce, *op. cit.*, I, pp. 104-105.

88 Monroe's speech to the Speakers of the General Assembly of Virginia, January 16, 1802, in S. M. Hamilton, ed., *op. cit.*, III, p. 329.

89 N. Y. *Commercial Advertising*, September 30, 1800, quoting a " Letter from ——— county to editor of a Fredericksburg paper."

and placed one open to the charge of hypocrite; and withal, no matter how many chains were placed upon the " monster," his stirring and writhing went on, to manifest itself not merely in flight or individual acts of terrorism, but also wholesale burnings, numerous poisonings, and serious schemes for revolutionary action, requiring the expenditure of much time, energy and effort to suppress.

A writer opposed to the " chains " policy remarked,[90] " I have dwelt upon this system of fetters and scourges, of deprivations and restrictions, because I perceive it as the favorite topic of the day," but, he warned, " When you make one little tyrant more tyrannical, you will make thousands of slaves impatient and vindictive." He proposed gradual emancipation.

The idea represented by this writer came the closest to realization in the South in this decade that it was ever again to come. The border states (Maryland, 1796, Kentucky, 1794, 1800, Tennessee, 1801) passed laws making manumission easier. Serious though futile, attempts were made in Kentucky and in Maryland in 1799 to enact laws for gradual emancipation.[91] At the formation of the Territory of Mississippi in 1798 an effort was made to keep slavery out, but this was opposed, probably with considerable sincerity, on the ground that by dispersing the slave population one lessened the danger of revolt and increased the possibility, in the long run, of emancipation. In 1802 a bill to forbid the importation for any purpose into Mississippi of male slaves passed the House but was defeated in the Council by two votes.[92]

90 Anonymous, *Letter to a Member of the General Assembly of Virginia*, pp. 10, 11, 16. As a complement to emancipation the writer urged colonization in the west, because, "Apt as we are to estimate by comparison, and to prize more highly the little we want, than the much we possess, it may be fairly inferred, that the negroes if once emancipated, would never rest satisfied with anything short of perfect equality."

91 W. Littell, *Statute Law of Kentucky*, I, pp. 246-47, 387; W. Kilty, *The Laws of Maryland*, II, Chap. LXVII; M. S. Locke, *op. cit.*, pp. 121-22; R. Hildreth, *op. cit.*, V, p. 316; G. Van Deusen, *op. cit.*, p. 21.

92 *Annals of Congress*, 6th Cong., 2nd Sess., 1309-1312; D. Rowland, ed., *op. cit.*, I, pp. 373-74; L. C. Gray, *op. cit.*, II, p. 688; D. R. Anderson, *William Branch Giles*, pp. 59-60.

As has previously been mentioned, an important cause of numerous acts restricting or forbidding the slave trade, was fear of slave rebellion. Such regulations were especially numerous and drastic during the crucial dozen years from 1790 through 1802. Examples are the Federal acts of 1794 and 1800, and the State acts of South Carolina, 1792, 1796, 1800, 1801, Georgia, 1793, North Carolina, 1794, Maryland, 1796, and the Louisiana prohibition against the trade following the unrest of 1795.[93]

The South Carolina acts of 1800 and 1801 were especially severe and had they been permitted on the books and been enforced, might well have checked the growth of slavery. In 1800 it was forbidden to bring any Negro in from beyond the United States, no one was to bring in over ten slaves from any part of the nation, and these slaves must have been owned for two years, and were not to be sold for two years after entrance. In 1801 this made made still more restrictive, for no one was to import over two slaves from within the United States, and these were to be for personal use only.[94]

Again indicative of what the Negro restlessness had done to enhance doubts concerning the wisdom of the institution of slavery, may be noted the sentiments of a resident of Louisiana expressing opposition to a projected reopening of the slave trade in that region. He felt [95]

that the embers of the servile insurrection which occurred in Louisiana in 1795 were still glowing; that the proposed reopening of the slave trade was a project conceived by foreigners for their own profit; and that, if the planters themselves were consulted they would raise a " terrible clamor " against the measure, and would paint a " fearful picture of the disorders to which the colony is a prey because of the insubordination of the slaves."

93 H. Marbury and W. Crawford, *Digest of the Laws of Georgia*, Savannah, 1802, pp. 440-41; Kilty, *op. cit.*, II, Chap. LXVII; M. S. Locke, *op. cit.*, p. 147; W. E. B. DuBois, *The Suppression of the African Slave Trade*, pp. 73, 84; E. Donnan, *op. cit.*, IV, p. 224; R. H. Taylor, *op. cit.*, p. 24.

94 J. Brevard, *Statute Law of South Carolina*, II, pp. 250, 256.

95 A. P. Whitaker, *The Mississippi Question*, p. 279 n.

But the Louisiana slave trade was reopened and was flourishing by 1802,[96] Mississippi did not forbid the importation of slaves, and by 1802 the legislature of South Carolina found the laws of 1800 and 1801, as it said, " to be too rigorous and inconvenient," and allowed the introduction from within the United States of any number of slaves for personal use, and by 1803, though the spectre of slave revolt was raised, the trade in human flesh was thrown wide open, except for slaves from South America and the West Indies.[97]

The masters of the South had made what was to prove, for them, an irrevocable decision. They had decided to keep the " monster " and they did this essentially because he now began to pay handsome dividends. As for Louisiana, sugar and cotton production were well-established there by the end of the eighteenth century. Increased settlement in western Pennsylvania, and Virginia, and in Upper Louisiana, Kentucky and Tennessee, and, in 1798, the " opening of the American deposit and the admission of neutral ships on advantageous terms " enhanced trade, and soon restored prosperity, so that by about 1801 Louisiana planters thought of the dire times from 1791 to 1797 as but a nightmare.[98]

In the lower south cotton was a staple product by the end of the eighteenth century. Thus, while in 1795 but 35,000 bales were being produced in 1801 over 210,000, and by 1806 about 345,000 bales were being produced to meet, especially, the ever-increasing demands of England and France. The first gin in Mississippi (made from a crude drawing by a skilled slave) was used in 1795, and she was soon an important cotton growing area, while, in 1803, the annexation of Louisiana helped fasten slavery upon the United States, and provided regions

96 *Ibid.*, p. 278.

97 J. Brevard, *op. cit.*, II, pp. 259-260; U. Phillips, *op. cit.*, pp. 136-37.

98 A. Whitaker, *op. cit.*, pp. 130-38; L. Pelzer, " Economic factors in the acquisition of Louisiana," *Proceedings of the Mississippi Valley Historical Association*, 1912-1913, VI, pp. 121-123.

like Virginia and North Carolina markets for surplus slaves.[99]

Anti-slavery, within most slave areas, was beaten and the policy of strict censorship of all such sentiment was begun [100] and, with minor exceptions, was not thrown off until the terror aroused by the Turner rebellion; and even then the expression of anti-slavery feeling lasted for about one year when it was once more effectively gagged by a slaveocracy revived by returning prosperity in 1832.

The Negroes, however, did not relinquish any phase of their struggle against enslavement. For some seven or eight years after the crushing of the 1802 plots there was a period of relative calm. This was, however, occasionally and sharply broken.

In February, 1803, the conviction of a Negro woman, Margaret Bradley, of attempting to poison two white people, precipitated serious trouble amongst the Negroes in York, Pennsylvania. They made several attempts to destroy the town by fire, and succeeded, within a period of three weeks, in burning eleven buildings. Patrols were established, strong guards set up, the militia dispatched to the scene of the unrest at Governor McKean's order, and a reward of three hundred dollars offered for the capture of the insurrectionists.[101]

Many Negroes were arrested. Several of their comrades attempted to rescue them by breaking down the jail, but they failed and were dispersed. After days of confusion and terror, about twenty Negroes were convicted of the crime of arson. On March 21 the Justices of the Peace issued a notice " to the inhabitants of York and its vicinity to the distance of ten miles" requiring such as had Negroes " to keep them at home under

99 W. B. Hesseltine, *A History of the South*, p. 249; U. Phillips, *op. cit.*, pp. 152-53, 160, 162, 163; M. B. Hammond, *The Cotton Industry*, p. 239; C. S. Sydnor, *Slavery in Mississippi*, p. 181.

100 See Charles Ambler, *Thomas Ritchie*, p. 25; U. Phillips, " The course of the South to secession," *Georgia Historical Quarterly*, 1937, XXI, p. 223. For the effects of this upon groups like the Quakers, see *ante*, p. 104.

101 W. C. Carter, and A. Glossbrenner, *History of York County*, new edition, edited by A. M. Aurand, Jr., pp. 139-41; R. G. Prowell, *History of York County*, I, p. 788; E. R. Turner, *The Negro in Pennsylvania*, pp. 152-153.

strict discipline and watch," and not to let them come to town on any pretense whatsoever without a written pass. Those who were in the town had to leave one hour before sundown " on pain of being imprisoned or at risk of their lives." Free Negroes were to get a pass from a Justice of the Peace so that they " might not be restrained from their daily labor."

A brief newspaper item presents all the evidence seen on an alleged uprising in North Carolina the same year. This reads: [102] " The Editor of the Kentucky Gazette acknowledges the receipt of a note from a gentleman in Warrenton, (North Carolina) without date, but which must have been subsequent to 25th April, which says—'The negroes rose in this town last night, and made great havoc—We had to fly'." Just what foundation, if any, existed for this statement is not known, but it may be said with some confidence that if slaves actually did create " havoc " in a North Carolina town in 1803 and caused white inhabitants to flee there would probably be more evidence of the occurrence than appears to exist.

In the year 1804 there was fairly serious trouble among the slaves in Orleans Territory as has already been noted. Their behavior in Savannah the same year aroused sharp alarm but the precise reasons for this are not clear,[103] while in February two slaves were imprisoned because of complicity in an attempt to destroy the city of Charleston, South Carolina by fire.[104]

The next year there were reports of slave plots or insurrections in North Carolina, Virginia, South Carolina, Maryland, and in New Orleans, but the known facts about most of them are few. In July two Negroes were tried before a special court of Oyer and Terminer in Cambridge, Maryland, for " having attempted to raise an insurrection." One, who was free, was

102 N. Y. *Eve. Post*, June 2, 1803.

103 See H. Aptheker, " Militant Abolitionism," in *The Journal of Negro History*, XXVI, pp. 442-43.

104 Item dated Charleston, February 11, 1804, in N. Y. *Eve. Post*, March 1, 1804. According to the Norfolk *Herald* of February 25, a disastrous fire, destroying hundreds of homes and six ships in that city, was of incendiary origin, but who were responsible was not stated. (*Ibid.*, March 7, 1804.)

sentenced to seven years' imprisonment at hard labor, while
the other, a slave, was condemned to hang [105] There seems to
have been some evidence that slaves in New Orleans, allegedly
aided by a Frenchman, planned to rebel on September 12, but
nothing of the nature occurred, and " the existence of a plot was
not fully ascertained." [106]

Columbia, South Carolina, was on edge the week before
Christmas of 1804, with cannon " placed on the eminence in
front of the State House," the militia on the alert, and patrols
everywhere, as the result of a report of an intended rebellion
during the holidays. The fear led to uneasy trigger fingers, one
of which caused the death of an innocent Negro. At least two
slaves believed to be the leaders in this affair were arrested,
and these arrests, the precautionary measures, and the show of
strength appear to have crushed this movement.[107]

Earlier that year a spirit of " insubordination among the negroes of Isle of Wight county " in Virginia was considered important enough for the Governor's notice. In April two slaves
of Stafford County, Cupid and Robin, were convicted of " Conspiracy and insurrection," the latter being sentenced to banishment, the former to hanging.[108] More important was the conspiracy of slaves at this time in Johnston, Sampson, and,
particularly, Wayne Counties, North Carolina to destroy their
enslavers by poison. Several whites actually were poisoned and
two " of our respectable men " died. About twenty slaves were

105 Letter dated Cambridge, July 21, in *ibid.*, August 12, 1805.

106 *Ibid.*, November 2, 1805. W. C. C. Claiborne, Governor of Orleans
Territory, wrote to James Madison, from Concordia, September 11, 1805:
"At the date of my last letter [August 27, 1805] every thing was Quiet at
New Orleans; There had been some little alarm in consequence of an attempt
made by a Frenchman to excite the Negroes to Insurrection. But the French-
man was arrested and the uneasiness had subsided."—Dunbar Rowland, ed.,
Official Letter Books of W. C. C. Claiborne, 1801-1816, III, p. 187.

107 Entries of December 19 and December 21, 1805 in the "Diary of
Edward Hooker," edited by J. F. Jameson, *Annual Report, Amer. Hist.
Assoc.*, 1896, I, pp. 881-82.

108 T. Newton to Governor of Virginia, Feb. 14, 1805, in *C.V.S.P.*, IX,
p. 437; MS. Council Journal, 1803-1806, p. 287. J. C. Ballagh, *op. cit.*, p. 109,
refers to a Virginia plot of 1805 involving free Negroes as well as slaves.

arrested, one, a woman, burned alive, three or four others hanged, one " was pilloried, whipped, his ears nailed down and then cut off," one was banished, and the others lashed.[109]

In April of the next year " considerable alarm " was aroused in Williamsburg, Virginia, because of " some suspicions . . . of an insurrection of the negroes." Students at William and Mary College experienced great excitement aiding in patrolling the town but apparently nothing further happened.[110] The Council Journal of the State on April 9, 1806, contains, however, the following interesting item: [111]

It appearing to the satisfaction of the board that two Negro men armed & on horseback have this day passed thro the City of Richmond bidding defiance to the Constables & others who endeavoured to arrest them & there being some reason to Suspect that their intentions may be of Such a nature as to endanger the Peace of Society—It is therefore advised that the Governor be requested to order out a Sufficient detachment from the Richmond Troop of Cavalry to apprehend . . . [them] . . . as soon as he may be able to discover the Route they had taken on leaving the City.

There is some evidence, not conclusive, pointing to the existence of a well-laid plan to capture the city of Savannah, Georgia in the fall of this year,[112] though the account may possibly have reference to the alarm of 1804, which has already been mentioned. A dozen of the rebel leaders were reportedly arrested, and the conspiracy nipped in the bud.

In the summer of 1807 some of the leading planters in Mississippi informed the Governor that they had reason to suspect

109 MS. Thomas Henderson Letter Book, 1810-1811, North Carolina Historical Commission, p. 12; A. R. Newsome, " Twelve North Carolina Counties," in *North Carolina Historical Review*, 1929, pp. 308-309. An account in the N. Y. *Eve. Post*, Sept. 3, 1805, is fairly accurate, but places the event in Waynesborough (Waynesboro), Georgia, instead of in North Carolina.

110 Letter dated Williamsburg, April 8, 1806, in *William and Mary College Quarterly*, 1900, (1) VIII, p. 219; C. W. Elliott, *Winfield Scott*, p. 6.

111 MS. Council Journal, 1803-1806, p. 421.

112 Charles W. Janson, *op. cit.*, p. 361 n.

an attempt at rebellion by their slaves and urged special precautionary measures. A patrol was established and a detachment
of soldiers of the United States Army forwarded to Fort Dearborn. The precise extent of the disaffection is not known, but it
was probably important in moving Governor Williams in his
message of December, 1807, to suggest the curtailment of the
slave trade. In 1808 Mississippi did regulate the importation of
slaves, placing a tax of five dollars on each Negro brought in,
and forbidding the introduction of criminal or " bad " slaves.[113]

In November and December, 1808, reports came to Governor
Tyler of Virginia telling of conspiracies and measures taken to
crush them in the cities of Norfolk and Richmond, and in the
counties of Nelson, Albemarle, and Chesterfield.[114] The fact
that the Governor, on the Council's advice, did not officially
inform the legislature of the circumstances in this case, and
that there appears to be extant no copy of the one hundred cir-
culars printed on December 21, 1808 in Richmond by Samuel
Pleasants, Jr., " respecting insurrection of negroes " makes it
impossible to accurately assess its importance. Certainly it was
considered serious enough to arouse great alarm not only in
Virginia, but in North Carolina, as well.

Disturbances of an undefined but apparently rather serious
nature occurred in the German coast region of the Territory of
Orleans a year later, in November, 1809. This caused commotion not only in the area immediately affected but also in New
Orleans, a city having among its population over nine thousand
slaves.[115]

113 Dunbar Rowland, *History of Mississippi*, II, p. 634.

114 *C. V. S. P.*, X, pp. 31, 62-63. See also Executive Papers, James Woods
to Governor, dated Nelson County, December 15, 1808; ten citizens of
Albemarle to Governor, December 17, 1808; note of December 20, 1808 on
Council's advice; Major William Brown to Governor, dated Chesterfield,
December 22, 1808; Earl G. Swem, *A Bibliography of Virginia*, part II,
p. 116; G. G. Johnson, *op. cit.*, p. 514. The indication of unrest in Charleston
at this time has been noted.

115 D. Rowland, ed., *Claiborne Letters*, III, p. 357; James E. Winston,
" The free Negro in New Orleans, 1803-1860," in *Louisiana Historical
Quarterly*, XXI, pp. 176, 178.

CHAPTER X

1810-1819

REBELLIOUS activity amongst the slaves entered a more intensive phase beginning in 1810 and lasting for six years, after which recurred, as usual, a short lapse of relative quietude. Economic depression, some evidence of which has been presented, was characteristic of most of the period for the South, largely induced by soil exhaustion, the embargo and non-intercourse acts, and the war itself, the last causing considerable devastation in eastern Maryland and Virginia, disorganizing the labor force, and rather effectively checking exportations while raising the prices of imported articles to high levels.[1]

Other events of a military nature affected the slave population during the period. There were revolts in East and West Florida and filibusters against Texas extending from 1810 to 1812. These brought dislocation and excitement to many areas of the South, together with widely spread revolutionary propaganda, so that appeals were made for men to join in the fighting against "the avowed enemies of republican liberty," or to help in "ameliorating the condition of an oppressed and subjugated people."[2]

In March, 1810, the discovery of two communications on a road in Halifax County, North Carolina, was reported. One was from a slave in Greene County, Georgia, to another slave, Cornell Lucas, of Martin County, North Carolina; another, likewise to and from slaves, had been sent from Tennessee and was intended for Brunswick County, Virginia. The contents of

1 Pertinent comments and data, in addition to that already given (*ante.*, p. 119), will be found in Henry Adams, *History of the United States During the Administrations of Jefferson and Madison*, VII, pp. 263-64; U. B. Phillips, *American Negro Slavery*, p. 177; L. M. Sears, *Jefferson and the Embargo*, pp. 126, 229-30, 238, 287; E. Q. Hawk, *Economic History of the South*, p. 260.

2 I. J. Cox, *The West Florida Controversy*, pp. 401, 406-407, 411; J. W. Pratt, *The Expansionists of 1812*, pp. 250-53.

both letters were declared to be similar, and one, that to Cornell Lucas, may be quoted in full:[3]

Dear Sir—I received your letter to the fourteenth of June, 1809 with great freedom and joy to hear and understand what great proceedance you have made, and the resolution you have in proceeding on in business as we have undertook, and hope you will still continue in the same mind. We have spread the sense nearly over the continent in our part of the country, and have the day when we are to fall to work, and you must be sure not to fail on that day, and that is the 22d April, to begin about midnight, and do the work at home first, and then take the armes of them you slay first, and that will strengthen us more in armes—for freedom we want and will have, for we have served this cruel land long enuff, & be as secret convaing your nuse as possabel, and be sure to send it by some cearfull hand, and if it happens to be discovered, fail not in the day, for we are full abel to conquer by any means.— Sir, I am your Captain James, living in the state of Jorgy, in Green county—so no more at present, but remaining your sincer friend and captain until death.

These letters were given to General Thomas Blount, a North Carolina Congressman, and he, believing them genuine, forwarded them to Governor Milledge of Georgia. This probably explains, at least in part, the passage in the latter's message to the legisature referring to information he had received [4] " from a source so respectable as to admit but little doubt of the existence of a plan of an insurrection being formed among our domestics and particularly in Greene County."

The final piece of information seen on this episode is contained in a letter [5] written by a resident of Augusta, Georgia, to a friend in Salem, Massachusetts, dated April 9, 1810. According to this:

The letter from " Captain James " is but a small part of the evidence of the disposition of the Blacks in this part of the country.

3 Published in the N. Y. *Evening Post*, April 30, 1810.

4 R. B. Flanders, *Plantation Slavery in Georgia*, p. 274.

5 N. Y. *Evening Post*, April 30, 1810.

The most vigorous measures are taking to defeat their infernal designs. May God preserve us from the fate of St. Domingo. The papers here will, for obvious reasons, observe a total silence on this business; and the mail being near closing, I can say no more on the subject at present.

Richard W. Byrd of Smithfield, Virginia, wrote on May 30, 1810, to Governor John Tyler concerning evidence of trouble in his neighborhood. This lengthy letter read, in part: [6]

An insurrection of the blacks, on the Saturday night, preceding Whit-Sunday, is much feared. As to myself, I am not satisfied that their plans are perfectly matured; but that such a scheme has been in contemplation, is beyond all doubt. Our unremitted vigilance may probably frustrate their designs in this neighborhood—but unless similar exertions are *generally* used, the consequences may be extremely fatal. A report that such an attempt would be made about Whit-Sunday, in North Carolina, has been very prevalent here for eight or ten days.

One " negro boy " after " receiving twenty lashes " stated, " that the operations were to commence in Carolina . . . that they were to fight with clubs, spikes and axes, and, if necessary, they (the Carolina negroes) would immediately come on here to help the Virginia negroes'." Mr. Byrd felt the slave preachers used their religious meetings as veils for revolutionary schemes and referred particularly to a " General Peter " of Isle of Wight who had been in communication with slaves of North Carolina.

In their messages the slaves referred to the planned revolt as an earthquake, and one Virginia slave had been heard to say " that there would be an earthquake here [as well as in North Carolina] on the same night, that he was entitled to his freedom, and he would be damned, if he did not have it in a

6 Executive Papers. On the back of this letter is written, presumably by Governor Tyler, " This paper is all founded in unreasonable fears." However, one hundred copies were printed and distributed to leading military officials east of the Blue Ridge Mountains. (MS. Council Journal, 1809-1810, June 2, 1810, p. 199). A printed copy is in the manuscript collection of the Library of Congress, Ac 5225 Broadsides: Virginia, May 30, 1810.

fortnight." Mr. Byrd concluded by remarking, "We have taken up many of these fellows and expect to go on in the same way. This course may possibly avert the dreadful calamity with which we are threatened," for he thought " it probable that we have broken the chain by which they were linked."

In June a slave named Sam, the property of John G. Pinner of Nansemond County, was convicted by an Isle of Wight court of conspiracy to rebel. A free Negro, Sam Scott, was an important witness against him, declaring that in May, while in his master's county, " the said prisoner asked the witness if he knew anything of the black people's rising to which the witness answered he did not; on which the prisoner said he did & he himself was one of the men." At the same time Lieutenant Colonel Sharp reported trouble in Norfolk, while somewhat later this month three slaves, two women and a man, were accused of arson activities in Culpeper. One of the women received fifteen lashes and the man, Glasgow, was hanged. The latter sentence was carried out at the written request addressed to the Governor of the five magistrates who condemned him for " In the present situation of our slaves, we are strongly impressed with the opinion that, his being either reprieved or sold, would have an injurious effect on the minds of the neighboring slaves." A similar request came from many citizens of Isle of Wight in connection with Sam, for it was again held " that the present situation of this Section of Country requires that examples by the Strict executions of law in Such Cases, are absolutely necessary for the Safety of Society." In this case, however, the Governor's judgment did not coincide with that of his petitioners, and on July 9 the State sold Sam, for three hundred dollars, together with five other slaves condemned for various reasons, to William Towles, slave-trader of Edgefield, South Carolina.[7]

7 Material based on manuscripts for June and July, 1810, in the Executive Papers. Lt. Col. Sharp's letter from Norfolk is condensed in *C. V. S. P.*, X, p. 83, but is there incorrectly dated June 6. For exaggerated reports of unrest at this time in Northern papers, see *ante*, p. 152.

At the end of November, 1810, "a dangerous conspiracy among the negroes was discovered" in Lexington, Kentucky. "A great many negroes were put in jail," but what became of them is not known.[8] Further indication of trouble is given by the fact that Kentucky passed a law in January, 1811, making conspiracy among slaves a crime punishable by death.[9]

There is evidence, in the form of an anonymous letter, dated merely January, 1811, and sent by " J.B." to " General T.R.", that white men were attempting to incite slave rebellion in Virginia. J.B. seems to have had trouble in enlisting as many slaves as he wished, and from the letter itself one is moved to declare that the slaves were shrewd in distrusting him.

He had offered to give twenty-five dollars to each rebel once Richmond had fallen, and had succeeded, so he wrote,[10] in getting " under our banner 100 or thereabout who is determined to fight for us. Keep every thing silent till that fatal night which will show to the world that Slavery will no longer exist in Virginia. The plans you laid down was good, you say you have 60 under you arm'd with guns side-blades &c I have

8 Entry of December 1, 1810 in the Diary of William L. Brown, published in the weekly edition of the Clarksville, Tennessee Leaf-Chronicle, October 5-16, 1916, and obtainable in the manuscript room of the New York Public Library. Brown was, at the time, a student at the University of Kentucky. He had a distinguished career, being one of Tennessee's commissioners (Felix Grundy was the other) in that State's border dispute with Kentucky, 1819-1820, and later serving in the Supreme Court of Tennessee.—See Joseph H. Parks, Felix Grundy, pp. 124, 157.

9 William Lettell, The Statute Law of Kentucky, IV, pp. 223-24.

10 Executive Papers. The letter is given (in condensed form and with minor variations and inaccuracies) in C.V.S.P., X, pp. 97-98. On the back of the letter is written " Recd Jany 10-1811 " and " To General T. R. Rocketts By Peter Procure Keg of Powder and continue making Balls." Rocketts is the name of a waterfront district in Richmond. Slaves were, of course, always exceedingly wary of the aid offered by white men, one of the reasons being that Negro stealing was a fairly common crime and often accomplished by promises of freedom. Earl G. Swem, in one of his invaluable bibliographical aids (A Bibliography of Virginia, Part II, p. 124) lists a circular printed in Richmond, January 12, 1811, by Samuel Pleasants called " Orders to militia officers in the different counties in consequence of an apprehension of an insurrection of the slaves," but no copy has been found.

20 arm'd with muskets the rest with old Swords Clubs." The first move was to fire Richmond and then attack. " I will divide my men in to 4 divisions, I will command 25 Peter the Bearer the second Bob the third and Henry the 4th ... You lay off your men, conduct every thing with secrecy and we trust in god, If We succeed We will be very rich—We are molding balls every night I am J.B.N.B. I have a small Keg of Powder." Nothing further concerning this plot is known except that militia officers were notified and ordered to be on the alert.

During the afternoon of January 9, 1811, the people of New Orleans were thrown into the " utmost dismay and confusion " on discovering wagons and carts straggling into the city, filled with people whose faces " wore the masks of consternation " and who told of having just escaped from " a miniature representation of the horrors of St. Domingo." They had fled from a revolt of slaves,[11] numbering about four or five hundred of St. Charles and St. John the Baptist Parishes, about thirty-five miles away from the city. These slaves, one of whose leaders, Charles Deslondes, was described as " a free mulatto from St. Domingo," rose in the evening of January 8, starting at the plantation of a Major Andry.

They were originally armed with cane knives, axes, and clubs. After killing Andry's son and wounding the Major, they took possession of a few guns, drums, and some sort of flags, and started marching from plantation to plantation, slaves everywhere joining them. They killed at least one other white man, and destroyed a few plantations.

11 Local press accounts and statements of the participants are in Richmond *Enquirer*, February 19, 22, March 12, 1811 ; the Hartford *Connecticut Courant*, February 20, 1811 ; N. Y. *Eve. Post*, February 14, 15, 19, 20, 26, 27, 1811 ; D. Rowland, ed., *Official Letter Books of W. C. C. Claiborne*, V, pp. 93-100, 107, 108, 110-111, 113-114, 123. See also, I. J. Cox, *op. cit.*, p. 575, who refers to a " series of insurrections." Compare Francis-Xavier Martin, *History of Louisiana*, II, pp. 300-301 ; Charles Gayerré, *History of Louisiana*, IV, pp. 267-68 ; A. Fortier, *A History of Louisiana*, III, pp. 78-79 ; A. Phelps, *Louisiana*, pp. 249-250 ; John S. Kendall, " Shadow Over the City " in *Louisiana Historical Quarterly*, XXII, pp. 142-44.

Major Andry, according to his own statement, organized about eight well-armed planters and, on the ninth of January, attacked the slaves, "of whom we made great slaughter." Many, however, escaped this first attack and continued their depredations. Andry ordered "several strong detachments to pursue them through the woods," and, he wrote, on January 11, "at every moment our men bring in or kill them."

Meanwhile, in New Orleans, Governor Claiborne had, on January 9, appointed seven aides for himself, called out the militia, and forbidden male Negroes from going at large. Brigadier-General Wade Hampton immediately left that city with four hundred militiamen and sixty United States Army men for the scene of action. Major Milton left Baton Rouge at about the same time with two hundred additional soldiers.

These forces, very early on the morning of the tenth, attacked the rebellious slaves and decimated them. Sixty-six were killed or executed on the spot, sixteen were captured and sent to New Orleans, and seventeen were reported as missing and were "supposed generally to be dead in the woods, as many bodies have been seen by the patrols." All those tried in the City were executed, at least one, a leader named Gilbert, by a firing squad; and their heads were strung aloft at intervals from New Orleans to Andry's plantation.

Hampton reported on January 11 that Milton had been posted in the neighborhood to aid "various companies of the citizens, that are scouring the country in every direction." At the same time a company of light artillery and one of the dragoons were sent up the river to suppress "disturbances that may have taken place higher up." Governor Claiborne, writing January 19, said he was "happy to find . . . so few Slaves are now in the woods. I hope this dreadful Insurrection is at an end and I pray God! we may never see another."

Precisely what else occurred cannot be said, but this paragraph from a Louisiana newspaper is suggestive: [12]

12 Unnamed, quoted in N. Y. *Eve. Post*, February 27, 1811. A law of April 25, 1811 provided for the payment by the Territory of $29,000 as

We are sorry to learn that a ferocious sanguinary disposition marked the character of some of the inhabitants. Civilized man ought to remember well his standing, and never let himself sink down to a level with the savage; our laws are summary enough and let them govern.

In March, 1811 occurred again a type of event that was never long absent in the ante-bellum South; an armed encounter between outlawed fugitive slaves and those whose purpose it was to retrieve or annihilate them. At this time a runaway community in Cabarrus County, North Carolina, whose inhabitants [13] " had bid defiance to any force whatever, and were resolved to stand their ground," was set upon by armed men, and in the ensuing struggle it was reported that two Negro men were killed, one wounded, and two Negro women captured.

The area in Orleans Territory known as the German Coast, which had been so severely disturbed in January 1811, was again uneasy in December of the same year. Governor Claiborne wrote to Major McRae, the commander of the Federal troops in the area, on the eleventh of December, directing him to exercise caution and dispatch arms to the zone of trouble, since he had heard [14] " that the Negros in the County of German Coast had again evidenced a disposition to rise in Insurrection, & that this spirit was supposed also to exist among the Negros " in New Orleans. Two days later he told the Secretary of the Navy, Paul Hamilton, " We are again disturbed by *apprehensions* of an insurrection among the Negroes. I believe them myself to be unfounded; But measures of precaution are nevertheless expedient and these have been directed."

compensation to the masters whose slaves were killed or executed in this rebellion. The sum was greater than the treasury balance and was therefore paid in installments.—D. Rowland, ed., *op. cit.*, V, p. 129; V. Moody, " Slavery on Louisiana sugar plantations " in *Louisiana Historical Quarterly*, VII, p. 223 n.

13 *Edenton Gazette*, March 22, 1811; G. Johnson, *op. cit.*, p. 514.

14 D. Rowland, ed., *op. cit.*, VI, pp. 17, 20.

There was disaffection in Kentucky in 1812. In January, several incendiary fires occurred in Lexington and contemporaries believed them to be the work of slaves intent upon destroying the town. Several were arrested and three were convicted, but only one, a Negro named Jack, seems actually to have been executed.[15]

A fugitive from Kentucky declared, years later, that his own master had been captain of a reserve corps of men over forty-five years of age, organized after the outbreak of the War of 1812, to aid in slave police duty, and that:[16] " at that time there were many colored people joined in a conspiracy to get their freedom, and wore as a mark a plait in the hair over the left eye. This was discovered,—many were whipped, and had the plait cut off. The conspiracy extended over three hundred miles, from Maysville to Henderson."

Two Justices of the Peace for Montgomery County, Virginia, Henry Edmundson and John Floyd (the latter was to be Governor and Secretary of War), presented the Council on April 10, 1812, with the interesting confession of a slave, Tom, who had killed his master, John Smith, and had fled.[17] Tom said that he, himself, knew of thirty or forty slaves anxious to

15 Letter from Georgetown, Ky. (twenty miles north of Lexington), in N. Y. *Eve. Post*, Feb. 11, 1812; extracts from the Lexington *Reporter*, Jan. 14, 21, Feb. 15, 22, March 21, 1812, and Lexington *Kentucky Gazette*, Jan. 14, 21, Feb. 18, 1812, kindly provided the present writer by Mr. J. Winston Coleman, Jr., of Lexington.

16 Story of J. C. Brown in Benjamin Drew, *A North-Side View of Slavery*, pp. 239-40. In November, 1815, a case came before the Supreme Court of Kentucky, in which two white men justified their killing of a slave on the ground that he had attacked them, while they were investigating an unlawful assembly of Negroes where the slaves " were combining to rise and rebel against the free white citizens of this commonwealth."—H. Catterall, ed., *op. cit.*, I, p. 290.

17 Executive Papers; also in *C. V. S. P.*, X, pp. 120-123. The Philadelphia *Freeman's Journal* (quoted in the N. Y. *Eve. Post*, June 12, 1812) reported a widespread plot in Northampton and Accomac Counties, Virginia, early in May, 1812, and declared that over two hundred slaves had been arrested. No confirmation of this has been seen. Evidence of alarm in South Carolina in June, 1812 has been presented, *ante*, p. 23.

rebel and that plans for this, under the leadership of a slave named Goomer, of Rockingham County, North Carolina, were being formed. These slaves " said they were not made to work for white people, but they (the white people), made to work for themselves; and that they (the negroes) would have it so." Tom informed a slave woman of these plans and " she said they could not rise too soon for her, as she had rather be in hell than where she was."

Floyd and Edmondson added this postscript: " Since the above discoveries the undersigned would further represent to y'r hon'r body, that from the most respectable information a spirit of rebellion is very obvious in this country, and in places where the greatest humility and obedience had hitherto been observed." It is pertinent to note, and this may have been more than coincidence, that the Raleigh, North Carolina *Register,* of June 6, 1812, declared [18] that a runaway slave recently apprehended had said " all should be free, and that he saw no reason why the sweat of his brow should be expended in supporting the extravagance of any man."

Notice has already been taken [19] of the serious situation in Mississippi Territory in the summer of 1812, and Governor David Holmes' lengthy letter to General Wilkinson of July 22 in which occurred the sentence: " Scarcely a day passes without my receiving some information relative to the design of those people to insurrect." A piece of evidence of a more specific nature appears in a letter the Governor wrote the next day to a planter named David Pannelli: [20]

I received your letter of this instant [not found] by your servant, and thank you for the attention you have shewn to the subject to which it relates. A negro of Mr. Madden's is now in jail upon suspicion of being concerned in a plan of insurrection. On tomorrow

18 Quoted by J. S. Bassett in *Slavery in the State of North Carolina,* p. 96.

19 *Ante,* pp. 24-25.

20 Letter sent from the town of Washington, in Clarence E. Carter, ed., *The Territorial Papers of the United States,* V, p. 301. From the names mentioned it is likely that this plot centered in Adams County.

an examination of several slaves from second creek upon similar charges will be had before Judge Simpson. I will therefore thank you to send to this place on tomorrow the slaves who have the information you have communicated, and also the negro belonging to Mr. Foot. I have no doubt his master will cheerfully assist in the development of this nefarious scheme. If you cannot have the servants sent here tomorrow, be pleased to forward to me the names of the witnesses, and of those who may be implicated, in order the legal process may issue to apprehend them.

A conspiracy involving slaves, free Negroes, and a few white men in New Orleans and the surrounding region was betrayed in the summer of 1812 by Lewis Bolah,[21] one of the slaves approached by the plotters. On the day Bolah talked, August 18, " The militia were ordered out which has completely frustrated their intentions. Some white men who were at their head are in prison; however a strong guard of the militia are still [August 25] ordered out every night." [22] One of these white men, Joseph Wood, was executed in the afternoon of September 13, at which time, " all the militia of the city were under arms—strong patrols were detailed for the night." It is clear that another of the whites implicated in this plot was named Macarty, and that he was jailed,[23] but what became of Mr. Macarty, or of the Negroes involved, is not known.

The years 1813 and 1814 were troublesome ones. In addition to the instances of alarms and indications of unrest in the Dis-

---

21 See petition to the Virginia Legislature of Lewis Bolah, dated Richmond, December 13, 1824, asking for permission to remain in the State though he had once left it and remained away for years—MS. Petitions, A9353, Virginia State Library. Mr. Bolah's action gained him his freedom. But he felt unsafe, and joined the United States Army serving through the War of 1812. Then he decided that " In Louisiana he could not remain with safety as he had every reason to believe that he might be the victim of disappointed Treason." Hayti occurred to him, but this too, would not be safe. So his freedom had "as yet only caused him to be an unhappy wanderer," and, apparently believing that his reputation had not reached the ears of the Virginia Negroes, he begged for permission to remain.

22 Local sources quoted in N. Y. Eve. Post, September 21, October 20, 1812.

23 H. T. Catterall, ed., op. cit., III, p. 449.

trict of Columbia, Maryland, Virginia, South Carolina and in Louisiana, to which reference has previously been made,[24] other similar occurrences may be noted.

Thus, on March 30, 1813, the Governor of Virginia heard from a Mr. Nathaniel Burwell of Gloucester County that, " we are threatened with an insurrection of our Negroes. Ten have been apprehended and are in jail for examination." Mr. Spencer George told the same official, on April 9, of an alarm in Lancaster. The militia was ordered out, and " Three negroes have been committed for conspiracy, and [are] waiting for trial." [25] Four days later Mr. Wardlaw wrote from Richmond to St. George Tucker: [26] " There are three slaves . . .now under sentence of Death in the jail of Wmsburg, [Williamsburg, James City County] condemned on a charge of conspiracy & insurrection and to be executed on the 23d inst." In July and in September like troubles disturbed Norfolk and Richmond.[27]

Virginia was rocked early in 1816 by an indigenous John Brown, one George Boxley. In appearancee he was anything but like Brown, but in ideas he seems to have been well-nigh identical. Boxley was between thirty and forty years of age, six feet one or two inches tall, with a " thin visage, of a sallow complexion, thin make, his hair light or yellowish, (thin on top of his head, and tied behind)—he stoops a little in his shoulders, has large whiskers, blue or gray eyes, pretends to be very religious, is fond of talking and speaks quick." [28]

Boxley had several times openly " declared that the distinction between the rich and the poor was too great; that offices were given rather to wealth than to merit; and seemed to be an advocate for a more levelling system of government. For many years he had avowed his disapprobation of the slavery

24 *Ante*, pp. 25-26, 92.

25 *C. V. S. P.*, X, pp. 217, 223.

26 Mrs. Georgia P. Coleman, ed., *Virginia Silhouettes*, p. 21.

27 *C. V. S. P.*, X, pp. 241, 279.

28 Governor's reward notice, in Richmond *Enquirer*, May 22, 1816.

of the negroes, and wished they were free." It was suggested that his failure to be elected to the state legislature, and to advance beyond the post of ensign in the War of 1812 may have embittered him.[29] His economic status was not high, and appears to have fallen precipitately between 1815 and 1816.[30]

Late in 1815 George Boxley decided to attempt to free the slaves and formed a conspiracy in Spotsylvania, Louisa, and Orange Counties. A few of the plotters obtained guns, and others swords and clubs. The rebels were to meet during harvest time at Boxley's house, to bring horses and what weapons they could, attack Fredericksburg first,[31] and then push on into Richmond.

Early in 1816, however, probably in February, a Negro woman belonging to Ptolemy Powell of Spotsylvania, betrayed the scheme, military and police measures were at once instituted, and about thirty slaves immediately arrested. Boxley, after vainly trying to organize a rescue party, fled. He finally surrendered and was imprisoned, but with the flame of a candle, and a file smuggled to him by his wife, escaped, in May, and

29 Letter from Walter Holladay and James M. Bell to Governor Nicholas, Spotsylvania County, March 1, 1816, marked "confidential intelligence" in Executive Papers. Condensed in *C.V.S.P.*, X, pp. 433-35.

30 According to the letter cited in above footnote, Boxley kept a general store in Spotsylvania. In the MS. Land Book of that County for 1815 he is listed as the owner of 459½ acres of land, having a total value of $345.78. The same is repeated for 1816. In the MS. Property Book for 1815 George Boxley is listed as the owner of three slaves, two horses, twenty-two cattle, two flour mills worth fifty dollars each, one side board worth under one hundred dollars, and one desk. He paid $6.76½ in taxes, below that paid by most others listed. In the 1816 Property Book he is listed as the owner of three slaves and two horses and nothing else, and he owed $2.46 in taxes, which he, of course, never paid. Archives, Virginia State Library.

31 The "confidential" letter of the two acting magistrates, W. Holladay and J. M. Bell, to the Governor of March 1, declared that the plot extended to Lynchburg, Fredericksburg, and Richmond. In the neighborhood of Fredericksburg a particularly disturbing fact had appeared — namely, the propagandizing of a Methodist preacher who "has spoken imprudently" concerning slavery and who "was *seen shaking hands with negroes*." Emphases in original.

though a reward of one thousand dollars was offered, he apparently was never recaptured. About six slaves were executed and, probably because of many appeals from white people for clemency, about six others condemned to hang were reprieved and banished.[22]

A favorite, but unnamed, slave belonging to a Colonel Chesnut, betrayed a plot involving many slaves in and around Camden, South Carolina, about one month after Boxley's escape. The Fourth of July was the day selected for the outbreak, which was to have been started by setting fire to several houses. Espionage was used to uncover the ramifications of this widespread conspiracy. A letter from Camden, dated July 4, stated that the Negroes had been discussing their scheme since the past December. It went on:[33]

Our gaol is filled with negroes. They are stretched on their backs on the bare floor, and scarcely move their heads; but have a strong guard placed over them;... This is really a dreadful situation to be in—I think it is time for us to leave a country where we cannot go to bed in safety. [This last sentence was deleted from the letter as published in the Richmond *Enquirer*, July 20, 1816.] Their thirst for revenge must have been very great—it was the wish of some to spare some of the whites, and they mentioned an old gentleman who is a preacher—he never owned a slave and has devoted much of his time to preach to them on the plantations, but even him they would not spare ... We are indebted to a slave for a discovery of this plan, but we shall never know who he is as he requested his master when he told him, never to tell his name—he said he did not wish to leave this country, and he knew the negroes would not let him live here. The negroes will never know who betrayed them, for they tried to engage all for a great distance round.

32 Based on letters and court records of March, 1816 in Executive Papers; Richmond *Enquirer*, May 22, 29, 1816; N. Y. *Eve. Post*, April 16, 1816. See also U. B. Phillips, *op. cit.*, p. 476; J. H. Johnston, *op. cit.*, pp. 166-67; H. Wish, *op. cit.*, p. 312; J. Carroll, *op. cit.*, pp. 74-76.

33 Letter to friend in Philadelphia, N. Y. *Eve. Post*, July 18, 1816.

The informer's status was, however, markedly changed as the legislature purchased his freedom for eleven hundred dollars and gave him a pension for life of fifty dollars.[34] Seven slave leaders were condemned to die, and six were hanged, one being pardoned " just before execution after all preparations had been completed." Another was sentenced to a year's imprisonment in irons, at the end of which time he was to be banished. The local paper reported that [35]

upon trial everyone who was most deeply implicated manifested the greatest apparent innocence, but upon conviction acknowledged the correctness of the Court's decision, nor did they evince the least compunction for having conceived and matured the design. It is melancholy to reflect that those who were most active in the conspiracy occupied a respectable stand in one of the churches, several were professors, and one a class leader.

At least two large-scale expeditions against communities of runaways which annoyed and harassed slaveowners were carried out in 1816. The account of the one near Ashepoo, South Carolina, given by Governor Williams in his legislative message of December, is worth quoting: [36]

A few runaway negroes, concealing themselves in the swamps and marshes contiguous to Combahee and Ashepoo rivers, not having been interrupted in their petty plunderings for a long time, formed the nucleus, round which all the ill-disposed and audacious near them gathered, until at length their robberies became too serious to be suffered with impunity. Attempts were then made to disperse them, which either from insufficiency of numbers or bad arrangement, served by their failure only to encourage a wanton

---

34 David J. McCord, *The Statutes at Large of South Carolina*, VI, p. 58.

35 Camden *Gazette*, July 4, 11, 1816, in T. J. Kirkland and R. M. Kennedy, *Historic Camden*, part two, Columbia, 1926, pp. 187-89; [E. C. Holland] *A Refutation of the Calumnies . . .*, pp. 74-77; H. T. Cook, *Life and Legacy of David R. Williams*, p. 130; H. M. Henry, *op. cit.*, p. 151. Harvey Wish (*op. cit.*, p. 315) mentions plots in North Carolina in 1816, and cites A. H. Gordon (*Journal of Negro History*, XIII, p. 332) but Gordon merely refers in general terms to plots in North Carolina early in the 19th century. So far as is known no conspiracies were reported in that State in 1816.

36 H. T. Cook, *op. cit.*, p. 130.

destruction of property. Their forces now became alarming, not less from its numbers than from its arms and ammunition with which it was supplied. The peculiar situation of the whole of that portion of our coast, rendered access to them difficult, while the numerous creeks and water courses through the marshes around the islands, furnished them easy opportunities to plunder, not only planters in open day, but the inland coasting trade also without leaving a trace of their movements by which they could be pursued ... I therefore ordered Major-General Youngblood to take the necessary measures for suppressing them, and authorized him to incur the necessary expenses of such an expedition. This was immediately executed. By a judicious employment of the militia under his command, he either captured or destroyed the whole body.

A fort erected by the British Colonel Nicholls at Appalachicola Bay, Florida, was occupied, after the English abandoned it, by the Seminoles. The latter were driven out by a band of about three hundred American fugitive slaves, men, women, and children, together with some thirty Indian allies. They took over the well-supplied fort and used it as a haven for other runaways, and as a base for marauding expeditions against slaveholders. The condition was very disturbing, and as has already been demonstrated,[37] was loudly condemned by the Southern press which clamored for the obliteration of the danger.

In July, 1816, United States troops, under Colonel Duncan Clinch, together with some friendly Indians, set out to destroy this stronghold. After a seige of about ten days, and the loss of four soldiers, the fort surrendered when an explosion resulting from a direct hit upon the magazine by a hot cannon shot killed about two hundred and seventy of the fugitives. Out of the original occupants, some forty survived.[38]

37 *Ante*, p. 31.

38 H. Aptheker, " Maroons within the present limits of the United States," *The Journal of Negro History*, XXIV, p. 173.

This period of rather serious concerted slave unrest produced, as usual, its crop of legal enactments aimed at the more secure maintenance of the institution of human bondage. The two schools, reformists and repressionists, again were in conflict, and once more the former came out second best. In Georgia, however, a few reform statutes came into existence.[39] It was there provided that the State might pay for the support of any old or infirm slaves abandoned by their owners, and charge them with the cost. In 1816 it declared that if any individual, not being the owner or his agent, were to hurt a slave without cause, or if the owner himself were cruel (a word left undefined) to the slave, he might be fined or imprisoned (no sum or period stated). The next year Georgia put the murder of Negroes, so far as the law books were concerned, on the same footing as the killing of whites.

Laws for added repression were much more numerous and more susceptible of enforcement. Thus, in 1811, the State of Delaware forbade the immigration of free Negroes. Any entering were to be given ten days' notice to leave, after which, not having left, they were to be subjected to a weekly fine of ten dollars. Any native free Negro who left the State and remained away over six months was to be considered a non-resident.[40] Georgia, in 1810, required incoming free Negroes to register and give full details concerning themselves and their reasons for entering the State.[41] In 1818 free Negroes were forbidden to enter that State, and those in it were required to register each year, and were neither to own slaves nor real estate. Manumission was forbidden, with any one attempting it liable to a fine of one thousand dollars. The next year the regulation concern-

---

39 Lucius Q. C. Lamar, *A Compilation of the Laws of the State of Georgia 1810 to 1819*, pp. 609, 616, 654, 802. The fact that Negroes could not testify against whites made convictions extremely difficult.

40 *Laws of the State of Delaware from January 7, 1806 to February 3, 1813*, IV, pp. 400-404.

41 *Acts of the General Assembly of the State of Georgia; passed at Milledgeville, November and December, 1810*, pp. 117 ff.

ing ownership of land or slaves was declared not to be retro-
active, and free Negroes were permitted to own real estate outside of Darien, Savannah, and Augusta. In December 1816,
South Carolina passed a drastic law forbidding the importation
of slaves from any part of the United States, but, repeating the
pattern followed during the last period of great unrest, this law
was repealed in 1818.[42]

Kentucky, in 1811, declared conspiracy or poisoning by
slaves, crimes punishable by death. In 1815 it forbade the introduction of slaves for sale. Georgia the next year declared the exciting, or attempting to excite, rebellion, a capital crime.[43]
Louisiana, in 1814 provided the death penalty for any slave
wilfully shedding the blood of a white. The same year it provided that for every thirty slaves on a plantation, there was to
be present at least one white adult male, and parish judges
were, twice a year, to visit the plantations to see that this law
was obeyed. Two years later this State provided that no slave
might serve as a witness against whites or free Negroes, unless
the latter were involved in a slave plot or outbreak. Any slave
shooting or stabbing a white was to die; and any guilty of
arson or administering poison was to be imprisoned in chains
and at hard labor for life. The Territory of Mississippi, in
1812, required each militia captain to form a patrol, and levied
a fine of five dollars against anyone not performing patrol duty,
or, in lieu of that, providing a substitute.[44]

The return of peace and some measure of prosperity were
again followed by a brief period of relative, though by no means
absolute, calm among America's slaves. Again, part of the explanation for this may have been an increased alertness on the

42 Lamar, *op. cit.*, 811 ff.; McCord, *op. cit.*, VI, pp. 34, 99.

43 Lettell, *op. cit.*, IV, pp. 223-24; V, pp. 293-94; Lamar, *op. cit.*, pp. 567, 614.

44 L. M. Lislet, *A General Digest of the Acts of the Legislature of Louisiana
passed from 1804 to 1827*, I, pp. 125-27; *Acts Passed at the Second Session
of the Seventh General Assembly of the Mississippi Territory*, November 2,
1812, pp. 42 ff. (photostat). Agitation for restrictions on the slaves' religious
activities became prominent; see Southern papers quoted by N. Y. *Eve. Post*,
August 7, 1816. The effect on the colonization movement will be noted later.

part of the ruling class reinforced by recent acts of repression, together with the growth of a feeling akin to exhaustion on the part of its victims. Occasional episodes of mass discontent were, however, reported.

On Easter Monday, April 7, 1817, several outbursts of slaves, possibly spontaneous, but believed by some contemporaries to have resulted from a preconcerted plan, occurred in St. Mary's County, Maryland. Approximately two hundred Negroes were involved, several whites were injured by sticks, brick-bats, " and other missiles," and two houses were sacked, before police and patrols restored order.[45]

Maroon activities of notable proportions disturbed South Carolina,[46] Virginia,[47] and North Carolina throughout the following year. The disturbances in Wake County of the latter state became serious enough, in November, to evoke considerable notice from the local press, which advised the " patrol to keep a strict look out." Later an attack upon a store " by a maroon banditti of negroes " led by " the noted Andey, alias Billy James, better known here by the name of Abaellino " was repulsed by armed residents. It was believed that the death of at least one white man, if not more, might accurately be placed at their hands. Though Governor Branch offered substantial

45 Report from Great Mill[s], Maryland, April 12, in N. Y. *Eve. Post*, April 21, 1817. In December, 1817 fires of suspicious origin disturbed Savannah. Rewards were offered, lynch law threatened, and a slave woman arrested—*ibid.*, Dec. 26, 29, 1817. The Charleston *Times*, Dec. 29, 1817, reported the arrest of 461 Negroes in the city who had bought some land and erected a church but had conducted themselves " in a manner contrary to the law." They were, however, released.

46 H. Catterall, ed., *op. cit.*, II, p. 307. One hundred and forty Negroes, free and slave, were arrested in Charleston in June, 1818, for having held a meeting at which no white was present, and which they had been told not to hold. Thirteen were fined, jailed or lashed—Charleston *Patriot*, June 10, in N. Y. *Eve. Post*, June 19, 1818.

47 A group of thirty outlawed slaves, together with some whites, caused grave alarm to planters in Princess Ann county in June, 1818—Norfolk *Herald*, June 29, in N. Y. *Eve. Post*, July 7, 1818; see also, *ibid.*, April 16, 1818.

rewards for the capture of eight specified outlaws there is no record of his having to make good the offers.[48]

In the spring of 1819 slaves of Augusta, Georgia entered into a conspiracy very much like that in Camden, South Carolina, three years before. This, too, was to start by firing the city, and this, too, was betrayed. A white man, Alexander Russel, not answering when hailed by one of the guards posted in the city on the occasion, was shot and killed. Several of the rebels were executed. The leader of the plot was a slave named Coot or Coco who had " arranged a pretty extensive plan of operations, and if it had got under way, would have caused much havoc of persons and property." During his trial he maintained a " bold and impudent effrontery, and not a muscle moved when the verdict of death was pronounced against him." [49] The punishment of another of the slaves involved, Paul, was described as follows : he was to receive twenty-five lashes every third day until he had received a total of two hundred and fifty, was then to be branded with the letter R on his left cheek, and to have his ears cut off.[50]

An outlaw community in Williamsburg County, South Carolina was attacked in July, 1919, with the result that three Negroes were killed, a few others were captured and one of the attacking white men was wounded.[51]

48 Raleigh *Register*, Nov. 13, 27, Dec. 18, 1818. Johnston county was also troubled at this time by maroons—G. G. Johnson, *op. cit.*, p. 514.

49 Unnamed Savannah paper of May 10, quoted in Niles' *Weekly Register*, Baltimore, May 22, 1819, XVI, p. 213.

50 Augusta *Herald*, May 14, in *the Louisiana Courier*, June 28, 1819. See also U. B. Phillips, *op. cit.*, p. 477. Late in November, 1819 a fire of incendiary origin causing damages estimated at $50,000 occurred in Augusta— N. Y. *Eve. Post*, December 3, 1819. A report from the same city dated February 1, 1820, told of the execution of two slaves who had killed a white man. One was burned alive, the other hanged and then decapitated, his head being put on public display—*ibid.*, February 12, 1820.

51 Entry of July 12, 1819 in diary of Dr. Henry Ravenal, St. John's Parish, S. C., in U. B. Phillips, ed., *Plantation and Frontier Documents 1649-1863*, II, p. 91.

CHAPTER XI

1820-1830

THE second decade of the nineteenth century is another period of sharply increased rebellious activity. This lasted for about a dozen years and had two great climaxes, that of 1822 conceived by Denmark Vesey, and that of 1831 conceived by Nat Turner.

Again the era is one of severe economic depression.[1] This encouraged the emigration of whites seeking better opportunities, and, by cutting the ground away from the domestic slave trade, tended to keep the Negro increment within the Old South. These factors resulted in a disproportionate population growth in that region, particularly in its most easterly sections. This piling up of a Negro population at a time of economic stress is undoubtedly important in accounting for rebelliousness.

The situation in Virginia may be examined as representative of the condition prevailing throughout the seaboard southern states. In percentages the Tidewater region of that State showed the following population development from 1820 to 1830: the number of whites increased 3.2; the number of slaves, 5.0; and the number of free Negroes, 25.5. The Piedmont area showed the same trend though in a much less sharp degree: there the number of whites increased 11.2; the number of slaves, 12.3; and the number of free Negroes, 26.5. In actual figures[2] this meant that during the decade the number of whites in the Tidewater increased by 5,314, and in the Piedmont by

1 *Ante*, p. 120.

2 These figures are calculated from the official " Census " in several pages of tables printed in *Documents Containing Statistics of Virginia Ordered to be Printed by the State Convention Sitting in the City of Richmond, 1850-1851, Richmond, 1851*, no pagination. Some contemporary and later writers have been in error regarding these figures, usually exaggerating the trend. See present writer's unpublished master's thesis " Nat Turner's Revolt," Columbia University, 1937, pp. 10-15.

21,170, while the number of Negroes (free and slave) increased by 15,864 in the former and by 27,885 in the latter. In the East as a whole (Tidewater plus Piedmont) there were 349,-173 whites in 1820 and 414,575 Negroes, while in 1830 the respective figures were 375,657 and 457,324.

The period was also one of world-wide revolutionary upheaval, such as had not been seen for a generation, particularly in the latter half of it, when outbreaks of major proportions occurred in Turkey, Greece, Italy, Spain, France, Belgium, Poland, South America, Mexico, and the West Indies. The last directly involved slaves, while in South America and in Mexico the upheavals resulted in furthering the anti-slavery cause, thus creating concern among the rulers of the Southern States. Another source of worry was the attempt made during these years by Mexico and Colombia, apparently backed by England and France, to get rid of slavery and Spanish rule in Cuba and Puerto Rico.[3]

Serious servile insurrections broke out during the twenties in Martinique, Puerto Rico, Cuba, Antigua, Tortola, Demerara, and Jamaica. These outbreaks, together with the democratic upsurge stirring England, revitalized her anti-slavery movement, and it not only grew quantitatively but changed qualitatively so that the demand increased for immediate emancipation.[4] This, together with economic depression in the Islands, and the complaints from staple producers in British India, where chattel slavery was forbidden, so advanced the cause that, in 1832 Parliament passed a gradual emancipation act.

John Quincy Adams, observing the movement, wrote in his diary on January 10, 1831, that this British development [5]

3 See speech of John Randolph, Senate, March 2, 1826, in *Register of Debates*, II, part 1, 114, 121; T. E. Burton, "Henry Clay," in Samuel F. Bemis, ed., *The American Secretaries of State and Their Diplomacy*, IV, pp. 134, 143.

4 G. W. Alexander, *Letters on the Slave Trade*, pp. 22-23; F. J. Klingberg, *The Anti-Slavery Movement in England*, p. 72; W. L. Mathieson, *British Slavery and its Abolition*, p. 197; R. L. Schuyler, *Parliament and the British Empire*, p. 163.

5 C. F. Adams, ed., *Memoirs of John Quincy Adams*, VIII, p. 269.

" may prove an earthquake upon this continent." The same years witnessed a growth in anti-slavery sentiment in the United States which, while by no means as considerable as that in Great Britain, was, nevertheless, relatively marked,[6] and also moved, somewhat belatedly, to an unequivocal demand for the abolition of slavery.

It is in such an atmosphere that the great unrest of the slaves of the United States for a dozen years after 1819 was displayed. It is probable that one affected the other, though precise evidence of this is rare,[7] but it is certain that without the entire picture in one's mind, the events themselves and the effects that flowed from them cannot be understood.

" The attention of the people " of Petersburg, Virginia, was " entirely engrossed by *an insurrection of the blacks* " [8] in February, 1820. Several attempts had been made to fire the town, and many Negroes together with a few suspicious whites were arrested, while armed guards patrolled the streets. White men slept with guns at their sides and " expecting to be roused either to stop the progress of the devouring element, or to quell insurrection." Nothing, however, other than the fires and a few arrests, seems to have occurred.

In March, 1820, slaves newly brought into Florida from Jamaica rebelled and were quickly subdued by a detachment of United States troops. In this process one Negro was killed, but what other casualties occurred, and what punishments were inflicted are not known.[9] In the spring of the same year maroons became especially troublesome in Gates County, North Caro-

6 Thus the output of anti-slavery writings in the twenties, while not to be compared to the flood of the thirties and the deluge of the next generation, was certainly markedly greater than that of the previous decade.

7 One such is the influence of the Missouri debates on certain of Vesey's followers; another is the presence of the Walker pamphlet in several southern states, and its alleged affect there.

8 Letters dated Petersburg, February 25, 29, in N. Y. *Eve. Post*, March 6, 1820, emphases in original.

9 Helen T. Catterall, *Judicial Cases Concerning the Negro and American Slavery*, II, pp. 327-28.

lina, and killed at least one white man. A hunting party succeeded in bagging Harry, a leader of the fugitives, whose head
was assessed at two hundred dollars. The paper reporting this
declared,[10] " It is expected that the balance of Harry's company
will very soon be taken."

Several months later there was similar difficulty near Georgetown, South Carolina, resulting in the death of one slaveholder
and the capture of three outlaws.[11] The activities of considerable
groups of these black Robin Hoods in North Carolina, aided by
some free Negroes, assumed the proportions of rebellion in the
summer of 1821.[12] There seem also to have been plans for joint
action between these maroons and the field slaves against the
slaveholders. About three hundred members of the militia of
the counties affected, Onslow, Carteret, and Bladen, saw service for about twenty-five days in August and September. Approximately twelve of these men were wounded when two companies of militia accidentally fired upon each other. The situation was under control by the middle of September, " although
the said malitia [sic] did not succeed in apprehending all the
runaways & fugitives, they did good by arresting some, and
driving others off, and suppressing the spirit of insurrection."
A newspaper item of 1824 discloses that the " prime mover " of
this trouble, Isam, " alias General Jackson," was among those
who escaped at the time, for he is there reported [13] as dying
from lashes publicly inflicted at Cape Fear, North Carolina.

Depression-ridden Charleston, South Carolina, whose census
of 1820 showed an actual decline in the number of its white inhabitants, and a rise in that of the Negroes until the latter

10 Edenton *Gazette*, May 12, quoted by N. Y. *Eve. Post*, May 17, 1820.

11 N. Y. *Eve. Post*, June 11, 1821.

12 See petition of John H. Hill, Colonel Commandant of the Carteret
militia, dated December 1825, and accompanying memoranda, in Legislative
Papers 1824-1825 (No. 366), North Carolina Historical Commission, Raleigh;
R. H. Taylor, " Slave conspiracies in North Carolina," *North Carolina Historical Review*, V, p. 24; G. G. Johnson, *Ante-Bellum North Carolina*, p. 514.

13 N. Y. *Eve. Post*, May 11, 1824.

comprised four-sevenths of its residents,[14] was the scene in 1822 of one of the most serious, widespread, and carefully planned conspiracies.[15] Since the leader of this plot, Denmark Vesey (born, it is reported, in Africa, and serving for several years aboard a slave-trader) had succeeded in purchasing his freedom in 1800 and thus was a member of the free Negro [16] group, it is especially interesting to observe that the rapid increase in that class of people [17] had aroused concern which several times found expression just prior to the discovery of the conspiracy, and which resulted in legislation aimed against the group.[18]

Vesey seems, however, to have been the only non-slave directly implicated in the plot. He and several other leaders, such as Peter Poyas and Mingo Harth, were urban artisans—carpenters, harness-makers, mechanics, and blacksmiths; they were

14 In his legislative message of December, 1821, Governor Bennett, whose own slaves were to be prominent rebel leaders, called attention to this disproportionate population trend.—T. D. Jervey, *Robert Y. Hayne*, p. 130.

15 All material, unless otherwise indicated, on the Vesey plot comes from two contemporary pamphlet accounts: [James Hamilton, Jr., Intendant of Charleston] *Negro Plot an Account of the Late Intended Insurrection among a Portion of the Blacks of the City of Charleston, South Carolina*; Lionel H. Kennedy and Thomas Parker, members of the Charleston bar, and the presiding magistrates of the Court; *An Official Report of the Trials of Sundry Negroes Charged with an Attempt to raise an Insurrection in the State of South-Carolina*.

16 Although often referred to by later writers as a mulatto, contemporary sources mention him as a "negro" or a "black"—Kennedy and Parker, *op. cit.*, p. 17; *Washington National Intelligencer*, July 6, 1822.

17 In 1790 there were 1,801 free Negroes in South Carolina; in 1820 there were 6,826. An important source of this marked increase was Quaker manumissions—H. M. Henry, *Police Control of the Slave in S. C.*, p. 177.

18 In 1820 and 1821, largely through the efforts of Col. John C. Prioleau, a member of the legislature whose favorite slave was to betray Vesey's plot, laws were passed forbidding manumission except with the legislature's approval, and prohibiting the immigration of free Negroes or the return of native free Negroes who left the State. And, in 1820, it was provided that anyone convicted of spreading anti-slavery ideas was to pay a fine of one thousand dollars. See Charleston *Courier*, Dec. 12, 1820; *Acts and Resolutions ... of S. C. passed Dec. 1820*, pp. 22-24; Henry, *op. cit.*, p. 155.

literate, and Vesey was master of several languages. He was the oldest of the plotters, being apparently in his late fifties.[19] Until the betrayal of the conspiracy, he wore a beard, but further than this little is known concerning his personal appearance.

Active organizational work was begun by Vesey in December, 1821, when he selected the leaders mentioned above. According to the *Official Report* of the trials:

In the selection of his leaders, Vesey showed great penetration and sound judgment. Rolla [slave of Governor Thomas Bennett] was plausible and possessed uncommon self-possession; bold and ardent he was not to be deterred from his purpose by danger. Ned's [owned by the same person] appearance indicated that he was a man of firm nerves and desperate courage. Peter [slave of James Poyas] was intrepid and resolute, true to his engagements, and cautious in observing secrecy where it was necessary; he was not to be daunted nor impeded by difficulties, and though confident of success, was careful in providing against any obstacles or casualties which might arise, and intent upon discovering every means which might be in their favor if thought of before hand. Gullah [slave of P. Pritchard] was regarded as a Sorcerer, and as such feared by the natives of Africa, who believe in witchcraft. He was not only considered invulnerable, but that he could make others so by his charms; and that he could and certainly would provide all his followers with arms. He was artful, cruel, bloody; his disposition in short was diabolical. His influence amongst the Africans was inconceivable. Monday [slave of John Gell] was firm, resolute, discreet and intelligent.

Appeals to the rights of man, couched in both theological and secular terms, were used by Vesey. Thus, he would read to the Negroes " from the bible how *the children of Israel were delivered out of Egypt from bondage,*" or if his companion were to bow " to a white person he would rebuke him, and observe that

19 Kennedy and Parker, *op. cit.*, p. 85, describe Vesey as an " old man." According to *Harper's Encyclopaedia of United States History*, X, p. 53, he was born about 1767, which agrees with A. H. Grimke's remark that, when executed, July 2, 1822, he was not over fifty-six years of age. — *Right on the Scaffold*, p. 10.

all men were born equal, and that he was surprised that any one would degrade himself by such conduct; that he would never cringe to the whites, nor ought any who had the feelings of a man." Affairs relating to enslavement were noted by him and called to the attention of the slaves, as the bitter debates in Congress over the Missouri question, or the success of the Haitians [20] in establishing and maintaining their independence.

Personal motives did not remain unexpressed. Thus, a slave reported that, " Vesey said the negroes were living such an abominable life, they ought to rise. I said I was living well— he said though I was others were not." He had not heeded the urgings of the slaveowners for free Negroes to go to Africa, *" because he had not the will, he wanted to stay and see what he could do* for his fellow creatures," including his own children who were slaves. Another slave reported of Peter Poyas: " I met him the next day according to appointment, when he said to me, we intend to see if we can't do something for ourselves, we can't live so."

Most of the other Negroes felt as did Poyas and Vesey. Two of the rebels said, " They never spoke to any person of color on the subject, or knew of any who had been spoken to by the other leaders, who had withheld his assent." The fear of betrayal, however, was great, so that, " In enlisting men the great caution observed by the leaders was remarkable. Few if any domestic servants were spoken to, as *they* were distrusted; . . . and Peter whilst he urged one of his agents to speak to others and solicit them to join, at the same time gave him this charge, ' but take care and don't mention it to those waiting men who receive presents of old coats, etc. from their masters, or they'll

20 *Ante*, pp. 81, 98. Note Thomas Jefferson's comment on the Missouri debates: " If Congress has the power to regulate the conditions of the inhabitants of the States, it will be but another exercise of that power to declare that all shall be free. Are we then to see again Athenian and Lacedemonian confederacies? To wage another Pelopeneasian war to settle the ascendency between them? Or is this the tocsin of merely a servile war? That remains to be seen; but not, I hope, by you or me." To John Adams, January 21, 1822, quoted by Gilbert Chinard, *Thomas Jefferson the Apostle of Americanism*, p. 503.

betray us; *I will speak to* them '." One agent did not receive, or did not benefit from, such advice and, on May 25, attempted to interest a favorite slave of Colonel Prioleau in the scheme. He immediately disclosed [21] the plan to a free Negro named Pencell who advised that he inform his master. This he did, and on May 30 the authorities took the first steps towards crushing the conspiracy by arresting Peter Poyas and Mingo Harth.

Vesey had set the date for the outbreak on the second Sunday in July, the Sabbath being selected since it was customary for many slaves to enter the city on that day, and the summer month because many whites would then be vacationing outside Charleston. The betrayal led him to put the date ahead one month, but Vesey could not communicate this to his country confederates, some of whom were as many as eighty miles outside the city. The two leaders, Peter and Mingo, though arrested, behaved " with so much composure and coolness " that " the wardens were completely deceived." Both were freed on May 31, but spies were detailed to watch their movements.

Another slave, William, now turned informer, and more arrests followed, the most damaging of which was that of Charles, slave of John Drayton, who agreed to act as a spy. This quickly led to complete exposure. One hundred and thirty-one Negroes of Charles were arrested and forty-nine were condemned to die. Twelve of these were pardoned and transported, while thirty-seven were hanged, the executions taking place from June 18 to August 9.[22]

21 The official report refers to the informer as Devany, but in the act granting him a reward he is called Peter; in both cases Col. J. C. Prioleau is given as the owner. The legislature freed him and gave him an annual pension of $50. He was living in 1857 when the yearly payment was raised to $200. The free Negro, Pencell was given $1,000.—J. C. Brevard, *Statutes at Large of South Carolina*, VI, p. 194; XII, p. 562; Henry, *op. cit.*, p. 17; J. C. Carroll, *Slave Insurrections in the United States, 1800-1865*, p. 102.

22 Washington *Daily National Intelligencer*, August 10, 13, 16, 1822. It may also be noted that Charles, the slave of John Drayton who had aided the State, was hanged on July 12. This adds credence to the charge made in Peter Neilson, ed., *The Life and Adventures of Zamba*, p. 238, where it

Although the leaders had kept lists of their comrades, only one list and part of another were found. Moreover, most of them followed the admonition of Peter Poyas, " Die silent, as you shall see me do," and so it is difficult to say how many Negroes were involved. One witness said sixty-six hundred outside of Charleston, another said nine thousand altogether were implicated. The plan of revolt, involving simultaneous attacks from five points and a sixth force on horseback to patrol the streets, further indicated a very considerable number of conspirators. The *Official Report* declared, " enough has been disclosed to satisfy every reasonable mind, that considerable numbers were involved . . . it extended to the North of Charleston many miles towards Santee, and unquestionably into St. John's Parish; to the South to James' and John's Islands; and to the West beyond Bacon's Bridge over Ashley River."

The preparations had been thorough. By the middle of June the Negroes had made about two hundred and fifty pike heads and bayonets and over three hundred daggers. They had noted every store containing any arms and had given instructions to all slaves who tended or could get horses as to when and where to bring the animals. Even a barber had assisted by making wigs and whiskers to hide the identities of the rebels. Vesey had also written twice to St. Domingo telling of his plans and asking for aid. All who opposed were to be killed for the creed of the Negroes was " he that is not with me is against me."

Following the arrests there was formulated a plan for the rescue of the prisoners; and, on the day of Vesey's execution, according to one source:[23] "Another attempt at insurrection was made but the State troops held the slaves in check. So determined, however, were they to strike a blow for liberty that it was found necessary for the federal government to send sol-

is said that Negroes were induced to talk by promises of reprieves, but were executed anyway. Vernon Loggins, however, doubts the authenticity of this work.—*The Negro Author*, p. 231.

[23] *Harper's Encyclopaedia of United States History*, pp. 53-55.

diers to maintain order." Contemporary evidence establishing the truth of the second point, that referring to federal reinforcements, has been seen.[24]

While the executions were proceeding in Charleston, activity among armed runaway Negroes was reported from Jacksonborough (now Jacksonboro) South Carolina, forty miles to the west. Three were captured, and hanged July 19. In August Governor Bennett offered a reward of two hundred dollars for the capture of about twenty maroons in the same region.[25] It is possible that these people had had some connection with Vesey's farflung plot. A laconic press item of late September reports another possible link in the scheme: [26] " It appears that an insurrection of the blacks was contemplated at Beaufort, South Carolina, and that ten negroes belonging to the most respectable families were arrested. The town council was in secret session. Particulars had not transpired."

The pattern of recommendations, and the enactments of new measures of restriction and repression following serious rebellious activity was copied in this case. Post-conspiracy literature

24 Charleston *Courier*, n. d., in Richmond *Enquirer*, August 3, 1822; Charleston *City Gazette*, n. d., in *ibid.*, August 23, 1822.

25 Washington *Daily National Intelligencer*, July 23, August 24, 1822.

26 *Niles' Weekly Register*, Baltimore, September 28, 1822, XXIII, p. 64. John H. Russell in *The Free Negro in Virginia, 1619-1865*, p. 169 declares: " Moses, a free negro of Goochland County, revealed a conspiracy of slaves in 1822." The cited source, a petition (dated December 18, 1822, Goochland, no. A7086) does not contain the information Russell gives. Moses, formerly the slave of a Mr. Peers, had purchased his own freedom in 1820 and petitioned for permission to remain in Virginia. To support his request he stated he was self-supporting and hard working. A statement to the same effect is made by Mr. Peers' son, who adds that Moses, as a slave, had " made communications... concerning insurrection." On this last point the petition of Moses reads: " In times when there were frequent alarms of insurrections of the Blacks, in the neighborhood, where there [sic] number was great being near large estates and extensive coal mines your Petitioner has more than once secretly made known to his Mistress the whispers of such Plots being agitated and concerning them he was always distressed and anxious to make discoveries."—Archives, Virginia State Library, Richmond.

stressed the wisdom of keeping down the number of free Negroes, and of making their lives more difficult. For [27]

the superior condition of the free persons of color, excites discontent among our slaves, who continually have before their eyes, persons of the same color, many of whom they have known in slavery, and with all of whom they associate on terms of equality —free from the controls of masters, working when they please, going whither they please, and expending their money how they please—the slave seeing this, finds his labor irksome; he becomes dissatisfied with his state, he pants for liberty!

Or more briefly put, the slaves seeing the free Negroes,[28] " naturally become dissatisfied with their lot, until the feverish restlessness of this disposition foments itself into insurrection."

Specific proposals called for ceasing to hire out slaves, keeping them out of cities, forbidding their instruction, and strengthening the military prowess of the community.[29] And, significantly, one influential commentator found dangerous and therefore lamentable the " indiscreet zeal in favor of universal liberty " that existed and found frequent expression in the United States.[30]

Action was taken. During the year following Vesey's conspiracy, laws were passed forbidding the hiring-out of slaves,

[27] Memorial of the citizens of Charleston to the Senate and House of Representatives of the State of South Carolina, 1822, in U. B. Phillips, ed., *Plantation and Frontier Documents*, II, pp. 108-109.

[28] [E. C. Holland] *op. cit.*, p. 83. These statements vividly contrast with those to come about ten years later and to last until the Civil Was as an important part of the pro-slavery argument, concerning the supposedly awful conditions of the free Negroes, North and South, so that, it was alleged, they were worse off than slaves.

[29] As note 27; South Carolina *State Gazette,* October and November, 1822; Charleston Grand Jury report in Charleston *Courier,* June 21, 1823; H. Henry, *op. cit.*, pp. 101, 167.

[30] "Achates " [General Thomas Pinckney] *Reflections Occasioned by the Late Disturbances in Charleston,* pp. 6-7. An anonymous pamphleteer, probably the Reverend Frederick Dalcho, suggested that Negroes be kept away from Fourth of July celebrations!—*Practical Considerations Founded on the Scriptures Relative to the Slave Population of South-Carolina,* pp. 33 n.

providing that every free Negro over fifteen years of age was to have a guardian whose function would be to serve as a control on his behavior, the congregating of slaves was forbidden, the instructing of Negroes in the arts of reading and writing was made a crime, slaves were ordered not to converge on Charleston every Sunday, and patrol regulations were made more severe.[31] It was, moreover, forbidden for any Negro from Mexico, the West Indies or South America to enter the State, and Negro crew members of any ship entering any harbor of South Carolina, were not to leave their boat on penalty of imprisonment, with the necessity of the captain paying the State the charges of his confinement, if he wished the seaman released.[32] In addition two extra-legal steps were taken when a volunteer military organization, under the leadership of Robert J. Turnbull, was formed July, 1823 in Charleston; and a Negro religious leader, Bishop Moses Brown, whose African Methodist Church in Charleston had three thousand members in 1822, was forced to leave the State.[33]

Of additional interest as an aftermath of the Vesey plot and its suppression is the fact that not a few Northern newspapers, like the New York *Daily Advertiser,* the Philadelphia *Gazette,* and the Boston *Recorder,* published articles in a deprecating tone to both the institution of slavery and the uprisings and

31 A special city guard of one hundred and fifty men was also provided for Charleston. *Acts and Resolutions of the General Assembly of the State of South-Carolina passed in December, 1822,* Columbia, 1822, pp. 9-11; David J. McCord, *The Statutes at Large of South Carolina, 1814-1838,* VI, pp. 179, 220.

32 The Negro Seamen's Act had interstate and international repercussions. But South Carolina, basing itself on its rights as a sovereign state, refused to modify or repeal the law. Other Southern states later passed such acts. The argument aroused by this law influenced the thinking of Thomas Cooper. See, Dumas Malone, *The Public Life of Thomas Cooper,* p. 285; H. Henry, *op. cit.,* pp. 124 ff.; Jervey, *Hayne, loc. cit.,* pp. 178-85; J. B. McMaster, *A History of the People of the United States,* V, pp. 200-205; Louis B. Boudin, *Government by Judiciary,* I, p. 310.

33 U. B. Phillips, *The Course of the South to Secession,* p. 102; C. G. Woodson, *The History of the Negro Church,* p. 78.

bloody repressions it called forth.[34] Even in South Carolina itself there is evidence of such a feeling,[35] and publicists in that State did not hesitate to rush to the defense of its action in repressing the conspiracy, and to the defense, *per se,* of the system of chattel slavery.[36]

The Charleston martyrs were hardly in their graves when other Negroes sprang forward to continue the efforts of their people for freedom. The Norfolk *Herald* of May 12, 1823, contains an unusually full account of maroons under the heading,[37] "A Serious Subject." It declares that the citizens of the southern part of Norfolk County, Virginia

have for some time been kept in a state of mind peculiarly harrassing and painful, from the too apparent fact that their lives are at the mercy of a band of lurking assassins, against whose fell designs neither the power of the law, or vigilance, or personal strength and intrepidity, can avail. These desperadoes are runaway negroes (commonly called outlyers) ... Their first object is to obtain a gun and ammunition, as well to procure game for subsistence as to defend themselves from attack, or accomplish objects of vengeance.

Several white men had already been killed by these militant slaves, one, a Mr. William Walker, very recently. This aroused great fear. " No individual after this can consider his life safe

34 See J. C. Carroll, *op. cit.,* pp. 109-111.

35 William Johnson, a South Carolinian and a Justice of the United States Supreme Court, adopted such an attitude and was, therefore, denounced by Thomas Cooper; see D. Malone, *op. cit.,* p. 269.

36 Charleston *City Gazette,* August 14, 15, September 22, 1822; Charleston *Courier,* November 15, 1822. It is to this that Edwin C. Holland had reference in his pamphlet's title, *A Refutation of the Calumnies Circulated Against the Southern & Western States Respecting the Institution and Existence of Slavery Amongst Them,* Charleston, 1822; see also, the Reverend Dr. Richard Furman's *Exposition of the Views of the Baptists, Relative to the Coloured Population of the United States, in a Communication to the Governor of South-Carolina,* especially p. 7; and [Frederick Dalcho] *op. cit., passim.* Though this evidence was not cited, it supports the view expressed by W. B. Hesseltine in " Some new aspects of the pro-slavery argument," *Journal of Negro History,* XXI, pp. 1-14.

37 Quoted in the N. Y. *Eve. Post,* May 15, 1823.

from the murdering aim of these monsters in human shape. Every one who has haply rendered himself obnoxious to their vengeance, must, indeed, calculate on sooner or later falling a victim " to them. Indeed, one slaverholder had received a note from these amazing fellows suggesting it would be healthier for him to remain indoors at night—and he did.

A large body of militia was ordered out to exterminate these outcasts and " thus relieve the neighbouring inhabitants from a state of perpetual anxiety and apprehension, than which nothing can be more painful." During the next few weeks there were occasional reports [38] of the killing or capturing of outlaws, culminating June 25 in the capture of the leader himself, Bob Ferebee, who, it was declared, had been a fugitive for six years. He was executed one month after capture. In October of this year runaway Negroes near Pineville, South Carolina, were attacked.[39] Several were captured and at least two, a woman and a child, were killed. One of the maroons was decapitated and his head stuck on a pole and publicly exposed as " a warning to vicious slaves."

The inhabitants of Edgecombe County, North Carolina were much distraught in December, 1825, " by the partial discovery of an insurrectionary plot among the blacks " who seemed to have believed that the national government had actually set them free. The patrol was strengthened, the militia called out, and the conspiracy crushed—but what that meant in human terms does not appear.[40]

In September, 1826, Edward and Howard Stone, slave-traders of Bourbon County, Kentucky, of ten years' experience, together with two hired men, David Cobb and Humphrey David of Lexington, were transporting seventy-seven slaves down the Ohio River for sale in the deep South. One other

38 *Ibid.*, May 29, June 5, 30, 1823.

39 Charleston *City Gazette*, in *ibid.*, October 24, 1823; Niles' *Weekly Register*, October 18, 1823, XXV, p. 112; T. J. Kirkland, and R. M. Kennedy, *op. cit.*, part two, p. 190.

40 See *ante*, p. 81.

white man, James M. Gray, of Woodville, Mississippi, was aboard the boat as a passenger. About ninety miles south of Louisville the slaves, in some manner, broke out of their confinement and, armed with clubs, axes, and knives, succeeded in killing the five white men. They then appropriated some money, sank the boat, and made their way to Indiana. All were reported as captured and five were publicly executed on November 29, 1826, while most of the others were sold into the South.[41]

The same year twenty-nine slaves being shipped from Maryland to Georgia aboard the *Decatur,* owned by Austin Woolfolk, one of the nation's leading slavetraders, rebelled, killed two members of the crew, and commanded another to take them to Haiti. The boat was captured and taken into New York, were in some unexplained way, every one of the rebels escaped. One, however, William Bowser, was later caught and executed in New York City on December 15, 1826. The occurrence moved the famous anti-slavery publicist, Benjamin Lundy, to denounce Mr. Woolfolk, whereupon the latter so beat up the former as to incapacitate him for several days. Lundy sued Woolfolk and the Baltimore Court awarded him damages totalling one dollar![42]

A news item dated New Orleans, October 7, 1826, reads:[43] " We have been informed that disturbances of rather a delicate

41 Hartford *Connecticut Courant,* October 16, 1826; Niles' *Weekly Register,* November 18, 1826, XXXI, p. 192; Charles S. Sydnor, *Slavery in Mississippi,* p. 149; J. Winston Coleman, Jr., *Slavery Times in Kentucky,* pp. 174-76. For a description of conditions on the boats of the internal slave trade see [Thomas Hamilton], *Men and Manners in America,* II, pp. 190-191.

42 N. Y. *Eve. Post,* May 26, 1826; [Thomas Earle], *Life, Travels and Opinions of Benjamin Lundy,* pp. 206-209; F. Bancroft, *Slave-Trading in the Old South,* p. 41.

43 N. Y. *Eve. Post,* November 7, 9, 1826. The year, 1826, also witnessed several incendiary fires, some serious, in Petersburg, Charleston, and Mobile, with slaves suspected as the authors. — Connecticut *Courant,* Jan. 17; Charleston *Gazette,* Jan. 16; Charleston *Courier,* June 25, N. Y. *Eve. Post,* Feb. 10, 14, 15, July 26, August 3, 1826. Joshua Coffin, *op. cit.,* p. 31, refers to trouble in Newbern, North Carolina in 1826, and this is followed by J. Carroll, *op. cit.,* p. 113. The date is erroneous, the event referred to occurring in 1830. See *post,* p. 290.

nature had taken place at three plantations on the coast above. Capt. Harney, with a detachment of United States' troops, provisioned for three days, left the city last evening, and will no doubt put matters on their former footing." A couple of days later, however, it was asserted that these military movements had been performed merely for purposes of " drill and exercise," so that the truth concerning this matter is obscure.

The existence of bothersome maroons at about the same time in South Carolina is established by the fact that in January, 1827, two cases appeared in a court of that State revolving around the killing of two outlying Negroes. In one case the action of the man firing the fatal shot was declared proper " on the ground that there were certain runaway negroes in the neighborhood . . . who were committing murders and other outrages, which kept the country in such a state of alarm." The other case also concerned a man who had been " one of a party who went in search of some runaway negroes who had been very mischievous in the neighborhood," and had killed one of the rebels.[44]

A lady in Georgia wrote to a friend in New York on June 6, 1827, as follows: [45]

A most dangerous and extensive insurrection of the blacks was detected at Macon a few days since. They had banded together to the number of 300, and were supposed to be instigated and headed by a French emigrant from the Mississippi. His slaves were in the plot. They had only arrested one of the rebels. The whole of the others, with the Frenchmen, have made their escape.

Where slaves might disappear to in this uncanny fashion is indicated in a report that came from Alabama about two weeks later: [46]

44 H. T. Catterall, ed., *op. cit.*, II, p. 335.

45 Washington, *African Repository and Colonial Journal*, July 1827, III, p. 157; R. Scarborough, *Opposition to Slavery in Georgia*, p. 89.

46 Mobile *Register*, June 20, 21, 1827, quoted in N. Y. *Eve. Post*, July 11, 12, 1827; U. B. Phillips in *The South in the Building of the Nation*, IV, p. 229. Fires of incendiary origin, at times ascribed to slaves, were

A nest of runaway negroes was discovered last week in the fork of the Alabama & Tombecke [Tombigbee] Rivers, by a party from the upper end of Mobile County, consisting of [five individuals are named] and some others. The negroes were attacked and after a very severe action they were conquered. Three negroes were shot ... several were taken prisoners and others escaped. They had two cabins, and were about to build a Fort. The encampment is probably broken up entirely. Some of these negroes have been runaways several years, and have committed many depredations on the neighbouring plantations. They fought desperately.

A later report declared that had they built the fort " a great number of negroes in the secret were to join them, and it is thought that in that event they could not be taken without bringing cannon to bear upon them." One of the whites in this engagement wrote, June 15, in part: " This much I can say that old Hal [a leader of the maroons] and his men fought like Spartans, not one gave an inch of ground, but stood, was shot dead or wounded fell on the spot. The negro man Pompey who is now living, tried to get his gun fresh primed to shoot after he was shot through the thigh." Because of the poor equipment of the slaves only one white was wounded.

In November of the same year a Negro woman returned to her master in New Orleans after an absence of sixteen years. She told of a maroon settlement some eight miles north of the city containing about sixty people. A drought prevailed at the time so it was felt [47] that " the uncommon dryness ... has made those retreats attainable ... and we are told there is another camp about the head of the bayou Bienvenu. Policy imperiously

reported in 1827 from Hanover County, Virginia, Moore County, North Carolina, and from Norfolk, Virginia, and Elizabeth City, N. C. See Richmond *Enquirer*, March 13, April 20; N. Y. *Eve. Post*, May 23; Boston *Independent Chronicle*, September 12, 1827.

47 N. Y. *Eve. Post*, December 4, 1827. In 1828 a man who had killed a slave was tried in North Carolina, and offered as an excuse " that good deal of alarm existed in the neighborhood, caused by depredations committed by runaway slaves."—H. T. Catterall, ed.,, *op. cit.*, II, p. 56. For notice of unrest in Texas in 1828, see *ante*, p. 32, 81.

calls for a thorough search, and the destruction of all such repairs, wherever found to exist."

Beginning in 1829 and persisting through 1831 there prevailed a period of extraordinary rebelliousness. Suspicious fires, frequently attributed to slaves, occurred in Mobile and in Huntsville, Alabama in January and February, 1829.[48] Early in April in Savannah and Augusta, Georgia, several attempts at arson were made. At the end of the month a disastrous fire swept Augusta and destroyed much of the arms stored there. This moved Governor John Forsyth to send, on May 6, " an urgent appeal to the Secretary of War (John Eaton) for arms to protect the people of the state in case of slave revolt;" and on the same day he sent a note to W. W. Montgomery, in command of the militia at Augusta, to be on his guard.[49]

An English visitor to Augusta early in 1830 wrote:[50]

There was a great fire in this city in the month of April last ... [1829]. The fire was believed to be the work of incendiaries among the people of colour. One slave, a female, was convicted, executed, dissected, and exposed, but she died denying the crime. Another, now with child, is sentenced to be executed in June [1830] but she still denies her guilt. I fear these unhappy creatures are convicted on what we should consider very insufficient evidence.

48 Huntsville *Southern Advocate*, January 30, February 6, 1830. A serious fire of allegedly incendiary origin hit Mobile in November, 1828—Mobile *Register*, November 7, in N. Y. *American*, November 29, 1828.

49 Huntsville *Southern Advocate*, April 24, May 8, 1829; C. Eaton, "A dangerous pamphlet in the old south," *Journal of Southern History*, II, pp. 325-26. David Walker's revolutionary *Appeal* had penetrated into Georgia, as well as North Carolina and Louisiana, and had provoked unrest. See *Journal of the House of Representatives of the State of Georgia ... 1829* (Milledgeville, 1830), p. 353; H. Aptheker, " Militant Abolitionism," in *The Journal of Negro History*, XXVI, pp. 446-48.

50 James Stuart, *Three Years in North America*, II, p. 123; see also James S. Buckingham, *Slave States of America*, II, pp. 47-50. Both Albert B. Hart (*Slavery and Abolition*, p. 116) and Ruth Scarborough (*op. cit.*, p. 89), incorrectly put the fire in 1830. In May, 1829, a slave woman tried for arson in Brownsborough, Alabama, was acquitted—Huntsville *Southern Advocate*, May 15, 1829.

Other fires [51] of incendiary origin occurred in the same city in October and November of this year, as well as in Frankfort, Kentucky, and Camden, South Carolina, the latter destroying eighty-five buildings.

A terrific fire swept New Orleans, January 13, 1830, causing damages estimated at three hundred thousand dollars. " The flames were discovered to burst out almost simultaneously on all sides of the square, which leaves no doubt of its being the work of malicious design." [52] That one resident at the time felt it was the " malicious design " of the slaves is clear, for he wrote [53]

The evils of this infernal system are beginning to re-act upon the Christians, who are latterly in a constant state of alarm, fearing the number and disposition of the blacks, which threaten at no distant period to overwhelm the south with some dreadful calamity. Three incendiary fires took place in New Orleans, during the month [January, 1830] I remained in that city, by which several thousand bales of cotton were consumed. The condition of the slaves on the sugar and rice plantations, is truly wretched.

The Maryland *Centreville Times* of July 10, 1830 asserted that two houses had recently been burned in Cambridge in that state, and " about 50 blacks had been committed to prison." The Easton *Gazette,* however, minimized the seriousness of the trouble and merely stated that since " the Citizens . . . are taking proper measures to investigate those infamous designs, we forbear, at present, to give any further particulars." [54]

The slaves did not restrict themselves to fire. Early in 1829 disaffection was reported from Louisiana. According to the

51 *Ibid.*, October 16, December 9, 1829; N. Y. *Eve. Post*, October 10, 17, December 5, 1829.

52 *Southern Advocate*, January 29, 1830; Richmond *Enquirer*, February 6, 1830.

53 S. A. Ferrall, *A Ramble . . . Through the United States*, p. 196.

54 Quoted in *The Genius of Universal Emancipation*, Washington, July, 1830, 3rd series, I, p. 52.

press,[55] " There has been a rising of the slaves on certain plantations about 40 miles from New Orleans, 'up the coast'. It created a general alarm, but was speedily suppressed, and two of the ringleaders hung." At about the same time, on March 17, 1829, Adjutant-General Roger Jones wrote to the commanding officer of the United States Army at Baton Rouge, from Washington, as follows: [56]

From the disquietude exhibited by the authorities and inhabitants of Louisiana, on account of the insurrectionary spirit manifested by the black population in that state, it is deemed proper by the executive [letter torn] and hold yourself in readiness to cooperate with the Governor of that State, in maintaining order, and suppressing any attempt of the Blacks, to put into execution [one word illegible] evil designs. The General in Chief directs that you will address a letter to the Governor of the State of Louisiana in New Orleans, informing him of the receipt of these instructions and furnish him a return of the force under your command. You will [letter torn] Governor of Louisiana may think proper to give in relation to this subject.

The agitation of western Virginia for a greater share in the governing of the State, which was accompanied by much talk about liberty and equality and which culminated in the constitutional convention of 1829-1830,[57] seems to have been taken

55 Niles' *Weekly Register*, March 21, 1829, XXXVI, p. 53; Philadelphia *Aurora and Pennsylvania Gazette*, March 6, 1829.

56 Ms. Personal Papers, Miscellaneous, J. Library of Congress.

57 There seems to have been but one memorial concerning the end of slavery prepared (whether received or considered is not known) for this convention. It was drawn up in July, 1829 by residents of the Valley county of Augusta " praying for the adoption of some provisions in the new constitution by which the slave population in the state may be checked, or reduced, and, if possible, ultimately done away with." Slavery was declared degrading and unprofitable, and further, it was feared that the whites " seem destined to become martyrs to their love of Virginia, exposed to foreign enemies, to civil feuds, and to domestic insurrections, without the physical ability indispensable to their own preservation." (Niles' *Weekly Register*, July 25, 1829, XXXVI, pp. 345, 356). In the convention itself emancipation was never broached, though the equalitarian speeches carried anti-slavery

seriously or perhaps one should say, seems to have been misinterpreted, by the slaves, and to have inspired them to plan their own liberation.[58] News of this leaked out and fear became widespread.[59] Coincident with, and multiplying the alarm, came the report of the killing of one white and the wounding of another in Hanover County on July 4th by about eight slaves.[60]

On August 4, 1829, Governor Giles " submitted the following preamble and advice " to the Council of Virginia which that Board adopted:[61]

The Executive have received sundry communications from different & distant quarters of the State which speak of rumors and alarms of an intended insurrection of Slaves on or about the first inst, which have spread widely and disquited [sic] the minds of many of the good Citizens of the Commonwealth—These rumours

implications. (See especially the speech of Mr. Cooke of Frederick County on Oct. 27, 1829, in *Proceedings and Debates of the Virginia State Convention of 1829-30*, Richmond, 1830, p. 55). Fears of the development of this sentiment appeared in the press (see Richmond *Enquirer*, Oct. 27, 1829) and in speeches of eastern delegates at the convention. Thus Mr. Barbour of Orange said (Oct. 29, 1829, *op. cit.*, p. 91) concerning the Bill of Rights, "if you give the language, all the force which the words literally import (and they are, I believe, but an echo of those in the Declaration of Independence) what will they amount to, but a declaration of universal emancipation, to a class of our population, not short of a moiety of our entire number, now in a state of slavery," And John Randolph (representing Charlotte County) declared: "There is nothing which so alarms me, as to see the existence of the fanatical spirit on this subject of negro slavery, as it is called, growing up in the land." (Speech of January 12, 1830, *ibid.*, p. 858.)

58 *Ante*, p. 82.

59 In July and August, 1829, letters telling of fears and requesting arms were sent to Gov. Giles from Gloucester, Mathews, Elizabeth City, Sussex, King and Queen, Chesterfield, Isle of Wight, and Hanover Counties.—See MS. Council Journal, 1828-29, pp. 133-139; in part in *C. V. S. P.*, X, pp. 567-69.

60 N. Y. *Even. Post*, July 18, 1829; Richmond *Whig*, August 3, 1829.

61 MS. Council Journal, 1828-29, pp. 138-39. In his legislative message the Governor declared: "A spirit of dissatisfaction and insubordination was manifested by the slaves in different parts of the country from this place [Richmond] to the seaboard."—Quoted by T. M. Whitfield, *Slavery Agitation in Virginia, 1829-1832*, p. 54.

have been much talked of by the Slaves themselves, & have probably increased the spirit of insubordination—Such a spirit has
certainly existed (it is believed however in a small degree) in some
of the Counties. . . . Therefore, it is advised that arms be distributed
to one volunteer Company belonging, or attached, to each Regiment
of Militia in the State; within the bounds of which the number of
Slaves is so great as to give just cause to apprehend danger of
insurrection; or make it proper to adopt measures of precaution.

A committee was set up to determine which counties fell into
this category, and three days later the newly-appointed body
advised the arming by the State of volunteer companies in practically every county of Eastern Virginia, from Amelia to Westmoreland—fifty-nine in all—and in the cities of Petersburg,
Norfolk, Lynchburg, and Richmond, an area whose population
was estimated at 459,324 whites and 421,019 Negroes.[62] These
energetic measures and the great show of strength that accompanied and followed them [63] appear to have effectively blocked,
for the time being, any maturing of the plans of the slaves.[64]

South Carolina planters also had their difficulties this year.
In the summer " a large gang of runaway negroes," who had
" infested the Parishes of Christ Church and St. James, for
several months, and committed serious depredations on the
properties of the planters " was accidentally discovered by a
party of deer hunters. One of the Negroes was wounded and
four others were captured. Several escaped, but the Charleston
Mercury hoped the citizens would " not cease their exertions
until the evil shall be effectually removed." [65]

62 MS. Council Journal, 1828-1829, pp. 141-143. In some of the counties
arms were supplied to two volunteer companies, as in Accomack, Bedford,
Culpeper, Fauquier, Norfolk, and Halifax.

63 See, for example, the anonymous article, " Richmond Light Infantry
Blues of Richmond, Virginia," in Tyler's *Quarterly Historical and Genealogical Magazine*, I, p. 14.

64 A free Negro, Jaspar Ellis, was tried for stirring up revolt among the
slaves in Richmond, but he was acquitted.—N. Y. *Eve. Post*, September 5,
1829; Niles' *Weekly Register*, September 12, 1829, XXXVII, p. 39.

65 Quoted in N. Y. *Eve. Post*, August 10, 1829.

The New York *Evening Post* of August 28, 1829 contains this very interesting item:

The alarming conspiracy detailed in the following article, taken from the New Haven (Con.) *Advertiser,* is news to us. The Southern papers do not notice the circumstances. " We learn by a letter, received in a neighboring town, that a dangerous conspiracy was formed among the blacks at Georgetown, S. C. to massacre the whites. The plan was matured in all its details, and the time fixed for its execution with such secrecy, that no doubts can be entertained of its certain and terrible success, had not one of the conspirators proved faint of heart, and betrayed the enterprise. . . . About 20 of the ring leaders have been arrested, the residue of the slaves disarmed, and a very active and vigilant police system adopted to disconcert any further measures the slaves may attempt."

Other evidence establishes the fact that this plot was several months old by the time it reached the northern press. Thus, it is clear that some time in April General Joseph W. Allston, a magistrate in Georgetown and a commander of the militia, had written the Attorney-General of the State, James L. Petigru, asking for legal advice in connection with the rebels' trials. It appears, too, that troops and arms had been rushed to Georgetown from Charleston and that the entire State was alarmed.[66]

On April 17, 1829, Mr. Petigru wrote General Allston that he regretted the latter's labors had been " so arduous . . . I am afraid you will hang half the country . . . You must take care and save negroes enough for the rice crop. It is to be confessed that your proceedings have not been bloody as yet, but the length of the investigation alarms us with apprehension that you will be obliged to punish a great many."

Amongst the leaders in this movement, all slaves, were Charles Prioleau, Nat, Robert, and Quico. It is known only that the last named was banished. His master tried to retain his property on the ground that the court which had sentenced him had not met until twelve days after his arrest, though the

66 James P. Carson, *Life, Letters and Speeches of James Louis Petigru,* p. 66.

law (of 1754) required it, in such cases, to meet within six days.[67] The higher court's reasons for rejecting this plea was revealing. " When the dreadful ... consequences of the insurrection of slaves in South Carolina are taken into consideration," said the Judge, " it appears to me that the judges of the superior court ought to be extremely cautious in interfering with the magistrates and freeholders." Moreover, the judges of the lower court had been ill, and so postponement was necessary, and " besides ... it was discovered that so many were concerned in the plot ... that the public safety required this delay, in order to find out the ramifications ...".

One August morning in 1829 two male slaves in a coffle of ninety men, women, and children recently bought in Maryland and being led to the South for sale, suddenly dropped their shackles, at a point between Greenup and Vanceburg, Kentucky, and began to deal blows to each other. William B. Petit, one of the three white men leading and guarding this valuable group of humans, rushed up at them with his whip ordering them to fall back into line. Instantly it became clear that, in some way, the shackles on each of the men slaves had been filed through, and they set upon and killed Mr. Petit. Another of the guards, Gabriel T. Allen, coming to the latter's aid, was also killed, and the owner, a well-known slave trader named Henry Gordon, was then attacked. He, however, with the assistance of a slave woman, managed to mount a horse and, though pursued, made good his getaway and rounded up aid.[68]

The posse thus formed is reported to have succeeded in capturing all the slaves, and six of the rebel leaders, five men and one woman, were sentenced to hang. The woman was found to be pregnant and permitted to remain in jail for several months until after the birth of the child, whereupon, on May 25, 1830, she was publicly hanged. The men were executed November

---

67 H. T. Catterall, ed., *op. cit.*, II, pp. 340-341.

68 *Southern Advocate* (Huntsville, Alabama), August 22, 1829; Niles' *Weekly Register*, September 5, 1829, XXXVII, pp. 18-19. This is mentioned in David Walker's *Appeal*.

20, 1829. The Portsmouth, Virginia, *Times* declared that [69] " they all maintained to the last, the utmost firmness and resignation to their fate. They severally addressed the assembled multitude, in which they attempted to justify the deed they had committed." According to Niles, one of the condemned Negroes,[70] " the instant before he was launched from the cart, exclaimed 'Death—death at any time in preference to slavery'."

Early in April, 1830, a conspiracy was reported from New Orleans and the leaders, two slaves, were executed. In July " dread of insurrection " prevailed in and around Dorchester, Maryland.[71] As has already been observed, too, reports of the discovery of Walker's *Appeal* began to recur in Georgia, Louisiana and North Carolina at about this time and added to the concern of the master class.[72] In September plots were reported from Wilmington, North Carolina, and from Nashville, Tennessee.[73] The next month a conspiracy embracing about one hundred Negroes, including a few who were free, was discovered in Plaquemines, a parish in Louisiana south of New Orleans.[74] Two companies of militia were pressed into service, with the result that the ringleaders were arrested, and it was reported, " were to be punished."

Maroons were important factors in causing slave insubordination in Onslow, Jones, Sampson, Bladen, New Hanover, and Dublin Counties, North Carolina, from September through December, 1830. Citizens of the last four counties petitioned the legislature on December 14, for aid because their " slaves are become almost uncontroulable. They go and come when and

69 Quoted in Richmond *Enquirer*, January 28, 1830.

70 *Weekly Register*, December 26, 1829, XXXVII, p. 277; see also J. W. Coleman, Jr., *op. cit.*, pp. 176-178. For a revolt aboard a domestic slave-trader in December, 1829, see *ante*, p. 98.

71 Niles' *Weekly Register*, April 24, 1830, XXXVIII, p. 157; *Genius of Universal Emancipation*, July, 1830.

72 *Ante*, p. 61, 82.

73 *The Genius of Universal Emancipation*, October, 1830.

74 *The Liberator*, January 1, 1831.

where they please, and if an attempt is made to stop them they immediately fly to the woods and there continue for months and years Committing depredations on our Cattle hogs and Sheep." And, said the petitioners, "patrols are of no use on account of the danger they subject themselves to," citing the fact that two patrolmen "not long since had their dwelling houses and other houses burnt down." In these areas militia bodies were strengthened and patrols pressed very frequently into service.[75]

One of these outlaws, Moses, who had been a fugitive for two years, was captured in November. From him was elicited the information [76] that an uprising was imminent, that the conspirators "had arms & ammunition secreted, that they had runners or messengers to go between Wilmington, Newbern & Elizabeth City to 'carry word' & report to them, that there was a camp in Dover Swamp of 30 or 40—another about Gastons Island, on Prince's Creek, several on Newport River, several near Wilmington." Arms were found in the place named by Moses

in possession of a white woman living in a very retired situation—also some meat, hid away & could not be accounted for—a child whom the party [of citizens] found a little way from the house, said that his mamy dressed victuals every day for 4 or 5 runaways, & shewed the spot ... where the meat was then hid & where it was found,—the place or camp in Dover was found, a party of neighbors discovered the camp, burnt 11 houses, and made such discoveries as convinced them it was a place of rendezvous for numbers (it is supposed they killed several of the negroes).

Newspaper accounts, indeed, referred to the wholesale shooting of fugitives. Thus, an item dated Milton, North Carolina, December 25, 1830, ran as follows: [77]

75 H. T. Catterall, ed., *op. cit.*, II, p. 60; G. G. Johnson, *op. cit.*, pp. 515-17; [Theodore Weld] *American Slavery As It Is*, p. 51.

76 See letter dated Newbern, November 15, 1830, by J. Turgwyn to Governor John Owen, in MS. Governor's Letter Book, XXVIII, pp. 247-49, and letter from J. I. Pasteur to Governor Owen, also dated Newbern, November 15, 1830, in MS. Governor's Papers, no. 60, Historical Commission, Raleigh.

77 Roanoke *Advertiser*, n. d., in *The Liberator*, January 15, 1831.

We have learned from authority of the most undoubted kind, that the inhabitants of Newbern, Tarborough, Hillsborough, and their vicinities, are considerably excited, with the anticipation of insurrectional movements among their slaves. Our informant, just from the latter place, states that considerable consternation exists among its citizens; that they have provided arms and ammunition, and are vigilantly patrolling every exposed position. The inhabitants of Newbern being advised of the assemblage of sixty armed slaves in a swamp in their vicinity, the military were called out, and surrounding the swamp killed the whole number. It appears from various rumors that Christmas morning had been selected as the period of rebellious motions.

From Wilmington, on January 7, 1831, came the report: [78] " There has been much shooting of negroes in this neighborhood recently, in consequence of symptoms of liberty having been discovered among them. These inhuman acts are kept profoundly secret—wherefore I know not. Two companies of troops have very lately been stationed here."

In Mississippi, too, the Woodville *Republican*,[79] on the day of the birth of the humble Prince of Peace, reported slave conspiracies, especially in Jefferson County, but, apparently, the only overt occurrence was an increase in the number of fugitive slaves.

A government document briefly states the essential facts in the period from early 1831 to the Turner outbreak of August [80]

78 N. Y. *Sentinel*, n. d., in *ibid.*, March 19, 1831. It may be noted that a Richmond paper on first hearing of the Turner Rebellion asked, concerning the rebels: "Were they connected with the desperadoes who harrassed N. Carolina last year?"

79 In Charles S. Sydnor, *op. cit.*, p. 116.

80 H. C. Corbin and F. T. Wilson, "Federal aid in domestic disturbances, 1787-1903," *Senate Document No. 209*, 57th Cong., 2nd Sess., p. 56. The report of the Major-General for 1831, dated November, in Document No. 2 of *Executive Documents*, 22nd Cong., 1st Sess., p. 55, makes it clear that troops were sent to Louisiana before the Turner revolt, but it is not clear about those sent to Fort Monroe. D. S. Freeman in *R. E. Lee*, I, pp. 111-112, citing only the latter source, states that five new companies arrived at the fort after the outbreak, but he apparently did not consult the first source noted above. It is possible that new troops arrived both before and after the uprising.

The year 1831 was one of unusual uneasiness throughout the slave-holding section of the country, consequent upon an apprehended rising of the negroes. Early in the spring of that year strong and urgent representations were made to the War Department by the authorities of Louisiana that a revolt was threatened by the slaves, and that the presence of a military force in New Orleans was necessary to the preservation of order and to allay the apprehensions of the people. To quiet these fears two companies of infantry were sent to that city and orders were given to neighboring posts to hold the troops in readiness for any emergency. Later in the same season similar reports of disorderly conduct upon the part of the slaves came from Delaware, Maryland, Virginia, and the Carolinas, and in order that a disposable force might be available to afford protection to such parts of the country as might require it, the garrison at Fort Monroe (Virginia) was augmented by five companies drawn from the northern seaboard.

The federal military activity was far from the only precautionary measures adopted by the slaveocracy as a result of the extraordinary manifestations of unrest characteristic of the past decade. The States themselves, as usual under such circumstances, passed many laws adding safeguards for the masters and restrictions upon the slaves and free Negroes.[81] These, like the preceding revolts and plots, were part of the background of southern life prior to the outbreak led by Nat Turner, and the panic and terror and insubordination that followed throughout the south until the end of the fateful year of 1831.

In 1830 North Carolina and Louisiana passed laws forbidding the teaching of the arts of writing and reading to slaves, while Georgia had extended a similar provision to all Negroes a year before. Virginia in April, 1831, prohibited the assembling of free Negroes for purposes of instruction in reading and writing. From 1829 to the spring of 1831 the states of Georgia, North Carolina, and Mississippi passed laws providing very heavy penalties for any individuals (death for Negroes) engaged in the dissemination of anti-slavery propaganda. During the same period North Carolina and Georgia enacted quarantine

81 These acts are often referred to as though they came after, and as a result of the Turner revolt. See, for example, G. H. Barnes, *The Anti-Slavery Impulse*, p. 51.

laws for all ships carrying free Negroes, the period of quarantine to last for 30 to 40 days respectively.[82]

Many precautionary acts of a miscellaneous character were passed during the same period. Thus, North Carolina passed laws punishing any who aided runaway slaves, providing for measures to combat maroons, forbidding the cohabitation of free Negroes and slaves, and the marriage of free Negroes and whites. Louisiana required all Negroes freed since 1825 to leave, and North Carolina ordered all Negroes emancipated after 1830 to leave within ninety days.[83]

There was another type of political activity relating to slavery during the period immediately preceding Turner's attempt at revolution. In Kentucky efforts were made during the closing months of 1829 to hold a constitutional convention. One of the objects of the unsuccessful backers of this movement was the abolition of slavery. In 1830 a bill for this purpose was introduced in the House of this State, but its consideration was postponed, indefinitely, by a vote of 18 to 11.[84]

The agitation over the question of a constitutional convention in Kentucky moved Hezekiah Niles, the influential Maryland publicist, to declare: [85] " We have no desire to meddle with the general question of slavery—it *must* be met sometime, though probably not in our day." Very shortly, and, to a considerable extent, because of the terror evoked by a diminutive, slavery-hating black man living near Jerusalem (now Courtland), Virginia, this idea of postponement, indifference, neutrality, was to lose ground, and the generation of crisis was to appear.

82 *Acts Passed by the General Assembly of N. C., 1830-31*, pp. 9-12, 16, 29, 119, 128-30; *Acts Passed at the First Session of the 9th Legislature of Louisiana, 1829*, pp. 38 ff.; *Acts Passed at a Gen. Ass. of Va., 1831*, p. 107 f.; Niles' *Weekly Register*, Jan. 16, 1830, XXXVII, p. 341; *The Liberator*, Jan. 8, 1831; *Laws of the State of Mississippi Passed at the 14th Session, 1830*, pp. 86 ff.; T. Alden and J. Van Hoesen, ed., *A Digest of Laws of Mississippi*, p. 767; G. Stroud, *Sketch of Laws Relating to Slavery*, p. 142.

83 In addition to references in above note, see Niles' *Weekly Register*, April 24, 1830, XXXVIII, p. 157; H. Wagstaff, *State Rights . . . in N. C.*, p. 57; J. Bassett, *Slavery in State of N. C.*, p. 100 f.

84 [Thomas Earle], *op. cit.*, p. 237.

85 Niles' *Weekly Register*, Jan. 16, 1830, XXXVII, p. 357.

CHAPTER XII

THE TURNER CATACLYSM

It has already been demonstrated that the decade preceding the Southampton Insurrection was one of economic depression throughout the South and, in the old South, especially eastern Virginia and eastern North Carolina, it was marked by a dangerously disproportionate rate of population growth, that of the Negroes distinctly outstripping that of the whites. To complete the picture of environmental conditions one should examine the specific locale of Turner's uprising.

Southampton is a tidewater county, located in the southeastern part of Virginia, bordering the state of North Carolina. Covering six hundred square miles, it was an important economic unit in the tidewater area. In 1830 it was second in the State in its production of potatoes and rice, and, in 1840, was the leading county in cotton production, in the value of its orchard produce, and in the number of its swine.[1] Its population trend was that of the section, i. e., a more rapid growth of the Negro than of the white element. Thus, one finds that while, in 1820, there were 6127 whites and 8043 Negroes in Southampton County, in 1830 the figures read 6574 whites and 9501 Negroes.[2] In 1830 out of a total of thirty-nine tidewater counties only three surpassed Southampton in the number of free Negroes, and only four in the number of slaves, and in the number of whites.[3]

[1] R. R. Howison, *A History of Virginia*, II, pp. 498-500.

[2] There is unusual agreement on these figures. They are so given in the first group of tables in *Documents ... of the Convention of 1850-51*; Niles' *Weekly Register*, Sept. 8, 1832, XLIII, p. 30; W. S. Drewry, *The Southampton Insurrection*, p. 108 n.; *The American Annual Register, 1830-31*, p. 381. Slight differences appear in J. H. Hinton, S. L. Knapp, J. O. Choulee, *The History and Topography of the United States*, II, p. 443; and S. B. Weeks, "The slave insurrection in Virginia," in *Magazine of American History*, XXV, p. 454 n.

[3] According to Drewry (*op. cit.*, p. 108) there were "numerous" Quakers in Southampton. A reviewer of Drewry's book repeats this—*Virginia Mag.*

In its economic decline Southampton is also typical of the condition in eastern Virginia during the period. Thus, for example, it ranked fifth in the State in 1810 in the amount of taxes it paid on the assessed valuation of its land and lots, but dropped to forty-fourth in 1820 and to forty-sixth in 1830.[4]

The situation, then, in the decade prior to the Southampton revolt is one of extraordinary *malaise* in the slaveholding area. It is marked by a considerable expansion and development of anti-slavery feeling, nationally and internationally (as part of an all-embracing upsurge of progressive and radical thought and action throughout the western world), by great and serious unrest among the slave populations, in the West Indies as well as on the Continent, by severe economic depression, and by the more rapid growth of the Negro population than the white throughout the old South. Testifying to the uneasiness of the master class there appear numerous precautionary measures for the purpose of overawing, or further restricting the activities of the slave population (which, in turn, very likely stimulated discontent), and, as a last resort, in order to assure the speedy suppression of all evidences of slave insubordination.

It was into such a situation (one is tempted to assert, though proof is, of course, not at hand, that it was *because* of such a situation) that the upraised dark arms of vengeance of Turner and his followers crashed in the summer of 1831.

Nat Turner was born October 2, 1800, and apparently lived all his life in Southampton County. At the time of the rebellion he was:[5]

Hist. & Biog., VIII, p. 222. It may also be noted that Southampton was the county where David Barrow, a leader of the Emancipating, or Anti-Slavery Baptists, lived until 1798. He founded churches of that faith there and spread his ideas widely. This, of course, was a generation before Turner's outbreak, and a few years before his birth, but it is possible that the activities of these people added a radical flavor to the atmosphere of Turner's neighborhood.— See J. C. Carroll, *op. cit.*, pp. 118-20; *The Negro in Virginia*, p. 99.

4 Table no. 4 in *Documents of the Convention of 1850-51*. In 1810 there were 1044 counties, in 1820 there were 110, and in 1830 there were 111 in Virginia.

5 Description accompanying reward notice ($500) for his capture, in Washington *National Intelligencer*, September 24, 1831.

5 feet 6 or 8 inches high, weighs between 150 and 160 pounds, rather bright complexion, but not a mulatto, broad shoulders, large flat nose, large eyes, broad flat feet, rather knockkneed, walks brisk and active, hair on the top of the head very thin, no beard, except on the upper lip and the top of the chin, a scar on one of his temples, also one on the back of his neck, a large knot on one of the bones of his right arm, near the wrist, produced by a blow.

Very naturally, William Lloyd Garrison, in commenting upon this description, pointed to these scars as important explanations for Turner's actions. But the Richmond *Enquirer* assured its readers that Turner got two of his bruises in fights with fellow slaves and one of them, that on his temple, through a mule's kick.[6] Drewry, notwithstanding the fact that his description of Turner hardly indicates a pugnacious individual, accepts [7] the explanation of the southern newspaper, and points out, correctly, that Turner himself stated that his last master, Joseph Travis, had not been severe. But he had had other masters—Benjamin Turner and Putnam Moore—and he had, in 1826 or 1827, run away from one of these after a change in overseers.[8]

However that may be, mere personal vengeance was not Nat Turner's motive. He had learned how to read—precisely when he did not know—and, when his labors permitted, he had immersed himself in the stories of the Bible. He was a keen, mechanically gifted man whose religion offered him a rationalization for his opposition to the status quo. Later writers have

6 *The Liberator*, Oct. 1, 1831; Richmond *Enquirer*, Oct. 25, 1831. W. B. Hesseltine in *A History of the South*, p. 251, erroneously calls Turner a free Negro. This is also done in a novel by P. Bouve, *Their Shadows Before*.

7 W. Drewry, *op. cit.*, p. 28. This work is seriously inadequate and unsatisfactory, particularly because of woefully inadequate documentation, and the deep anti-Negro prejudice of the author.

8 T. R. Gray, *The Confessions of Nat Turner*, pp. 7, 11, 18. Hereafter cited as *The Confessions*. This is the basic work for a study of the revolt. See bibliography for remarks concerning it. The body of the pamphlet is printed, with minor changes, as an appendix to E. S. Abdy's *Journal of a Residence*, and in Harriet Beecher Stowe's *Dred*.

described [9] him as an overseer or foreman, and while no convincing support for this has been found, it is certain that his considerable mental abilities were recognized and appreciated by his contemporaries. He was a religious leader, often conducting services of a Baptist nature and exhorting his fellow workers. It appears that even white people were influenced, if not controlled, by him, so that, as he said,[10] he immersed one Ethelred T. Brantley [11] and prevailed upon him to " cease from his wickedness."

Turner became convinced that he " was ordained for some great purpose in the hands of the Almighty." In the spring of 1828, while working in the fields, he " heard a loud noise in the heavens, and the Spirit instantly appeared to me and said the Serpent was loosened, and Christ had laid down the yoke he had borne for the sins of men, and that I should take it on and fight against the Serpent, for the time was fast approaching when the first should be last and the last should be first." [12]

The slave waited for a sign from his God. This came to him in the form of the solar eclipse of February 12, 1831.[13] Then

9 Drewry, *op. cit.*, p. 27; Phillips, *American Negro Slavery*, p. 480.

10 *The Confessions*, pp. 7-9, 11.

11 There are two Brantleys listed in Turner's parish (Nottoway) in Southampton County, in the property book for that area for 1831. These were named Elisha and James. Both are listed as owning no land and no property. No Ethelred Brantley was found. MS. Property Book, Nottoway Parish, Southampton County, 1831, Virginia State Library.

12 *The Confessions*, pp. 9, 11.

13 The fact that Turner saw these apparitions and was affected by the solar eclipse moves not a few historians to ridicule his so-called "negro intelligence" (J. C. Ballagh, *op. cit.*, p. 94 n.) or to dismiss Turner as a "Crazy Negro" (W. H. T. Squires, *Through Centuries Three*, p. 416). One must remember, however, that Turner lived in early nineteenth century rural America where superstition and mysticism were common for white and Negro. Thus, at that time many North Carolina farmers carried on their work according to the signs of the Zodiac (G. G. Johnson, *op. cit.*, p. 48). Olmsted quoted a Charleston paper of 1855 to the effect that the poor whites were "totally given up to a species of hallucination" and "nearly all believed implicitly in witchcraft." (F. L. Olmsted, *A Journey in the Seaboard Slave States*, I, p. 389). Indeed, the eclipse that influenced Turner moved a New

apparently for the first time, he told four other slaves of his plans for rebellion. All joined him, and these American Negroes selected the Fourth of July as the day on which to strike for liberty, a choice which led a later commentator to curse them because they had " perverted that sacred day." [14]

Turner was ill on the " sacred day," and the conspirators waited for another sign. This appeared to them on Saturday, August 13, in the " greenish blue color " of the sun.[15] According to Drewry,[16] Turner the next day exhorted at a religious meeting of Negroes in the southern part of Southampton County (not in North Carolina, as has been said) [17] where some of the slaves " signified their willingness to co-operate with him by wearing around their necks red bandanna handkerchiefs." There was, certainly, a meeting of plotters in the afternoon of Sunday, August 21, and it was then decided to start the revolt that evening.

Appreciating the value of a dramatic entrance, Turner was the last to join this gathering. He noticed a newcomer in the group, and declared: [18]

I saluted them on coming up, and asked Will how came he there, he answered, his life was worth no more than others, and his liberty as dear to him. I asked him if he meant to obtain it? He said he would, or loose his life. This was enough to put him in full confidence.

York City white preacher to say that " the whole city South of Canal Street would sink. Some persons actually went to the upper part of the city."— N. Y. *Patriot*, n. d., quoted in *Liberator*, February 19, 1831.

14 W. H. Parker, " The Nat Turner Insurrection," in *Old Virginia Yarns*, 1893, I, p. 18—copy in Virginia State Library.

15 N. Y. *Eve. Post*, August 26, 1831; S. B. Weeks, *op. cit.*, p. 451; W. S. Forrest, *Historical and Descriptive Sketches of Norfolk*, p. 192.

16 W. Drewry, *op. cit.*, p. 157. Drewry cites no source.

17 N. Stevens, " The 100th anniversary of the Nat Turner Revolt," in *The Communist*, 1931, X, p. 739.

18 *The Confessions*, p. 12. A much longer and more formal speech, of similar sentiments, was ascribed to Turner by. G. W. Williams, *History of the Negro Race*, II, pp. 87-88, and occasionally repeated as an historical fact—H. P. Wilson, *John Brown*, pp. 360-61. Mr. Williams was more novelist than historian in this instance.

These six slaves, then, started out, in the evening of August 21, 1831, on their crusade against bondage. Their first blow—delivered by Turner himself—struck against person and family of Turner's master, Joseph Travis, who were killed.[19] Some arms and horses were taken, the rebels pushed on, and everywhere slaves flocked to their standard;[20] a result which Turner, starting out with but a handful of followers, must have had excellent reasons to anticipate. Within twenty-four hours approximately seventy slaves were actively aiding in the rebellion. By the morning of August 23rd, at least fifty-seven whites —men, women, and children—had been killed, and the rebels had covered about twenty miles.[21]

19 *The Confessions*, and the press, especially the Richmond *Enquirer* and the Richmond *Whig* are the basic sources for the proceedings of the rebellion itself, bearing in mind, of course, that all are hostile to the cause Turner espoused. No attempt will be made to detail these since accuracy is impossible. Moreover, Drewry made the attempt in forty pages (*op. cit.*, pp. 35-74) and his account entered the realm of fantasy, as when he declared (p. 36) that one infant was temporarily spared because it "sweetly smiled" at its assailant. A search for Joseph Travis' name in land or property books was unsuccessful. However, a Joseph Travis was married in Southampton County on October 5, 1829 to Sarah W. Moore, perhaps the widow of Putnam Moore a former owner of Nat Turner. MS. Marriage Register, Southampton, 1750 to 1853, part 2, p. 402. The Southampton Land Book for 1831 does list a Benjamin Travis as the owner of 250 acres, worth with the buildings, about $695, some fifteen miles north of Jerusalem. A Pegg Travis, owner of 2 acres of land worth $24, is also listed.

20 It was later claimed that some of these slaves were forced to join. This is possible though Turner nowhere mentions anything like that. As Thomas Wentworth Higginson pointed out ("Nat Turner's insurrection," *The Atlantic Monthly*, VIII, pp. 180-181) it was to be expected that once the movement had been crushed that would be offered as an extenuating circumstance.

21 Neither contemporaries nor later commentators agree as to the number of casualties, or, and here the discrepancies are especially great, the number of rebels. Detailed evidence for the estimates made above covers several pages of the present writer's master's thesis, "Nat Turner's Revolt," Columbia University, 1937. Death alone met the victims of the slaves' vengeance and wrath. Historians find great difficulty in accounting for the fact that, so far as the evidence shows, there was no instance of rape or attempted rape by Turner's followers. R. R. Howison (*op. cit.*, II, p. 444) is reduced to saying: " Remembering the brutal passions of the negro [sic] we can only account for

Turner declared [22] that "indiscriminate slaughter was not their intention after they obtained a foothold, and was resorted to in the first instance to strike terror and alarm. Women and children would afterwards have been spared, and men too who ceased to resist." According to Governor John Floyd the slaves "spared but one family and that was one so wretched as to be in all respects upon a par with them." [23]

In the morning of the twenty-third Turner and his followers set out for the county seat, Jerusalem,[24] where there was a considerable store of arms. When about three miles from this town several of the slaves, notwithstanding Turner's objections, insisted upon trying to recruit the slaves of a wealthy planter named Parker. Turner, with a handful of followers, remained at the Parker gate while the rest went to the home itself, about half a mile away. Once at the Parker home many of the slaves appear to have slacked their thirst from its well-stocked cellar

this fact by supposing the actors to have been appalled by the very success of their hideous enterprise." Drewry (*op. cit.*, p. 117) on the other hand, while having no evidence to controvert this, states that women were insulted and offers further, without reference, some romantic nonsense about Turner promising to save a fair white damsel if she would but marry him. J. C. Ballagh (*op. cit.*, p. 93) goes still further and writes, "strange to say only a single well authenticated case of attempted violation of a female occurred," a statement repeated by Arthur Y. Lloyd (*The Slavery Controversy*, p. 105) who cites Ballagh. But "strange to say" the latter historian did not feel called upon to cite any authority for his statement, in opposition, incidentally, to Drewry, to whom Ballagh turned as an authority for everything else he had to say about this event.

22 Richmond *Enquirer*, November 8, 1831. Higginson, *op. cit.*, p. 176, gave this without quotation marks, and as having been stated by the editor. As a matter of fact, the editor makes it clear that he is paraphrasing Turner's words.

23 John Floyd to Governor James Hamilton, Jr. (he who had been intendant of Charleston during the Vesey plot), dated November 19, 1831, in Papers of John Floyd, Library of Congress. See also, Charles H. Ambler, "Life of John Floyd," in *John P. Branch Historical Papers*, V, p. 87.

24 In the interesting work, *The Negro in Virginia*, p. 179, it has been suggested that Turner may have read and been moved by this sentence in his Bible: "From that time began Jesus to show unto his disciples, that he must go unto Jerusalem, and suffer many things of the elders and chief priests, and scribes, and be killed."

and to have rested. Turner became impatient and set out to get his tardy companions. The eight or nine slaves remaining at the gate were then attacked by a volunteer corps of whites of about twice their number. The slaves retreated, but upon being reinforced by the returning Turner and his men, the rebels pressed on and forced the whites to give ground. The latter, however, were in turn reinforced by a company of militia and the Negroes, whose guns, according to the Richmond *Compiler* of August 29, were not " fit for use," fled.[25]

Though Turner later tried to round up sufficient followers to continue the struggle, his efforts were futile and this battle at Parker's field was the crucial one. Late in the day of this encounter the commander at Fort Monroe, Colonel Eustis, was requested by the Mayor of Norfolk to send aid. By the morning of the 24th, three companies of artillery with a field piece and one hundred stands of spare arms, together with detachments of men from the warships *Warren* and *Natchez* were on their way to the scene of the trouble. They made the sixty miles in one day, and met hundreds of other soldiers from volunteer and militia companies of the counties, in Virginia and in North Carolina, surrounding Southampton.[26]

Massacre followed. Phillips simply notes, " a certain number of innocent blacks shot down," and Ballagh asserts, "A most impartial trial was given to all, except a few decapitated " in Southampton, while Drewry thought " there was far less of this indiscriminate murder than might have been expected." [27] Just how much " indiscriminate murder " one ought to " expect " is not clear, but this statement by General Eppes, the officer in command of the affected county, leads one to believe that these historians were rather uncritical in dealing with this phase of the event: [28]

25 *The Confessions*, pp. 15-16; W. Drewry, *op. cit.*, pp. 61-66.

26 H. Corbin and F. Wilson, *op. cit.*, pp. 56, 261; D. Freeman, *op. cit.*, I, p. 111.

27 U. B. Phillips, *op. cit.*, p. 481; J. C. Ballagh, *op. cit.*, p. 93; Drewry, *op. cit.*, p. 36.

28 Richmond *Enquirer*, September 6, 1831.

He [the General] will not specify all the instances that he is bound to believe have occurred, but pass in silence what has happened, with the expression of his deepest sorrow, that any necessity should be supposed to have existed, to justify a single act of atrocity. But he feels himself bound to declare, and hereby announces to the troops and citizens, that no excuse will be allowed for any similar acts of violence, after the promulgation of this order, and further to declare, in the most explicit terms, that any who may attempt the repetition of such acts, shall be punished, if necessary, by the rigors of the articles of war. The course that has been pursued, he fears, will in some instances be the means of rendering doubtful the guilt of those who may have participated in the carnage.... This course of proceeding dignified the rebel and the assassin with the sanctity of martyrdom, and confounds the difference that morality and religion makes between the ruffian and the brave and the honorable.

The editor of the Richmond *Whig* also referred " with pain " to this " feature of the Southampton Rebellion ... We allude to the slaughter of many blacks without trial and under circumstances of great barbarity." He thought that about forty had thus been killed. A Reverend G. W. Powell, writing August 27, when the reign of terror was by no means over, reported, " many negroes are killed overy day. The exact number will never be known." [29] The reverend gentleman was correct, but it appears certain that more, many more, than forty were massacred. The Huntsville, Alabama, *Southern Advocate* of October 15, 1831, declared that over one hundred Negroes had been killed in Southampton. It seems accurate to say that at least twice as many Negroes were indiscriminately slaughtered in that county, as the number of white people who had fallen victim to the vengeance and bondage-hating spirit of the slave.

That some considered themselves martyrs, as General Eppes suggested, is indicated by Governor Floyd's comment that [30]

29 Richmond *Whig*, September 3, 1831; N. Y. *Atlas*, September 17, 1831; N. Y. *Eve. Post*, September 5, 1831; *The Liberator*, October 22, 1831. See also Samuel Warner, *Authentic and Impartial Narrative*, p. 15.

30 Governor Floyd to Governor Hamilton, Jr. of South Carolina, November 19, 1831, in Papers of John Floyd, Library of Congress.

"All died bravely indicating no reluctance to lose their lives in such a cause;" and a letter to Judge Thomas Ruffin of North Carolina declared,[31] " some of them that were wounded and in the aggonies of Death declared that they was going happy fore that God had a hand in what they had been doing."

Nat Turner eluded his pursuers from the end of August until October 30, when he was caught, armed only with an old sword, by Benjamin Phipps. During those weeks there had been rumors that he was caught, that he was a runaway in Maryland, that he was drowned, but as a matter of fact he never left his native county. He forsook his hiding place only at night for water, having supplied himself with food.[32]

Turner was tried and, though pleading not guilty, since, as he said, he did not feel *guilty,* he was condemned to hang. The honorable Jeremiah Cobb pronounced sentence on November 5, in these words: " The judgement of the Court, is that you be taken hence to the jail from whence you came, thence to the place of execution, and on Friday next, between the hours of ten A. M. and 2 P. M. be hung by the neck until you are dead! dead! dead! and may the Lord have mercy upon your soul." About sixteen other slaves and three free Negroes had previously been executed, and on November the eleventh, 1831, their leader, the Prophet, he who had inspired them to value liberty above life, went calmly to his death.[33]

Some of the first contemporary accounts of the revolt stated that it was led by about three whites, but this was later denied, and no good evidence has been seen to demonstrate that any but Negroes were implicated in the uprising itself.[34] There is, how-

31 From E. P. Guion, dated Raleigh, August 28, 1831, in J. G. deRoulhac Hamilton, ed., *The Papers of Thomas Ruffin*, II, p. 45.

32 *The Confessions*, p. 16; Richmond *Enquirer*, October 18, 1831; Niles' *Weekly Register*, October 29, 1831, XLI, p. 162.

33 Drewry, *op. cit.*, p. 100 n.; N. Y. *Eve. Post*, November 19, 1831.

34 Richmond *Enquirer*, August 26, 1831; Niles' *Weekly Register*, August 27, 1831, XL, p. 456; September 3, 1831, XLI, p. 4. Though several contemporaries and later commentators have asserted that Abolitionists were responsible for the Turner uprising, no good evidence of any such connection

ever, evidence of joint activity in the troubles and plots immediately following the outbreak. Governor Floyd of Virginia in
his legislative message of December 6, 1831, darkly hinted [35]
that the unrest was " not confined to the slaves." The best evidence observed concerning this, in Virginia, is a semi-literate
letter from a white person, Williamson Mann, dated Chesterfield County, August 29, 1831, to a slave, Ben Lee, reading: [36]

My old fellow
Ben—

You will tell or acquaint every servant in Richmond and adjoining countys they all must be in strict readiness, that this occurrence
will go throug Virginia with the slaves and whites if there had
never been an association—a visiting with free and slaves this
would never of been. They are put up by the free about their liberation. I've wrote to Norfolk, Amelia, Nottoway and to sevel other
countys to different slaves bob and bill Miller Bowler john ferguson
—and sevel other free fellows been at Dr. Crumps—and a great
many gentlemens servants how they must act in getting their
liberation they must set afire to the city [Richmond] beginning at
Shokoe Hill then going through east west north south Set fire to
the bridges they are about to break out in Goochland and in
Mecklenburg and several other countys very shortly. now their is
a barber here in this place—tells that a methodist of the name
edmonds has put a great many servants up to how they should
do and act by setting fire to this town. I do wish they may succeed by so doing we poor whites can get work as well as slaves
or collord. this fellow edmonds the methodist says that judge T. F.
—is no friend to the free and your Richmond free associates that
your master Watkins Lee brockenberry Johnson Taylor of Norfolk
and several other noble delegates is bitterly against them all—
servants says that billy hickman has just put him up how to do to

exists. Turner himself explicitly denied being influenced by any other person.
For a full discussion of this point, see the present writer's unpublished
master's thesis, " Nat Turner's Revolt " (Columbia, 1937), pp. 46-49.

35 See Henry Wilson, *History of the Rise and Fall of the Slave Power*,
I, p. 191.

36 Executive Papers, Virginia State Library; quoted by J. H. Johnston,
op. cit., p. 163.

revenge the whites—edmonds says so you all ought to get revenge
—every white in this place is scared except myself and a few
others this methodist has put up a great many slaves in this place
what to do I can tell you so push on boys push on

Your friend Williamson Mann

Some evidence pointing to white participation or, at least,
sympathy with the plotting of slaves in North Carolina just
after the Turner rebellion, exists. Thus, a Mr. Nathan B. Whitfield of Union County wrote [37] to Governor Montfort Stokes
on September 12, 1831, concerning serious trouble in Sampson
and Duplin Counties and of uneasiness in his own area leading
to the mobilization of the militia. He added, as a postscript: " I
am inclined to believe that the insurrectionary feeling is generally disseminated among the blacks in the lower or eastern
counties of the state—I have just learnt though I cannot rely
on it that these marauders are assisted by some rascally
whites."

Later in September the commander of the militia of Hyde
County, North Carolina, informed the Governor that [38] " unusual night assemblies " of the slaves had recently occurred,
excitement was great, strong patrols were out every night, and
a fresh supply of arms would be welcome. He added, however,
that when it came to getting men for patrol duty difficulties
were encountered for " there are many in this County who are
quite refractory & scarcely can be brought to do their turn of
service and their pleas are that it is uncertain whether they
shall get pay for their service & that they have no slaves of
their own & therefore ought not to be interrupted about the
slaves of others." Finally, a Baltimore publication, reporting [39]
the plots in North Carolina, added the ominous note, that the
" extensive and organized plan to bring about desolation and

37 Governor's Papers, vol. 62, North Carolina Historical Commission,
Raleigh.

38 Colonel Benjamin Watson to Governor Stokes, dated Hyde County,
September 25, 1831, ibid.

39 Niles' Weekly Register, October 15, 1831, XLI, p. 80.

massacre ... it may be awfully believed was not altogether confined to the slaves."

With the news of this outbreak panic flashed through Virginia. The uprising was infectious and slaves everywhere became restless (or, at least, it was believed that they had become
restless) so that the terror, momentarily localized in Virginia,
spread up to Delaware and through Georgia, across to Louisiana and into Kentucky. This naturally led some to believe that
Turner had concerted measures for rebellion over a wider area
than his own county. Thus, Governor Floyd wrote: [40] " From
all that has come to my knowledge during and since this affair
—I am fully convinced that every black preacher in the whole
country east of the Blue Ridge, was in the secret," and again,
" In relation to the extent of the insurrection I think it greater
than will ever appear." A few other contemporary statements
of similar purport appeared,[41] and some later writers have
adopted [42] the same viewpoint.

The final authority on this question, however, is Nat Turner
himself and he affirmed that the revolt he led was local, and
that his activities had been confined to his own neighborhood.
He added: [43] " I see, sir, you doubt my word but can you not

40 Governor Floyd to Governor Hamilton, November 19, 1831, Papers of
J. Floyd.

41 Samuel Warner, *op. cit.*, p. 18; N. Y. *Atlas*, September 17, 1831. A Mr.
H. Borlund told Governor Stokes of North Carolina, in a letter dated
Murfreesborough, Hertford County, N. C., September 18, 1831, that the
slaves in the areas around Southampton were in on the plot but did not act
with Turner for they had understood the date for the outbreak to be the
last Sunday in August, not August 21. He added: "There was during the
alarm here, a negroman taken out shot and beheaded, his master's residence
some fifteen miles south & west of this place, he had procured a forged
pass and made a bold attempt to reach the neighborhood where the massacre
was committed in Southampton,—having told a negro, before he left home,
there would be a war between the black and white people; a negro-man is
now in jail found travelling through the country in woman's dress and in
that garb is known to have been passing in the neighborhood of Edenton."

42 H. M. Wagstaff, *op. cit.*, p. 57; James McSherry, *History of Maryland*,
pp. 78-79, 151-160, is confusing and contradictory on this point.

43 *The Confessions*, p. 17. It is possible that Turner insisted on this in order
to protect others. It is also possible that his early associates in the plot, in

think the same ideas and strange appearances about this time in the heavens might prompt others, as well as myself, to this undertaking?" In the absence of any evidence of equal weight to the contrary, one must conclude that Turner possessed the characteristic of great leaders in that he sensed the mood and feelings of the masses of his fellow beings, not only in his immediate environment but generally. The years immediately preceding his effort had been marked by a great rumbling of discontent and protest. Turner's act, itself carrying that rumbling to a high point, caused an eruption throughout the length and breadth of the slave South—which always rested on a volcano of outraged humanity.

The Richmond *Enquirer* of August 26, 1831, while assuring the world that in its city there was " no disturbance, no suspicion, no panic," did note the fact that " a patrol turns out in our city every night." Two days later a resident of Richmond wrote to his New York friends that [44] " the question now arises, if the slaves in that county, would murder the whites, whether they are not ready to do it in any *other county* in the State; and whether the reports that may spread among the slaves in other parts of the State, may not *excite* those to insurrection that never thought of such a thing before." Somewhat later, " A Friend of Precaution " wanted to know,[45] " how can a remedy be provided? the safety of our wives and children, and their lives be preserved?"

These thoughts kept recurring and, together with the incessant stream of other slave plots and outbursts, developed a truly feverish state of mind. A niece of George Washington declared,[46] " it is like a smothered volcano—we know not when,

the weeks prior to the outbreak, may have spread word of what was to come. Such news via the almost uncanny underground telegraph of the slaves could travel great distances in a short time.

44 N. Y. *Eve. Post*, September 2, 1831, emphases in original.

45 Richmond *Enquirer*, September 13, 1831.

46 Mrs. Lawrence Lewis to Mayor Harrison Gray Otis of Boston, dated October 17, 1831, in Samuel R. Morison, *Life and Letters of Harrison Gray Otis*, II, p. 260.

or where, the flame will burst forth but we know that death in the most horrid forms threaten us. Some have died, others have become deranged from apprehension since the South Hampton affair." And a gentleman in Virginia wrote to an acquaintance in Cincinnati: [47]

These insurrections have alarmed my wife so as really to endanger her health, and I have not slept without anxiety in three months. Our nights are sometimes spent in listening to noises. A corn song, or a hog call, has often been the subject of nervous terror, and a cat, in the dining room, will banish sleep for the night. There has been and there still is a *panic* in all this country. I am beginning to lose my courage about the melioration of the South. Our revivals produce no preachers; churches are like the buildings in which they worship, gone in a few years. There is no principle of life. Death is autocrat of slave regions.

The Richmond *Compiler* of September 3, 1831, contained this paragraph:

Some rumors are still afloat; but we know not on what authority they rest, and we hope they are very much exaggerated; as, of a deposit of guns, pistols, and knives, being found in Nansemond— though a late letter from that county says all alarm had subsided. Yet we now and then hear of a suspected slave taken up in Nansemond and Surry—and we hear a report of a Patrol going upon an estate in Prince George and upon the overseer's pointing out five whom he suspected, shooting two who were attempting to escape, and securing the other three and throwing them into jail.

A little later were reported the convictions of about eleven slaves in the three eastern counties of Nansemond, Prince George, and Sussex. Then came the arrest and subsequent release of twelve in Norfolk, the conviction of one in Fredericksburg, and the jailing of forty more in Nansemond.[48] Reports,

47 Cincinnati *Journal*, n. d., quoted in *The Liberator*, January 28, 1832.

48 Richmond *Enquirer*, September 20, 1831; Washington *National Intelligencer*, September 21, 1831; Niles' *Weekly Register*, September 24, November 18, 1831, XLI, pp. 67, 221. Population figures on some of the Virginia counties near Southampton help explain the fear of the ruling group. As

no doubt greatly exaggerated, were current that two or three thousand Negroes were hiding in the Great Dismal Swamp, which extends from Southampton into North Carolina.[49] The entire man-power of the State and much, if not all, its military might, infantry, artillery, cavalry, either in volunteer or regular militia units, were pressed into service throughout the Tide-water and the Piedmont areas, while the non-combatant population moved into garrisons, forts or blockhouses.[50] Two slaves attempting to avoid arrest were shot and killed in Charles City County in September. The next month several slaves imprisoned in Sussex attempted to escape. One succeeded, one was killed, "another severely wounded—the remainder were secured without injury. On Friday [October 21] four of them were hung." [51]

The residents of Georgetown and Sussex, Delaware, and Easton and Seaford, Maryland, were panic-stricken, and slaves

examples may be cited the following counties (the data are for 1830, the figure first given (the larger one in every instance) is for Negroes (free and slave), the second is for the whites): Greensville, 5013, 2104; Isle of Wight, 5494, 5023; Nansemond, 6641, 5143; Surry, 4244, 2865; Sussex, 8602, 4118. These are from "The Census" in *Documents Containing Statistics of Virginia, loc. cit.*; Drewry, *op. cit.*, p. 109 n. incorrectly gives the number of whites in Isle of Wight as 7023, an error repeated by S. B. Weeks, *op. cit.*, p. 454 n.

49 Niles' *Weekly Register*, September 17, 1831, XLI, p. 35; S. Warner, *op. cit.*, p. 12. This swamp was a favorite haunt of runaway slaves. See Edmund Jackson, "Virginia Maroons," in *The Pennsylvania Freeman*, January 1, 1852; present writer, *The Journal of Negro History*, XXIV, p. 168.

50 See Auditor's Records, Box 165, folders 10, 14; Box 166, folder 10, Archives Division, Virginia State Library, showing expenditures for state militia in various counties. See also, Niles' *Weekly Register*, September 17, 1831, XLI, p. 35; N. Y. *Eve. Post*, August 29, 1831; and the Richmond press generally for August and September, 1831. A youngster of fifteen, a native of Southampton, distinguished himself in these trying days by serving as a courier between garrisons. As a reward President Andrew Jackson appointed him a cadet at West Point. This individual, as General George Thomas, was influential in destroying slavery by his labors for the Union side during the Civil War.—See Lloyd Lewis, *Sherman*, p. 57.

51 Niles' *Weekly Register*, September 10, 1831, XLI, p. 19; N. Y. *Eve. Post*, November 1, 1831.

in those regions were arrested by the scores.[52] Excitement in eastern North Carolina was as widespread and intense as in Virginia, indeed, it was so great that it led to the deaths of three white men, due to heart failure.[53] Typical letters from this area told of the mobilization of the man-power, the need for more arms, the arrests of dozens of slaves, and the lashing or hanging of many.[54] One from Murfreesboro dated August 31, told of the arrest of five slaves, two of whom, London Gee and Sam Brantley, were supposed to be Baptist preachers. A show of force was still needed to convince the Negroes that revolt was hopeless. " Religion has been brought to their aid. Their leaders, who you know are preachers, have convinced many of them that to die in the cause in which they are engaged affords them a passport to heaven—many have said so when about to die." [55] Another letter, this dated Sampson County, September 13, addressed to the Governor, and signed by William Blanks and four other citizens, read: [56]

Sir the inhabitants of Sampson have been alarmed with an insurrection of the Negroes—We have ten or fifteen negroes in Jail, & we have such proof that most of them will be bound over to our Supr. Court We have testimony that will implicate most of the negroes in the county.... The people of Duplin County have examined ten or fifteen negroes & found two guilty, & have put them to *death*, there never was such excitement in Sampson & Duplin before.

A later communication from Hyde County contains more graphic details. The Governor is informed that the Colonel [57]

52 Richmond *Enquirer*, October 4, 1831 ; Niles' *Weekly Register*, October 20, 1831, XLI, p. 141 ; S. Warner, *op. cit.*, p. 26.

53 See letter from H. Borlund to Governor Stokes, dated Murfreesboro, September 18, 1831, N. C. Hist. Commission.

54 Numerous letters from almost every point in eastern North Carolina, mostly addressed to the Governor, dated from August 23, to October 14, 1831, are in the collection of Governor's Papers at Raleigh.

55 Solon Borlund to his brother, in *ibid*.

56 Governor's Papers, Raleigh.

57 Isaiah Spencer to Gov. Stokes, dated Hyde County, September 20, 1831, *ibid*.

has obeyed orders and has commanded the Guards to travole all night long and to whip all slaves which they cetch off there owners plantations without a pas from his or her owner. . . . I will give you a state of the alarm First there was a store broken open an 5 or 6 bags shot & powder Second ther has been found in posseson of slave Guns & ammonition thirdly there has been many threats by the slaves which has been [one word illegible] fourthly we have had two slaves preecher tride by a Single[?] Maistrate and the Evidence against one was that he went[?] to one Mr. Gibbs and asked him if he would join them for they ware about to rise.

This letter ends with a plea to the Governor (who is addressed as " your majesty "!) to forward arms to the county. A company of artillery of the United States Army was dispatched to Newbern, early in September,[58] martial law was declared in Raleigh,[59] and the panic, exaggerated reports,[60] arrests, beatings, executions, and lynchings lasted well into November, 1831.

Olmsted, in the late fifties, recorded his conversation with two poor whites of Mississippi, almost certainly referring to these stirring days:[61]

" Where I used to live (Alabama) I remember when I was a boy — mus ha' been about twenty years ago — folks was dreadful frightened about the niggers. I remember they built pens in the woods where they could hide, and Christmas time they went and got into the pens 'fraid the niggers was rising." " I remember the same time where we was in South Carolina," said his wife, " we had all our things put in a bag so we could tote 'em, if we heard they was comin' our way."

58 Report of United State Major-General, November, 1831, *op. cit.*, p. 55.

59 Niles' *Weekly Register*, Sept. 24, 1831, XLI, p. 67. In addition to sources already cited see, for the trouble in North Carolina, Richmond *Enquirer*, Sept. 20, November 25, 1831; Washington *National Intelligencer*, Sept. 21, October 5, 1831; N. Y. *Eve. Post*, Sept. 20, 24, October 19, 29, 1831; *The Liberator*, Oct. 15, 1831.

60 J. S. Bassett, *op. cit.*, p. 97, has suggested the possibility that exaggerated reports of slave disturbances and of Abolitionist propaganda may have had a political origin. See also G. H. Ambler, *Thomas Ritchie*, p. 167.

61 F. L. Olmsted, *A Journey in the Back Country*, p. 203.

Fears were expressed in October, 1831, of a revolt of the slaves, assisted by Indians, in Alabama. It was reported that "the infection is pretty general with the negroes," many of whom were arrested. In Laurens County, South Carolina, at least two slaves were executed for plotting rebellion at this time. Some hint of what was occurring in Mississippi is provided by the fact that a runaway slave in that State in 1839 declared that his scars were " caused from severe whipping with a cow skin, at the time of the South-Hampton insurrection." [62]

The *Messenger* of Macon, Georgia apologized " for the barrenness of the present paper " and offered as an excuse the fact that its staff was on patrol duty. In October, 1831, six slaves were arrested on a charge of conspiracy in Dublin, Georgia, of whom four were executed. The same month arms were distributed to the citizens of Milledgeville, and four slaves of that city were arrested but, after examination, released. Trouble was also reported from Jones County in this State, but details are unknown. [63]

A conspiracy was, at the end of the year, reported from Fayetteville, Tennessee. The object of the slaves [64] " was to set fire to some building, and amidst the confusion of the citizens, to seize as many guns and implements of destruction as they could procure, and commence a general massacre. Many of those who were engaged in this infernal conspiracy, have been slashed with all the severity, which the iniquity of their diabolical schemes, so justly deserved."

No specific instance of outbreak among Louisiana slaves directly after the Turner rebellion has been seen, though refer-

62 *The Liberator*, October 29, 1831; H. M. Henry, *op. cit.*, p. 153; C. S. Sydnor, *op. cit.*, p. 92.

63 *The Liberator*, October 22, 1831; R. B. Flanders, *op. cit.*, p. 153; C. S. Sydnor, *op. cit.*, p. 92.

64 *The Western Freeman*, n. d., Shelbyville, Tenn., quoted by Niles' *Weekly Register*, January 7, 1832, XLI, p. 340. Higginson, *op. cit.*, p. 181, refers to a plot at this time in Louisville, Kentucky; this however has not been seen elsewhere. Coleman, *op. cit.*, p. 297, notes evidence of increased unrest among Kentucky slaves in 1831, *before* Turner's uprising.

ence to their "insurrectionary disposition," and the special precautions therefore taken by the Federal government, has already been made.[65] A resident of that State wrote a revealing letter to a friend, a Congressman, after the Turner event. Though federal reinforcements had already been forwarded to his State, he was apparently unaware of this. He wrote:[66]

The late occurrences in Virginia has awakened a deep solicitude here as to the perils of our own situation. You will have seen from the papers that our Govr. [A. B. Roman] has called the Legislature for the 14 of next month. It is understood that the principal object in making this call, is the expectation, that some effective steps, may be taken for the safety of the State. We can do nothing, worth doing, without some help. So many have an interest in the preservation of the country, as well as ourselves, that we have every possible claim on all the aid that can be given.

He went on to suggest that an effective police force would be two steamboats filled with well-armed federal troops regularly plying between New Orleans and St. Francisville. " No one at all acquainted with the country can doubt that there wd be great security in such a force, against any rising happening, or if it occur, that they would then prove most efficient arms of defence. Let me ask you to make such inquiry as will enable you to inform me, how far we might count on the co-operation of the Federal Gov. in this or any other scheme." A somewhat similar suggestion, comprising unannounced tours by " from ten to fifteen companies of Infantry artillery or Riflemen," was made to Governor Roman by the commanding officer of the Western Army of the United States.[67]

The basic idea represented by these communications, a stiffening and sharpening—once more—of the apparatus of sup-

65 *Ante*, pp. 99-100.

66 Robert Carter Nicholas to Nicholas Trist, dated October 22, 1831, letter postmarked Donaldson [Louisiana] in Nicholas Trist Papers, Library of Congress.

67 Major-General Edmund P. Gaines to Governor Roman, New Orleans, November 16, 1831, in Personal Papers, Miscellaneous, G, Library of Congress.

pression and terrorism, was instituted, following these outbreaks and plots of 1831, in city, state, and territory. This took,
in the main, three forms : repression of the free Negro,[68] repression of the slave,[69] and attempts at the amelioration of the social
unrest, resulting essentially in greater efforts at African colonization, and in the repression of anti-slavery opinion and
thought in the South.

To exemplify the flood of legislation, two states, Maryland
and Virginia, will be examined in detail. The General Assembly
of Maryland meeting from December 1831 to March 1832 enacted the following pertinent laws. The immigration of free
Negroes was forbidden. Any who did enter were not to be
given employment, and if remaining over ten days were to pay
fines of fifty dollars per week. No free Negro was to possess any
weapons. Slaves and free Negroes were permitted to hold religious services only if whites were present. No foodstuff, tobacco, or spiritous liquors were to be bought from any Negro,
nor were the latter to be sold to a Negro. The importation of
slaves *for sale* after June 1, 1832 was forbidden.[70] The Maryland State Colonization Society was incorporated and a Board
of Managers, of three persons, was to be appointed by the Governor and Council. This Board was to spread propaganda detailing the alleged delights of Liberia, and to remove free Negros from the State. Twenty thousand dollars were given for
1831 and permission to subsequently borrow up to two hundred
thousand dollars (the last sum was not " appropriated ").[71]
If not enough Negroes volunteered to leave to use up the avail-

68 " Various severe measures are contemplated against the free people of
color "—Niles' *Weekly Register*, November 19, 1831, XLI, p. 221.

69 " It is charged against the slaves lately condemned that a number of
them were ' preachers of the gospel '—and that those who had been the
most kindly treated and were the best informed, were most prominent. The
bearing of these remarks is easily seen, and will add to the burthen of the
suffering "—*idem*.

70 Laws of this type were early and often passed in various states, and
seem to have always been practically impossible to enforce. See G. M.
Stroud, *op. cit.*, pp. 88 ff.

71 As reported in Niles' *Weekly Register*, April 7, 1832, XLII, p. 93.

able money, force was to be used. Moreover, the Congressmen from Maryland were memorialized to do what they could to obtain a grant from the federal government for colonization purposes, and if they deemed this unconstitutional to work for a constitutional amendment making the action possible, for [72] " recent occurrences in this State, as well as in other states of our Union, have impressed more deeply upon our minds, the necessity of devising some means, by which we may facilitate the removal of the free persons of color from our state."

Though, as has been shown, Virginia passed many restrictive measures in the years immediately preceding Turner's revolt, her Assembly did find it possible to enact new regulations in the 1831-1832 meeting. It was then provided that " no slave, free negro, or mulatto, whether he shall have been ordained or licensed, or otherwise, shall hereafter undertake to preach, exhort, or conduct, or hold any assembly or meeting, for religious or other purposes, either in the day time, or at night," under a penalty of not over thirty-nine lashes. Whites, however, were allowed to take Negroes to their own services, and a licensed white preacher was permitted to address Negroes during the daytime. No free Negro was to possess weapons. If any Negro should commit assault on a white person with intent to kill, death without benefit of clergy was to be his punishment. No one was to sell liquor to or purchase it from a slave, and no Negro was to sell liquor within one mile of a public assembly. An act which went into operation July 1, 1832 provided that any Negro attending a seditious meeting or saying anything of such a nature was to be whipped not over thirty-nine times, while a white person so guilty was to be fined from one hundred to one thousand dollars. Another act, passed March 5, 1832, though as the influential editor, Thomas Ritchie remarked,[73] " applicable to one county only," was " deemed sufficiently im-

---

72 *Laws Made and Passed by the General Assembly of the State of Maryland ... 1831 ... 1832*, Annapolis, 1832, Chapters 281, 325, and Resolution No. 124.

73 T. M. Whitfield, *Slavery Agitation in Virginia, 1829-1832*, p. 114.

portant, (as affecting the general policy of the state,) to be inserted among the acts of a public nature." This provided that the fifteen thousand dollars pledged for the cause of colonization at a mass meeting in Northampton was to become part of the public debt of that county.[74]

But what this legislature did not do, and why, and what various citizens inside and outside the honorable body thought it ought to do, and what was said to and in, and reported about and asked of, this body are of greater significance than the laws it passed. In the twenties, with the prevailing depression, the acute fear of the Negroes, and the frequent manifestations of slave unrest, there had developed in the South, as has been indicated, a growing perplexity and doubt concerning the wisdom of slavery. Prior to the Turner rebellion this had been, on the whole, expressed in a hushed sort of way. Thus, Thomas Ritchie who, at least formally, was, prior to 1832, anti-slavery, urged western Virginians at the constitutional convention of 1829-30 to avoid emancipationist utterances.[75]

74 *Acts Passed at the General Assembly of the Commonwealth of Virginia, 1831-1832*, Richmond, 1832, pp. 20, 21, 23, 24; see also, J. C. Ballagh, *op. cit.,* pp. 93, 147. Practically all other regions in the South passed restrictive legislation. This is true of Delaware, the Carolinas, Georgia, Florida Territory, Alabama, Mississippi, Louisiana, Tennessee, and Kentucky. These data are detailed in the present writer's unpublished master's thesis on Nat Turner, Columbia, 1937, pp. 88-96. This writer does not, however, feel free to declare categorically, that the lot of the Negro slave was worsened considerably by these laws. He does incline to agree with Carter G. Woodson that the last generation of the institution of slavery, particularly because of the industrial revolution which tended to emphasize the commercial aspects of human slavery, probably saw more severe treatment than did the eighteenth century as a whole. See C. G. Woodson, *The Education of the Negro Prior to 1861*, p. 2; and his review of a book by U. B. Phillips in *The Mississippi Valley Historical Review*, 1919, V, pp. 480-482. A contrary opinion will be found expressed by some contemporaries, see Harriet Martineau, *Society in America*, I, p. 380; F. L. Olmsted, *A Journey in the Seaboard Slave States*, I, p. 108; F. Bremer, *The Homes of the New World*, II, pp. 449-450; James G. Birney in (MS.) An anti-slavery album of contributions from friends of freedom 1834-1858, Manuscript room Library of Congress, Ac5191, p. 109—dated September 29, 1837.

75 Ambler, *op. cit.*, pp. 100, 120-21; see also, A. D. Adams, *The Neglected Period of Anti-Slavery in America, 1805-1831*, p. 41.

The Turner cataclysm, however, succeeded in ripping up, for one year, the lid of censorship applied by the slaveocracy. This is especially true of the state most directly affected by that event, and the question of slavery was publicly debated for weeks in Virginia's legislature during the 1831-32 session. The western representatives, grieved at their section's inferior political position as compared with the east, and, restrained by no considerable body of slave-holding constituents, used anti-slavery utterances and sentiments—which were here expressed as deeply and as fully as they were ever to be in Ohio or Massachusetts—as a weapon in their sectional battle.

The extent and power of this anti-slavery influence have been greatly exaggerated, and it has often been declared that slavery's abolition came within a very few votes of accomplishment in Virginia at this time.[76] Many writers under this illusion ascribe the failure only to annoyance and fear caused by the agitation of the northern Abolitionists,[77] who are dragged in to explain everything. Thus, the Turner revolt itself was a result of their nefarious activities. Though the vehemence of anti-slavery pronouncements in the Virginia legislature following that event is explained by the " fact " that Abolitionist propaganda had not yet really begun the defeat of any emancipation measure is promptly blamed upon resentment at Northern interference. The sensitive slaveholders, one is asked to believe, although actually desiring to relinquish their property, refused to do so in order to spite the meddling Abolitionists![78]

76 As a few examples see, J. H. Russell, op. cit., pp. 80-81; W. C. Cabell, Below the James, pp. 152-53; L. C. Bell, The Old Free State, I, p. 496; Marquis James, The Raven, p. 374.

77 As examples, see G. T. Curtis, Life of James Buchanan, II, pp. 278-279; [James Buchanan], Mr. Buchanan's Administration on the Eve of the Rebellion, pp. 3-4; T. N. Page, The Old South, p. 38; B. H. Wise, The Life of Henry A. Wise of Virginia, p. 46; B. B. Munford, Virginia's Attitude Toward Slavery and Secession, pp. 41-59; H. A. Herbert, The Abolition Crusade, pp. 12, 61 ff.; L. P. Stryker, Andrew Johnson, p. 50.

78 The remarks of George M. Weston are to the point: " No man is ever restrained from pursuing a course in harmony with his own wishes and opinions, merely because he is advised to it by others; although it is common

But there is no evidence to show a connection between Turner's efforts and those of the Abolitionsts, and it is not true that the Virginia legislature, following his rebellion, came close to abolition. It, in this session, came close to passing a colonization bill [79] (introduced by W. H. Brodnax, of Dinwiddie, a Piedmont County) modeled on that already passed by Maryland,[80] and it next year did appropriate eighteen thousand dollars for such a purpose, but to identify this with the abolition of slavery, as does, for example, Edward Channing,[81] is erroneous. And it is to be noted that Brodnax's bill passed the eastern controlled House of Delegates, but, because no provision was made in it for those Negroes who might be emancipated without sufficient funds for transportation, it was defeated in the Senate by *Western* opposition.[82]

enough, to make the manner of disagreeable advice, the pretext for the purpose, already pre-determined, to disregard it "—*The Progress of Slavery*, p. 184. The brutal frankness of James Hammond, a leading South Carolina politician, in his "Letters on Slavery" written in 1845 is refreshing. He remarks about the bitterness of the words of the slaveholders and of the Abolitionists, and to the latter says: "But if your course was wholly different—if you distilled nectar from your lips, and discoursed sweetest music, could you reasonably indulge the hope of accomplishing your object by such means? Nay, supposing that we were all convinced, and thought of Slavery precisely as you do, at what era of 'moral suasion' do you imagine you could prevail on us to give up a thousand millions of dollars in the value of our slaves, and a thousand millions of dollars more in the depreciation of our lands, in consequence of the want of laborers to cultivate them?'", in E. N. Elliot, ed., *Cotton Is King, and Pro-Slavery Arguments*, pp. 140-141.

79 In the bound volume called the *Virginia Slavery Debate of 1832*, in the Virginia State Library, there is an appendix by Brodnax explaining this bill; see also his speech of January 19, 1832, printed in pamphlet form by Thomas White in Richmond in 1832; and also the Richmond *Whig*, January 28, 1832.

80 In that State during 1832, 1833, 1834, a total of 219 Negroes were sent to Africa at an expense of about $16,000—J. R. Brackett, *The Negro in Maryland*, p. 239.

81 E. Channing, *History of the United States*, V, pp. 144-45; see also *The Virginia Magazine of History and Biography*, XI, p. 331.

82 Richmond *Whig*, March 12, 1832; Niles' *Weekly Register*, March 21, 1832, XLII, p. 78. This answers a point made by E. L. Fox, *The American Colonization Society*, p. 102. The vote in the Senate seems to have been 18

The only anti-slavery activity, outside of talk and the receipt of petitions,[83] developed when a Mr. Witches moved that consideration of the slavery question be indefinitely postponed.[84] This was voted down, 71 to 60, and therefore a select committee on slaves, free Negroes, and the recent insurrection, was appointed. This committee, in the person of its chairman, Mr. Goode of Mecklenberg, resolved that " it is not expedient " to legislate on the question of emancipation, and asked to be absolved from further consideration of that subject. Two amendments, *as to what the committee ought to consider,* were offered. Mr. Preston suggested it was " expedient " for it to consider the problem. This was defeated by a vote of 73 to 58. Mr. Thomas J. Randolph then offered an elaborate plan for gradual emancipation which he thought the committee would do well to ponder. This seems never to have come to a vote.[85] Nothing was done.

It may also be pointed out that while it is true the legislative halls and newspapers were filled with very nearly all the arguments against slavery that were ever to be used, it is far off the mark to say, for example,[86] " The Richmond *Inquirer* [sic] urged that slavery be abolished," or that Ritchie, its editor, " favored the abolition of negro slavery in 1832." [87] True, that

to 14, as reported in the Richmond *Whig*, March 12, 1832. A tradition has arisen (among those who label the bill a move for abolition) that it was defeated by one vote—see sources cited in footnotes 76, 77.

83 One of these, that from ladies in Fluvanna County, is very inaccurately given by Drewry, *op. cit.*, p. 165 n. Words are altered, and whole sentences are omitted, though this is not indicated. It is quite long, but worth reading. See Niles' *Weekly Register*, December 10, 1831, XLI, p. 273.

84 Richmond *Whig*, January 28, 1832.

85 See *Journal of the House of Delegates, 1831-1832, passim.* Goode's report and Randolph's plan were printed in full in a pamphlet of the latter's speech delivered January 21, 1832, and printed that year in Richmond. For the action of Mr. Preston see The Richmond *Whig*, January 28, 1832. See present writer's thesis, *op. cit.*, pp. 99 ff.; and Joseph C. Robert, " The Road from Monticello," *Historical Papers of the Trinity College Historical Society,* Series XXIV, *passim.*

86 L. P. Stryker, *op. cit.*, p. 45.

87 C. H. Ambler, *Ritchie*, pp. 165, 295.

paper shouted [88] " something must be done," but what, concretely, what, did it suggest? " In fine, by *great discretion, the utmost respect for private property, great perseverance, by an active and increased police,* we may rid ourselves, in some long and distant times, of an evil, which, if left to itself, will 'grow with our growth, and strengthen with out strength'!" [89] That is the high point in the " emancipationist " feeling of this influential paper, and it is difficult to ascertain whether the writer is deploring slavery, or asking that its too rapid growth be checked.

And while anti-slavery letters abounded in the press, pro-slavery letters were certainly not rare, but now being considered vulgar, they are often overlooked by commentators in evaluating articulate Southern opinion. One, signed "A Slaveholder and No Politician," declared: " Some people seem very anxious to devise some scheme for the gradual emancipation of our slaves; if they know what was good for themselves they had better let that question rest; for as I live, *for one,* they will have to take them at the point of the bayonet. I do not mean to go into a discussion of the subject, but merely to state that public sentiment is against *any scheme* of emancipation." A letter from Richard Hughes told of the decision of his neighbor, one Colonel Lee, to free his slaves and hire white men:

they'll be cheaper, he says: and he can make more money on his plantation than he does now. Colonel, says I, the white laborers must be better fed, and clothed, and lodged, than your negroes—and you'll have to pay them wages, too :—how can you make more money then? But the negro children, says he—the white men will have their children, too, says I; and if you think they can work harder than the blacks, I reckon you'll be out—for no people will

88 Richmond *Enquirer*, January 7, 1832. See also the Richmond *Whig* for the month of January, 1832, especially Jan. 13, 28, 31, and also March 12, 1832, in which this occurs, " all things relating to free negroes, escept insofar as a change may be effected by the police bill, remain *in statu quo ante bellum.* All goes for nothing, a ridiculous *finale,* all things considered."

89 Richmond *Enquirer*, January 19, 1832. See also W. S. Jenkins, *Pro-Slavery Thought in the Old South,* p. 82.

work more, or ought to work more than our negroes do—they'll do their work well too, if the master or overseer be good for anything—but this last I didn't say to him.

As a final example there is a blunt letter from "A.B.C. of Halifax City": [90]

This one thing we wish to be understood and remembered,—that the Constitution of this State, has made Tom, Dick, and Harry, *property*—it has made Polly, Nancy, and Molly, *property*; and be that property an evil, a curse, or what not, we intend to hold it. Property, which is considered the most valuable by the owners of it, is a nice thing; and for the right thereto, to be called in question by an unphilosophical set of political mountebanks, under the influence of supernatural agency or deceit, is insufferable.

And in 1832 there appeared, in reply to the agitation of western Virginians, a classical pro-slavery paper, that by Thomas R. Dew.[91] Using historical, anthropological, and theological arguments that had already been generally accepted in the lower South, and denying the possibility or advisability of solving the slavery problem by colonization, he gave to many former anti-slaverites, like Thomas Ritchie, James Paulding, Joseph Gales, and Edmund Ruffin,[92] rationalizations for affirming slavery to be, *per se,* a " good." Dew did not fail to notice the immediate interests of the slaveholders, for he remarked, " wonderful to relate, Virginia slaves are now higher than they have been for many years in the past." Returning prosperity was, indeed, the clinching pro-slavery argument.

90 These letters are, respectively, in Richmond *Whig*, January 28, 1832; Richmond *Enquirer*, March 1, 1832; Richmond *Whig*, April 13, 1832; emphases as in original.

91 *Review of the Debate in the Virginia Legislature,* first published in Richmond in 1832, many times reprinted. L. P. Stryker, *op. cit.,* p. 50, gives its date of appearance as 1835, which helps his argument that Abolitionist propaganda stopped emancipation in Virginia, but the date and the argument are erroneous.

92 See, J. S. Bassett, *op. cit.,* pp. 100-101 ; Avery Craven, *Edmund Ruffin,* pp. 108-109; C. Ambler, *op. cit.,* pp. 164-66.

By 1830 slave prices [93] had begun to rise from their low of $400 and had reached, at the end of the year, about $425 for a prime field hand. In 1831, $460 was the average, and by 1832 the price hit $500, a rise of twenty-five per cent in three years. It kept going up until it reached $1,100 in 1837. This rise in prices, due to " the increased demand for slaves in the south-western states," [94] and " improved methods of agriculture ... better means of intercommunication ... and the employment given negro slaves upon works of internal improvements and in factories, revived the economic interest in negro slaves " [95] in eastern Virginia and in the old South generally. The Southern rulers, reassured and gaining vigor, reinstituted their strict censorship of anti-slavery opinion, and " resentment at northern interference ...as being more chivalrous ... [was] the reason alleged in public debates, and in newspaper paragraphs" [96] for this policy.

The era of crisis takes form: remaining groups of anti-slavery people, as Quakers, leave or alter their sentiments; [97] emancipationist societies disappear in the South, and spring up by the hundreds in the North.[98] Anti-slavery agitators " in any shape, or under any pretext, are furious fanatics or knaves or hypocrites; and we hereby promise them, upon all occasions which may put them in our power, the fate of the pirate, the incendiary, and the midnight assassin," [99] while in the North there begins to develop the feeling that [100] " all who are not

93 U. B. Phillips, *Life and Labor in the Old South*, p. 177.

94 E. A. Andrews, *Slavery and the Domestic Slave Trade*, p. 180.

95 Charles Ambler, *Sectionalism in Virginia*, p. 187.

96 E. A. Andrews, *op. cit.*, p. 180.

97 H. Aptheker, " The Quakers and Negro slavery," *The Journal of Negro History*, 1940, XXV, pp. 358-59.

98 G. G. Johnson, *op. cit.*, p. 356; [Thomas Earle], *op. cit.*, pp. 218, 247, 296.

99 Resolution of a mass meeting in Camden, S. C., in 1834, given in LaRoy Sunderland, *Anti-Slavery Manual*, p. 50.

100 Harriet Martineau, *op. cit.*, I, p. 390.

with the abolitionists are against them; for silence and inaction are public acquiescence in things as they are."

The decade of the twenties was a period of growth for the colonization movement, which was further accelerated by the Turner revolt. Some who became interested in it probably felt sincerely that it might end slavery.[101] But, on the whole the purpose was to strengthen slavery by removing dangerous elements among the Negroes, keeping the growth of the free Negro population down, and confusing the anti-slavery movement. The attitude is exemplified in a letter from Dr. John Ker, a leader in the movement in Mississippi. He admitted that colonization might lead to some manumission, but felt sure these would be made only by indulgent masters. This, he argued, would be desirable: [102]

Will it not ... benefit other slave holders, rather by removing some examples of loose and injuriously indulgent discipline, the effect of mistaken feelings of Humanity? Will it not have the effect, also, of enhancing the value of those who may be left? Will not the hands of slavery be strengthened as to those who shall remain, except from the only ground of hope to the slave, the voluntary act of his master?

But this concept of colonization was not, it appears, seriously held by many people, particularly after Dew demonstrated the extreme difficulty, indeed, impossibility, as he thought, of accomplishing it; an argument that appeared [103] to John Quincy Adams, as to most others, to be " conclusive." Another, and decisive, factor in the decline of the colonization movement was the almost unanimous opposition of the Negroes, who felt,[104]

101 E. L. Fox, op. cit., p. 92; African Repository, Nov. 1831, VII, p. 281.

102 Dated July 25, 1831, in Pub. of Miss. Hist. Soc., IX, p. 350; see also D. L. Dumond, ed., Letters of James G. Birney, I, pp. 25, 34, 46-48, 50, 71; S. E. Morison, op. cit., II, pp. 266-67.

103 C. F. Adams, ed., Memoirs of John Quincy Adams, entry of Oct. 13, 1833, IX, p. 23.

104 David Walker's Appeal, p. 73. For a few examples of this opposition at various times, see G. Barnes and D. Dumond, eds., Weld-Grimké Letters, I, p. 253; Mississippi Valley Historical Review, XVIII, p. 386; Charles H. Wesley, Richard Allen, p. 161; E. A. Andrews, op. cit., p. 57.

"America is more our country, than it is the whites—we have enriched it with our *blood and tears."* It is to be observed that the collapse here mentioned, which set in about 1836 and was permanent, refers to the movement for the colonization of free Negroes, not of the freed Negroes, which was to develop later, and still lives, though feebly.[105]

Following the Turner uprising there was some expulsion of free Negroes,[106] and for a time it was feared [107] too that a mass exodus of non-slaveholding whites, in addition to the Quakers, might occur, but this did not develop. The same event, by precipitating a vehement discussion of the slavery question, and by bringing to the foreground one of its persistent dangers, stimulated the feeling of sectionalism in Virginia.[108] Suggestions for the splitting of the State recurred but a much greater upheaval than the one begun by the slave of Southampton was needed to accomplish that.

This decade of great slave unrest which culminated in the outbreaks and conspiracies of 1831, and which resulted in a sharpening and strengthening of the machinery of repression, was followed by three years of surface calm, so far as rebellions and plots were concerned. An apparently unimportant excep-

105 See, for example, the United Press dispatch, "Liberia welcomes American Negroes," in N. Y. *World-Telegram*, July 8, 1936.

106 See item about influx of free Negroes into Ohio in N. Y. *Atlas*, X, November 19, 1831; also, W. E. B. DuBois, *The Philadelphia Negro*, p. 239; Benjamin Drew, *A North-Side View of Slavery*, p. 332; W. Drewry, *op. cit.*, p. 172 n.

107 Niles' *Weekly Register*, October 15, December 10, 1831, XLI, pp. 80, 266; J. C. Ballagh, *op. cit.*, p. 93.

108 N. Y. *Eve. Post*, November 19, 1831; C. Ambler, *Sectionalism*, p. 192; R. T. Stevenson, *The Growth of the Nation, 1809-1837*, p. 328, being vol. XII, of *The History of North America*, edited by G. C. Lee. Benjamin Brawley declared the outbreaks of 1831 "made more certain the carrying out of the policy of the Jackson administration to remove the Indians of the South to the West"—*A Social History of the American Negro*, p. 148. No substantiation of this has been seen. It is conceivable that the reports of Indian alliance with Negro conspirators in Alabama (as previously noted) were concocted to further the drive for their forced removal.

tion occurred in the summer of 1833 in Fairfax, Virginia, where fears were aroused by a " suspicious character," a white carpenter named John Windover, who was thought to be provoking a servile insurrection.[109] Some nine or ten slaves were arrested, but their disposition is unknown. Available evidence, which is slight, indicates that this affair was of minor proportions.

109 G. Millan to Governor, dated Fairfax, September 9, 1833, Executive Papers; in *C. V. S. P.*, X, p. 587.

CHAPTER XIII

1835-1849

THE year 1835 witnessed the reopening of this never-long interrupted drama of the organized struggle of an enslaved people to throw off their yoke. This particular act lasted until 1842 after which, once more, a momentary intermission occurred. The locale of the first scene was the lush, new soil in the heart of Mississippi, Madison and Hinds counties. To this region, in the thirties, came thousands of men on the make intent upon cashing in on the fluffy gold that might be produced, and bringing more thousands of slaves, torn from every state in the South, and often from all persons and associations dear to them.[1]

The preoccupation of these slave-drivers with the alchemy of procuring wealth by selling the white product of black men's toil was rudely interrupted in June, 1835, when rumors of an impending Negro insurrection began to fly around. In that month a lady of Madison county reported to her neighbors that she had overheard the following alarming statements of one of her slaves: " she wished to God it was all over and done with; that she was tired of waiting on *white folks,* and wanted to be

1 James K. Polk wrote his wife on Sept. 26, 1834, that he had decided to purchase land in Mississippi and ship his slaves there. " The negroes have no idea they are going to be sent to the South, and I do not wish them to know it, and therefore it would be best to say nothing about it at home, for it might be carreyed back to them "—J. S. Bassett, *The Southern Plantation Overseer,* p. 78. The rate of increase of slaves in Hinds and Madison counties was greater than that for any other county in the State from 1830 to 1840. In the former year slaves formed 39.4 percent of the population, in the latter year this had jumped to 68.8 percent—L. C. Gray, *History of Agriculture in the Southern United States,* II, p. 903. In 1837 there were 3,675 whites and 11,238 Negroes in Madison county—D. Rowland, *History of Mississippi,* II, p. 783. According to the report of the vigilance committee that suppressed the plot, the Negroes outnumbered the whites by fifty to one in the immediate area of its origin — Livingston and Beatie's Bluff — H. Howard, *The History of Virgil Steward,* appendix, p. 233.

her own mistress the balance of her days, and clean up her own house."

A favorite slave was sent among the others as a spy and soon accused one Negro. This man " after receiving a most severe chastisement " confessed that a plot for revolt had been formed and implicated a Mr. Ruel Blake, a local slaveholder, and his slaves. One of that individual's slaves " was severely whipped by order of the [vigilance] committee, but refused to confess anything—alleging all the time, that if they wanted to know what his master had told him, they might whip on until they killed him; that he had promised him that he would never divulge it." Other slaves were tortured and it was finally determined, to the committee's satisfaction, that there existed a general plot of the slaves and that a number of white men were implicated. By the decision of this extra-legal body about fifteen slaves and six white men were hanged in the month of July. At least two of the latter, William Saunders and Joshua Cotton, appear to have been members of a gang of desperadoes and bandits led by John Murrell, one of whose specialties was the stealing and reselling of slaves. Others, however, notably, Ruel Blake, and A. L. Donovan, reportedly from Kentucky, appear to have taken part in the plot because of a sincere wish to aid in liberating the Negroes.[2]

There is evidence indicating that the vigilance committee, or some members of it, operating under the name of Regulators, got out of hand and began directing their violence against wealthy people, particularly a Judge Patrick Sharkey, who barely escaped with his life. The Governor was told that " un-

[2] H. R. Howard, *op. cit.*, pp. 224-233. See also *A Memoir of S. S. Prentiss*, edited by his brother, I, pp. 161-62; Niles' *Weekly Register*, August 8, 1835, XLVIII, pp. 403-404; *The Liberator*, August 8, 15, 1835 and Robert M. Coates, *The Outlaw Years*, book IV. *The Liberator* for Nov. 21, 1835 tells of another slave being executed in Livingston for conspiracy. Extracts from the Tuscaloosa, Ala., *Flag of the Union*, July 25, 1835, and the Jackson *Mississippian*, July 17, 1835, dealing with the plot have been kindly supplied to the present writer by Dr. Clement Eaton. See his account in *Freedom of Thought in the Old South*, pp. 96-99.

less there is a stop put to the shedding of blood, confusion and revolution must shortly reign over the land." [3] By the end of July, however, relative order was restored.

Before the year was ended acute alarm had been experienced in Georgia, South Carolina, North Carolina, Virginia, Maryland, Alabama, Louisiana, and Texas.[4] In August the town of Charlestown, Maryland, was thrown into " an uproar for several days " because of suspicion of an impending uprising stimulated by a white man. The community was " guarded every night by armed men of the first respectability ", but just what foundation existed for the fear is uncertain.[5]

That same month a white man named Brady was arrested near Charleston, South Carolina, for allegedly attempting to interest slaves in an uprising, while another named Robinson was hanged near Lynchburg, Virginia, for the same offense. Suspicions were aroused in September concerning the behavior of slaves working in mines in Lumpkin County, Georgia, while three whites were lynched in Aiken, South Carolina, and Jefferson County, Georgia, for seditious activity, and another was, for the same reason, driven out of Twigg County, Georgia.[6]

3 James B. Kilborn and Patrick Sharkey to Governor Runnels, dated Fleetwood, Hinds County, July 7, 1835, in archives of Mississippi at Jackson (from notes kindly given the writer by Dr. Eaton). Several other pertinent letters are preserved there, as from the Committee of Safety of Hinds and Clinton Counties to Governor, July 11, 1835, and from George Wyche to Governor, Fleetwood, July 8, 1835.

4 For the facts concerning Texas, see *ante*, p. 93.

5 Letter from Charlestown, Maryland, dated August 17, in *The Liberator*, September 5, 1835.

6 Selma Alabama *Free Press*, August 29, September 5, 1835; *The Liberator* (citing southern papers) September 19, 26, October 3, 1835; *The Friend of the African*, London, 1844, no. 9, p. 131; W. Sherman Savage, *The Controversy Over the Distribution of Abolition Literature*, pp. 14, 35; Ralph F. Bates, *Plantation Slavery in Georgia*, p. 275. Something approaching a veritable reign of terror spread throughout the South in this mail-burning year of anti-Abolitionist hysteria. This was used to provoke anti-Catholic feeling by certain writers who claimed there existed a Catholic-Negro alliance to destroy white Protestants. Bishop John England of Charleston was almost mobbed and forced to close a school for free Negroes which the church had

The high pitch of the excitement in the slave area is revealed by an episode that occurred in September, in Buckingham County, Virginia. A group of slaves marching along the road and carrying across their shoulders what appeared to be weapons precipitated panic, sent children and adults scampering and produced a hurried call for the militia. It soon developed that the slaves were carrying nothing but tools, and were marching nowhere but off to work in nearby mines.[7]

What appears to have been a bona fide conspiracy was uncovered in October, 1835, in Elizabeth City, North Carolina. Free Negroes were declared to be involved as well as slaves, and the contemporary press asserted the excitement was as great as it had been in 1831. The slaves involved were banished and the free Negroes were also forced to leave the State.[8]

An old domestic slave revealed that same month a plan for rebellion comprising slaves in Georgia and in South Carolina. Northern lumbermen were believed to be the instigators of this movement.[9] From press accounts the Georgia counties of Monroe and Jones appear to have been the centers of disaffection, and a " considerable number " of slaves were arrested. Two of the ringleaders were selected for punishment, that meted out to one being death, while the other was "whipped, branded, cropped." [10]

recently established. See Peter Guilday, *The Life and Times of John England*, II, pp. 151-52; R. A. Billington, *The Protestant Crusade, 1800-1860*, p. 127. Dr. Billington errs when he asserts the Catholic school in Charleston was for *slaves*. See also H. Aptheker, " Militant Abolitionism " in *The Journal of Negro History*, XXVI, p. 452; and C. H. Wesley, " The Negro in the organization of abolition," in *Phylon*, II, p. 235, n. 60.

7 Richmond, *Compiler*, n. d., in *The Liberator*, October 10, 1835.

8 Elizabeth City *Herald*, October 3, in *ibid.*, October 17, 1835; Richmond *Whig*, October 20, 1835, see *ante*, p. 83.

9 Emily P. Burke, *Reminiscences of Georgia*, p. 157; R. B. Flanders, *op. cit.*, p. 274.

10 Milledgeville *Journal*, n. d., and Macon *Messenger*, n. d., in *The Liberator*, October 31, December 12, 1835.

In December a fairly serious effort at rebellion was nipped by the disclosures of a " confidential servant " of a planter living in East Feliciana, Louisiana.[11] Once again whites, this time two, were believed to be implicated, as well as " a great many of the most favorite confidential servants " which made it all the more disturbing. Arms were found in the possession of about forty slaves, great excitement prevailed in St. Francisville and in East and West Feliciana, armed patrols swept over the countryside, and some of the planters moved into New Orleans for greater safety. The fate of the slaves involved is unknown.[12]

Negroes of Missouri were overheard, in the spring of 1836, " communicating their designs to other slaves, and by this means were detected before their scheme was ripe for execution. The plan was to murder their masters, take whatever money they could find, and make for Canada." Their punishment is laconically indicated [13] in the line, " This destination was changed for the South." In June of this year maroon bands were especially active and dangerous in Gates County, North Carolina, and in the Cypress Swamp, near New Orleans.[14]

11 Letter dated New Orleans, December 29, 1835, in Niles' *Weekly Register*, January 16, 1836, XLIX, p. 331.

12 A letter dated Clinton, Parish of East Feliciana, April 7, 1836, told of two slaveholders being sued by a third because they punished his slaves as well as their own, " for rebellious indications " without his permission. The aggrieved slaveholder was awarded $350 damages. It is probable that this developed from the plot of December, 1835. Louisville *Journal*, April 15, in *The Liberator*, May 14, 1836.

13 St. Louis *Republican*, n. d., in N. Y. *Observer*, May 7, 1836.

14 Louisiana *Advertiser*, June 8, 1836, in *The Liberator*, July 2, 1836; H. T. Catterall, ed., *op. cit.*, II, p. 75. In September a Negro named Parker was jailed in Mobile, Alabama, because he possessed a copy of a radical Abolitionist paper, *The Struggler*, published by Negroes in Philadelphia— Mobile *Register*, September 7, 1836, in W. S. Savage, *op. cit.*, p. 35. According to U. B. Phillips, *American Negro Slavery*, p. 485, there was great uneasiness among slaveholders in Georgia and in Tennessee in December, 1836. No other reference to this has been seen. On December 11, 14, and 15, attempts were made to set fire to Winchester, Virginia and the citizens were " greatly alarmed." It was reported that " Two negroes have been committed to jail on suspicion of being concerned in these attempts." — Baltimore American, n. d., in N. Y. *Eve. Post*, December 23, 1836.

The next year [15] slave disaffection of an organized nature seems to have centered in Louisiana. In July 1837 came reports of the killing of an outlaw slave leader, Squire, near New Orleans, whose band had been responsible for the deaths of several white men. Squire's career had lasted for years. A guard of soldiers was sent to the swamp for his body, which was exhibited for a few days in the public square of the city.[16] A conspiracy, " said to have been better planned and managed than any known before " was betrayed in October by a slave, Lewis,[17] belonging to a Mr. Compton of Rapides Parish, Louisiana. The revolt was supposed to begin in Alexandria, but the rebels had disagreed as to whether all the whites should be killed, or the women and children should be spared. This caused delay, and the betrayal by Lewis squelched the uprising before it could begin. About fifty or sixty slaves and at least three free Negroes were arrested. The free Negroes and at least nine of the slaves were hanged, while several others were sentenced to life imprisonment. Two companies of United States troops were stationed in the disaffected region and succeeded in restoring order.[18]

15 The year 1837 marks the beginning of a severe economic depression that lasted for about five or six years, and bank failures and repudiations were common, the latter being resorted to by the State of Mississippi. See *ante*, p. 121; N. Y. *Eve. Post*, for April, 1837; *The Liberator*, July 13, 1838. In addition a long drought and insect ravages crippled the cotton crop in 1839, while the sugar crop of that year sold at extremely low prices, falling below 3½ cents in the spring of 1840. See J. L. Watkins, " Production and price of cotton for one hundred years " Department of Agriculture, *Miscellaneous Series, Bulletin*, No. 9, p. 10; L. C. Gray, *op. cit.*, II, p. 744.

16 New Orleans *Picayune*, July 19, 1837. This year also witnessed the start of the Second Seminole War, or the Florida War, destined to last six years, to cost the lives of about fifteen hundred soldiers and an undetermined number of Indians and their Negro allies. For a brief notice of this affair, and sources, see H. Aptheker, in *The Journal of Negro History*, XXIV, p. 180.

17 The State purchased his freedom and gave him five hundred dollars so that he might establish himself in some distant community where he would be safe.—U. B. Phillips, *op. cit.*, p. 485.

18 New Orleans *American*, n. d., in N. Y. *Eve. Post*, October 27, 1837 (where it is said that two whites, one of whom was killed, were also implicated); Niles' *National Register*, October 28, 1837, LIII, p. 129; V. A.

The zone of greatest trouble moved to the border area in 1838. In the District of Columbia reports of a serious plot arose in May. Armed citizens and regular police patrols came out in force, arrested several slaves and a few white men, and broke up, according to the press, some " infamous dens " in which the schemes had been hatched.[19]

At Florence in Boone County, Kentucky, a conspiracy to rebel was uncovered and the movement thwarted in November. Six of the insurgent leaders, apparently aided by white men, managed to escape and safely made their way into Canada.[20] The next month " a concerted plot, entered into by a large number of negroes of Williamson and Rutherford Counties ", Tennessee, was discovered and suppressed.[21]

Some slave trouble of an unspecified nature was reported in February, 1839, from Iberville Parish, Louisiana. " A vigilant patrol " was instituted and " tranquillity " finally prevailed.[22] In the same month several attempts at the destruction of Macon, Georgia, by fire was made. A resident wrote:

Suspicion falls mainly on the slaves. I can give you no accurate or satisfactory information as to the particulars, as the alarm and danger are too great to allow us to make investigation at present. No person feels a disposition to sleep again to-night; and not only the police but citizens generally, as well as sailors, are extremely vigilant, and greatly excited.[23]

A report of a general conspiracy of the slaves of Memphis, Tennessee, swept through the city in March. A vigilance commit-

Moody, " Slavery on Louisiana sugar plantations," in *The Louisiana Historical Quarterly*, VII, p. 223. In 1837 a free Negro named M'Donald was tried by the Alabama Supreme Court for attempting to provoke an insurrection, but he was released.—H. T. Catterall, ed., *op. cit.*, III, pp. 126, 141.

19 The Georgetown *Advocate*, May 30, 1838; Washington *National Intelligencer*, n. d., in *The Liberator*, June 8, 1838.

20 Paris, *Western Citizen*, November 16, 1838, in Coleman, *op. cit.*, p. 88.

21 Nashville *Banner*, n. d., in *The Liberator*, December 28, 1838.

22 Baton Rouge *Gazette*, n. d., in *ibid.*, March 1, 1839.

23 Letter dated Macon, February 19, originally in the Franklin, Tennessee *Review*, n. d., in *ibid.*, April 12, 1839.

tee was appointed, and on March 17, at a public meeting, it reported that the rumors were gross exaggerations, and that only a few slaves had actually planned vengeance upon the whites, by the use of poison. Their fate is not known.[24] A similar rumor pervaded Louisville, Kentucky, in December and about forty Negroes were arrested. Military precautions were taken, but precisely why this concern existed is not clear.[25]

The slaves were disturbing in widely dispersed areas in 1840, uneasiness being reported from Washington, Maryland, Virginia, North Carolina, Alabama,[26] and, above all, Louisiana. In June or July panic pervaded the counties of Southampton and Westmoreland in Virginia. Military precautions were taken, and some slaves were arrested, but apparently no conclusive evidence of conspiracy was uncovered.[27] In the summer "considerable alarm" pervaded Craven County, North Carolina, "on account of a supposed conspiracy of the Negroes", and there were reports, too, from Petersburg, Virginia, of a similar nature which led to the taking of special measures of control.[28]

A few Negroes were arrested in August in Charles County, Maryland, "upon suspicion of having been engaged in insurrectionary movements, one of whom confessed that a plot had been made up to commence an attack on Washington city, ' on the night of the 30th August ' for the purpose, as was alleged, of ' obtaining their rights '." The Mayor of that city summoned civil and military authorities, and the streets were carefully patrolled. Rumors of serious impending trouble circulated.[29] One gentleman suggested to the President that he station " a

24 Greenfield, Tennessee *Gazette*, n. d., and the Boston *Post*, n. d., in *The Liberator*, April 19, 26, 1839.

25 Letter from Louisville, December 18, 1839, in *ibid.*, April 24, 1840. The writer remarks: " But all is mum in the press."

26 The trouble in Alabama in December has been observed, *ante*, pp. 83.

27 *The Liberator*, July 31, 1840; N. Y. *Eve. Post*, August 27, 1840.

28 N. Y. *Eve. Post*, August 28, 1840; G. G. Johnson, *op. cit.*, pp. 520-21.

29 *The Liberator*, September 18, 1840.

full company of U. S. troops" at the arsenal for call at any instant for: "It is notoriously true that the public mind is seriously agitated with apprehension of Negroe insurrections and that it is becoming more and more so. We have reason to know that we in this district feel that apprehension and have cause to dread its consequences." [30] The local press asserted that the danger had been magnified and that the arrest of a few whites—"vagrants"—and some Negroes restored quiet.[31]

In September and October large-scale conspiracies involving hundreds of Negroes were reported from seven parishes in Louisiana, Avoyelles, Rapides, St. Landry, Lafayette, Iberville, Vermillion, and St. Martin. Many slaves and a few whites were arrested, scores were lashed, a considerable number were executed or lynched, and at least two of the Negro leaders committed suicide.

According to the New Orleans *Picayune* of September 1, about four hundred slaves in Iberville alone " were induced ... to rise against their masters, but they were easily put down, forty were placed in confinement and twenty sentenced to be hung." Four " white abolition rascals " were implicated in this region. Six slaves were sentenced to death in Lafayette but one, Eugene, the leader, cheated the gallows by drinking poison. In addition, another conspirator of that Parish received fifty lashes, was sentenced to the stocks for two years, and to wear iron for another two years. The leader of the slaves in St. Martin also committed suicide. Two whites were held to have aided the slaves in this Parish and in St. Landry but, since Negro testimony was not legal against them, they were lashed at the command of a lynch court and ordered " to leave the state at the peril of their lives."[32]

30 T. L. Smith to President Van Buren, dated Washington, September 11, 1840, in Martin Van Buren Papers, Library of Congress.

31 Washington *National Intelligencer*, n. d., in N. Y. *Eve. Post*, September 8, 1840.

32 Other accounts in Southern papers are reprinted in *The Liberator,* September 18, 25, October 30, November 20, 1840; N. Y. *Eve. Post*, September 11, 12, 14, 1840; Niles' *National Register*, September 19, October 10, November 14, 1840, LIX, pp. 39, 88, 176. See C. S. Sydnor, " The Southerner and the laws " in *The Journal of Southern History*, VI, p. 11.

In Rapides and Avoyelles Parishes the Negroes had planned a mass flight, with Mexico as the goal, but when all preparations had been made the leader, Lew Cheney, "in order to curry favor with his master" betrayed the plot. "The fugitives were surrounded . . . carried in chains to Alexandria [in Rapides] and hung by the populace. Not only those but many who were suspected, though entirely innocent, were taken from the field and from the cabin, and without the shadow of process or form of trial hurried to the scaffold." A regiment of soldiers was required to stop the slaughter. "Lew Cheney escaped, and was even rewarded for his treachery . . . his name is despised and execrated by all his race throughout the parishes of Rapides and Avoyelles." [33]

A carefully conceived conspiracy was discovered among the slaves of Augusta, Georgia, in February, 1841. Several Negroes were arrested, as was a young white teacher named Hawes. Plans had been laid for the seizure of the arsenal and the destruction of the city by fire. At least one of the rebel leaders was executed, but nothing further is known concerning the fate of those involved. [34] Reports originating in New Orleans in July told of widespread plots in West Feliciana, Louisiana, and in the neighborhood of Woodville, Mississippi, and some slaves were jailed. They were, however, soon released and there appears to have been little foundation for the stories. [35]

Somewhat later a New Orleans newspaper [36] editorialized on the fact that " enmity between the white and black race is rap-

33 Solomon Northup, *Twelve Years a Slave*, pp. 246-48. In October an unspecified number of slaves on one plantation in Anne Arundel County, Maryland, rebelled, apparently spontaneously, seriously wounded an overseer, and resisted the police. The slaves, one of whom was shot, were all, with one exception, captured, but their punishment is unknown—*Baltimore Sun*, n. d., in *The Liberator*, October 16, 1840, and the Howard Md. *Free Press*, Oct. 17, in *ibid.*, Oct. 23, 1840.

34 U. B. Phillips, *op. cit.*, p. 486 (citing letter in private hands) ; R. B. Flanders, *op. cit.*, p. 275; *The Liberator*, March 6, 1841.

35 Niles' *National Register*, August 7, 14, 1841, LX, pp. 368, 384; *The Liberator*, August 27, 1841.

36 New Orleans *Advertiser*, n. d., in *The Liberator*, October 15, 1841.

idly maturing " and pointed to " the late repeated attacks of the
negro upon the white man in our city." These, said the paper,
" should excite our suspicions whether they be not the piquet
guard of some stupendous conspiracy among the blacks to fall
upon us unawares." The writer urged, " Let us always be on
our guard, and grant no indulgences to the negro, but keep him
strictly within his sphere." Action in line with his suggestions
was shortly taken.[37]

Maroon activity was prominent during the year. Thus, in
January, armed runaways repulsed an attack near Wilmington,
North Carolina, after killing one of the whites. A posse captured three of the Negroes and lodged them in the city jail.
One escaped but two were taken from the prison by about
twenty-five whites and lynched.[38] Late in September two companies of militia were dispatched in search of a body of slave
outlaws some forty-five miles north of Mobile, Alabama. " It is
believed that these fellows have for a long time been in the
practice of theft and arson, both in town and country . . . A
force from above was scouring down, with bloodhounds, &c to
meet the Mobile party." A month later frequent attacks upon
white men by runaway Negroes were reported from Terrebonne
Parish, Louisiana.[39]

A paragraph in a New Orleans newspaper published a year
later indicates that this maroon problem was persistent, serious
and had grave possibilities. It declared that in November, 1842
some excitement prevailed in the parishes of Concordia, Madison,

37 In October, 1841 the City of New Orleans passed a regulation forcing
all free Negroes present contrary to the law of March, 1830 (see *ante*, p. 292)
to leave, and in April, 1842 Louisiana enacted a law forbidding free Negro
seamen to disembark from their ships when putting in at any port of the
State—see *ibid.*, November 5, 1841; April 29, 1842.

38 Wilmington *Chronicle*, January 6, 1841, in *The Liberator*, January
22, 1841.

39 New Orleans, *Bee*, October 4, in *ibid.*, October 29, 1841, Lafourche, La.,
Patriot, n. d. *ibid.*, November 12, 12, 1841. Note J. Bassett's comment on
the existence of runaway settlements in Tennessee, Virginia, the Carolinas,
and Florida, in *op. cit.*, p. 78.

and Carroll, in consequence of the discovery of a contemplated rising of the negroes. There are now in the swamps of that region about 300 runaway negroes belonging to said parishes, all armed, it is presumed. Some fifteen or twenty negroes have been arrested and examined, and from the facts elicited, it is believed that an insurrection was contemplated about Christmas. The plot seems to have been extensive, embracing negroes from nearly every plantation in the three parishes.[40]

There were reports, of an incomplete and indefinite nature, of plots among slaves in Marshall County, Tennessee, and in the northern section of Alabama early in the summer, and again in Fulton, Missouri, in the fall of 1842.[41]

The remainder of the forties were relatively quiet years, though occasional reports of mass unrest recurred. There were, for example, several notices of difficulties with militant Negro outlaws. Thus, near Hanesville, Mississippi, in February, 1844, some armed planters set an ambush for fugitive outlaws who had been exceedingly troublesome. Six Negroes, " part of the gang ", were trapped, but three managed to escape. Two were wounded and one was killed.[42] In November, 1846, about a dozen armed slaveholders surprised "a considerable gang of runaway negroes" in St. Landry Parish, Louisiana. The maroons refused to surrender and fled. Two Negroes, a man and a woman, were killed, and two Negro women were " badly wounded." The others escaped.[43] Early in 1848 fugitive slaves living in the Dismal Swamp between Virginia and North Carolina were similarly attacked and a few were captured.[44]

40 New Orleans *Picayune*, November 17, 1842 ; V. A. Moody, *op. cit.*, p. 231.

41 *The Liberator*, July 15, 1842 ; The Nashville *Union*, June 28, in *ibid.*, July 22, and the Missouri *Sentinel*, Oct. 26, in *ibid.*, Nov. 25, 1842. In January, 1843 reports of an intended insurrection disturbed Donaldsonville, Louisiana, but they seem to have had slight foundation—*The Liberator*, February 2, 1843.

42 Hanesville *Free Press*, March 1, in *The Liberator*, April 5, 1844.

43 New Orleans *Picayune*, n. d., in *ibid.*, December 4, 1846.

44 *The Non-Slaveholder*, Philadelphia, May, 1848, III, p. 115.

A fairly serious outbreak occurred in Maryland in July, 1845. An account in a paper of that State declares that a group of slaves numbering about seventy-five men from St. Mary's, Charles, and Prince George's Counties set out in marching order for the free State of Pennsylvania. One of the slaves had a gun, another a pistol, and the rest carried scythe blades, swords, and clubs. They went six abreast " headed by a powerful negro fellow, sword in hand." Intercepting parties from several directions set out in pursuit, and caught up with, surrounded, and attacked the rebels near Rockville, in Montgomery County, about twenty miles north of Washington, and but fifty miles from Pennsylvania. " Several of the negroes were shot, thirty-one were captured and lodged in Rockville jail, five of them were wounded, one severely." [45] A free Negro was found guilty of complicity in this affair and was sentenced to forty years' imprisonment; one slave, a leader named William Wheeler, was hanged, and most of the others were sold out of Maryland by their masters.[46]

In the summer of 1845 there were two attempts at rebellion among the slaves of Louisiana, one in the neighborhood of Campti and the other about fifteen miles south of Sligo. In each case the slaves were armed, but the superior equipment of the master class led to the quick suppression of the outbreaks.[47]

Conspiracies and outbreaks were reported in 1846 from Florida,[48] Louisiana, Virginia, and Tennessee. The reports [49] from

45 Niles' *National Register,* July 12, 1845, LXVIII, p. 293; *The Liberator,* July 18, 1845.

46 J. R. Brackett, *op. cit.,* p. 96; Baltimore *Patriot,* n. d., in *The Liberator,* Oct. 10, 1845. In January of this year an apparently spontaneous outbreak occurred in Tennessee when several patrols broke into a meeting of about one hundred Negroes. The slaves, some of whom were crudely armed, resisted, and a general melee resulted, the precise outcome of which is not clear —Nashville *Banner,* n. d., in *The Liberator,* January 31, 1845.

47 New Orleans *Republican,* n. d., the Sligo *Shield,* n. d., in *ibid.,* August 29, September 12, 1845.

48 The plot in Florida has already been described, *ante,* p. 93.

49 New Orleans *Delta,* February 13; New Orleans *Tropic,* February 16, in *The Liberator,* February 27, March 13, 1846; letters from Richmond dated May 17 and June 4, in *ibid.,* July 3, 1846.

Louisiana and Virginia were contradictory, the earlier one giving details pointing to grave trouble, but the later accounts tended to minimize the disturbance. It is certain only that some cause of alarm did exist near New Orleans in February, and near Richmond in May, 1846. In the latter part of the year, probably in December, a conspiracy to rebel, which got no further than the destruction of one house by fire, was discovered in Memphis, Tennessee, and led to the arrests of several Negroes.[50]

An event occurred in Fayette County, Kentucky, in August, 1848, which was very similar to the break for freedom made by Maryland slaves three years before. On Sunday, August 5, about seventy-five slaves from that county, led by a young white man named Patrick Doyle, a student at Centre College in Danville, Kentucky, armed themselves with guns and crude weapons and boldly set forth for the Ohio River and liberty. A reward of five thousand dollars was offered for the group's capture and well over one hundred white men—one account said three hundred—set out to apprehend them. Two pitched battles were fought, in which one Negro and one of the pursuing white men were killed, while another of the latter was wounded. Apparently all, or nearly all the rebels, including Patrick Doyle, were finally captured. Three of the Negro leaders, Shadrack, Harry, and Prestley, were hanged, and Patrick Doyle was sentenced to serve twenty years in prison.[51] In the month of these convictions, October, a plot among forty slaves in Woodford County, Kentucky, to emulate the actions of the Fayette Negroes was discovered and frustrated.[52]

About three hundred slaves in the region of St. Mary's, Georgia, which is close to the sea and at the Florida border, had planned in July, 1849, to rebel and seize a steamboat, the *Wil-*

50 New Orleans *Jeffersonian*, n. d., in *ibid.*, January 15, 1847.

51 Lexington, Ky., *Atlas*, August 11, in *ibid.*, September 1, 1848; J. W. Coleman, *op. cit.*, p. 88.

52 J. W. Coleman, *op. cit.*, p. 106; William E. Connelley and E. M. Coulter, *History of Kentucky*, II, p. 807 (here the event is erroneously put in 1849).

liam Gaston. With this they had intended to reach the British West Indies, but a delay in the boat's arrival at St. Mary's led to the plot's exposure and suppression.[53] There were also indications of trouble at about the same time in South Carolina.[54]

53 Jacksonville, Fla., *Republican*, July 12, and the Wakulla, Fla., *Times*, July 18, in *The Liberator*, August 3, 1848.

54 In the collection of MS. Letters to Garrison in the Boston Public Library is one dated July 21, 1849 from " Placido ". This individual states that he "lived in Charleston from my birth untill (sic) a very few years [ago]," and that he is a friend of well-known Abolitionists like Robert Purvis and James McKim of Philadelphia and William C. Nell of Boston. The letter tells of a " late insurrection " in his native city, declares that three slaves, Nicholas, George, and John were sentenced to hang, and that the city guard was used in suppressing the slaves. He mentions enclosing a news item about this, but none was found. An attack on maroons in South Carolina in 1849 is noted by H. T. Catterall, ed., *op. cit.*, II, p. 434.

CHAPTER XIV

1850-1860

The pre-Civil War decade witnessed an increased straining by the Negro people against the degradation and oppression of their enslavement.[1] Statements of a general nature supporting this were made in widely scattered regions of the South during the period.

Thus, a lady in Burke County, North Carolina, observing a spirit of insubordination among her slaves, admitted, in April, 1850, " I have not a single servant at my command." [2] A Virginia newspaper in 1852 commented,[3] " It is useless to disguise the fact, its truth is undeniable, that a greater degree of insubordination has been manifested by the negro population, within the last few months, than at any previous period in our history as a State." A year later a traveller in the South observed [4] " in the newspapers, complaints of growing insolence and insubordination among the negroes." Early in 1858 a Louisiana paper [5] noted " more cases of insubordination among the negro population . . . than ever known before ", while the next year a Missouri newspaper remarked [6] upon the " alarmingly frequent " cases of slaves killing their owners. It added that " retribution seems to be dealt out to the perpetrators with dispatch and in the form to which only a people wrought up to the highest degree of indignation and excitement would resort."

Examples of such retribution with their justifications are also indicative of the current of unrest present in Southern life.

1 Reasons for this have previously been offered, *ante*, pp. 84-85, 111-12, 122-23.

2 G. G. Johnson, *Ante-Bellum North Carolina*, p. 496.

3 Fredericksburg *Herald*, n. d., in *The Pennsylvania Freeman* (Philadelphia) August 7, 1852.

4 F. L. Olmsted, *A Journey in the Seaboard Slave States*, I, p. 32.

5 Franklin *Sun*, n. d., in *The Liberator*, January 29, 1858.

6 St. Louis *Democrat*, n. d., in *ibid.*, July 8, 1859.

Olmsted tells of the burning of a slave near Knoxville, Tennessee, for the offense of killing his master and quotes the editor of a " liberal " paper as justifying the lynching as a " means of absolute, necessary self-defense." He remarks that the same community shortly found six legal slave executions necessary to the stability of its social order.[7] Similarly, a slave in August, 1854, killed his master at Mt. Meigs, Alabama, and, according to the hastily-formed vigilance committee, boasted of his deed. This Negro, too, was burned alive, by the decision of a meeting of that committee, constituted, said a local paper, of " men of prudence, deliberation and intelligence." These men acted " from an imperative sense of the necessity of an example to check the growing and dangerous insubordination of the slave population." Precisely the same things happened in the same region in April, 1856, and in January, 1857.[8] Again, on the night of August 1, 1855, a patrolman in Louisiana killed a slave who did not stop when hailed, and this was considered proper since [9] " recent disorders among the slaves in New Iberia had made it a matter of importance that the laws relative to the police of slaves, should be strictly enforced."

Probably behind these tantalizingly incomplete statements and generalizations there lurked, at least in some cases, organized schemes for rebellion. There were, in addition, numerous specific cases of conspiracy and revolt from 1850 to the outbreak of the Civil War.

In January, 1850, there was " great excitement " in Lewis County, Missouri, because of an " attempt of the negroes to run away and rise in insurrection." [10] About thirty slaves, men and

7 F. L. Olmsted, *A Journey in the Back Country*, pp. 445-46.

8 The Montgomery *Journal*, cited in the N. Y. *Weekly Tribune*, September 16, 1854, April 19, 1856, February 7, 1857.

9 Helen T. Catterall, ed., *Judicial Cases Concerning American Slavery and the Negro*, III, pp. 648-49

10 The Canton, Lewis County, *Reporter*, n. d., in *The Liberator*, January 18, 1850. The local paper's account is very full for, it said, " as many reports are in circulation . . . we deem it our duty to publish a true statement of the matter as it occurred."

women, of four different owners, had armed themselves with knives, clubs, and three guns, and set out for a free State. They were pursued by a group of men possessing thirty guns among them, and were overtaken. The Negroes halted and " made their dispositions for an obstinate defense. Their pursuers marched toward them in regular order with presented guns. When near enough they asked them to surrender—they refused." Once more the whites advanced, when John, a leader of the slaves, " a very powerful negro and fierce as a grisly (sic) bear ", armed with club and knife, rushed forth to meet them. Two shots rang out and John fell dead. " Undismayed by the occurrence, the negroes still maintained the same hostile attitude. Five minutes were given them to consider of their surrender. The women first gave up and implored the men to do likewise." They did, " were bound and brought to Canton. The leaders have been shipped to St. Louis and sold." Other slaves had fled at the same time, and " It has been ascertained that it was intended to be a general insurrection, and, to that end, it is believed that nearly all the slaves in the county had notice."

A Richmond, Virginia, newspaper reported, a few months later, " the discovery of a contemplated servile insurrection " in Monroe County, and asserted that free Negroes were also involved. About fifteen of the leaders were jailed, but the final outcome is not known.[11] Trouble, perhaps of a serious nature, appears in the terse note of a New Orleans paper that " the plantation slaves near that city manifest a spirit of insubordination, and a few nights since made an attack on the patrol." [12]

In September, 1850, several hundred former Florida maroons fled from their abode in present Oklahoma to Mexico, and accomplished this by routing a body of Creek Indians sent to oppose them.[13] Mass flights of slaves from Texas at about this time seem to have reached the stage of rebellion. Thus, an

11 Richmond *Times*, May 13, in *ibid.*, May 24, 1850.

12 New Orleans *True Delta*, n. d., in *ibid.*, September 6, 1850.

13 Joshua R. Giddings, *The Exiles of Florida*, p. 316; Laurence Foster, *Negro-Indian Relationships in the Southeast*, p, 42.

item in *The Liberator* of April 18, 1851, declares: "Galveston dates to the 28th say that a large number of negroes in Colorado county have succeeded in escaping into Mexico; and the late extensive plot was only partly frustrated." It was later reported that about fifteen hundred former American slaves were aiding the Comanchee Indians of Mexico in their fighting,[14] and it is a fact that Texan slaveholders, in the fifties, made several unsuccessful expeditions into Mexico in order to recover fugitive slaves, during which the Texans suffered several casualties.[15]

A "rumor of servile disturbances" brought the arrests and punishment (in what manner was not disclosed) of "several negroes" in Pitt County, North Carolina, in September, 1851.[16] During the same year there occurred two pitched battles resulting in "bloodshed and death" between maroons and whites in Grayson County, Virginia.[17] Evidence of considerable unrest in 1852 in Princess Anne County, Virginia, has already been noted.[18]

George Wright, a free Negro of New Orleans, was asked in June, 1853, by a slave named Albert to join in a rebellion. He declared his interest and was brought to a white man, a teacher by the name of Dyson, who had come to Louisiana about a dozen years before from Jamaica. Dyson trusted Wright, as-

14 Houston *Telegraph*, n. d., in *The Pennsylvania Freeman*, October 30, 1851.

15 Giddings, *op. cit.*, p. 334; Foster, op. cit., p. 45. Giddings declared that at the time he was writing (1858) maroons in southern Florida were again causing trouble, *ibid.*, p. 337. F. L. Olmsted gave evidence of Negro outlaw troubles in the 1850's in Virginia, Louisiana, and northern Alabama — Seaboard, I, p. 177; *Back Country, op. cit.*, pp. 30, 55. See also J. F. Rippy, *The United States and Mexico*, pp. 173, 179.

16 *The Liberator*, October 10, 1851.

17 G. G. Johnson, *op. cit.*, p. 577. In Atlanta, Georgia this same year nine slaves were arrested on suspicion of conspiring to rebel, but apparently no concrete evidence was found.—R. B. Flanders, *Plantation Slavery in Georgia*, p. 275; and letter from Professor Flanders to the present writer, October 2, 1940, clearing up a typographical error in the cited work.

18 *Ante*, p. 148.

serted that one hundred white men had agreed to aid the Negroes in their bid for freedom, and urged him to join. Wright did—verbally. He almost immediately betrayed the plot and led the police to Albert. The slave, at the time of arrest, June 13, carried a knife, a sword, a revolver, one bag of bullets, one pound of powder, two boxes of percussion caps, and eighty-six dollars. The patrol was ordered out, the city guard strengthened, and Dyson together with twenty slaves were arrested.

According to Albert about twenty-five hundred slaves were involved, but he named none. In prison he declared that " all his friends had gone down the coast and were fighting like soldiers. If he had shed blood in the cause he would not have minded the arrest." It was, indeed, reported that " a large number of negroes have fled from their masters and are now missing ", but no actual fighting was mentioned. Excitement was great along the coast, however, and the arrest of one white man, a cattle driver, occurred at Bonnet Claré. A fisherman, Michael McGill, testified that he had taken Dyson and two slaves carrying what he thought were arms to a swamp from which several Negroes emerged. The Negroes were given the arms and disappeared.

The New Orleans newpapers tended to play down the trouble, but did declare that the city contained " malicious and fanatical " whites, " cut-throats in the name of liberty—murderers in the guise of philanthropy ", and commended the swift action of the police, while calling for further precautions and restrictions. The last piece of information concerning this is an item telling of an attack by Albert upon the jailer in which he caused " the blood to flow ". The disposition of the rebels is not known.[19]

In May and June, 1854, reports of " insubordination and outbreak among the slaves " in Campti and Grappes Bluff, Natchitoches Parish, Louisiana, caused great alarm, and led to the establishment of vigilance committees. Whites were supposed to

19 New Orleans *Picayune*, June 14, 15, 16, 23, 1853; and *The Liberator*, June 24, July 1, 8, 1853, citing other local papers.

be implicated, but nothing further than the fact that sixteen slaves were imprisoned is known.[20]

There was considerable fear of slave rebellion during Easter of 1855 in the eastern shore region of Maryland, particularly in Dorchester County. Citizens armed themselves and the hovels of the slaves were carefully searched. The incident, however, was ridiculed by the press, and just what basis existed to explain the extraordinary measures taken is not clear.[21] In August of this year a slave conspiracy was uncovered in Gerlandsville, Jaspar County, Mississippi. " Several negroes " were arrested and " severely whipped." Two whites, unnamed, were implicated and it was asserted [22] that " the conspiracy extended throughout a large section of the country." A letter of October 17, 1855, from Baton Rouge, Louisiana, mentioned a " state of great excitement " there as a result of reports of Negro unrest. The news " spread like wildfire, and our citizens turned out in large numbers, armed to the teeth, and the streets and suburbs were patrolled all night." The only concrete result mentioned was that a Negro barber, Joe Craig, " president of a negro association ", was forced to leave the city.[23]

The year 1856 was one of tremendous servile unrest. The first serious trouble was caused by maroons in North Carolina. A letter [24] of August 25, 1856, to Governor Thomas Bragg signed by Richard A. Lewis and twenty-one others informed him of a " very secure retreat for runaway negroes " in a large swamp between Bladen and Robeson Counties. In that area

---

20 Natchitoches *Chronicle*, June 24 in *The Liberator*, July 14, 1854.

21 Baltimore *Sun*, April 13, 1855; Cambridge, Md., *Democrat*, n. d., in *The Liberator*, May 5, 1855; J. R. Brackett, *op. cit.*, p. 97. *The Federal Union* of Milledgeville, Georgia, March 20, 1855, told of incendiary fires set by slaves that month in South Carolina and in three counties of Georgia. Property damage was extensive and "many persons were seriously injured" —U. B. Phillips, ed., *Plantation and Frontier Documents*, II, p. 125.

22 Merion, Miss., *Republican*, n. d., in *The Liberator*, September 7, 1855.

23 New Orleans *Delta*, n. d., in *ibid.*, November 9, 1855.

24 MS. Governor's Letter Book, No. 43, pp. 514-515, Historical Commission, Raleigh.

" for many years past, and at this time, there are several runaways of bad and daring character—destructive to all kinds of
stock and dangerous to all persons living by or near said
swamp." Slaveholders attacked these maroons August 1, but
accomplished nothing and saw one of their own number killed.
" The negroes ran off cursing and swearing and telling them to
come on, they were ready for them again." The Wilmington,
North Carolina, *Journal* of August 14 mentioned that these
Negroes " had cleared a place for a garden, had cows &c in the
swamp." Mr. Lewis and his friends were " unable to offer sufficient inducement for negro hunters to come with their dogs
unless aided from other sources." The Governor suggested that
magistrates call for the militia, as prescribed by law, but
whether this was done or not is not known.

A plot involving over two hundred slaves and supposed to
mature on September 6, 1856, was discovered in Colorado
County, Texas, shortly before that date. Many of the Mexican
inhabitants of the region were declared to be implicated, and
it was felt " that the lower class of the Mexican population are
incendiaries in any country where slaves are held." They were
arrested and ordered to leave the county within five days and
never to return " under the penalty of death ", while another
white person whose name, William Mehrman, certainly indicates
non-Mexican descent, was similarly dealt with. It was reported [25] that arms were in the slaves' possession. Every one of
the approximately two hundred slaves arrested was severely
whipped, two dying under the lash. Three leaders were hanged,
while another, Frank, was not captured.

Trouble involving some three hundred slaves and a few white
men, one of whom was named James Hancock, was reported
in October from two counties, Ouchita and Union, in Arkansas,
and two parishes, Union and Claiborne, across the border in
Louisiana. The outcome here, however, went entirely unre-

25 Austin *State Gazette*, September 27, 1856; other local papers are quoted
in F. L. Olmsted, *A Journey Through Texas*, pp. 503-504. See also *ante*, p. 111.

ported.[26] On November 7 " an extensive scheme of negro insurrection" was discovered in Lavaca, De Witt, and Victoria
counties, in the southeastern part of Texas. A letter from Victoria of that date asserted that "the negroes had killed off all
the dogs in the neighborhood and were preparing for a general
attack", when betrayal came. Whites again were involved, one
being "severely horsewhipped", and the others driven out of
the country. What became of the slaves is not stated.[27]

One week later a plot was disclosed in St. Mary Parish,
Louisiana. It was believed that "favorite family servants"
were the leaders, and slaves throughout the parish were arrested. In addition one free Negro and three white men were
jailed. The slaves were lashed and returned to their masters,
but the fate of the other four is obscure.[28] One local paper declared that the free Negro "and at least one of the white men,
will suffer death for the part taken in the matter." [29]

And early in November trouble was reported from Tennessee. A letter of November 2 told of the arrest of thirty
slaves, and a white man named Williams, in Fayette County at
the southwestern tip of the State. It was believed that the plot
extended to "the surrounding counties and States." Confirmation of this soon came. Within two weeks unrest was noticed in
Montgomery County in the north-central part of the State, and
across the border in the iron foundries of Louisa, Kentucky.
Again many slaves and one white man were arrested. Shortly
thereafter conspiracies were discovered in Obion, at Tennessee's
western tip, and in Fulton, Kentucky, as well as in New Madrid
and Scott Counties, Missouri.[30]

In December plots were reported, occasionally outbreaks occurred, slaves and a few white allies were arrested, tortured,

26 Ouchita, La., *Register*, n.d., in N. Y. *Weekly Tribune*, November 15, 1856.

27 Austin *State Gazette*, November 15, 1856; New Orleans *Picayune*,
Nov. 16, 1856.

28 New Orleans *Picayune*, November 27, 1856.

29 Franklin, La., *Register*, Nov. 22 in *ibid.*, December 2, 1856.

30 Local papers in *The Liberator*, November 28, December 12, 1856.

banished, and executed in virtually every slave state. The discontent forces its way through notwithstanding clear evidences of censorship. Thus, a Georgia paper confessed [31] that slave disaffection was " a delicate subject to touch " and that it had " refrained from giving our readers any of the accounts of contemplated insurrections." The Washington correspondent of the New York *Weekly Tribune* wrote on December 20 that " the insurrectionary movement in Tennessee obtained more headway than is known to the public—important facts being suppressed in order to check the spread of the contagion and prevent the true condition of affairs from being understood elsewhere." Next week the same correspondent stated that he had " reliable information " of serious trouble in New Orleans leading to the hanging of twenty slaves, " but the newspapers carefully refrain from any mention of the facts." Indeed, the New Orleans *Picayune* of December 9 had itself admitted that it had " refrained from publishing a great deal which we receive by the mails, going to show that there is a spirit of turbulence abroad in various quarters." On December 23 it said the same thing about " this very delicate subject ", but added that there had been unearthed plots for rebellion during the Christmas holidays " in Kentucky, Arkansas and Tennessee, as well as in Mississippi, Louisiana, and Texas ", and that recent events " along the Cumberland river in Kentucky and Tennessee and the more recent affairs in Mississippi, approach very nearly " to " positive insurrection."

To this may be added Maryland, Alabama, Virginia, North Carolina, South Carolina, Georgia, and Florida. Features of the conspiracies are worth particular notice. Arms were found in the possession of slaves in Tennessee, Kentucky, and Texas. Preparations for blowing up bridges were uncovered. Attacks upon iron mills in Kentucky were started, but defeated, and in the town of Hopkinsville of that State telegraph poles were cut. At least three whites were killed by slave attacks in that same

31 Milledgeville *Federal Union*, quoted in U. B. Phillips, ed., *op. cit.*, II, p. 116.

State. The date for the executions of four slaves in Dover, Tennessee, was pushed ahead for fear of an attempt at rescue, and a body of one hundred and fifty men was required to break up a group of about the same number of slaves marching to Dover for that very purpose.[32]

Free Negroes were directly implicated as well as slaves in Kentucky, in one city of which, Cadiz, Solomon Young, a free Negro preacher, was hanged. They were, as a class, driven out of several cities, as Paducah, Kentucky; Murfreesboro, Tennessee, and Montgomery, Alabama. Whites, too, were often declared to be involved. The Galveston, Texas, *News* of December 27 reported the frustration of a plot in Houston County and stated, " Arms and ammunition were discovered in several portions of the county, given to them, no doubt, by white men who are now living among us, and who are constantly inciting our slaves to deeds of violence and bloodshed." Two were forced to flee from Charles County, Maryland, one was arrested in Obion, Tennessee, one was hanged and another whipped in Cadiz, Kentucky. The Reverend Thomas Donegan received five hundred lashes in Waxahatchie, Texas, a Mr. Hurd is reported to have suffered the almost incredible number of one thousand strokes in Arkansas, while in Lavaca County, Texas, a white named Davidson, allegedly from Ohio, was treated to one hundred blows—all for complicity in slave conspiracies.[33]

32 The data in this and in the following paragraph are based on: MS. Letter Books of the Governor of North Carolina, Thomas Bragg, no. 43, 25, 26, 1856; Richmond *Daily Dispatch*, December 9, 10, 11, 12, 15, 1856; N. Y. *Weekly Tribune*, December 13, 20, 1856, January 3, 1857; *The Liberator*, December 12, 1856; *Annual Report of the American Anti-Slavery Society, 1857-58*, pp. 76-79; F. L. Olmsted, *Back Country*, pp. 474-75; James Stirling, *Letters From the Slave States*, pp. 51, 59, 91, 294, 297-98; Laura White, " The South as seen by British consuls," in *The Journal of Southern History*, I, pp. 43-44; Harvey Wish, " The slave insurrection panic of 1856 " in *ibid.*, V, pp. 208-214; J. W. Coleman, Jr., *op. cit.*, pp. 107-110.

33 In addition many whites were driven from various areas in the South simply because of their anti-slavery feelings. See *Annual Report of the American Anti-Slavery Society, 1858-59*, pp. 4-14, 123. The decade 1850-1860 witnessed a great growth in the number of militant abolitionists. There is some

A letter,[34] passed along by whites as well as slaves, found December 24, 1856, on a slave employed on the Richmond and York Railroad in Virginia, is especially interesting because of the light it throws on white cooperation and because it demonstrates, too, a desire on the part of the Negroes for something more than bare bodily freedom. It reads:

My dear friend—You must certainly remember what I told you —you must come up to the contract—as we have carried things thus far. Meet at the place where we said and d'ont let any white man know any-thing about it, unless he is trust-worthy. The articles are all right and the country is ours certain. Bring all your friends; tell them, if they want freedom, to come, D'ont let it leak out; if you should get in any difficulty send me word immediately to afford protection. Meet at the crossing and prepare for Sunday night for the neighbourhood—

P. S.   Dont let anybody see this   Freedom – Freeland
                                           Your old friend
                                           W. B.

The next two years were comparatively quiet. In March, 1857, there occurred a fight between outlawed fugitives and slaveholders in the vicinity of Bovina, Mississippi. The reported result was the capture of three men and one woman. About this time there were acute fears of slave revolt in Prince George County, Maryland, but no overt action seems to have transpired. Similarly there were reports of " some mischief " amongst slaves in Texas in 1857, but details are lacking.[35]

evidence that one of these, John Fairfield, a native of Virginia and a white man, was active in the Tennessee plots of 1856. See, *Reminiscences of Levi Coffin*, pp. 428-446; and H. Aptheker, " Militant Abolitionism," in *The Journal of Negro History*, XXVI, p. 482.

34 Copied by Richard H. Coleman, in a letter asking for arms, dated Bowling Green, Caroline County, Dec. 25, 1856, to Governor Henry Wise, in Executive Papers, Archives, Virginia State Library. Other letters in this collection show that the Governor in December, 1856, received requests from and sent arms to fifteen counties.

35 Vicksburg *Whig*, n. d., in *The Liberator*, April 3, 1857; J. R. Brackett, *op. cit.*, p. 97; H. T. Catterall, ed., *op. cit.*, V, pp. 299-300.

A news item dated Chicago, February 5, 1858, referred to a
" fearful insurrection " in Arkansas, " said to have been incited
by two white men." According to the story, for which, be it
noted, no further substantiation has been found, twenty-three
whites and seven slaves were killed in fierce fighting, and
eighteen Negro leaders were arrested.[36] In August, 1858, about
fifty-five slaves on the plantation of an ex-First Lady of the
Land, Mrs. James K. Polk, near Coffeesville, Mississippi, decided they would no longer submit to whippings, and became
unmanageable. The overseer obtained assistance from his neighbors, but the slaves, armed with axes, hatchets, clubs, scythes,
and stones, barricaded themselves, " bid defiance to the overseer
and his friends, and swore they would die to a man before one
of their party should be whipped." One white man was severely
injured in attempting to get at the rebellious Negroes. It was
only when, after a few days, some seventy-five armed men came
to the plantation from surrounding communities that the slaves
were overpowered. All were " whipped according to their several deserts " and four, the leaders, were held for trial. At least
two, Giles and Emanuel, were condemned to die.[37]

A slave woman betrayed a plot near Clarksburg, Virginia
(now West Virginia), in July, 1859. Arms were found in the
possession of the slaves, ten of whom were arrested, but their
fate is unknown.[38] During the same month a similar event
created " much excitement " in Daviess County, Kentucky, and
resulted in the banishment of seven slaves.[39] Early in October
(prior to Brown's raid of the sixteenth) there were two pitched
battles between slaveholders and armed runaway Negroes. One
occurred in Chester, Illinois, where runaway Missouri slaves
fought valiantly for their freedom. Most of them made good

36 *The Liberator*, February 12, 1858.

37 Coffeeville *Intelligencer*, n.d., in *The Liberator,* September 17, 1858,
January 28, 1859; H. T. Catterall, ed., *op. cit.*, III, p. 358. J. S. Bassett noted
the fact that Mrs. Polk sold her Mississippi plantation in January, 1860, but
did not mention this outbreak—*The Southern Plantation Overseer*, p. 46.

38 Clarksburg *Register*, July 15 in *The Liberator*, July 29, 1859.

39 *Idem.*

their escape, but one was killed and two, wounded, were captured. At about the same time there was a minor engagement with maroons in Nashe County, North Carolina, resulting in the wounding of three Negroes.[40]

Of the indomitable band under old John Brown little may be said that has not oft been told. It should, however, be remarked that to draw the lesson from the attempt's failure that the slaves were docile, as has so often been done,[41] is absurd. And it would be absurd even if one did not have the record of the bitter struggle of the Negro people against slavery.

This is so for two main reasons. In the first place, Brown's raid [42] was made in the northwestern part of the State of Virginia where slavery was of a domestic, household nature, and where slaves were relatively few; in the second place, Brown gave the slaves absolutely no foreknowledge of his attempt. The slaves had, thus, no way of judging Brown's chances, or even his sincerity, and, in that connection, let it be remembered that slave-stealing was a common crime in the old South.

The event aroused truly tremendous excitement. The immediate result is well indicated in this paragraph: [43]

A most terrible panic, in the meantime, seizes not only the village, the vicinity, and all parts of the State, but every Slave State in the Union ... Rumours of insurrection, apprehensions of invasions, whether well-founded or ill-founded, alters not the proof of the inherent and incurable weakness and insecurity of society, organized upon a slaveholding basis.

Many of these rumors were undoubtedly false or exaggerated, both by terror and by anti-" Black Republican " politicians.[44]

40 *The Day Book*, Norfolk, October 13, 1859.

41 See, as examples, Frederic Bancroft, *The Life of William H. Seward*, I, p. 498; W. B. Hesseltine, *A History of the South 1607-1936*, p. 425.

42 For a brief notice of the role of the Negro people in that event see H. Aptheker, "American Negro Slave Revolts" in *Science & Society*, I, p. 533.

43 *Principia*, N. Y., December 17, 1859.

44 See *ante*, p. 153.

Bearing this in mind there yet remains good evidence of real and widespread disaffection among the slaves.

Late in November, 1859, there were several incendiary fires in the neighborhood of Berryville, Virginia. Two slaves, Jerry and Joe, belonging to Colonel Frances McCormick, were arrested on the charge of conspiracy and were convicted. An effort was made to save these slaves from hanging for it was felt that the evidence against them was not conclusive, and that, since, " We, of the South, have boasted that our slaves took no part in the raid upon Virginia, and did not sympathize with Brown ", it would appear most inconsistent to now hang two slaves for the same crime. Others, however, urged their executions as justified by the evidence, and necessary as an example for " there are other negroes who disserve just as much punishment." The slaves' sentences were commuted to imprisonment, at hard labor, for life.[45]

Negroes in Bolivar, Missouri, revolted in December, 1859, and attacked their enslavers with sticks and stones. A few whites were injured and at least one was killed. " A mounted company was ranging the woods in search of negroes. The owner of some rebellious slaves was badly wounded, and only saved himself by flight. The greatest excitement prevailed, and every man was armed and prepared for a more serious attack." Later advices declared that " the excitement had somewhat subsided." [46]

Early in July, 1860, fires swept over and devastated many cities in northern Texas. Slaves were immediately suspected and arrested. White men were invariably reported as being impli-

---

45 Material on this is in Executive Papers, archives division, State Library, Richmond. The quotations are from letters to Governor John Letcher from P. Williams, dated January 5, 1860 and from C. C. Larue, dated January 17, 1860. Panic pervaded Cynthiana, Kentucky in November, 1859, and reports of slave unrest were rife, but the actual facts here are obscure—J. W. Coleman, Jr., *op. cit.*, p. 112.

46 Missouri *Democrat*, quoted in Principia, N. Y., January 7, 1860. Karl Marx read reports of this uprising. See his comment and the reply of Frederick Engels, in their *The Civil War in the United States*, p. 221.

cated, and frequent notices of their being lashed and executed with slaves occur. Listing the counties in which plots were reported, cities burned and rebels executed will give one an idea of the extensiveness of the unrest and help explain the abject terror it aroused: Anderson, Austin, Dallas, Denton, Ellis, Grimes, Hempstead, Lamar, Milan, Montgomery, Rusk, Tarrant, Walker, and Wood. The reign of terror lasted for about eight weeks.[47]

And before it was over, reports of disaffection came from other areas. In August a conspiracy among the slaves, again with white accomplices, said to have been inspired by a nearby maroon band, was uncovered and crushed in Talladega County, Alabama. About one hundred miles south of this, in Pine Level, Montgomery County, of the same State, in that same month, the arrest of a white man, a harness maker, was reported [48] for "holding improper conversations with slaves." Soon, as shall be observed, serious difficulties embarrassed that region.

Meanwhile, still in August, plots were uncovered in Whitfield, Cobb, and Floyd Counties in northwest Georgia. Said the Columbus, Georgia, *Sun* of August 29: "By a private letter from Upper Georgia, we learn that an insurrectionary plot has been discovered among the negroes in the vicinity of Dalton and Marietta and great excitement was occasioned by it, and still prevails." The slaves had intended to burn Dalton, capture a train and crash on into Marietta some seventy miles away.

47 Austin *State Gazette*, July 14, 28, August 4, 11, 25, 1860. Other local papers are quoted in John Townsend, *The Doom of Slavery*, pp. 34-38; *Principia*, N. Y., August 11, 25, September 8, 27, 1860; *Twenty-Eighth Annual Report of the American Anti-Slavery Society, for the year ending May 1, 1861*, pp. 200-208. During this election year, as in 1856, many whites suspected of pro-Lincoln and anti-slavery leanings were forced to leave the South—see last cited work, pp. 192-198.

48 *The Liberator*, August 24, 1860; Laura White, *op. cit.*, p. 47; see *ante*, p. 160 for the remarks of the editor of the Montgomery *Mail* on the seriousness of the trouble in his State, and the policy of censorship that prevailed. It is worth noting that drought and crop failures brought the spectre of famine before the inhabitants of Alabama, Georgia, and parts of Mississippi from 1860 to 1861—Henry C. Hubbart, *The Older Middle West, 1840-1880*, p. 154.

Thirty-six of the slave leaders were imprisoned and the entire area took on a war-like aspect. Again, it was felt that " white men instigated the plot ", but since Negro testimony was not acceptable against whites the necessary proof to convict them was missing. Another Georgia paper of the same month, the Augusta *Dispatch,* while admitting, " We dislike to allude to the evidences of the insurrectionary tendency of things ", nevertheless did deign to barely mention the recent discovery of a plot among the slaves of Floyd County, about forty miles northwest of Marietta.[49]

A slave girl betrayed a conspiracy the next month in Winston County, Mississippi. Approximately thirty-five slaves were arrested and once again it was asserted that whites were involved. At least one slave was hanged as well as one white man, described as " an ambrotypist named G. Harrington." Somewhat later another plot was uncovered in the same State, near Aberdeen, which was to have matured on the day of Abraham Lincoln's inauguration. Those involved " were all captured and flogged severely, the leaders so severely, that it was thought they would die."[50]

Late in October a plot first formed in July was disclosed among the slaves of Norfolk and Princess Anne Counties, Virginia, and Currituck County, North Carolina. Jack and Denson, slaves of a Mr. David Corprew of Princess Anne, were among the leaders, others of whom were named Jonas, Andrew, William, Leicester, and Daniel. These men planned to start the fight for freedom with their spades, axes, and grubbing hoes. And it was understood, according to a slave witness, that " white folks were to come in there to help us ", but in no way could the slaves be influenced to name their allies. The Norfolk *Argus* did, however, report that a white man named Flynn was killed and a free Negro named Dick Smith had been seriously

49 See *The Liberator,* August 24, 1860; *Twenty-Eighth Annual Report of the American Anti-Slavery Society,* p. 212.

50 *The Liberator,* October 26, 1860; *Twenty-Eighth Annual Report,* pp. 211-212.

injured for complicity in this affair. The slave leaders were banished from the State.[51]

At the same time there was tremendous excitement in the neighborhood of Plymouth, Washington County, North Carolina. Quite a few slaves were arrested and it was asserted that the conspiracy called for three hundred slaves to set out one night and [52]

march towards Plymouth, murder & destroy all they might encounter on the road, set fire to the town, kill all the inhabitants that might oppose them, seize what money there might be, also what ammunition & weapons they might acquire, then take possession of such vessels as they required for their purpose & go in them where they might think proper ... The leader of the negroes was a man belonging to a Mr. Baker of Norfolk ... Some persons, but few however, thought those charged should have been hung without Judge or Jury. Some of the country people were said to have been so much excited & alarmed as to avow themselves as ready to slaughter the negroes indiscriminately ... The timidity that exists among the whites in the Southern country is almost inconceivable ... I have evidence sufficient to satisfy me of the correctness of your remark, that in case of a panic on the subject of insurrectionary designs, the negroes are in much more danger from the non slave holding whites than the whites are from the negroes.

Crawford and Habersham Counties, Georgia, were the locales of plots in November. In both places whites were involved. In Crawford a white man described as a northern tinsmith was executed, while the white implicated in Habersham County was given five hours to leave. The number of slaves concerned in these events is not known and, according to the local press, the

51 Material on this is in Executive Papers for November, 1860, archives, Va. St. Lib. The Norfolk *Argus* is quoted in the *Twenty-Eighth Annual Report*, p. 213.

52 William S. Pettigrew to James C. Johnston, dated Magnolia, October 25, 1860, in the Pettigrew Papers, University of North Carolina, Chapel Hill, photostat in author's possession.

rebels were merely " severely whipped ", none being hanged.[53]

December found the trouble back again in the heart of Alabama, in Pine Level, Autaugaville, Prattville, and Haynesville. A resident of the area declared it involved " many hundred negroes ", and that " the instigators of the insurrection were found to be the low-down, or poor, whites of the country." It was found that the plot called for the redistribution of " the land, mules, and money." The Montgomery, Alabama, *Advertiser* of December 13 asserted: "We have found out a deep laid plan among the negroes of our neighborhood, and from what we can find out from our negroes, it is general all over the country. . . . We hear some startling facts. They have gone far enough in the plot to divide our estates, mules, lands, and household furniture." The crop of martyrs in this particular conspiracy numbered at least twenty-five Negroes and four whites. The names of but two of the latter are known, namely, Rollo and Williamson.[54]

According to James R. Gilmore, a wealthy merchant and, under the name of Edmund Kirke, a well-known publicist of mildly emancipationist views, there existed in December, 1860, within South Carolina a far-flung secret organization of slaves dedicated to the objective of freedom. In Gilmore's words: ". . . there exists among the blacks a secret and wide-spread organization of a Masonic character, having its grip, password, and oath. It has various grades of leaders, who are competent and *earnest* men and its ultimate object is FREEDOM."

Gilmore warned one such leader, Scipio, that such an organization meant mischief. No, said the Negro, " it meant only RIGHT and JUSTICE." The slaves saw the impending war between the States and sang:

53 R. B. Flanders, *op. cit.*, p. 275; *Twenty-Eighth Annual Report*, p. 213. At about this time trouble was also reported from Louisiana, but its precise nature is not clear—See Lloyd Lewis, *Sherman*, p. 134.

54 Laura White, *op. cit.*, p. 47; and accounts from local sources in N. Y. *Daily Tribune*, January 3, 10, 11, May 29, August 5, 1861.

And when dat day am come to pass
We'll all be dar to see!
So shut your mouf as close as death,
And all you niggas hole your breafh,
And do de white folks brown!

Or, in more sober prose, Scipio told Mr. Gilmore that the South would be defeated " 'cause you see dey'll fight wid only one hand. When dey fight de Norf wid de right hand, dey'll hev to hold de nigga wid de leff." His parting words were a plea that Gilmore let the North know that the Negroes were panting for freedom and that the poor whites, too, were unhappy victims of the same exploiting system.[55]

---

[55] Edmund Kirke, *Among the Pines*, pp. 20, 25, 59, 89, 90-91, 301. Gilmore was, during the Civil War, a close associate of Abraham Lincoln. See Carl Sandburg, *Abraham Lincoln The War Years*, I, pp. 401-403, 559-560, 569; II, pp. 195-97, 285, 368, 375, 391-93, 421, 548, III, pp. 164-66. According to *The Liberator* of January 11, 1861 several slaves were arrested in Manchester, Virginia, on suspicion of conspiring to rebel.

CHAPTER XV
THE CIVIL WAR YEARS

No matter how often or how vehemently politicians and publicists might deny that the status of the Negro people was in any way involved or concerned in the War between the States, they themselves immediately sensed that their enslavement and the social order based thereon were the centers around which everything revolved. They knew, more clearly and earlier than others, that the Army of Lincoln was to be an Army of Liberation. They, therefore, assisted it. Nightly prayers arose from ten thousand huts for its success. Hourly its encampments were reached by scores of fugitives, and even early spurning could not stop the flow which soon reached flood proportions. From this came two hundred thousand workers for the Union Army —to fell trees and dig trenches and cook food and drive wagons.

Regularly came offers to serve in the ranks, and finally these were accepted. Then came twelve times ten thousand Southern Negroes to take part in the contest as to whether this nation " might long endure "; men who, in the words of their Commander-in-Chief,[1] " with silent tongue, and clenched teeth, and steady eye, and well-poised bayonet . . . helped mankind on to this great consummation ", though some forty thousand did not live to see it. And as spies, scouts, and pilots they served as eyes and ears for the advancing strangers.

Added to this wholesale flight were all the other means by which, for generations, the Negro people had fought back against enslavement—sabotage, strikes, " insubordination ", individual acts of violence, and conspiracy and rebellion. These things occurred notwithstanding the fact that the measures of precaution and repression characteristic of the slave society were tightened and added to at a dozen points, and notwith-

1 Carl Sandburg, *Abraham Lincoln The War Years*, II, p. 382.

standing the fact that the entire South was now one huge *mobilized* military camp.[2]

There is evidence to demonstrate that the years of the Civil War witnessed considerable activity on the part of militant fugitive slave outlaws, frequently operating together with the guerrilla bands formed by deserters from the Confederate Army. Just prior to the outbreak of hostilities there were reports of depredations committed by " a gang of runaway slaves " acting together with two white men along the Comite River in Louisiana. An expedition was set " on foot to capture the whole party ", but what success it had, if any, is not known.[3]

There appeared in the Marion, South Carolina, *Star* of June 18, 1861, an unusually detailed account of a maroon camp under the heading, " Runaways ". The account, in part, follows: [4]

Last Tuesday a party of gentlemen from this place went in search of runaways who were thought to be in a swamp two miles from here. A trail was discovered which, winding about much, conducted the party to a knoll in the swamp on which corn, squashes, and peas were growing and a camp had been burnt. Continuing the search, another patch of corn, etc., was found and a camp from which several negroes fled, leaving two small negro children, each about a year old ... There were several guns fired at the negroes who fled from the camp but none proved effectual. The camp seemed well provided with meal, cooking utensils, blankets, etc. The party returned, having taken the two children, twelve guns and one axe ... Means should immediately be taken for the capture of these runaways, as they are probably lurking about the place.

Confederate Brigadier-General R. F. Floyd asked Governor Milton of Florida on April 11, 1862, to declare martial law in

2 Note Lincoln's remark to John Hay, November 24, 1863: " The society of the Southern States is now constituted on a basis entirely military. It would be easier now than formerly to repress a rising of unarmed and uneducated slaves "—*ibid.*, II, p. 27. For a summary of precautionary measures see H. Aptheker, *The Negro in the Civil War*, pp. 12-15.

3 N. Y. *Daily Tribune*, March 11, 1861.

4 Quoted by H. M. Henry, *The Police Control of the Slave in South Carolina*, p. 121.

Nassau, Duval, Clay, Putnam, St. John's and Volusia Counties [5] " as a measure of absolute necessity, as they contain a nest of traitors and lawless negroes." In October, 1862, a scouting party of three armed whites, investigating a maroon camp containing one hundred men, women, and children in Surry County, Virginia, were killed by these fugitives.[6] In January, 1863, Governor Shorter of Alabama asked Secretary of War Seddon to dispatch reinforcements to the southeastern region of his State which, he said,[7] was " the common retreat of deserters from our armies, tories and runaways," and at the same time commissioned J. H. Clayton to destroy these disturbing elements.

Colonel Hatch of the Union Army reported in August, 1864, that " 500 Union men, deserters, and negroes were . . . raiding towards Gainesville ", Florida. The same month a Confederate officer, John K. Jackson, declared [8] that " Many deserters . . . are collected in the swamps and fastnesses of Taylor, LaFayette, Levy and other counties [in Florida], and have organized, with runaway negroes, bands for the purpose of committing depredations upon the plantations and crops of loyal citizens and running off their slaves. These depredatory bands have even threatened the cities of Tallahassee, Madison, and Marianna."

A Confederate newspaper noticed similar activities in North Carolina in 1864. It reported [9] it

difficult to find words of description . . . of the wild and terrible consequences of the negro raids in this obscure . . . theatre of the war . . . In the two counties of Currituck and Camden, there are said to be from five to six hundred negroes, who are not in the

5 *Official Records of the Rebellion* . . . Series I, Vol. LIII, p. 233.

6 *C. V. S. P.*, XI, pp. 233-36.

7 J. G. Shorter to J. A. Seddon, Montgomery, January 14, 1863, in *Official Records of the Rebellion*, Series I, vol. XV, p. 947; Georgia L. Tatum, *Disloyalty in the Confederacy*, p. 63.

8 G. L. Tatum, *op. cit.*, p. 88; *Off. Recd. of the Rebell.*, Series, I, vol. XXV, part II, p. 607.

9 *Daily Richmond Examiner*, January 14, 1864.

regular military organization of the Yankees, but who, outlawed and disowned by their masters, lead the lives of banditti, roving the country with fire and committing all sorts of horrible crimes upon the inhabitants.

This present theatre of guerrilla warfare has at this time, a most important interest for our authorities. It is described as a rich country ... and one of the most important sources of meat supplies that is now accessible to our armies.

Attempts at rebellion among slaves who had not managed to flee were also far from rare during the war years. In addition to several concrete instances of this one finds statements pointing to the existence of widespread disaffection and unrest, but these are couched in such general or indecisive terms as to create hesitancy in joining them with the more clearly established cases. Thus, a short time before the firing upon Fort Sumter it was reported from Charleston, South Carolina: [10]

There has recently been a stampede of about 100 slaves from the interior of this State, about which but little is said, and of which, I dare say, you will see nothing in the local papers. The demoralization consequent on the political disorders of the day has extended to the slave population. There is a manifest uneasiness in this respect.

Again, on May 30, 1861, an individual in New Orleans wrote to an English friend: [11]

The agricultural population, which in other countries furnishes the fighting masses, is here, of course, ineligible for the purpose and ever requires armed power to keep it in order. There have been very alarming disturbances among the blacks; on more than one plantation, the assistance of the authorities has been called in to overcome the open resistance of the slaves.

10 Special correspondent, Charleston, March 14, 1861, in N. Y. *Daily Tribune*, March 19, 1861. A similar item dated Savannah, Georgia, February 15, is in *ibid.*, February 20, 1861. See also *ante*, p. 160.

11 London *Daily News*, n. d., in *ibid.*, July 3, 1861.

Several reports of this nature came from Mississippi. From Jackson County in August, 1862, Governor Pettus heard warnings that no more men could be spared for service against the external foe. It was maintained that if this were not heeded [12] "we may as well give it to the negroes ... now we have to patrol every night to keep them down." Six weeks later a Confederate officer wrote his superior from the same region that there were not sufficient white men on the plantations for proper control of the slaves, and that [13] " pernicious influences have already been manifested upon many of these plantations." In the spring of the next year the slaves in Mississippi were declared [14] to be "much demoralized ... On some of the places the negroes are almost in a state of insurrection." Later in this year of 1863 uneasiness and alarm prevailed in Alabama, while in the summer of 1864 there had been " manifestations of insubordination and rebellion among the Negroes " in Bolivar County, Mississippi. [15]

Concrete instances of conspiracy or revolt come from practically all of the slave states. From January through April, 1861, there were persistent reports of unrest in South Carolina. In the first month a plot headed by a white stone cutter of Ger-

12 C. F. Howell to Governor Pettus, August 23, 1862, in Bell I. Wiley, *Southern Negroes 1861-1865*, p. 36.

13 Brigadier-General D. Ruggles to General S. Cooper, Jackson, October 3, 1862, in *Off. Recds. of the Rebell.*, Series I, vol. XV, p. 821. The Confederacy's first conscription act, of 1862, exempted one white, owner or overseer, for every twenty slaves. This was important in creating hostility among non-slaveholding whites.

14 Confederate Brigadier-General S. D. Lee to Major J. J. Reeve, Rolling Fork, April 12, 1863, *ibid.*, Series I, vol. XXIV, part I, p. 505; Harvey Wish, " Slave disloyalty in the Confederacy," in *The Journal of Negro History*, XXIII, p. 443. See also W. H. Stephenson, "A quarter-century of a Mississippi plantation," in *Mississippi Valley Historical Review*, XXIII, pp. 355 ff.

15 B. I. Wiley, *op. cit.*, pp. 67-76, gives these and several other instances in Texas, Tennessee, South Carolina, and Virginia. See also, for Louisiana, J. C. Sitterson, " Magnolia plantation, 1852-1862 " in *Mississippi Valley Historical Review*, XXV, pp. 207-209.

man descent was discovered among the Negroes of Columbia.[16] From Charleston a correspondent wrote on March 29, 1861 : [17]

A conversation, which I could not help hearing, at the Charleston hotel last night, convinces me that the disaffection among the slaves is more general than even I imagined. A member of the [constitutional] Convention, who comes from the District of Prince George, was relating to a friend circumstances of a plot which he had discovered, the ramifications of which extended for miles around, and in which the servants of some score of planters were concerned.

The leading rebels were unmercifully lashed.

There is evidence indicating an attempted rebellion near Charleston in April, 1861, resulting in the hanging of seven slave leaders. During the same month there were rumors of trouble in Lexington, Kentucky, while in May these seem to have become realities in a short-lived uprising in Owen and Gallatin Counties of that State.[18] The river counties of Mississippi, particularly Jefferson, were distracted in May by the discovery of a slave plot supposed to mature on the Fourth of July. About five whites were implicated with the Negroes. The Governor was urged not to remove militia or volunteer companies from the area and the incident set one resident " to thinking where I could be of the most service to my County *at home* or *in the army* you will see nothing but eternal Vigilance will keep down the enemy at home as well as [at] our frontier . . ." Several of the Negroes were hanged.[19] Others involved in a plot in Charles

16 N. Y. *Daily Tribune*, February 1, 7, 1861. The latter issue cites a private letter dated Columbia, January 31, 1861.

17 *Ibid.*, April 2, 1861.

18 *The Liberator*, May 10, 1861; N. Y. *Daily Tribune*, May 3, 11, 1861; N. Y. *Principia*, May 18, 1861. In May occurred General B. F. Butler's offer to Gov. Andrew of Maryland to aid in suppressing an expected servile insurrection. This aroused much opposition in anti-slavery circles—see especially *The Liberator*, May 24, 1861.

19 J. D. L. Davenport to Governor J. J. Pettus, May 14, 1861, in Executive Papers, Archives of the State of Mississippi, Jackson (note kindly supplied

City County, Virginia, again in May, got off more easily, receiving a stern warning and thirty lashes apiece.[20]

20 W. Eppes to Hill Carter, May 25, 1861, in C. Eaton, *op. cit.*, p. 105. A dozen ships were burned while at anchor in New Orleans early in May, and "there was nobody in the city who felt any doubt" that slaves were responsible—N. Y. *Daily Tribune*, May 13, 1861.

In June, 1861, a plot was discovered in Monroe, Arkansas, and three of the leaders were executed. Reports of a similar nature recurred during the year,[21] but of greater importance was the tremendous fire that swept Charleston in December and destroyed about six hundred buildings, causing seven million dollars' damage. This was generally ascribed to the slaves, and usually, though not always, to their deliberate work.[22] Several fires were set by slaves in Henry County, Kentucky, destroying "numerous houses and barns" the same month. It was reported [23] that "a general feeling of insecurity prevails throughout the entire community", and that, in New Castle, some sixty slaves had, on December 24, paraded "singing political songs, and shouting for Lincoln", while no one dared put them down.

Adams County, in the southwestern corner of Mississippi, was the center, in 1862, of a serious slave plot. The leader was a Negro named Orange, belonging to a Colonel Mosby. The field slaves had communicated their plans to nearby maroons, and it was asserted, too, that a white man, painted like a Negro,

by Dr. Clement Eaton); and other letters cited in C. Eaton, *Freedom of Thought in the Old South,* pp. 105-106. This is erroneously put in Louisiana by B. I. Wiley, *op. cit.*, p. 82. In June, according to the N. Y. *Daily Tribune,* June 12, 1861, six slaves were executed near Brandon, Mississippi after confessing to a conspiracy.

21 *American Annual Cyclopaedia,* 1861, p. 25; Memphis *Bulletin, n. d.*, in N. Y. *Daily Tribune,* June 21, 1861: G. L. Tatum, *op. cit.*, p. 38; A N. Y. *Tribune* correspondent wrote from Jonesborough, Tenn., on July 28th that great fears of rebellion prevailed and rumors concerning actual outbreaks in that State were rife, but he could offer no opinion as to their veracity— issue of August 16, 1861.

22 N. Y. *Principia,* Dec. 21, 1861; St. Julien Ravenal, *Charleston,* p. 496; C. Sandburg, *op. cit.*, I, p. 383.

23 Frankfort, Kentucky, *Yeoman,* January 17, in N. Y. *Daily Tribune,* January 23, 1862. *Ante,* p. 94.

was implicated. A few guns were found among the rebels, and several of their leaders were hanged. Their bodies were left on public display for months, the idea being to induce "docility" by adding this delightful bit to the scenery and atmosphere of the area.[24]

General Butler, stationed at New Orleans, declared on August 2, 1862, that:[25] "An insurrection broke out among the negroes, a few miles up the river, which caused the women of that neighborhood to apply to an armed boat, belonging to us, passing down, for aid; and the incipient revolt was stopped by informing the negroes that we should repel an attack by them upon the women and children." In November serious uprisings occurred amongst slaves about fifteen miles north of Thibodeaux in Louisiana.[26] The facts concerning the conspiracy in Culpeper County, Virginia, in October of this year, have already been detailed.[27]

Disaffection among the slaves laboring in the vital Tredegar Iron Works in Richmond, Virginia, sprang up in May, 1863. It is known only that "the leaders were punished."[28] Again few details are known about a plot in Hancock County, Georgia,

24 Pencilled notes of the lynch court, in possession of Mrs. Lemuel P. Connor of Natchez, Mississippi, in C. Eaton, op. cit., pp. 106-107. In this State there were two minor outbreaks in July, 1862—See B. I. Wiley, op. cit., p. 82.

25 N. Y. Daily Tribune, August 14, 1862.

26 Brigadier-General G. Weitzel to Asst. Adjutant-General G. C. Strong, dated "near Thibodeaux," November 5, 1862, in Off. Recds. of the Rebell., Series I, vol. XV, p. 172. This Union officer, General Weitzel, expressed disinclination to accept command of Negro troops on the ground that they created terror among the Confederates! General Strong, writing from New Orleans, November 6, 1862, told him that slavery, not Negro troops, brought servile insurrections, that the Negroes knew the Union Army was bringing freedom, that the slaves were in a state of rebelliousness before Negro troops were enrolled, that the terror these troops inspired in the enemy was an asset to the United States, and that the way to end slave insurrections was by defeating the Confederacy—ibid. It was General Weitzel and his Negro troops who first entered Richmond two and a half years later.

27 Ante, p. 95.

28 Kathleen Bruce, Virginia Iron Manufacture in the Slave Era, p. 399.

in October, 1863, other than the fact that as a result of its disclosure eighteen slaves were imprisoned.[29] Earlier this year, in
Florida and in South Carolina, plots and uprisings, with the
aim of getting to Union forces, were discovered and suppressed
by detachments of the Confederate Army.[30]

The conspiracy in Richmond in June, 1864, and the large-
scale incendiary activities among slaves in Yazoo City, Mississippi at about the same time have previously been noted.[31] The
uncovering of a plot in Brooks County, Georgia, in August,
1864, led to a public meeting, the appointment of an investigating committee of twelve and the hanging, at that committee's
decision, of one white man and three slaves.[32] The next month,
in Amite County, Mississippi, a group of about thirty armed
slaves was attacked, and most of them killed by Confederate
troops.[33] Plans for a widespread rebellion in the region of Troy,
Alabama, were revealed in December, 1864, and it was declared
that white men, " deserters and escaped Yankee Prisoners "
were prominent in their formulation.[34]

And that, so far as is known, was the last slave conspiracy
within the present borders of the United States, and brings to
an end the narrative of the numerous plots and rebellions that
persistently rocked American slave society for over two centuries.

29 B. I. Wiley, *op. cit.*, p. 82. The discovery by the Confederacy of alleged
plans for a general rebellion in 1863 has been referred to before.

30 See letters of Confederate officers, Major T. W. Brevard, dated Camp
Finegan, East Florida, April 2, 1863; Major W. P. Emanuel, dated Between
Ashepoo and Combahee, June 6, 1863; Captain J. F. Lay, dated Charleston,
June 24, 1863, in *Off. Recds. of the Rebell.*, Series I, vol. XIV, pp. 303, 401.

31 *Ante*, p. 95.

32 B. I. Wiley, *op. cit.*, pp. 68, 82; R. B. Flanders, *op. cit.*, p. 275. The
incendiary fire caused by slaves in President Davis' official Richmond
residence has been referred to before—p. 147. Notices of arson in the Confederacy were frequent, but it is not possible to fix responsibility for this. See,
as examples, Arthur C. Cole, *The Irrepressible Conflict*, p. 399; K. Bruce,
op. cit., pp. 359-360, 366; Kate M. Rowland and Mrs. M. L. Croxall, eds.,
The Journal of Julia LeGrande, 1862-1863, pp. 58-59.

33 B. I. Wiley, *op. cit.*, p. 68.

34 *Southern Recorder*, December 27, 1864, in *ibid.*, p. 82.

CHAPTER XVI

CONCLUSION

THERE are few phases of ante-bellum Southern life and history that were not in some way influenced by the fear of, or the actual outbreak of, militant concerted slave action. In some cases the influences were of a minor, if not of a merely formal, nature. Such appears to be the case when Southerners appealed for the annexation of Louisiana in order to take it out of the hands of a possibly hostile and apparently revolutionary France, which might use that possession as a means of arousing slave rebellion in the United States. Similar arguments were used to justify other annexations, as those of East and West Florida and Texas, and pronouncements of imperialistic designs, such as the Ostend Manifesto. Another argument, however, used in all the territorial advancements of the slave society, to the effect that the South needed new lands in order to lessen the danger of revolt by checking the concentration of Negroes within a limited area, seems to have been a rather important consideration in the minds of Southern leaders.[1]

Associated with this latter idea was the colonization movement which attempted to attack the problem of Negro concentration either by persuading or by forcing the free Negroes to leave, thus ridding the slave society of a living refutation of its rationalizations. The Governor of North Carolina, for example, was urged to further the cause of the American Colonization Society, because it might " rid us more expeditiously of our greatest pest and danger—the free people of colour." [2] It is this that explains the fact that, as has been shown, the discovery of slave conspiracies or the suppression of insurrections, as in 1800, 1816, 1831, brought a resuscitation of this colonization

1 *Ante*, pp. 33-34.

2 Calvin Jones to Governor John Owen, Wake Forest, North Carolina, December 28, 1830, in MS. Governor's Papers, no. 60, Historical Commission, Raleigh. See also, *ante*, p. 322.

movement. Thus, one of the first proposals of such a plan, that coming from New Jersey in 1772, was put forward by one moved to write because of a recent plot in his own neighborhood.[3] Yet, although most " respectable " channels of propaganda were friendly to it,[4] and although governments and wealthy individuals liberally provided it with funds, the movement was an utter failure.[5] An essential reason for this was the bitter and well-nigh unanimous opposition of the Negro people themselves to any movement seeking to remove them from their homes.

Another line of approach to the problem of curtailing Negro concentration was through restrictions on slave importations. Measures having this as their inspiration were frequently passed by colonial, state, and federal governments, as has been noted, and such action generally occurred during or immediately following periods of considerable servile unrest. But these efforts were also, in large part, ineffective, undoubtedly because of the powerful economic interests which profited by defying their provisions.[6]

The prime motive, on the part of the slaveholders of the antebellum South, was the maintenance of its type of social order. Internally, the ultimate threat to this stability was disaffection and unrest on the part of the slaves, particularly organized, militant activity threatening the order's security. Thus it came about that a basic consideration in the formulation of the legal, social, and theological aspects of pre-Civil War Southern life was how best to prevent or how most efficiently to suppress mass Negro rebelliousness.

3 *Ante*, p. 194.

4 There were exceptions. See, for example, Whitemarsh B. Seabrook, *A Concise View of the Critical Situation and Future Prospects of the Slaveholding States, in Relation to their Coloured Population*, Charleston, 1825, pp. 9-10.

5 For figures on numbers colonized see Carter G. Woodson, *The Negro in Our History*, p. 293.

6 A desire to raise slave prices was also present in moves looking towards curtailing importation.

Thus was fostered the colossal myth of the sub-humanity of the Negro, a myth basic to the entire social order,[7] and which demanded the corruption of political science, theology, and anthropology. Acceptance of this idea had to be demonstrated by all, Negro and white, in their daily behavior, their mode of eating and speaking, their demeanor, their occupations and activities, their worshipping and love-making, their every feature and phase of living had to acknowledge the immutability, indeed, the divine origin of the status quo. Failure to abide by this meant—for the white—ostracism, both social and economic, explicit warning, or overt punishment, tar and feathers, lashing, imprisonment, hanging; for the Negro, sale, torture, death.

This was the foundation. Upon this was reared the structure itself. Laws hampered and penalized the free Negro, and finally called for his removal or enslavement. They told the slave where he might go, how, and when. They forbade him to learn to read or write, or to testify against a white man, or to possess weapons, or to resist the demands and commands of his master. The slaveocracy supplied overseers and patrolmen and city guards and militiamen and volunteer armed groups and federal soldiers, but these were not always sufficient to allay the terror that ever underlay that life, like some dark brooding evil spirit, and that became reality at the first intimation—" The slaves are plotting —the Negroes have risen!" Instant action—blood, burning flesh, swaying bodies—was then the cry and nothing else would do, so that vigilance committees and lynchings were so common as to become institutionalized.[8]

7 Thus, in the House of Delegates of Virginia on January 16, 1832, William Preston said, "if those who are slaves here, were not what they are; if, Mr. Speaker, they were white men in oppression and bondage, I would rejoice in a revolution here"—Richmond *Enquirer*, February 9, 1832. And a young slaveholder admitted to a distinguished English visitor, that "if it would be proved that negroes are more than a link between man and brute, the rest follows of course, and he must liberate all his."—Harriet Martineau, *Society in America*, I, p. 371.

8 Edwin L. Godkin reported that when he mentioned lynchings in the South, " The only answer to this I found to be declamation upon the horrors

An outstanding characteristic of ante-bellum Southern economic life was its predominantly agrarian nature. Undoubtedly the fact that the institution of slavery froze billions of dollars of capital into human beings was of great importance in maintaining this way of life. But the belief that urban, proletarian Negroes were difficult to control was a factor not to be overlooked [9] in explaining the reluctance of the Southern rulers to do more than they did to bring their section's life closer into line with the prevailing trend of the nineteenth century.

Philosophically, too, the effect was considerable. It has been demonstrated that the prevalence of revolutionary sentiments and slogans frequently reached the consciousness of America's slaves and affected their behavior. The irreconcilability of a progressive political ideology with the persistence of a commercial-

that might result from slave rebellion."—Rollo Ogden, *Life and Letters of Edwin Lawrence Godkin*, I, p. 124. Frederick Law Olmsted found the same thing to be true. A Methodist preacher remarked to him in Tennessee in reference to a recent lynching of a rebellious slave: "'Had we been there we should have taken a part, and even suggested the pinching of pieces out of him with red-hot pincers—the cutting off of a limb at a time, and then burning them all in a heap."—F. L. Olmsted, *A Journey in the Back Country*, p. 446. Professor Charles S. Sydnor emphasizes the inefficiency of Southern legal machinery (since the testimony of Negroes in relation to whites had no validity in the eyes of a court) as provoking resort to extra-legal means of punishment.—See "The Southerner and the laws," in *The Journal of Southern History*, VI, pp. 3-23. Notice has been taken of the fact that servile rebelliousness at times aided the "liberal" school which believed that reforms were wise, and even led occasionally to the passage of such laws, as in South Carolina in 1739, and in Louisiana in 1795.

9 See *ante*, pp. 116, 130; Chauncey S. Boucher, "The ante-bellum attitude of South Carolina towards manufacturing" in *Washington University Studies*, 1916, III, pp. 255-56; also R. B. Flanders, *op. cit.*, p. 205. The leading proponent of manufacturing in the slave South pointed to the identity between capital and labor which he saw in slavery as its greatest virtue. Said he: "In all...manufacturing States, labor and capital are assuming an antagonistical position. Here it cannot be the case; capital will be able to control labor, even in manufactures with whites, for blacks can always be resorted to in case of need."—Broadus Mitchell, *William Gregg*, p. 143. But see C. G. Memminger's disapproving comment in a letter to J. H. Hammond, dated April 28, 1849, quoted in C. S. Boucher, *op. cit., idem*. See also Arthur C. Cole, *The Irrepressible Conflict, 1850-1865*, p. 284; and compare Kathleen Bruce, *Virginia Iron Manufacture in the Slave Era*, p. 334.

ized plantation slavery was well understood by many Southern leaders. The fear that the former would lead to the destruction of the latter did much to hasten the South in its repudiation of Jeffersonian equalitarian doctrines.[10] Back in 1794 a Virginia aristocrat pointed out that the democrats favored the common, poor people and asked,[11] " Who so poor as our slaves, who therefore so fit to participate in the spoils of the rich and to direct the affairs of the nation? " To the slaveocracy of the nineteenth century the Declaration of Independence became but the mouthings of an irresponsible and dangerous fanatic, a ridiculous, high-sounding concoction of obvious absurdities. In the words of Bishop Elliot, uttered in Savannah, February 23, 1862, the American people following the Revolution [12]

declared war against all authority ... The reason of man was exalted to an impious degree and in the face not only of experience, but of the revealed word of God, all men were declared equal, and man was pronounced capable of self-government ... Two greater falsehoods could not have been announced, because the one struck at the whole constitution of civil society as it had ever existed, and because the other denied the fall and corruption of man.

Freedom—for Negroes and poor whites—was nothing but a shadow, and an aspiration, in the South.

And the maintenance of the slave system in the South, in the midst of a nation founded upon a deep democratic faith, required—or was believed to require—repressive measures in the North as well as in the South. Silence on the subject of slavery was demanded, and an attack was made on the freedom of the mails, and the rights of assembly and petition. Negro seamen, of foreign nations and of the free states, were discriminated against and maltreated. Actions of a pro-slavery cast, like the

10 See Clement Eaton, *Freedom of Thought in the Old South, passim.*

11 Charles A. Beard, *Economic Origins of Jeffersonian Democracy,* p. 235, quoting Marcellus, *Letters from the Virginia Gazette.*

12 Quoted by W. S. Jenkins, *Pro-Slavery Thought in the Old South,* p. 240. See also the quotation from the Muskogee, Ga. *Herald* of 1856 following title page of Arthur C. Cole's *Irrepressible Conflict.*

seizing of fugitive slaves, the employment of the Army for slave control duties, the enunciation of expansionist sentiments, and the support of annexationist adventures, though distasteful to many citizens, were pressed forward.

The anti-slavery struggle broadened into a battle for the security of the democratic rights of the white people. This development was probably the most important force strengthening the entire Abolitionist movement. And one of the great causes of this was the fear of slave plots or rebellions and the measures taken to prevent or subdue them. A more direct impetus to the movement came from the fact that the acute fear of rebellion that pervaded the South, and the frequent justification for that fear in actual conspiracy or uprising, offered valuable agitational material. Surely, it was pointed out, this terror was a peculiar condition for the mental state of custodians of a delightful patriarchal system, and certainly these plots and insurrections were inexplicable modes of behavior for docile, contented " servants ". Moreover, it was asked, exactly where do bleeding backs, cropped ears, banishments and hangings, fit into the dream of the Paradise that is Dixie? [13]

It is very interesting to observe how frequent were the occasions when the slaves had received aid from white people, generally in the lower economic groups, and this notwithstanding the fact that the slaveholders deliberately attempted to weed out and to destroy anti-slavery individuals and associations. Moreover, slave rebellions themselves, and the elaborate and expensive systems of control needed for the maintenance of a slave society fostered opposition among the non-slaveholding whites to the lords of the country. The expense comprised in compensating masters of executed or banished slaves, of maintaining patrols, guards, and the entire military machine necessary for police purposes, was met in part by non-slaveholders and was often resented by them. In addition, patrol duty itself was rarely pleasant and frequently dangerous, and fell most heavily upon

[13] See, as an example, the editorial in the N. Y. *Weekly Tribune*, December 13, 1856.

poor whites who were unable to pay the fine imposed upon those who failed to perform it.[14]

The weakness, from a military standpoint, of the slave area was a prominent consideration in the minds of southern and national leaders. And, in times of stress, as during the Revolution, the War of 1812, and the Civil War, the measures taken in an attempt to insure continued subordination or to suppress evidences of unrest, resulted in serious weakening of the prowess of the South. This, as has been shown, entered prominently into the discussions, pro and con, among the dominant class in the 1850's, and down to the moment of decision, as to the advisability of pursuing the policy of secession. One of the important causes aggravating the already severe strain placed on the acquiescence of the poorer whites in continued domination by the Bourbons were certain of the precautionary measures thought necessary by the Confederacy, particularly that which exempted from military service in the first conscription act one white (owner or overseer) for every twenty slaves, and which was later changed to one for every fifteen slaves.

This study has attempted to meet the need, which has become increasingly evident in recent years, of depicting in realistic terms the response of the American Negro to his bondage. The data herein presented make necessary the revision of the generally accepted notion that his response was one of passivity and docility. The evidence, on the contrary, points to the conclusion that discontent and rebelliousness were not only exceedingly common, but, indeed, characteristic of American Negro slaves.

14 *Ante*, p. 303. Hinton R. Helper, *The Impending Crisis of the South*, p. 368.

BIBLIOGRAPHY

PRIMARY SOURCES

MANUSCRIPT MATERIAL

Boston Public Library:

The Papers of William Lloyd Garrison.

The Papers of Lysander Spooner.

The Library of Congress:

An Anti-Slavery Album of Contributions from Friends of Freedom, 1834-1858.

Autobiography of a Negro Slave (Jan. 23, 1847), Slave papers, 2, no. 24-folder Ac 342.

Floyd, John, Papers of, particularly item marked "Extract letter J. Marryatt, M.P. received per packet 18 Dec. 1823"; and letter from Floyd to Governor James Hamilton, Jr. of South Carolina, dated Richmond, November 19, 1831.

Gaines, Edmund P., to Governor A. B. Roman, dated New Orleans, November 16, 1831, Personal Papers, Miscellaneous, G.

Jefferson, Thomas, Papers of.

Jones, Roger, to (Colonel Duncan A. Clinch?) dated Washington, March 17, 1829, in Personal Papers, Miscellaneous, J.

Macomb, Alexander, to Nathan Morse, dated Washington, October 12, 1831, in Personal Papers, Miscellaneous, M.

Madison, James, Papers of.

Monroe, James, Papers of.

Trist, Nicholas, Papers of, particularly letter to Trist from Robert Carter Nicholas (letter postmarked Donaldson, Louisiana), dated October 22, 1831.

Ruffin, Edmund, Diary of, particularly vol. I, entries of December 25 and 28, 1856, vol. IV, entry of September 5, 1860.

Van Buren, Martin, Papers of, particularly W. B. Lewis to Van Buren, dated Washington, September 11, 1840.

Virginia State Library, Richmond:

Auditor's Papers, Boxes 164, 166, 187.

Executive Papers.

Council Journals.

Land, Property, Marriage Books—various counties.

Manuscripts from British Record Office, Sainsbury, especially volumes VIII, IX.

Petitions, various counties and dates.

Register of Certs. & Warrants Issued for Slaves Executed (1783-1814).

Middlesex County Order Book, 1680-1694.

York County Records, 1694-1697.

Mississippi State Library, Jackson:
    Extracts from Executive Papers kindly supplied present writer by **Dr.**
        Clement Eaton of Lafayette College.
North Carolina Historical Commission, Raleigh:
    Governors' Letter Books.
    Governors' Papers.
    Legislative Papers.
Maryland Historical Society, Baltimore:
    Letter from Stephen Bordley to Matt Harris, Annapolis, January 30,
        1739. Photostat in author's possession.
South Carolina Historical Commission, Columbia:
    Council Journals.
    Journals of the Commons House of Assembly.
    Public Records.
Virginia Historical Society, Richmond:
    Photostats of sentences passed against rebel slaves in 1722 and 1723, in
        possession of author.
Library of the University of North Carolina, Chapel Hill:
    Letter from William S. Pettigrew to James Johnston, dated Magnolia,
        October 25, 1860, photostat in author's possession.

PUBLISHED MATERIAL

The annual compilations of the acts of the legislatures of the slave
states were examined, the extensive collection in the law library of Columbia University being the depository that was used for this purpose. The
Journals of the two houses of these legislatures were also examined, material of particular value being found in those for Georgia, South Carolina,
and Virginia. In addition the following law digests were valuable:
    Delaware, Laws of the State of—to 1813, 4 vols. (Wilmington, 1816,
        Bradford and Porter).
    Georgia, Digest of the Laws of, by Horatio Marbury and W. H. Craw-
        ford (Savannah, 1802, Seymour, Woolhopter, Stebbins).
    Georgia, A Compilation of the Laws of, by Lucius Q. C. Lamar, cover-
        ing the years 1810-1819 (Augusta, 1821, Hannon).
    *Louisiana, A General Digest of the Acts of the Legislature of, 1804-
        1827,* 2 vols. (New Orleans, 1829, Levy).
    Maryland, The Laws of, 2 vols., by William Kilty (Annapolis, 1800,
        Green).
    Kentucky, The Statute Law of, to 1815, 5 vols., by W. Littell (Frank-
        fort, 1819, Hunter).
    South Carolina, Statutes at Large of, by Thomas Cooper, vols. V, VI,
        (Columbia, 1839, Johnston).
    South Carolina, An Alphabetical Digest of the Public Statute Law of,
        vol. II (Charleston, 1810), by Joseph Brevard.
    Virginia, The Statutes at Large of, by William W. Hening, 11 vols.
        (Richmond, 1799-1814).
    Virginia, The Statutes at Large of, 1792-1806, continuation of Hening,
        by Samuel Shepherd, 3 vols. (Richmond, 1835).

COLONIAL STATE AND FEDERAL RECORDS

Catterall, Helen T., ed., *Judicial Cases Concerning American Slavery and the Negro*, 5 vols. (Washington, 1926-37).

Headlam, C., ed., *Calendar of State Papers, Colonial Series, America and West Indies*—of particular value were the volumes for 1710-1711, 1720-1721, 1722-1723.

Candler, Allen D., W. J. Northen, L. L. Knight, eds., *The Colonial Records of the State of Georgia*, 24 vols. (Atlanta, 1904-1919).

Hill, Roscoe R., ed., *Descriptive Catalogue of the Documents Relating to the History of the United States in the Papeles Procedentes de Cuba Deposited in the Archivo General de Indias at Seville* (Washington, 1916).

Appendix to an Account of Louisiana, being an Abstract of Documents, in the Offices of the Departments of State, and of the Treasury (n.p., n.d.).

Padgett, James A., ed., " A decree for Louisiana issued by the Baron of Carodelet, June 1, 1795 ", in *The Louisiana Historical Quarterly* (1937), XX, pp. 590-605.

Porteus, Laura L., ed., " Index to the Spanish Judicial records of Louisiana ", in *The Louisiana Historical Quarterly* (1937), XX, pp. 840-865.

Browne, William H., ed., *Archives of Maryland*, vols. VI, XXVIII, XXXI (Baltimore, 1888-1908).

Steiner, Bernard C., ed., " Proceedings of the Provincial Court 1658-1662 ", vol. XLI, *Archives of Maryland* (Baltimore, 1922).

Carter, Clarence E., ed., " The Territory of Mississippi, 1798-1817 ", vol. V, *The Territorial Papers of the United States* (Washington, 1937).

Rowland, Dunbar, ed., *The Mississippi Territorial Archives 1789-1803*, 2 vols. (Nashville, 1909).

Clark, Walter, ed., *State Records of North Carolina*, 20 vols. (Winston, Goldsboro, 1895-1914).

Saunders, W. L., ed., *Colonial Records of North Carolina*, 10 vols. (Raleigh, 1886-1890).

Egle, William F., ed., *Pennsylvania Archives*, 2d series, XV (Harrisburg, 1890).

Hazard, Samuel, ed., *Pennsylvania Archives*, 1st series, IV (Philadelphia, 1853).

Minutes of the Provincial Council of Pennsylvania, from the Organization to the Termination of the Proprietary Government, IV (Harrisburg, 1852).

Nelson, William, ed., *Archives of the State of New Jersey*, 1st Series: " Extracts from American Newspapers ", 8 vols., Paterson, 1894-1906; " Documents relating to revolutionary history of New Jersey ", 5 vols. (Trenton, 1901-1917).

O'Callaghan, E. B., ed., *Documents Relative to the Colonial History of the State of New York*, 15 vols. (Albany, 1853-87).

Paltsits, Victor H., ed., *Minutes of the Commissioners for Detecting and Defeating Conspiracies in the State of New York, Albany County Sessions, 1778-1781*, 3 vols. (Albany, 1909).

Sullivan, James, ed., *Minutes of the Albany Committee of Correspondence 1775-1781*, 3 vols. (Albany, 1923).

Salley, A. S., ed., *Journals of the Commons House of Assembly of South Carolina for 1702* (Columbia, 1932).

Documents Containing Statistics of Virginia, Ordered to be Printed by the State Convention Sitting in the City of Richmond 1850-51 (Richmond, 1851).

House of Delegates, 1852, Virginia, Documents 21-89 (Virginia State Library).

McIlwaine, H. R., ed., *Legislative Journals of the Council of Colonial Virginia*, 3 vols. (Richmond, 1918).

——, *Executive Journals of the Council of Colonial Virginia*, 3 vols.

——, *Journals of the Council of the State of Virginia*, 5 vols. (Richmond, 1931-39).

——, *Minutes of the Council and General Court of Colonial Virginia, 1622-1632, 1670-1676 with notes and excerpts from original Council and General Court Records, into 1683, now lost* (Richmond, 1924).

——, *Journals of the House of Burgesses of Virginia, 1712-1714, 1715, 1718, 1720-22, 1723-26* (Richmond, 1912).

Palmer, William P., S. McRae, H. W. Flournoy, eds., *Calendar of Virginia State Papers and other Manuscripts Preserved in the Capitol at Richmond*, 11 vols. (Richmond, 1875-1893).

Annals of Congress . . . 1789-1824 (Washington, 1834-56).

Congressional Globe . . . 1833-73 (Washington, 1834-73).

Executive Documents, First Session, Twenty-Second Congress, No. 2, November, 1831, report of the Major-General.

Executive Documents, Second Session, Twenty-Seventh Congress, Vol. V, Nos. 282, 286, August, 1842, communications from the Secretaries of War and the Navy.

Force, Peter, ed., *American Archives, Consisting of a Collection of Authentick Records, State Papers, Debates, and Letters and other Notices of Publick Affairs* (4th and 5th series, 9 vols., Washington, 1837-53).

War of the Rebellion, The: A Compilation of the Official Records (Washington, 1880-1901, 128 vols.).

Wilson, Frederick T., " Federal Aid in domestic disturbances 1787-1903 ", prepared under the direction of Major-General Henry C. Corbin, *Senate Document, No. 209, Second Session, Fifty-Seventh Congress*, Vol. XV.

PERIODICALS AND NEWSPAPERS

(Those of particular value are starred)

African Repository and Colonial Journal, Washington, III, VII, VIII, 1827, 1831, 1832.

American Annual Register, 1830-1831, Boston, N. Y., 1832.

American Annual Register, 1831-1832, N. Y., 1835, 2d edit.

American Anti-Slavery Almanac, The, for 1836, Boston.

American Moral & Sentimental Magazine, I, 1797, N. Y.

American Museum, VI, XII, 1789, 1791, Philadelphia.

Annual Register, The, 1768, London.

Anti-Slavery Examiner, The, I, XI, 1836, 1845, N. Y.

Friend of the African, The, IX, 1844, London.

Gentleman's Magazine and Historical Chronicle, The, X, XI, XIX, 1740, 1741, 1749, London.

Austin, Texas, *State Gazette**

Baltimore: *Genius of Universal Emancipation; Maryland Journal and Baltimore Advertiser; Sun: Niles' Weekly* (later, *National*) *Register**

Boston: *Chronicle; Independent Chronicle and Boston Patriot; Columbian Centinel; The Liberator*; Weekly News-Letter*; Gazette.*

Charleston: *City Gazette; South Carolina State Gazette.*

Columbus, Mississippi Southern *Argus* (extracts kindly provided by Dr. Clement Eaton).

Edenton *Gazette and North Carolina Advertiser.*

Fredericksburg *Virginia Herald.*

Hartford: *American Mercury; Connecticut Courant**.

Huntsville, *Alabama Southern Advocate**.

Jackson *Mississippian* (extracts kindly provided by Dr. Eaton).

Lexington: *Kentucky Reporter; Gazette* (extracts kindly provided by Mr. J. Winston Coleman, Jr.).

New Orleans: *Daily Picayune*; Louisiana Courier.*

New York: *American Citizen and General Advertiser; American; Commercial Advertiser; Evening Post*; Herald; Minerva and Mercantile Evening Advertiser; National Anti-Slavery Standard; Observer; Principia; Spectator; Tribune** (Weekly and Daily).

Norfolk, Virginia *Day Book.*

Philadelphia: *Gazette of the United States; General Advertiser (Aurora)*; *Pennsylvania Freeman.*

Raleigh *Register and North Carolina State Gazette**.

Richmond: *Argus; Daily Dispatch; Enquirer*; Examiner; Recorder*; Virginia Gazette and General Advertiser; Whig**.

Savannah *Republican.*

Selma, Alabama *Free Press* (extracts kindly provided by Dr. Eaton).

Tuscaloosa, Alabama *Flag of the Union* (extracts kindly provided by Dr. Eaton).

Washington *National Intelligencer**

Wilmington, *North Carolina Chronicle.*

PAMPHLETS

Adams, John Quincy, *Speech of, on the joint resolution for distributing rations to the distressed fugitives from Indian hostilities in the States of Alabama and Georgia*, delivered in the House of Representatives, Wednesday, May 25, 1836 (Washington, 1836).

[Alexander, Ann], *An Address to the Inhabitants of Charleston, South Carolina* (Phila., 1805).

[Allen, John], *An Essay on the Policy of Appropriations being made by the Government of the United States, for Purchasing, Liberating and Colonizing without the territory of the said states, the slaves thereof ... by* a citizen of Maryland (Baltimore, 1826).

Alston, William J., *Speech of, in the House of Representatives,* April 18, 1850 (n.p., n.d.) Mr. Alston was from Alabama.

An Address to the People of North Carolina on the Evils of Slavery, by the Friends of Liberty and Equality (signed by Amos Weaver, chairman), (Greensborough, 1830, William Swaim), (Virginia State Library).

Annual Reports of the American Anti-Slavery Society, by the Executive Committee, for the Years Ending May 1, 1857, and May 1, 1858 (N. Y., 1859).

Anonymous, *Letter to a Member of the General Assembly of Virginia, on the Subject of the Late Conspiracy of the Slaves; with a Proposal for their Colonization* (Baltimore, 1801), (New York Public Library).

Anonymous, *Tyrannical Libertymen. A Discourse upon Negro-Slavery: Composed at ——, in Newhampshire on the late Federal thanksgiving day* (Hanover, 1795, N. Y. P. L.).

Anonymous, *The South: A Letter from a Friend in the North with special reference to the Effects of Disunion upon Slavery* (Philadelphia, 1856).

Benezet, Ant[hony]; *A Caution to Great Britain and Her Colonies in a Short Representation of the Calamitous State of the Enslaved Negroes in the British Dominions,* new edition (Philadelphia, London, 1784).

Brown, Edward, *Notes on the Origin and Necessity of Slavery* (Charleston, 1826).

Byrd, Richard W., *Letter from of Smithfield [Virginia], to John Tyler [Governor] Relating to a Projected Insurrection of Slaves ("Peter's Insurrection"), dated May 30, 1810* (Broadsides: Virginia, May 30, 1810, Ac 5225, Library of Congress).

Carey, Matthew, *Letters on the Colonization Society; and of its probable results, 4th edit.* (Philadelphia, 1832, first issued December, 1831).

[Dalcho, Frederick?], *Practical Considerations Founded on the Scriptures Relative to the Slave Population of South-Carolina* by a South Carolinian (Charleston, 1823).

Dew, Thomas R., *Review of the Debate in the Virginia Legislature of 1831 and 1832* (Richmond, 1832).

Dwight, Theodore, *An Oration Spoken Before the Connecticut Society, for the Promotion of Freedom and the Relief of Persons Unlawfully Holden in Bondage Convened in Hartford on the 8th Day of May, A. D. 1794* (Hartford, 1794).

Edwards, Jonathan, *The Injustice and Impolicy of the Slave Trade, and of the Slavery of the Africans: illustrated in a sermon preached before the Connecticut Society for the Promotion of Freedom, and for the Relief of Persons Unlawfully Holden in Bondage, at their Annual Meeting in New Haven, September 15, 1791* (3rd edit., New Haven, 1833).

Elliott, Benjamin, *A Sketch of the Means and Benefits of Prosecuting This War Against Britain* (Charleston, 1814).

Furman, Richard, *Exposition of the Views of the Baptists, Relative to the Coloured Population of the United States, in a Communication to the Governor of South Carolina* (Charleston, 1823), (Library of Congress).

Garretson, Freeborn, *A Dialogue Between Do-Justice and Professing-Christian. Dedicated to the respective and collective abolition societies, and to all other benevolent, humane philanthropists in America* (Wilmington, circa 1825, printed by Peter Brynberg), (N. Y. P. L.).

Garrison, William L., *An Address Delivered in Marlboro' Chapel, Boston, July 4, 1838* (Boston, 1838).

Gray, Thomas R., *The Confessions of Nat Turner, the Leader of the Late Insurrection in Southampton, Va.* As fully and voluntarily made to Thomas R. Gray, in the prison where he was confined, and acknowledged by him to be such when read before the court of Southampton; with the certificate, under the seal of the court convened at Jerusalem, Nov. 5, 1831, for his trial. Also an authentic account of the whole insurrection, with lists of the whites who were murdered, and of the Negroes brought before the court of Southampton, and there sentenced, etc. (Baltimore: published by Thomas R. Gray. Lucas & Deaver, print. 1831).

This is the main source of an account of Turner's rebellion. It appears that about 50,000 copies were issued (see *The Liberator,* December 17, 1831; The Huntsville *Southern Advocate,* December 3, 1831; Thomas W. Higginson, *Travellers and Outlaws* (Boston, 1889, p. 330), but it is now exceedingly scarce. It is not, however, quite so scarce as J. W. Cromwell (*Journal of Negro History,* V, p. 217n.), and B. Brawley (*A Social History of the American Negro,* N. Y., 1921, p. 406) make it, for they say it is not even in the Virginia State Library. The copy used for this work is located in that library, there is another in the 135th Street Branch of the New York Public Library, and one in the Harvard College Library. According to Cromwell (*op. cit.*) the Richmond *Enquirer* (he gives no date; the item was not found by the present writer) doubted that Turner used such "classically expressed" language, but no doubts were cast upon the contents of the pamphlet. W. S. Drewry (*The Southampton Insurrection,* Washington, 1900, p. 169n.) states that its sale was forbidden in the South. So far as this writer knows it is genuine.

[Hamilton, James, Jr.], *Negro Plot An Account of the Late Intended Insurrection Among a Portion of the Blacks of the City of Charleston, South Carolina.* Published by the authority of the Corporation of Charleston (2d edit., Boston, 1822).

[Holland, Edwin C.], *A Refutation of the Calumnies Circulated Against the Southern & Western States Respecting the Institution and Existence of Slavery Among Them, to which is added a minute and particular account of the actual state and condition of their Negro population. Together with historical notices of all the insurrections that have taken place since the settlement of the country,* by a South Carolinian (Charleston, 1822).

382 BIBLIOGRAPHY

Horsmanden, Daniel, *The New York Conspiracy, or A History of the Negro Plot, with the Journal of the Proceedings against the Conspirators at New York in the years 1741-42 together with several interesting tables* ... (2d edit., N. Y., 1810, reissued in 1851).

Horton, George M., *Poems by a Slave* (2d edit., Philadelphia, 1837, originally issued as *The Hope of Liberty*, in Raleigh, 1829, by Joseph Gales).

Kennedy, Lionel H., and Thomas Parker, members of the Charleston bar, and the presiding magistrates of the Court; *An Official Report of the Trials of Sundry Negroes Charged with an Attempt to Raise an Insurrection in the State of South-Carolina: preceded by an introduction and narrative; and in an appendix, a report of the trials of four white persons, on indictments for attempting to excite the slaves to insurrection.* Prepared and published at the request of the Court (Charleston, 1822).

Mann, Horace, *Speech of——, of Massachusetts on the Subject of Slavery in the Territories, and the Consequences of a Dissolution of the Union,* delivered in the House of Representatives, Feb. 15, 1850 (Boston, 1850).

May, Samuel J., *A Discourse on Slavery in the United States, delivered in Brooklyn, July 3, 1831* (Boston, 1832). The Brooklyn here mentioned was in Connecticut.

Mifflin, Warner, *A Serious Expostulation with the Members of the House of Representatives of the United States* (Philadelphia, 1793).

Miller, Samuel, *A Discourse, delivered April 12, 1797, at the request of and before the New York Society for Promoting the Manumission of Slaves, and Protecting such of them as have been or may be liberated* (N. Y., 1797).

M'Leod, Alexander, *Negro Slavery Unjustifiable A Discourse* (N. Y., 1802).

Miner, Charles, *The Olive Branch; or, The Evil and the Remedy* (Philadelphia, 1856).

Minutes of the Proceedings of the Seventh Convention of Delegates from the Abolition Societies Established in Different Parts of the United States, Assembled at Philadelphia, June 3-6, 1801 (Philadelphia, 1801).

Paxton, J. D., *Letters on Slavery, Addressed to the Cumberland Congregation, Virginia, by their former pastor* (Lexington, Ky., 1833).

[Pinckney, Thomas], " Achates ", *Reflections Occasioned by the Late Disturbances in Charleston* (Charleston, 1822).

Quincy, Josiah, *Address Illustrative of the Nature and Power of the Slave States, and the Duties of the Free States,* Delivered at the Request of the Inhabitants of the Town of Quincy, Mass., June 5, 1856 (Boston, 1856).

Rankin, John, *Letters on American Slavery, Addressed to Mr. Thomas Rankin, merchant at Middlebrook, Augusta County, Va.* (Boston, 1833).

Raymond, Henry J., *Disunion and Slavery. A Series of Letters to Hon. W. L. Yancey, of Alabama* (N. Y., 1860).

Rice, David, *Slavery Inconsistent with Justice and Good Policy; Proved by a speech delivered in the Convention, held at Danville, Kentucky* (originally published in Philadelphia, 1792, reprinted in London, 1793).

Scott, Orange. *The Wesleyan Anti-Slavery Review, Containing an Appeal to the Methodist Episcopal Church* (Boston, 1838).

Seabrook, Whitemarsh B., *A Concise View of the Critical Situation, and Future Prospects of the Slave-Holding States, in Relation to Their Coloured Population*, read before Agricultural Society of St. John's Colleton, on the 14th of September, 1825, and published at their request (Charleston, 1825, 2d edit.) Rare Book room, Library of Congress.

Stevens, Thaddeus, *Speech of——, Pennsylvania, in the House of Representatives, Feb. 20, 1850* (N.P., n.d.).

[Townsend, John], *The Doom of Slavery in the Union: Its Safety Out Of It* (Charleston, 1860).

Tucker, St. George, *A Dissertation on Slavery: With a Proposal for the Gradual Abolition of It, in the State of Virginia* (Philadelphia, 1796).

Virginia Slavery Debate of 1832 (bound volume of pamphlets in Virginia State Library, printed in Richmond, 1832, by T. W. White), containing the letters of " Appomattox " (B. W. Leigh) to the people of Virginia; and the speeches of Henry Berry of Jefferson, Jan. 20; P. A. Bolling of Buckingham, Jan. 11; W. H. Brodnax of Dinwiddie, Jan. 19; J. T. Brown of Petersburg, Jan. 18; J. A. Chandler of Norfolk, Jan. 17; C. J. Faulkner of Berkeley, Jan. 20; J. McDowell, Jr., of Rockbridge, Jan. 21; T. Marshall of Fauquier, Jan. 14; T. J. Randolph of Albemarle, Jan. 21; and an appendix by W. H. Brodnax explaining his colonization bill.

Walker's (David) *Appeal, in four articles together with a preamble to the coloured citizens of the world, but in particular, and very expressly to those of the United States of America, written in Boston, State of Massachusetts, September 28, 1829.* (Three editions, Boston, 1829-30—located in Boston Public Library).

Warner, Samuel, *Authentic and Impartial Narrative of the Tragical Scene which was witnessed in Southampton County (Virginia), on Monday the 22d of August last* (N. Y., 1831).

[Weld, Theodore D.], *American Slavery As It Is: The Testimony of One Thousand Witnesses* (N. Y., 1839).

Whipple, Charles K., *The Non-Resistance Principle: with particular application to the help of slaves by abolitionists* (Boston, 1860).

Williams, Thomas, *The Negro in American Politics. A Speech delivered at Lafayette Hall, Pittsburgh, Sept. 29, 1860* (Pittsburgh, n.d.).

Wright, Elizur, *The Lesson of St. Domingo How to make the war short and the peace righteous* (Boston, 1861).

Wright, Henry C., *The Natick Resolution; or, resistance to slaveholders the right and duty of southern slaves and northern freemen* (Boston, 1859).

[Young, Robert A.], *The Ethiopian Manifesto, Issued in defence of the Black Man's Rights, in the scale of universal freedom* (N. Y., 1829).

LETTERS, DIARIES, MEMOIRS

Adams, Charles F., ed., *Memoirs of John Quincy Adams Comprising Portions of his Diary from 1795 to 1848*, 12 vols. (Phila., 1874-77).

——, *Letters of Mrs. Adams, the Wife of John Adams*, 2 vols. (Boston, 1841).

——, *The Works of John Adams*, 10 vols. (Boston, 1856).

American Historical Review, I (1895), p. 89, " Letter from Col. William Byrd to Lord Egmont, July 12, 1736."

American Historical Review, XVI, (1910), pp. 64-101, " Letters of Toussaint Louverture and of Edward Stevens, 1798-1800."

Asbury, Rev. Francis, *The Journal of, Bishop of the Methodist Episcopal Church*, 3 vols. (n.d., N. Y., Cincinnati).

Barker, Eugene C., ed., *The Austin Papers, October 1834-January 1837*, III (Austin, n.d.).

Bassett, J. S., ed., *Southern Plantation Overseer as Revealed in his Letters* (Northampton, 1925).

Bowers, Claude G., ed., *The Diary of Elbridge Gerry, Jr.* (N.Y., 1927).

Brock, Robert A., ed., *The Official Records of Robert Dinwiddie, Lieutenant-Governor of Virginia 1751-1758*, 2 vols. (Richmond, 1884).

" Brown, William L., Diary of ", printed in the Clarksville (Tenn.) *Leaf-Chronicle*, weekly edition, October 5-26, 1916 (MS. Room, N. Y. P. L.).

Burke, Emily P., *Reminiscences of Georgia* (Oberlin, 1850).

Calendar of the Correspondence of James Monroe, Bulletin of the Bureau of Rolls and Library of the Department of State (Washington, 1893).

Cobbett, William, *Porcupine's Works; Containing Various Writings and Selections, Exhibiting a Faithful Picture of the U. S. A.*, 12 vols. (London, 1801).

Coffin, Levi, *Reminiscences of, the Reputed President of the Underground Railroad; being a brief history of the labors of a lifetime in behalf of the slave*, etc. (London, Cincinnati, 1876).

Colden, Cadwalleder, *The Letters and Papers of —*, 9 vols. (N. Y., 1932-37).

Coleman, G. P., ed., *Virginia Silhouettes: Contemporary Letters Concerning Negro Slavery in the State of Virginia* (Richmond, 1934).

Collections of the Connecticut Historical Society, XXI, " The Wyllys Papers " (Hartford, 1924).

Collections of the South-Carolina Historical Society, I, p. 252, " Abstract of a letter of June 24, 1720 " (Charleston, 1857).

Ibid., II, p. 270, " Letter from William Bull, Oct. 5, 1739 " (Charleston, 1858).

Donnan, Elizabeth, ed., " Papers of James Bayard, 1796-1815 ", *Annual Report of the American Historical Association for 1913* (Washington, 1915).

Ford, Paul L., ed., *The Writings of Thomas Jefferson* (N. Y., 1892-99, 10 vols.).

Fitzpatrick, John C., ed., *The Diaries of George Washington* (Boston, 1929, 4 vols.).

Ford, Worthington C., ed., *The Writings of George Washington* (N. Y., 1889-1893, 14 vols.).

——, "Letters of William Vans Murray to John Q. Adams", *Annual Report of American Historical Association, 1912* (Washington, 1914).

Galpin, W. F., ed., "Conditions in Savannah during the War of 1812", in *The Georgia Historical Quarterly,* 1924, VIII, pp. 325-26.

Hamilton, Stanislaus, ed., *The Writings of James Monroe* (N. Y., 1898-1903, 7 vols.).

Hoes, R. R., "Letter of June 23, 1712", *New York Genealogical and Biographical Record,* 1890, XXI, pp. 162-63.

Hunt, Gaillard, ed., *The Writings of James Madison* (N. Y., 1900-1910, 9 vols.).

Jones, J. B., *A Rebel War Clerk's Diary* (Swiggett, ed., N. Y., 1935, 2 vols.).

Kemble, Frances A., *Journal of a Residence on a Georgian Plantation in 1838-1839* (London, 1863).

Jameson, J. F., ed., "Diary of Edward Hooker", *Annual Report of the American Historical Association for the Year 1896,* I (Washington, 1897).

King, Charles, ed., *Life and Correspondence of Rufus King* (N. Y., 1897, 6 vols.).

"Lee, Charles The —— Papers", *Collections of the New York Historical Society* (4 vols, 1871-74).

Lodge, Henry C., ed., *Works of Alexander Hamilton* (N. Y., London, 1904, 12 vols.).

Martin, Isabella D., and M. L. Avery, eds., *A Diary from Dixie, As Written by Mary Boykin Chesnut* (N. Y., 1905).

"Mason, Jonathan, Diary of the Hon.", in *Proceedings of the Massachusetts Historical Society, 1885-86,* Second Series, II.

Nicolay, John G., and John Hay, eds., *Abraham Lincoln, Complete Works, Comprising his Speeches, Letters, State Papers, and Miscellaneous Writings,* 2 vols. (N. Y., 1920).

Northrup, Solomon, *Narrative of ——; Twelve Years a Slave, Kidnapped and Rescued in 1853, from a Cotton Plantation near the Red River, in Louisiana* (Auburn, Buffalo, London, 1853).

Phillips, U. B., ed., "The Correspondence of Robert Toombs, Alexander H. Stephens, and Howell Cobb", *Annual Report of the American Historical Association for 1911,* 2 vols. (Washington, 1913).

Phillips, U. B., and James D. Glunt, eds., *Florida Plantation Records from the Papers of George Noble Jones* (St. Louis, 1927).

Pickard, Kate E. R., *The Kidnapped and the Ransomed, being the Personal Recollections of Peter Still and his wife, Vina, after Forty Years of Slavery* (3rd edit., Syracuse, Auburn, N. Y., 1856).

Prentiss, S. S., *A Memoir of, edited by his brother,* 2 vols. (N. Y., 1856).

Richardson, James D., ed.; *The Messages and Papers of the Presidents* (N. Y., 1897, Vols. I-VIII).

Rowland, Dunbar, ed., *Official Letter Books of W. C. C. Claiborne, 1801-1816,* 6 vols. (Jackson, 1917).

Rowland, D., ed., *Jefferson Davis Constitutionalist His Letters, Papers and Speeches*, 10 vols. (Jackson, 1923).

Rowland, Kate M., and M. L. Croxall, eds., *The Journal of Julia Le Grand* (Richmond, 1911).

Russell, William H., *My Diary North and South* (Boston, 1863).

South Carolina Historical and Genealogical Magazine, The (1903), IV, p. 209. " Letter from Henry Laurens to Stephen Bull, March 16, 1776."

South Carolina Historical and Genealogical Magazine, The (1907), VIII, pp. 7-8. " Letter from Lafayette to H. Laurens, March 11, 1778."

South Carolina Historical and Genealogical Magazine, The (1930), XXXI, p. 219, " Letter from H. Laurens to James Coles, March 21, 1748."

Steward, Austin, *Twenty-Two Years a Slave and Forty Years a Freeman* (Rochester, 1857).

Uhlendorf, Bernhard A., ed., *The Seige of Charleston with an Account of the Province of South Carolina: Diaries and Letters of Hessian Officers from the von Jungkenn Papers* (University of Michigan Publication on History, XII, Ann Arbor, 1938).

Virginia Historical Register and Literary Notebook, The (Richmond, 1851), IV, p. 63—speech of Governor Drysdale, 1723.

Virginia Magazine of History and Biography (Richmond, 1924), XXXII, pp. 322-23—Governor Gooch's letters to the Bishop of London, 1727-49.

Virginia Magazine of History and Biography (1928), XXXVI—Virginia Council Journals, 1726, 1753.

Wagstaff, H. H., ed., " The Harris Letters ", in *The James Sprunt Historical Publications*, vol. XIV, no. 1, Durham, 1916.

Washington, H. A., ed., *The Writings of Thomas Jefferson*.

William and Mary College Quarterly Historical Magazine (1900), 1st Series, VIII, p. 219, letter from Williamsburg, April 8, 1806.

William and Mary College Quarterly Historical Magazine (1912), XX, p. 275, letter from John J. Maund, Richmond, November 9, 1793.

William and Mary College Quarterly Historical Magazine (1901), X, pp. 5-24, " Missouri Compromise. Letters to James Barbour, Senator of Virginia in the Congress of the United States."

Williams, John R., ed., *Philip Vickers Fithian Journal and Letters, 1767-1774*, I (Princeton, 1900).

Wright, L. B., and M. Tinling, eds., *The Secret Diary of William Byrd of Westover, 1709-1712* (Richmond, 1941).

TRAVEL ACCOUNTS AND CONTEMPORARY HISTORIES

Abbott, John S. C., *South and North; or, Impressions Received during a Trip to Cuba and the South* (N. Y., 1860).

Abdy, E. S., *Journal of a Residence and Tour in the United States from April, 1833, to October, 1834* (3 vols., London, 1835).

Adams, Nehemiah, *A South-Side View of Slavery; or, Three Months at the South, in 1854* (Boston, N. Y., 1855, 3rd edit.).

Andrews, E. A., *Slavery and the Domestic Slave-Trade in the United States* (Boston, 1836).

Aughey, John H., *The Iron Furnace; or, Slavery and Secession* (Philadelphia, 1863).

Baily, Francis, *Journal of a Tour in Unsettled Parts of North America in 1796 & 1797* (London, 1856).

Bernard, John, *Retrospections of America, 1797-1811,* edited from the manuscript of Mrs. Bayle Bernard with an introduction, notes, and index by Laurence Hutton and Brander Matthews (N. Y., 1887).

Birkbeck, Morris, *Notes on a Journey in America, from the Coast of Virginia to the Territory of Illinois* (2d edit., London, 1818).

Blane, W. W., *An Excursion through the United States and Canada during the Years 1822-1823, by an English gentleman* (London, 1824).

Bremer, Frederika, *The Homes of the New World Impressions of America* (3 vols., trans. M. Howitt, London, 1853).

Buckingham, James S., *The Slave States of America* (2 vols., London, Paris, 1842).

Chambers, William, *American Slavery and Colour* (London, N. Y., 1857).

Cobb, Joseph B., *Mississippi Scenes; or, Sketches of Southern and Western Life and Adventure* (Phila., 1851).

Davis, John, *Travels of Four Years and a Half in the United States during 1798, 1799, 1800, 1801, and 1802* (first published, London, 1803; N. Y., 1909).

DeBow, J. D. B., ed., *The Industrial Resources, etc., of the Southern and Western States* (3 vols., New Orleans, 1852).

Drew, Benjamin, *A North-Side View of Slavery. The Refugee; or the Narratives of Fugitive Slaves in Canada related by themselves* (Boston, N. Y., Cleveland, London, 1856).

Dumond, Dwight L., ed., *Southern Editorials on Secession* (N. Y., London, 1931).

Elliot, E. N., ed., *Cotton is King and Pro-Slavery Arguments* (Augusta, 1860).

Enmale, Richard, ed., *The Civil War in the United States,* by Karl Marx and Frederick Engels (N. Y., 1937).

Ferrall, S. A., *A Ramble of Six Thousand Miles Through the United States of America* (London, 1832).

Gilmore, James R. (Edmund Kirke), *Among the Pines; or, South in Secession-Times* (N. Y., 1862).

Goodwin, Thomas S., *The Natural History of Secession; or Despotism, and Democracy at Necessary, Eternal Exterminating War* (N. Y., 1865, c. 1864).

Hall, Basil, *Travels in North America, in the Years 1827 and 1828* (3 vols., 3rd edit., Edinburgh, London, 1830).

Helper, Hinton R., *The Impending Crisis of the South* (N. Y., 1860).

Hewatt, Alexander, *An Historical Account of the Rise and Progress of the Colonies of South Carolina and Georgia* (2 vols., London, 1779).

Hildreth, Richard, *Despotism in America; an Inquiry into the Nature, Results, and Legal Basis of the Slave-Holding System in the United States* (Boston, Cleveland, London, 1854).

Howard, H. R., *The History of Virgil A. Stewart, and his Adventure in Capturing and Exposing the great "Western Land Pirate" and his gang . . . also of the trials, confessions, and execution of a number of Murrell's associates in the State of Mississippi during the Summer of 1835* . . . (N. Y., 1836).

Ingraham, Joseph H., *The Southwest by a Yankee* (2 vols., N. Y., 1835).

Janson, Charles W., *The Stranger in America: Containing Observations Made During a Long Residence in that Country* (London, 1807).

Lac, Perrin du, *Travels Through the Two Louisianas and among the Savage Nations of the Missouri* (translated and published, London, 1807, Vol. VI of A Collection of Modern and Contemporary Voyages).

Liancourt, Duke de la Rochefoucault, *Travels through the United States of North America, the country of the Iroquois, and Upper Canada, in the Years 1795-1797* (translated by H. Neuman, 2 vols., London, 1799).

Martineau, Harriet, *Society in America* (2 vols., 4th edit., N. Y., London, 1837).

Martyn, Benjamin, " An impartial inquiry into the state and utility of the province of Georgia. London: 1741 " in *Collections of the Georgia Historical Society* (Savannah, 1840), I, pp. 170-73.

——, " An account, showing the progress of the colony of Georgia, in America, from its first establishment ", *Collections of the Georgia Historical Society* (1841), II, pp. 301-302.

Olmsted, Frederick L., *A Journey in the Seaboard Slave States in the Years 1853-1854 with remarks on their economy*, originally issued in 1856, with a biographical sketch by F. L. Olmsted, Jr., and an introduction by William P. Rent, 2 vols. (N. Y., London, 1904).

——, *A Journey in the Back Country* (London, 1860).

——, *A Journey through Texas; or, a Saddle-Trip on the Southwestern Frontier: with a statistical appendix* (N. Y., 1860).

Parkinson, Richard, *The Experienced Farmer's Tour in America: Exhibiting in a Copious and Familiar View, the American System of Agriculture* (2 vols., London, 1805).

Phillips, Ulrich B., ed., *Plantation and Frontier Documents: 1649-1863* (2 vols., Cleveland, 1909).

——, " The public archives of Georgia ", *Annual Report of the American Historical Association for the Year 1903*, I (Washington, 1904).

Pratz, Le Page Du, *The History of Louisiana, and of the Western Parts of Virginia and Carolina* (new edit., London, 1774).

Priest, William, *Travels in the United States of America, Commencing in the Year 1793, and ending in 1797* (London, 1902).

Proceedings of the New Jersey Historical Society, 1874, p. 179—sentence of Negro rebels, 1741.

Redpath, James, *The Roving Editor; or, Talks with Slaves in the Southern States* (N. Y., 1859).

Russell, William H., *Pictures of Southern Life, Social, Political, and Military* (N. Y., 1861).

Stirling, James, *Letters from the Slave States* (London, 1857).

Stoddard, Amos, *Sketches, Historical and Descriptive of Louisiana* (Phila., 1812).

Strickland, W., *Observations on the Agriculture of the United States of America* (London, 1801).

Stuart, James, *Three Years in North America* (2 vols., Edinburgh, London, 1833).

Sutcliff, Robert, *Travels in Some Parts of North America in the Years 1804, 1805 & 1806* (York, London, 1811).

Torrey, Jesse, Jr., *A Portraiture of Domestic Slavery in the United States with reflections on the practicability of restoring the moral rights of the slave, without impairing the legal privileges of the possessor*, etc., (Phila., 1817).

Weld, Isaac, Jr., *Travels through the States of North America, and the Provinces of Upper and Lower Canada, during the years 1795, 1796, and 1797* (2 vols., London, 1799, 2d edit.).

William and Mary College Quarterly Historical Magazine (1901-02), X, pp. 177-78. Sentence of a Negro rebel, 1688.

SECONDARY SOURCES

Abernethy, Thomas P., *From Frontier to Plantation in Tennessee; A Study in Frontier Democracy* (Chapel Hill, 1932).

Adams, Alice D., *The Neglected Period of Anti-Slavery Agitation in America, 1808-1831* (Radcliffe College Monograph, No. 14, Boston, London, 1908).

Adams, Henry, *History of the United States During the Administrations of Jefferson and Madison*, 9 vols. (N. Y., 1890-91).

——, *John Randolph*, being volume XVI of *American Statesmen*, edited by John T. Morse, Jr. (Boston, N. Y., 1882).

Adams, James T., *Provincial Society, 1690-1763*, being volume III of *A History of American Life*, edited by D. R. Fox and A. M. Schlesinger (N. Y., 1927).

Alexander, Herbert B., " Brazilian and United States slavery compared ", in *The Journal of Negro History*, 1922, VII, pp. 349-364.

Ambler, Charles H., *Sectionalism in Virginia from 1776 to 1861* (Chicago, 1910).

——, *Thomas Ritchie, A Study in Virginia Politics* (Richmond, 1913).

——, *George Washington and the West* (Chapel Hill, 1936).

——, " Life of John Floyd ", in *John P. Branch. Historical Papers of Randolph-Macon College*, V, 1918.

Ames, Susie M., *Studies of the Virginia Eastern Shore in the Seventeenth Century* (Richmond, 1940).

Anderson, Dice R., *William Branch Giles: A Study in the Politics of Virginia and the Nation from 1790 to 1832* (Menasha, 1914).

Andrews, Matthew P., *Virginia The Old Dominion* (Garden City, 1937).

Anonymous, " Negro plot in New York, 1741 ", in *The National Magazine, A monthly journal of American history*, 1893, XVIII, pp. 128-131.

——, "Richmond Light Infantry Blues, of Richmond, Va." in *Tyler's Quarterly Historical and Genealogical Magazine*, 1919, I, pp. 1-14.

Aptheker, Herbert, "American Negro Slave Revolts", in *Science & Society*, 1937, 1938, I, pp. 512-538, II, pp. 386-392.

——, "Nat Turner's Revolt: the environment, the event, the effects", unpublished master's thesis, Columbia University, 1937.

——, "Negro History: A cause for optimism", in *Opportunity*, August, 1941, p. 228-31.

——, "Militant Abolitionism", in *The Journal of Negro History* (1941), XXVI, pp. 438-484.

——, *The Negro in the Civil War* (N. Y., 1938).

——, *Negro Slave Revolts in the United States, 1526-1860* (N. Y., 1939).

——, "Maroons within the present limits of the United States", in the *Journal of Negro History* (1939), XXIV, pp. 167-184.

——, "The Quakers and Negro Slavery", in *The Journal of Negro History* (1940), XXV, pp. 331-362.

——, *The Negro in the American Revolution* (N. Y., 1940).

——, "They bought their way to freedom", in *Opportunity*, June, 1940, pp. 180-82.

Armstrong, Margaret, *Fanny Kemble A Passionate Victorian* (N. Y., 1938).

Asbury, Herbert, *A Methodist Saint, The Life of Bishop Asbury* (N. Y., 1927).

Ashe, Samuel A., *History of North Carolina*, 2 vols. (Greensboro, 1908).

—— and L. G. Tyler, *Secession, Insurrection of the Negroes and Northern Incendiarism* (revised and reprinted from *Tyler's Quarterly Historical and Genealogical Magazine*, July, 1933).

Atkinson, Joseph, *The History of Newark, New Jersey, being a Narrative of Its Rise and Progress* (Newark, 1878).

Baker-Crothers, Hayes, *Virginia and the French & Indian War* (Chicago, 1928).

Baldwin, Alice M., *The New England Clergy and the American Revolution* (Durham, 1928).

Ballagh, James C., *A History of Slavery in Virginia* (Baltimore, 1902, Johns Hopkins University Studies, extra volume XXIV).

——, "Anti-slavery sentiment", *South Atlantic Quarterly*, 1902, I, pp. 107-117.

Bancroft, Frederic, *The Life of William H. Seward*, 2 vols. (N. Y., London, 1900).

——, *Slave-Trading in the Old South* (Baltimore, 1931).

Barber, J. W., *Incidents in American History* (N. Y., 1847).

Barker, Charles A., *The Background of the Revolution in Maryland*, Yale Historical Publications, XXXVIII, edited by L. W. Labaree (New Haven, 1940).

Barnes, Gilbert H., *The Anti-Slavery Impulse, 1830-1844* (N. Y., London, 1933).

Bassett, John S., *Slavery and Servitude in the Colony of North Carolina* (Baltimore, 1896, Johns Hopkins University Studies, XIV).

——, *Slavery in the State of North Carolina* (Baltimore, 1899, Johns Hopkins University Studies XVII).

——, *The Life of Andrew Jackson* (2 vols. N. Y., 1916).

Bassett, John S., *The Federalist System, 1789-1801*, being volume XI of *The American Nation Series*, edited by Albert B. Hart (N. Y., London, 1906).

Batten, J. M., " Governor John Floyd " in *John P. Branch Historical Papers of Randolph-Macon College*, 1913, IV.

Bauer, R. A. and A. H., " Day to Day Resistance to Slavery," in *The Journal of Negro History* (1942), XXVII, pp. 388-419.

Beard, Charles and Mary, *The Rise of American Civilization* (new edition, two volumes in one, N. Y., 1936).

Beard, Charles A., *Economic Origins of Jeffersonian Democracy* (N. Y., 1915).

Bell, Landon C., *The Old Free State, A Contribution to the History of Lunenberg County and Southside Virginia*, 2 vols. (Richmond, 1927).

Bell, Whitfield, J., Jr., " The relation of Herndon and Gibbon's Exploration of the Amazon to North American slavery, 1850-1855 ", in *The Hispanic American Historical Review* (1939), XIX, pp. 494-503.

[Bibb, Henry?], *The Late Contemplated Insurrection in Charleston, S. C., with the Execution of Thirty-Six of the Patriots: the Death of William Irving, the Provoked Husband: and Joe Devaul, for Refusing to be the slave of Mr. Roach: with the Capture of the American Slaver Trading between the Seat of Government and New Orleans: together with an Account of the Capture of the Spanish Schooner Amistad.* By a Colored American (N. Y., 1850), in Library of Congress.

Biel, H., " Class conflicts in the Old South, 1850-1860 ", in *The Communist* (1939), XVIII, pp. 170-181, 274-79.

Billington, Ray A., *The Protestant Crusade, 1800-1860* (N. Y., 1938).

Bontemps, Arna, *Black Thunder* (N. Y., 1936).

Booth, Mary L., *History of the City of New York* (2 vols., N. Y., 1867).

Boucher, Chauncey S., " The ante-bellum attitude of South Carolina towards manufacturing ", *Washington University Studies*, 1916, III, pp. 243-270.

Bouve, P. C., *The Shadows Before* (Boston, 1899).

Brackett, Jeffrey R., *The Negro in Maryland A Study of the Institution of Slavery* (Baltimore, 1889, Johns Hopkins University Studies, extra volume VI).

Brawley, Benjamin, *The Negro Genius A New Appraisal of the Achievement of the American Negro in Literature and the Fine Arts* (N.Y., 1937).

——, *Negro Builders and Heroes* (Chapel Hill, 1937).

——, *A Social History of the American Negro Being a History of the Negro Problem in the United States* (N. Y., 1921).

Brevard, Caroline M., *A History of Florida from the Treaty of 1763 to our Own Times*, edited by J. A. Robertson (2 vols., Deland, 1924).

Bridenbaugh, Carl, *Cities in the Wilderness, 1625-1742* (N. Y., 1938).

Brookes, George S., *Friend Anthony Benezet* (Phila., 1937).

Brothers, Thomas, *The United States of North America as They Are: Not as They Are Generally Described: being a cure for Radicalism* (London, 1840).

Brown, John H., *History of Texas from 1685 to 1892* (2 vols., St. Louis, 1893).

Brown, Sterling A., "Unhistoric history" in *The Journal of Negro History,* 1930, XV, pp. 134-161.

Bruce, Kathleen, *Virginia Iron Manufacture in the Slave Era* (N. Y., London, 1937).

Bruce, Philip A., *Institutional History of Virginia in the Seventeenth Century, An Inquiry into the Religious, Moral, Educational, Legal, Military, and Political Condition of the People based on Original and Contemporaneous Records* (N. Y., London, 1910, 2 vols.).

——, *Economic History of Virginia in the Seventeenth Century,* (2 vols., N. Y., 1896).

Bruce, William C., *Below the James, A Plantation Sketch* (N. Y., 1918).

——, *John Randolph of Roanoke, 1773-1833* (2 vols., N. Y., London, 1922).

Bryan, William B., *A History of the National Capitol* (2 vols., N. Y., 1916).

Bryant, William C. and S. H. Gay, *A Popular History of the United States* (4 vols., N. Y., 1881).

Buchanan, James, *Mr. Buchanan's Administration on the Eve of the Rebellion* (N. Y., 1866).

Buckmaster, Henrietta, *Let My People Go* (N. Y., 1941).

Bunner, E., *History of Louisiana from its First Discovery and Settlement to the Present Time* (N. Y., 1842).

Burgess, John W., *The Middle Period, 1817-1858* (N. Y., 1898, The American History Series).

Burke, John (continued by S. Jones and L. Girardin), *The History of Virginia From its First Settlement to the Present Day* (4 vols., Petersburg, 1804-1816, Virginia State Library).

Burton, Theodore, "Henry Clay" in Samuel F. Bemis, ed., *The American Secretaries of State and Their Diplomacy,* IV (N. Y., 1928).

Carroll, Joseph C., *Slave Insurrections in the United States, 1800-1860* (Boston, 1939).

Carson, James P., *Life, Letters and Speeches of James Louis Petigru, the Union Man of South Carolina* (Washington, 1920).

Carter, Hollie E., "Negro insurrections in American history, 1639-1860", unpublished master's thesis, Howard University, 1936.

Carter, W. C., and A. J. Glossbrenner, *History of York County, Pa., from its Erection to the Present Time (1729-1834)*, new edition; with additions, edited by A. M. Aurand, Jr. (Harrisburg, 1930).

Cartland, Fernando G., *Southern Heroes or the Friends in War Times* (Cambridge, 1895).

Chandler, Julian A., *Representation in Virginia* (Baltimore, 1896, Johns Hopkins University Studies, XIV).

Channing, Edward, *A History of the United States* (6 vols., N. Y., 1905-25).

Chinard, Gilbert, *Thomas Jefferson the Apostle of Americanism* (Boston, 1929).

Cobb, Thomas R., *An Inquiry into the Law of Negro Slavery in the United States to which is prefixed a historical sketch of slavery* (Phila., Savannah, 1858).

Coffin, Joshua, *A Sketch of the History of Newbury, Newburyport, and West Newbury from 1635-1845* (Boston, 1845).

——, *An Account of Some of the Principal Slave Insurrections, and Others, which have occurred, or been attempted, in the United States and elsewhere, during the last two centuries, with various remarks* (N. Y., 1860). This was originally published as an appendix to Amos A. Phelps, *Letters on Slavery* (Boston, 1833).

Cole, Arthur C., *The Irrepressible Conflict* (N. Y., 1934, being volume VII of *A History of American Life*, edited by D. R. Fox and A. M. Schlesinger).

Coleman, J. Winston, Jr., letter from to present writer, dated Lexington, Kentucky, April 30, 1941.

——, *Slavery Times in Kentucky* (Chapel Hill, 1940).

Conway, Moncure D., *Testimonies Concerning Slavery* (London, 1864).

——, *Omitted Chapters of History Disclosed in the Life and Papers of Edmund Randolph* (N. Y., London, 1888).

Cook, Harvey T., *The Life and Legacy of David Rogerson Williams* (N. Y., 1916).

Cooke, John E., *Virginia, A History of Her People* (American Commonwealths Series, edited by H. E. Scudder, Boston, 1883).

Cooley, Henry S., *A Study of Slavery in New Jersey* (Baltimore, 1896, Johns Hopkins University Studies, XIV).

Cotterill, Ralph S., *The Old South* (Glendale, 1936).

Coulter, E. Merton, *The Civil War and Readjustment in Kentucky* (Chapel Hill, 1926).

Cox, Isaac J., " The Louisiana-Texas Frontier ", in *The Southwestern Historical Quarterly*, 1913, XVII, pp. 1-42.

——, *The West Florida Controversy, 1798-1813, A Study in American Diplomacy* (Baltimore, 1918).

Crane, Verner W., *The Southern Frontier 1670-1732* (Phila., 1929, Doctor's dissertation, University of Pennsylvania).

Craven, Avery, *Soil Exhaustion as a Factor in the Agricultural History of Virginia and Maryland, 1606-1860* (Urbana, 1926, University of Illinois Studies in Social Sciences, XIII).

——, *Edmund Ruffin Southerner, A Study in Secession* (N. Y., London, 1932).

Cromwell, John W., *The Negro in American History Men and Women Eminent in the Evolution of the American of African Descent* (Washington, 1914).

——, " The aftermath of Nat Turner's insurrection ", *The Journal of Negro History* (1920), V, pp. 208-34.

Curlee, Abigail, " The history of a Texas slave plantation 1831-63 " in *The Southwestern Historical Quarterly*, 1913; XVII, pp. 79-127.

Curtis, George T., *Life of James Buchanan, Fifteenth President of the United States* (2 vols., N. Y., London, 1883).

Cutler, James E., *Lynch-Law, An Investigation into the History of Lynching in the United States* (N. Y., London, 1905).

Davidson, Philip G., " Virginia and the Alien and Sedition Laws ", in *American Historical Review*, 1931, XXXVI, pp. 36-42.

Davidson, Philip, *Propaganda and the American Revolution, 1763-1783* (Chapel Hill, 1941).

Darling, Arthur B., *Our Rising Empire 1763-1803* (New Haven, 1940).

Davis, Charles S., *The Cotton Kingdom in Alabama* (Montgomery, 1939).

Davis, T. F., " United States troops in Spanish East Florida, 1812-1813 ", in *The Florida Historical Society Quarterly*, 1930-31, IX, pp. 3-42.

Davis, William W., *The Civil War and Reconstruction in Florida* (N. Y., 1913).

Dodd, William E., *The Cotton Kingdom A Chronicle of the Old South* (being volume XXVII of *Chronicles of America*, edited by Allen Johnson, New Haven, 1919).

——, " The emergence of the first social order in the United States ", in *American Historical Review*, 1935, XL, pp. 217-231.

——, *The Old South Struggles for Democracy* (N. Y., 1937).

Doyle, Bertram W., *The Etiquette of Race Relations in the South, A Study in Social Control* (Chicago, 1937).

Drewry, William S., *The Southampton Insurrection* (Washington, 1900; also published as *Slave Insurrections in Virginia*, same place and date).

DuBois, W. E. B., *The Suppression of the African Slave-Trade to the United States of America 1638-1870* (N. Y., 1896, Harvard Historical Studies, I).

——, *John Brown* (Phila., 1909, American Crisis Biographies, edited by E. P. Oberholtzer).

——, *Black Reconstruction* (N. Y., 1935).

——, *The Philadelphia Negro* (Phila., 1899).

Dubose, John W., *The Life and Times of William Lowndes Yancey A History of Political Parties in the United States from 1834 to 1864; especially as to the Origin of the Confederate States* (Birmingham, 1892).

Dumond, Dwight L., *The Secession Movement* (N. Y., 1931).

Dunlap, William, *History of the New Netherlands, Province of New York, and State of New York, to the Adoption of the Federal Constitution* (2 vols., N. Y., 1839).

Earle, Thomas, *The Life, Travels and Opinions of Benjamin Lundy including his Journeys to Texas and Mexico* (Phila., 1847).

Eaton, Clement, " A dangerous pamphlet in the old South ", in *The Journal of Southern History*, 1936, II, pp. 323-334.

——, *Freedom of Thought in the Old South* (Durham, 1940).

Eckenrode, H. J., *The Revolution in Virginia* (Boston, N. Y., 1916).

——, " Negroes in Richmond in 1864 ", in *The Virginia Magazine of History and Biography*, 1938, XLVI, pp. 193-200.

Edwards, George W., *New York as an Eighteenth Century Municipality, 1731-1776* (N. Y., 1917).

Elliott, Charles W., *Winfield Scott The Soldier and the Man* (N. Y., 1937).

Ellis, S. M., *The Solitary Horseman, or the Life & Adventures of G. P. R. James* (Kensington, Eng., 1927).

Fish, Carl R., *The American Civil War An Interpretation*, edited by W. E. Smith (London, N. Y., 1937).

Fiske, John, *Old Virginia and Her Neighbours* (2 vols., Boston, N. Y., 1897).

Fite, Emerson D., *The Presidential Campaign of 1860* (N. Y., 1911).

Flanders, Ralph B., *Plantation Slavery in Georgia* (Chapel Hill, 1933).

——, letter from to present writer, dated October 2, 1940.

Fleming, Walter L., *Civil War and Reconstruction in Alabama* (N. Y., 1905).

Forrest, William S., *Historical and Descriptive Sketches of Norfolk and Vicinity including Portsmouth and the Adjacent Counties, during a period of two hundred years* (Phila., 1853).

Fortier, Alcee, *A History of Louisiana* (4 vols., N. Y., 1904).

Foster, Laurence, *Negro-Indian Relationships in the Southeast* (Phila., 1935).

Fox, E. L., *The American Colonization Society 1817-1840* (Baltimore, 1919, Johns Hopkins University Studies, XXXVII).

Frazier, E. Franklin, *The Negro Family in the United States* (Chicago, 1939).

Freeman, Douglas S., *R. E. Lee A Biography* (4 vols., N. Y., London, 1934).

Fuller, Herbert B., *The Purchase of Florida, Its History and Diplomacy* (Cleveland, 1906).

Gaines, Francis P., *The Southern Plantation A Study in the Development and Accuracy of a Tradition* (N. Y., 1925).

Garland, Hugh A., *The Life of John Randolph of Roanoke* (2 vols., in 1, 11th edition, N. Y., 1857).

Garrison, W. P. and F. J., *William Lloyd Garrison 1805-1879 The Story of His Life* (4 vols., N. Y., 1885).

Gayarré, Charles, *History of Louisiana* (4 vols., New Orleans, 1903, 4th edition).

Gewehr, Wesley M., *The Great Awakening in Virginia, 1740-1790* (Durham, 1930).

Gibbs, George, *Memoirs of the Administrations of Washington and John Adams,* edited from the papers of Oliver Wolcott (2 vols., N. Y., 1846).

Giddings, Joshua R., *The Exiles of Florida* (Columbus, 1858).

Gilman, Daniel C., *James Monroe in his Relations to the Public Service during Half a Century 1776-1826* (Boston, 1888, American Statesmen Series, edited by J. T. Morse, Jr.).

Goodloe, Daniel R., *The Southern Platform: or Manual of Southern Sentiment on the Subject of Slavery* (Boston, 1858).

Gordon, Asa H., " The struggle of the slave for freedom ", in *The Journal of Negro History*, 1928, XIII, pp. 22-36.

Granger, Mary R., Letter from, to the present writer, dated Savannah, August 8, 1940.

Gray, Lewis C., assisted by L. K. Thompson, *History of Agriculture in the Southern States to 1860* (Washington, 1933, 2 vols.).

Greene, Evarts B., and V. D. Harrington, *American Population Before the Federal Census of 1790* (N. Y., 1932).

——, *Provincial America* (N. Y., 1906, being vol. 6 of the American Nation Series edited by Albert B. Hart).

Greene, Lorenzo J., *The Negro in Colonial New England, 1620-1776* (Ph.D. thesis, Columbia University, 1941).

Grimke, Archibald H., *William Lloyd Garrison The Abolitionist* (N. Y., London, 1891).

——, *Right on the Scaffold, or The Martyrs of 1822* (Washington, 1901).

Guild, Jane P., *Black Laws of Virginia, A Summary of the Legislative Acts of Virginia Concerning Negroes from Earliest Times to the Present* (Richmond, 1936).

Guilday, Peter, *The Life and Times of John England, 1786-1842* (2 vols., N. Y., 1927).

Hacker, L. M., *The Triumph of American Capitalism* (N. Y., 1940).

Hammond, Matthew B., *The Cotton Industry, An Essay in American Economic History* (Ithaca, 1897).

Harlow, Ralph V., *Gerrit Smith, Philanthropist and Reformer* (N. Y., 1939).

Harper's *Encyclopaedia of United States History* (N. Y., 1902).

Harris, N. D., *The History of Negro Servitude in Illinois* (Chicago, 1904).

Hart, Albert B., *Slavery and Abolition 1831-1841* (being vol. 16, of the American Nation Series edited by A. B. Hart, N. Y., 1906).

Hartz, Louis, " Otis and anti-slavery doctrine ", in *The New England Quarterly*, 1939, XII, pp. 745-747.

Hatfield, Edwin F., *History of Elizabeth, New Jersey, including the early history of Union County* (N. Y., 1868).

Hawk, Emory Q., *Economic History of the South* (N. Y., 1934).

Henry, H. M., *The Police Control of the Slave in South Carolina* (Emory, 1914).

Herbert, Hilary A., *The Abolition Crusade and its Consequences* (N. Y., 1912).

Herskovits, Melville J., Letter by, in *The South Atlantic Quarterly*, 1940, XXXIX, pp. 350-351.

——, *The Myth of the Negro Past* (N. Y., 1941).

Hesseltine, William B., " Some new aspects of the pro-slavery argument ", in *The Journal of Negro History*, 1936, XXI, pp. 1-14.

——, *A History of the South 1607-1936* (N. Y., 1936).

Hicks, John D., *The Federal Union, A History of the United States to 1865* (Boston, 1937).

Higginson, Thomas W., " Denmark Vesey ", in *Atlantic Monthly*, Boston, 1861, VII, pp. 728-744.

——, " Gabriel's Plot ", in *Atlantic Monthly*, 1862, X, pp. 337-345.

Higginson, Thomas W., *Travellers and Outlaws Episodes in American History* (Boston, N. Y., 1889).

——, *Contemporaries* (Boston, N. Y., 1899).

Hildreth, Richard, *The History of the United States of America* (6 vols., revised edition, N. Y., 1879).

Hill, Helen, *George Mason: Constitutionalist* (Cambridge, 1938).

Hinton, J. H., S. L. Knapp, and J. O. Choules, *The History and Topography of the United States of North America* (2 vols., 2d edit., Boston, 1846).

Holst, H. von, *The Constitutional and Political History of the United States,* J. J. Lelor, trans., 7 vols. (Vol. II, Chicago, 1879).

Hosmer, J. K., *The Appeal to Arms* (being vol. 20 of the American Nation series, edited by A. B. Hart, N. Y., 1906).

Howell, George, and J. Tenney, *History of the County of Albany, New York from 1609-1886* (N. Y., 1886).

Howison, Robert R., *A History of Virginia from its Discovery and Settlement by Europeans to the Present Time* (2 vols., Richmond, N. Y., London, 1848).

Howren, Alleine, " Causes and origin of the decree of April 6, 1830 ", in *The Southwestern Historical Quarterly,* 1913, XVI, pp. 378-422.

Hubbart, Henry C., *The Older Middle West 1840-1880* (N. Y., London, 1936).

Hudnot, Ruth and Hayes Baker-Crothers, " Acadian transients in South Carolina ", in *American Historical Review,* 1938, XVI, pp. 378-422.

Jackson, Luther P., " Manumission in certain Virginia cities ", in *The Journal of Negro History,* 1930, XV, pp. 278-314.

——, " Religious instruction of Negroes, 1830-1860, with special reference to South Carolina ", in *The Journal of Negro History,* 1930, XV, pp. 72-114.

——, " Religious development of the Negro in Virginia from 1760 to 1860 ", in *The Journal of Negro History,* XVI, 1931, pp. 168-239.

James, Bartlett B., edits and continues, *History of Maryland by James Mc-Sherry* (Baltimore, 1904).

James, C. L. R., " History of Negro Revolt ", in *Fact,* London, 1938, No. 18.

James, G. P. R., *The Old Dominion, A Novel* (London, N. Y., new edition, 1858).

James, Marquis, *The Raven, A Biography of Sam Houston* (N. Y., 1929).

Jansen, Mary L., " Agriculture in Virginia in the post-colonial period ", unpublished master's thesis, Columbia University, 1935.

Jenkins, William S., *Pro-Slavery Thought in the Old South* (Chapel Hill, 1935).

Jervey, Theodore D., *Robert Y. Hayne and His Times* (N. Y., 1909).

Johnson, Guion G., *Ante-Bellum North Carolina* (Chapel Hill, 1937).

Johnson, Rossiter, *A Short History of the War of Secession 1861-1865* (Boston, N. Y., 1889).

Johnson, James W., *Black Manhattan* (N. Y., 1930).

Johnston, James H., " The Participation of White men in Virginia Negro insurrections ", in *The Journal of Negro History,* 1931, XVI, pp.

Johnston, Mary, *Prisoners of Hope, A Tale of Colonial Virginia* (Boston, N. Y., 1899).

Kendall, John S., "Shadow over the city" in *The Louisiana Historical Quarterly*, 1939, XXII, pp. 142-165.

King, Henry T., *Sketches of Pitt County, A Brief History of the County 1704-1910* (Raleigh, 1911).

Kirkland, Thomas J., and R. M. Kennedy, *Historic Camden, part two, Nineteenth Century* (Columbia, 1926).

Klingberg, F. G., *The Anti-Slavery Movement in England* (New Haven, 1926).

Koontz, Louis K., *The Virginia Frontier, 1754-1763* (Baltimore, 1925, Johns Hopkins University Studies, XLVII).

Kraus, Michael, "Social classes and customs", in Alexander C. Flick, ed., *History of the State of New York*, II, pp. 375-410 (10 vols., N. Y., 1933).

Lamb, Martha J., *History of the City of New York: Its Origin, Rise, Progress* (2 vols., N. Y., Chicago, 1877).

Lee, Francis B., *New Jersey as a Colony and as a State* (4 vols., N. Y., 1902).

Lefler, Hugh T., *Hinton Rowan Helper Advocate of a "White America"* (J. D. Eggleston, ed., Southern Sketches, No. 1, Charlottesville, 1935).

Lewis, Lloyd, *Sherman Fighting Prophet* (N. Y., 1932).

Lober, J. W., "Slavery in New Jersey from the first settlement to the Civil War", unpublished bachelor's paper (Princeton University, 1939).

Locke, Mary S., *Anti-Slavery in America from the Introduction of African Slaves to the Prohibition of the Slave Trade (1619-1808)*, (Radcliff College Monographs, XI, Boston, 1901).

Lokke, Carl L., "Jefferson and the Leclerc expedition", in *American Historical Review*, 1928, XXXIII, pp. 322-331.

Lonn, Ella, *Desertion During the Civil War* (N. Y., London, 1928).

Lossing, Benson J., *The Pictorial Field Book of the War of 1812* (N. Y., 1869).

Lowery, Woodbury, *The Spanish Settlements within the Present Limits of the United States 1513-1561* (N. Y., London, 1901).

Lundin, Leonard, *Cockpit of the Revolution, The War for Independence in New Jersey* (Princeton, 1940).

Lyon, E. Wilson, *Louisiana in French Diplomacy 1759-1804* (Norman, 1934).

Macy, Jesse, *The Anti-Slavery Crusade, A Chronicle of the Gathering Storm* (being vol. 28 of The Chronicles of America, edited by A. Johnson, New Haven, 1921).

Magoffin, Dorothy S., "A Georgia planter and his plantations 1837-1861", *The North Carolina Historical Review* (1938), XV, pp. 354-377.

Malone, Dumas, *The Public Life of Thomas Cooper 1783-1839* (New Haven, 1926).

Martin, Francois-Xavier, *The History of Louisiana from the Earliest Period* (2 vols., New Orleans, 1827, 1829).

——, *The History of North Carolina from the Earliest Period* (2 vols., New Orleans, 1829).

Mather, F. G., "Slavery in the Colony and State of New York", *Magazine of American History* (N. Y., 1884), XI, pp. 408-420.

Mathieson, W. L., *British Slavery and Its Abolition* (London, N. Y., 1926).

Matlack, Lucius C., *The Antislavery Struggle and Triumph in the Methodist Episcopal Church* (N. Y., Cincinnati, 1881).

Maverick, Maury, *A Maverick American* (N. Y., 1937).

Mayo, Bernard, *Henry Clay, Spokesman of the New West* (Boston, 1937).

Mazyck, Walter H., *George Washington and the Negro* (Washington, 1932).

M'Call, Hugh, *The History of Georgia Containing Brief Sketches of the Most Remarkable Events, up to the Present Day* (2 vols., Savannah, 1811).

McCrady, Edward, "Slavery in the Province of South Carolina, 1670-1770", *Annual Report of the American Historical Association*, 1895 (Washington, 1896).

——, *History of South Carolina Under the Royal Government 1719-1776* (N. Y., 1901).

McDougle, Ivan E., *Slavery in Kentucky 1792-1865* (reprinted from *The Journal of Negro History*, Washington, 1918, III).

McMaster, John B., *A History of the People of the United States from the Revolution to the Civil War* (N. Y., 1883-1913, 8 vols.).

Meigs, William M., *The Life of John C. Calhoun* (2 vols., N. Y., 1917).

Mellick, Andrew D., Jr., *The Story of an Old Farm, or Life in New Jersey in the Eighteenth Century* (Somerville, 1889).

Mellon, Matthew T., *Early American Views on Negro Slavery from the Letters and Papers of the Founders of the Republic* (Boston, 1934).

Mereness, Newton D., *Maryland as a Proprietary Province* (N. Y., 1901).

Meriwether, Robert L., *The Expansion of South Carolina 1729-1765* (Kingsport, Tenn., 1940).

Minor, Robert, "The black ten millions", in *The Liberator* (1924), VII, pp. 7-9.

Mitchell, Broadus, *William Gregg, Factory Master of the Old South* (Chapel Hill, 1928).

Mitchell, Stewart, *Horatio Seymour of New York* (Cambridge, 1938).

Moody, V. A., "Slavery on Louisiana sugar plantations", in *The Louisiana Historical Quarterly* (1924), VII, pp. 191-301.

Moore, George H., *Notes on the History of Slavery in Massachusetts* (N. Y., 1866).

Moore, John W., *History of North Carolina from its Earliest Discoveries to the Present Time* (2 vols., Raleigh, 1880).

Morgan, Edwin V., *Slavery in New York* (N. Y., London, 1892).

Morgan, George, *The Life of James Monroe* (Boston, 1924).

Morison, Samuel E., *The Life and Letters of Harrison Gray Otis, Federalist 1765-1848* (2 vols., Boston, N. Y., 1913).

Munford, Beverley B., *Virginia's Attitude Toward Slavery and Secession* (N. Y., London, 1909).

Nearing, Scott, *Black America* (N. Y., 1929).

Nevins, Allan, *The Evening Post, A Century of Journalism* (N. Y., 1922).

——, *Hamilton Fish The Inner History of the Grant Administration* (N. Y., 1936).

——, *The American States During and After the Revolution 1775-1789* (N. Y., 1924).

——, *Thirty Years of American Diplomacy* (N. Y., 1930).

Newsome, A. R., " Twelve North Carolina Counties in 1810-1811 ", in *The North Carolina Historical Review* (1929), VI, pp. 308-309.

Northrup, A. Judd, *Slavery in New York, A Historical Sketch* (Albany, 1900, New York State Library Bulletin History No. 4).

Odum, Howard W., *An American Epoch Southern Portraiture in the National Picture* (N. Y., 1930).

Ogden, Rollo, *Life and Letters of Edwin Lawrence Godkin* (2 vols., N. Y., 1907).

Olson, Edwin, " Negro slavery in New York, 1626-1827 ", unpublished doctor's dissertation, New York University, 1938.

O'Neall, John B., and John A. Chapman, *The Annals of Newberry* (Newberry, S. C., 1892).

Osgood, Herbert L., *The American Colonies in the Eighteenth Century* (4 vols., N. Y., 1924).

——, *The American Colonies in the Seventeenth Century* (3 vols., N. Y., 1904).

Ostrander, Stephen M., *A History of the City of Brooklyn and Kings County* (2 vols., Brooklyn, 1894).

Page, Thomas N., *The Old South Essays, Social and Political* (N. Y., 1892).

Park, Robert E., " The conflict and fusion of cultures with special reference to the Negro ", in *The Journal of Negro History* (1919), IV, pp. 111-133.

Parker, William H., " The Nat Turner Insurrection ", *Old Virginia Yarns* (1893), I, pp. 14-29. There is no title page—the preceding is written in pencil. Copy in the Virginia State Library.

Parton, James, *Life of Andrew Jackson* (3 vols., Boston, 1860).

——, *General Butler in New Orleans* (N. Y., 1864, 13th edit., c. 1863).

Patterson, Caleb P., *The Negro in Tennessee, 1790-1865* (University of Texas Bulletin, No. 2205, 1927).

Pelzer, Louis, " Economic factors in the acquisition of Louisiana " in *Proceedings of the Mississippi Valley Historical Association 1912-1913*, VI, pp. 109-128.

Pennington, Edgar L., " The Reverend Francis Le Jau's work among Indians and Negro slaves ", in *The Journal of Southern History* (1935, I).

Perkins, Haven, " Religion for slaves ", *Church History*, 1941 X, pp. 228-45.

Peterson, Victor H., " The position of the free person of color in Mississippi, Louisiana and Alabama before the Civil War ", unpublished master's thesis, University of Chicago, 1939.

Phelps, Albert, *Louisiana, A Record of Expansion* (American Commonwealth Series, Boston, N. Y., 1905).

Phelps, Amos A., *Lectures on Slavery and its Remedy* (Boston, 1834).

Phillips, Ulrich Bonnell, *Georgia and State Rights, A Study of the Political History of Georgia from the Revolution to the Civil War with particular regard to Federal Relations* (Washington, 1902).

——, *Racial Problems, Adjustments and Disturbances in the Ante-Bellum South*, reprinted from *The South in the Building of the Nation*, IV, pp. 194-241 (Richmond, 1909).

——, " The slave labor problem in the Charleston district ", in *Political Science Quarterly* (1907), XXII, pp. 416-439.

——, *American Negro Slavery, A Survey of the Supply, Employment and control of Negro labor as determined by the plantation regime* (N. Y., London, 1918).

——, *Life and Labor in the Old South* (Boston, 1931).

——, " The South Carolina Federalists II ", in *The American Historical Review* (1909), XIV, pp. 731-743.

——, *The Course of the South to Secession, An Interpretation,* edited by E. Merton Coulter (N. Y., London, 1939).

Pinckney, Charles C., *Life of General Thomas Pinckney* (Boston, N. Y., 1895).

Poole, William F., *Anti-Slavery Opinions Before the Year 1800* (Cincinnati, 1873).

Posey, W. B., " Influence of slavery upon the Methodist Church in the early south and southwest ", in *The Mississippi Valley Historical Review* (1931), XVII, pp. 530-542.

——, *The Development of Methodism in the Old Southwest, 1783-1824* (Tuscaloosa, 1933).

Pratt, Julius W., *The Expansionists of 1812* (N. Y., 1925).

Prince, Walter F., " New York ' Negro Plot ' of 1741 ", published in the *Saturday Chronicle,* New Haven, Conn., June 28-August 23, 1902 (type-written copy in the New York Public Library).

Prowell, R. George, *History of York County, Pennsylvania* (2 vols., Chicago, 1907).

Quincy, Edmund, *Life of Josiah Quincy of Massachusetts* (Boston, 1868).

——, *Memoir of the Life of John Quincy Adams* (Boston, 1858).

Ranck, James B., *Albert Gallatin Brown Radical Southern Nationalist* (N. Y., London, 1937).

Randall, James G., *The Civil War and Reconstruction* (N. Y., Boston, 1937).

Rappoport, Stanley, " Slave struggles for freedom ", *The Crisis,* September, 1936, pp. 264, 265, 274, 284-86.

Ravenal, St. Julien, Mrs., *Charleston, The Place and the People* (N. Y., 1906).

Reddick, L. D., " A new interpretation for Negro history ", in *The Journal of Negro History* (1937), XXII, pp. 17-28.

Redpath, James, *The Public Life of John Brown* (London, 1860).

Rhodes, James F., *History of the United States from the Compromise of 1850,* Vol. I, 1850-1854 (N. Y., 1896).

Riddell, William R., " Slavery in early New York ", in *The Journal of Negro History* (1928), XIII, pp. 53-86.

Riley, F. L., "A contribution to the history of the colonization movement in Mississippi,", *Publications of the Mississippi Historical Society* (1906), IX, pp. 337-414.

Rippy, J. Fred, *Rivalry of the United States and Great Britain Over Latin America (1808-1830)*, (Baltimore, 1929).

——, *The United States and Mexico* (c. 1926, N. Y., 1931).

——, *Joel R. Poinsett Versatile American* (Durham, 1935).

Robert, Joseph C., *The Tobacco Kingdom Plantation, Market and Factory in Virginia and North Carolina, 1800-1860* (Durham, 1938).

——, *The Road from Monticello, A Study of the Virginia Slavery Debate of 1832* (Historical Papers of the Trinity College Historical Society, Series XXIV, Durham, 1941).

Robertson, James A., *Louisiana Under the Rule of Spain, France, and the United States, 1785-1807* (2 vols., Cleveland, 1911).

Rowland, Dunbar, *History of Mississippi the Heart of the South* (2 vols., Chicago, Jackson, 1925).

Russell, John H., *The Free Negro in Virginia 1619-1865* (Baltimore, 1913, Johns Hopkins University Studies, XXXI).

Sanborn, Frank B., *The Life and Letters of John Brown, Liberator of Kansas, and Martyr of Virginia* (Boston, 1891).

Sandburg, Carl, *Abraham Lincoln The War Years* (4 vols., N. Y., 1939).

Savage, W. Sherman, *The Controversy Over the Distribution of Abolition Literature 1830-1860* (Washington, 1938).

Savannah Unit, Federal Writers' Project, compiled and written by—*Savannah* (Savannah, 1937).

Saxon, Lyle, *Old Louisiana* (N. Y., London, 1929).

Scarborough, Ruth, *The Opposition to Slavery in Georgia Prior to 1860* (Nashville, 1933, George Peabody College of Teachers Contributions to Education, no. 97).

Scharf, J. Thomas, *History of Maryland from the Earliest Times to the Present Day* (3 vols., Baltimore, 1879).

Schluter, Herman, *Lincoln, Labor and Slavery, A Chapter from the Social History of America* (N. Y., 1913).

Schoen, Harold, "The free Negro in the Republic of Texas", in *Southwestern Historical Quarterly* (1937), XLI, pp. 101, 107, 171.

Schouler, James, *History of the United States of America Under the Constitution* (6 vols., revised edit., N. Y., 1906).

Schurz, Carl, *Life of Henry Clay* (2 vols., American Statesmen series, Boston, N. Y., 1890).

Schuyler, R. L., *Parliament and the British Empire* (N. Y., 1929).

Sears, Louis M., *Jefferson and the Embargo* (Durham, 1927).

Shanks, Henry T., *The Secession Movement in Virginia, 1847-1861* (Richmond, 1934).

Siebert, Wilbur H., "Slavery and white servitude in East Florida, 1726 to 1776", in *The Florida Historical Society Quarterly* (1931), X, pp. 3-23, 139-161.

——, *Loyalists in East Florida 1774-1785* (2 vols., Deland, 1929).

Simkins, Frances B., and J. W. Patton, *The Women of the Confederacy* (Richmond, N. Y., 1936).

Simms, Henry H., *Life of John Taylor* (Richmond, 1932).

——, *The Rise of the Whigs in Virginia, 1824-1840* (Richmond, 1929).

Smith, Henry A., "Willtown or New London", in *South Carolina Historical and Genealogical Magazine* (1909), X, pp.

Smith, W. R., *South Carolina as a Royal Province 1719-1776* (N. Y., 1903).

Snider, Denton J., *The American Ten Years' War 1855-1865* (St. Louis, 1906).

Snowden, Yates, and H. G. Cutter, *History of South Carolina* (5 vols., Chicago, N. Y., 1920).

Squires, W. H., *Through Centuries Three, A Short History of the People of Virginia* (Portsmouth, 1929).

Stanard, Mary N., *Richmond, Its People and Its Story* (Phila., London, 1923).

Stevens, N., "The 100th anniversary of the Nat Turner revolt", *The Communist* (1931), X, pp. 737-743.

Stevens, William B., *A History of Georgia from its First Discovery by Europeans to the Adoption of the Present Constitution in 1798* (2 vols., Phila., 1859).

Stowe, Harriet Beecher, *Dred; A Tale of the Great Dismal Swamp* (2 vols., Boston, 1856).

Strickland, Reba C., *Religion and the State in Georgia in the 18th Century* (N. Y., 1939).

Stroud, George M., *A Sketch of the Laws Relating to Slavery in the Several States of the United States of America* (2d edit., Phila., 1856).

Stryker, Lloyd P., *Andrew Johnson, A Study in Courage* (N. Y., 1929).

Styron, Arthur, *The Cast-Iron Man, John C. Calhoun, and American Democracy* (N. Y., Toronto, 1935).

Sunderland, La Roy, *Anti-Slavery Manual, Containing a Collection of Facts and Arguments on American Slavery* (N. Y., 1837, 2d edit.).

Sydnor, Charles S., *Slavery in Mississippi* (N. Y., London, 1933).

——, "The Southerner and the laws", in *The Journal of Southern History* (1940), VI, pp. 3-23.

Swaney, Charles B., *Episcopal Methodism and Slavery with Sidelights on Ecclesiastical Politics* (Boston, 1926).

Swem, E. G., *A Bibliography of Virginia*, Part II (Richmond, 1917, Virginia State Library Bulletin, No. 10).

Swem, E. G., *Virginia Historical Index* (2 vols., Roanoke, 1934-36).

Tatum, Georgia L., *Disloyalty in the Confederacy* (Chapel Hill, 1934).

Taylor, R. H., "Slaveholding in North Carolina: an economic view", *James Sprunt Historical Publications*, XVIII (Chapel Hill, 1926).

——, "Slave conspiracies in North Carolina", in *North Carolina Historical Review* (1928), V, pp. 20-34.

——, "Humanizing the slave code of North Carolina", *North Carolina Historical Review* (1925), II, pp. 323-331.

——, " The gentry of ante-bellum South Carolina ", *North Carolina Historical Review* (1940), XVII, pp. 114-131.

Tiernan, Mary S., *Homoselle* (Boston, 1881).

Treudley, Mary, " The United States and St. Domingo, 1789-1866 ", *Journal of Race Development* (1917), VII, pp. 83-148.

Trexler, Harrison A., *Slavery in Missouri 1804-1865* (Baltimore, 1914, Johns Hopkins University Studies, XXXII).

Tuckerman, Bayard, *William Jay and the Constitutional Movement for the Abolition of Slavery* (N. Y., 1894).

Turner, Edward R., *The Negro in Pennsylvania: Slavery—Servitude—Freedom 1639-1861* (Washington, 1911).

Turner, Frederick J., " The South, 1820-1830 ", in *The American Historical Review* (1906), XI, pp. 559-573.

Turner, Lorenzo D., *Anti-Slavery Sentiment in American Literature Prior to 1865* (Washington, 1929).

Van Deusen, Glyndon G., *The Life of Henry Clay* (Boston, 1937).

Van Tyne, Claude H., *The War of Independence American Phase* (Boston, N. Y., 1929).

Villard, Oswald G., *John Brown 1800-1859, A Biography Fifty Years After* (N. Y., 1911).

Virginia Magazine of History and Biography (1901), VIII, pp. 221-222, unsigned review of W. S. Drewry's *The Southampton Insurrection*.

——, (1904), XI, p. 331, " Genealogy of Bruce family."

——, (1928), XXXVI, p. 227, " Genealogy of Harrison of James River."

Wagstaff, H. M., *State Rights and Political Parties in North Carolina, 1776-1861* (Baltimore, 1906, Johns Hopkins University Studies, XXIV).

Wallace, David D., *The Life of Henry Laurens* (N. Y., London, 1915).

——, *The History of South Carolina* (4 vols., N. Y., 1934).

Washington, Booker T., *The Story of the Negro* (2 vols., N. Y., 1909).

Washington, L. B., " The use of religion for social control in American slavery ", unpublished master's thesis, Howard University, Washington, 1939.

Watkins, James L., " Production and price of cotton for one hundred years " *United States Department of Agriculture Miscellaneous Series, Bulletin No. 9* (Washington, 1895).

Weatherford, W. D., and C. S. Johnson, *Race Relations: Adjustment of whites and Negroes in the United States* (N. Y., 1934).

Weeks, Stephen B., *Southern Quakers and Slavery, A Study in Institutional History* (Baltimore, 1896, Johns Hopkins University Studies, XV).

——, " The slave insurrection in Virginia, 1831, known as ' Old Nat's War ' ", *Magazine of American History* (1891), XXV, pp. 448-458.

Wertenbaker, Thomas J., *The Planters of Colonial Virginia* (Princeton, 1922).

——, *Norfolk Historic Southern Port* (Durham, 1931).

Wesley, Charles H., *Negro Labor in the United States 1850-1925, A Study in American Economic History* (N. Y., 1927).

——, *Richard Allen, Apostle of Freedom* (Washington, 1935).

Weston, George M., *The Progress of Slavery in the United States* (Washington, 1857).

Whitaker, Arthur Preston, *The Spanish-American Frontier 1783-1795* (N. Y., Boston, 1927).

——, *The Mississippi Question 1795-1803* (N. Y., London, 1934).

——, "The commerce of Louisiana and the Floridas at the end of the 18th century", in *The Hispanic-American Historical Review* (1928), VIII, pp. 19-203.

White, Laura, "The South in the 1850's as seen by British consuls", in *The Journal of Southern History* (1935), I, pp. 29-48.

Whitehead, William A., *Contributions to the Early History of Perth Amboy and Adjoining Counties* (N. Y., 1856).

Whitfield, Theodore M., *Slavery Agitation in Virginia 1829-1832* (Baltimore, 1930, Johns Hopkins University Studies, extra volume no. 10).

Wiley, Bell I., *Southern Negroes, 1861-1865* (L. W. Labaree, ed., Yale Historical Publications, XXXI, New Haven, 1938).

William and Mary College Quarterly Historical Magazine (1915), XXIV, p. 52, "Genealogy of the Lee family".

Williams, George W., *History of the Negro Race in America from 1619 to 1880* (2 vols., N. Y., 1883).

Wilson, Henry, *History of the Rise and Fall of the Slave Power in America* (3 vols., Boston, 1872).

Wilson, Hill P., *John Brown Soldier of Fortune, A Critique* (Lawrence, 1913).

Winston, James E., "The free Negro in New Orleans, 1803-1860", in *Louisiana Historical Quarterly* (1938), XXI, pp. 1075-1085.

Wise, Barton H., *The Life of Henry A. Wise of Virginia 1806-1876* (N. Y., London, 1899).

Wish, Harvey, Letter from, to present writer, dated Chicago, April 20, 1940.

——, "American slave insurrections before 1861", in *The Journal of Negro History* (1937), XXII, pp. 229-320.

——, "Slave disloyalty in the Confederacy", in *The Journal of Negro History* (1938), XXIII, pp. 435-450.

——, "The slave insurrection panic of 1856", in *The Journal of Southern History* (1939), V, pp. 206-222.

Wolfe, John H., "Jeffersonian Democracy in South Carolina", (*James Sprunt Historical Publications*, XXIV, Chapel Hill, 1940).

Woodson, Carter G., review of U. B. Phillips' *American Negro Slavery* in the *Mississippi Valley Historical Review* (1919), V, pp. 480-482.

——, *The Education of the Negro Prior to 1861* (N. Y., London, 1915).

——, *The History of the Negro Church* (2d edit., Washington, 1921).

——, *The Mind of the Negro as Reflected in Letters Written During the Crisis* (Washington, 1926).

——, *The Negro in Our History* (5th edit., Washington, 1928).

——, *Negro Orators and their Orations* (Washington, 1925).

Woodward, C. Vann, *Tom Watson Agrarian Rebel* (N. Y., 1938).

INDEX